Theological Aesthetics

Theological Aesthetics

God in Imagination,
Beauty, and Art

RICHARD VILADESAU

UNIVERSITY PRESS

OXFORD

UNIVERSITY PRESS

Oxford University Press is a department of the University of Oxford.
It furthers the University's objective of excellence in research, scholarship,
and education by publishing worldwide.

Oxford   New York

Auckland   Cape Town   Dar es Salaam   Hong Kong   Karachi
Kuala Lumpur   Madrid   Melbourne   Mexico City   Nairobi
New Delhi   Shanghai   Taipei   Toronto

With offices in

Argentina   Austria   Brazil   Chile   Czech Republic   France   Greece
Guatemala   Hungary   Italy   Japan   Poland   Portugal   Singapore
South Korea   Switzerland   Thailand   Turkey   Ukraine   Vietnam

Oxford is a registered trade mark of Oxford University Press
in the UK and certain other countries.

Published in the United States of America by
Oxford University Press
198 Madison Avenue, New York, NY 10016

First issued as an Oxford University Press paperback, 2013.

Library of Congress Cataloging-in-Publication Data
Viladesau, Richard.
Theological aesthetics : God in imagination, beauty, and art /
Richard Viladesau.
p.   cm.
Includes bibliographical references and index.
ISBN 978-0-19-512622-8 (hardcover); 978-0-19-995976-1 (paperback)
1. Aesthetics—Religious aspects—Christianity.
2. Christianity and the arts. I. Title.
BR115.A8V55   1999
230—dc21   98-25261

Printed in the United States of America
on acid-free paper

To Marie and Jason

Acknowledgments

Quotation from Karl Barth. *Church Dogmatics*. Copyright © of the German original version of Karl Barth *Die Kirchliche Dogmatik* III/3, 3rd edition 1979 Theologischer Verlag Zurich. Used by Permission.

Lyrics from Arnold Schoenberg used by permission of Belmont Music Publishers, Pacific Palisades, CA 90272.

Text of "Betelgeuse" by Humbert Wolfe from *The Unknown Goddess* (New York: Harcourt, Brace and Co., 1925) reprinted by permission of the Peters Fraser & Dunlop Group Ltd.

Portions of chapter 6 first appeared as the article, "Natural Theology Aesthetics" in *Philosophy and Theology,* vol. 3, no. 2 (winter, 1988); used here by permission of Marquette University Press.

Text from *Acathist of Thanksgiving* by Gregory Petrov, trans. by Mother Thekla Reprinted by Permission of G. Schirmer, Inc. o/b/o Chester Music Ltd. International Copyright Secured. All Rights Reserved. Reprinted by Permission.

Haiku "Old pond" by Matsuo Bashō from *An Introduction to Haiku* by Harold G. Henderson. Copyright © 1958 by Harold G. Henderson. Used by permission of Doubleday, a division of Bantam Doubleday Dell Publishing Group, Inc.

"Deer Fence" by Wang Wei, translation from *The Heart of Chinese Poetry* by Greg Whincup, copyright © 1987 by Greg Whincup. Used by permission of Doubleday, a division of Bantam Doubleday Dell Publishing Group, Inc. World rights by gracious permission of Greg Whincup.

Text from Fyodor Dostoievsky, *The Idiot,* translated by Constance Garnett (New York: Bantam Books, 1983).

Figure 1. Michelangelo Buonarroti. Detail of Christ Child. *Bruges Madonna.* Notre Dame, Bruges, Belgium.

Figure 2. "God and Adam," from the cathedral of Chartres, is reproduced by the gracious permission of Éditions Houvet, Chartres, France.

Figure 3. "Persimmons" by Mu Ch'i is reproduced from Jean A. Keim, *Chinese Art. III. Southern Sung and Yuan. Petite Encyclopédie de l'art,* 39 (Paris: Fernand Hazan, 1961), by gracious permission of Fernand Hazan, Editeur, Paris.

Figure 4. Giotto di Bondone. *Crucifixion.* Lower church, S. Francesco, Assisi, Italy. Alinari/Art Resource, N.Y.

Figure 5. Grünewald, Matthias. "Crucifixion" from the *Isenheim Altarpiece.* Musée Unterlinden, Colmar, France. Giraudon/Art Resource, N.Y.

Preface

Professor Mary Gerhart has argued that "a sea change is needed in the field of religious studies, one that must take place in the nexus of the field of theology, the field of art, literature and religion, and the field of science and religion."[1] In recent years, the interdisciplinary engagement of which she speaks has begun taking place. Within religious studies, there has been increasing scholarly engagement with religion as ideology and as spirituality,[2] with a correlative interest in the aesthetic and communicative dimensions of religious practice and thought. Particular areas of theology have for some time been involved with topics and methods that have a connection either directly with the "aesthetic" realm or with its study; one may think, for example, of the use of literary theory in scriptural studies and in theological hermeneutics in general, or the study of symbolism in sacramental and liturgical theology. And, finally, a few recent works have explicitly undertaken the task of formulating a religious and/or theological approach to aesthetics.[3]

It is the purpose of this work to approach the aesthetic from the point of view of a "fundamental" theology. My starting point is explicitly theological; I write from a confessional and spiritual stance. At the same time, my attempt is to engage in the particular kind of Christian theology that attempts with methodical self-consciousness to "give answer" for faith's presuppositions, viewpoint, and content. In terms of method, this book owes a great deal to "transcendental" theology, especially as practiced by Lonergan and Rahner. From one point of view, its content might be described as a transcendental theology of revelation examined in relation to the different dimensions of the aesthetic realm: feeling and imagination, beauty, and art.

A study of this kind could hardly fail to take into account the monumental *Theological Aesthetics* of Hans Urs von Balthasar; and in fact, Balthasar's theology will figure prominently here, particularly in the definition of the task. Nevertheless, although Balthasar's work is invaluable, it will not be my central focus; as the first chapter will explain, my desire is neither to repeat nor to recapitulate what Balthasar and his followers have done, but to engage in a different—and I hope complementary—approach to "fundamental theology." Indeed, it seems to me that the study of the aesthetic dimension of theology should form a point of mediation between a more "transcendental" type of theology, like Rahner's, and a more "hermeneutical" type, like Balthasar's.

I am acutely aware of the incompleteness of this study, from the point of view of theology as well as that of aesthetics. I have already adverted to the possibility and legitimacy of dealing with the subject as a whole by a totally different method, represented especially by Balthasar. Indeed, as Frank Burch Brown remarks, "it makes no sense to speak of a single, uniform relation between aesthetics and theology, as if every theology would need or want to engage in aesthetics in the same manner. Any such uniform approach is further ruled out by the simple fact that theology takes many forms."[4] Because I have consciously adopted a "fundamental" theological approach, I have not dealt in depth with a number of issues that would be important in either a more "systematic" or a more "practical" approach to Christian theology. Several of the recent texts noted above have explored such topics. On the aesthetic side, I have not attempted to survey the various contemporary theories of aesthetics or of postmodern "anti-aesthetics," nor to formulate a theory of aesthetics, nor to deal with the reasons there has historically been a gap between aesthetics and theology. Brown's *Religious Aesthetics* deals admirably with these issues, as well as with a number of others that are complementary to the topics in this book.

Even within the limits of the approach I have chosen, there is room for much expansion. I do not attempt to produce, even in outline form, a complete "theological aesthetics," but only to look at certain limited theological questions within each of the three areas designated by the word "aesthetics." This volume would be inadequate in size for a thorough examination of any one of these three senses in relation to theology, even if the latter is restricted to its specialization of "foundations." I have barely scratched the surface in dealing with the mutual relationships of theology and the nonverbal arts, for example, and have not treated the vast realm of literary theory at all. Happily, these topics are ones that promise to engage theologians increasingly, and more detailed and adequate treatments will no doubt appear both to complement and advance the positive aspects of my introductory and schematic study, and to correct its errors.

The last remark brings to light another limitation. I am clearly not well versed in the many fields besides theology that are involved in a theological aesthetics. Those who are experts in one or another field may find my treatments simplistic— or worse. As Balthasar remarked of his own work, the theologian's choice to speak about aesthetics "appears to betray in him who chooses it an idle amateur among such busy experts."[5] This is a risk, however, that is probably endemic to interdisciplinary studies. It is my hope that this preliminary treatment may give rise to questions that will advance the dialogue.

The reader will note that each chapter of the book is introduced by a prologue: a presentation and/or a discussion of art, music, or literature that raises in "aesthetic" form the question to be dealt with in the chapter. These introductory pieces—like the art works cited within the various chapters—are not intended merely as "illustrations." They are, rather, instances of "aesthetic theology": a reflection on and communication of theological insight in a way irreducible to abstract conceptual thought. In one sense, indeed, one might say that the rest of the book is commentary on what is said by the works of art. Theological discourse about art and beauty is, of course, quite different from allowing art and beauty themselves speak theologically. It is my hope that this book may function, at least to some extent, on both levels, engaging the reader in an "aesthetic" as well as an intellectual pattern of experience. I cannot, unfortunately, provide music along with the text; but where appropriate, I have referred in the notes to relevant recordings.

A problem arises with regard to works in languages other than English. As Gadamer says, "every translation is at the same time an interpretation. . . . Where a translation is necessary, the gap between the spirit of the original words and that of their reproduction must be accepted. It is a gap that can never be completely closed."[6] This gap is particularly significant in poetry. On the other hand, many English-speaking readers would find at least some of the poetry quoted inaccessible if it were simply given in the original. I have compromised by translating the texts as literally as possible, and including the original texts of the most important poems in an appendix. Where I have occasionally quoted from non-English sources in the text, I have provided translations in the notes. (Unless otherwise noted, translations are my own.) I have left untranslated some material in the notes that will be of interest primarily to scholars; likewise, where possible I have attempted to include the original of significant technical terms used in translated quotations from theological sources.

I wish to thank Fordham University and my colleagues in the Department of Theology for providing the faculty fellowship that allowed me to complete this book. My gratitude goes also to those who aided in its preparation and production: in particular, to Liana MacKinnon and Ronnie Rombs, who aided in bibliographical searches and in the pursuit of sources; to Prof. Frank Burch Brown, who read an earlier version of the manuscript and made many valuable suggestions; and to Cynthia Read of Oxford University Press, who guided it to publication. My special thanks go to my parents and my family, who taught me in many ways the love of beauty and its connection with God.

Contents

Abbreviations

CSM   *Encyclopedia of Theology. The Concise Sacramentum Mundi,* ed. Karl Rahner (New York: The Seabury Press, 1975).

DS   *Enchiridion Symbolorum, Definitionum et Declarationum de Rebus Fidei et Morum,* ed. Henricus Denzinger and Adolfus Schönmetzer, S.J., XXXIII ed. (Freiburg in Bres.: Herder, 1965).

EP   *Enchiridion Patristicum. Loci SS. Patrum, Doctorum Scriptorum Ecclesiasticorum,* ed. M. J. Rouët de Journel, S.J., 23 ed. (Freiburg in Brisg.: Herder, 1965).

JBC   *The Jerome Biblical Commentary,* ed. Raymond E. Brown, S.S., Joseph A. Fitzmyer, S.J., Roland E. Murphy, O. Carm. (London: Geoffrey Chapman, 1968).

LThK   *Lexikon für Theologie und Kirche*

Mansi   *Sacrorum conciliorum nova et amplissima collectio,* 31 vols., ed. J. D. Mansi (1757–1798).

PG   *Patrologiae Cursus Completus, Series Graeca,* ed. Jacques-P. Migne (Paris: 1857ss.).

PL   *Patrologiae Cursus Completus, Series Latina,* ed. Jacques-P. Migne (Paris: 1844ss.).

ST   Thomas Aquinas, *Summa Theologiae,* Leonine text, ed. Petrus Caramello (Torino: Marietti, 1952).

TDNT   G. Kittel, ed., *Theological Dictionary of the New Testament* (Grand Rapids, 1964).

TI   Karl Rahner, *Theological Investigations,* 23 vols. (New York: Crossroad, 1982–1992).

WM   Hans-Georg Gadamer, *Wahrheit und Methode* (Tübingen: J. C. B. Mohr, 1975).

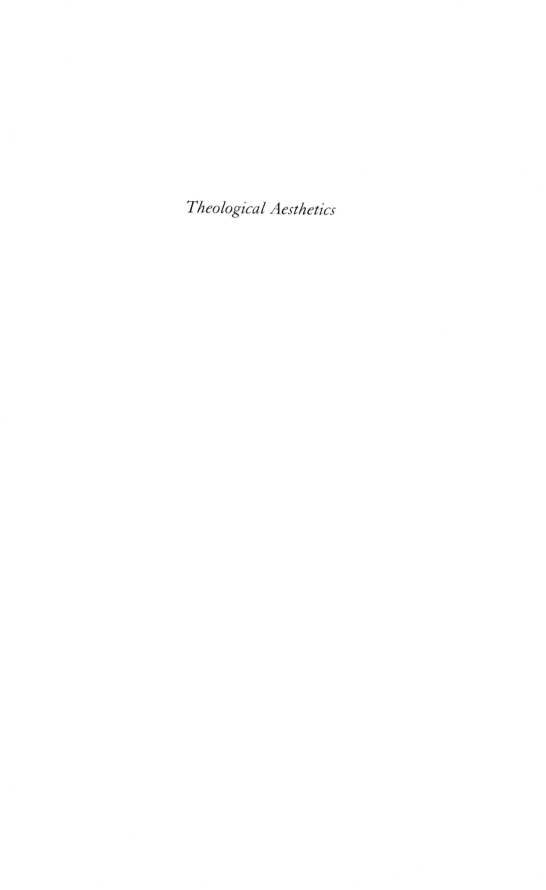

Theological Aesthetics

CHAPTER I

Theology and Aesthetics

Prologue: Karl Barth on Mozart's Place in Theology

Here[1] I must speak about Wolfgang Amadeus Mozart. Why and in what respect can one call this man "incomparable"?[2] Why is it that, with almost every measure that went through his head and that he brought forth on paper, he produced, for those who can receive it, music that it is an understatement to call "beautiful"?—music that for the saved is not entertainment, not enjoyment, not exaltation, but rather food and drink; music full of comfort and admonishment, as we need them; music that is never dominated by technique, nor ever sentimental, but always "moving," free and freeing, because it is wise, strong, and sovereign music. Why can one hold that Mozart has a place in theology (especially in the doctrine of creation, and then again in eschatology)—even though he was no Father of the Church, nor even, apparently, a particularly assiduous Christian (and who was a Catholic, besides!), and who, when he was not actually working, seems to our way of thinking to have lived somewhat superficially? One can say that Mozart belongs in theology because precisely in this matter, namely the goodness of creation in its totality, he knew something that neither the real Fathers of the Church, nor our Reformers, neither the Orthodox nor the Liberals, neither the adherents of natural theology nor those powerfully armed with the Word of God, and certainly not the Existentialists, knew as he knew it—or at least they did not know as he did how to express it and show its worth; something moreover that the other great musicians before and after him likewise did not know the way he did. In this matter he was pure of heart, head and shoulders above both optimists and pessimists. 1756–1791! It was just during this time that the theologians and other honest folk were having a hard time defending the good Lord, who was placed in the dock because of the Lisbon earthquake. But in the face of the problem of Theodicy, Mozart had the peace of God, which surpasses all reason—whether praising or blaming, speculative or critical. The problem caused him no struggle— it simply lay behind him. Why concern himself with it? He had heard—and he allows those who have ears, even to this day, to hear—what we shall only see at the end of time: the total coherence of the divine dispensation. As though from this end, he heard the harmony of creation: a harmony to which the darkness also

3

belongs, but in which the darkness is not blackness; where there is deficiency, but without being a defect; sadness, without becoming despair; gloom that nevertheless does not degenerate to tragedy; infinite sadness that nevertheless is not forced to make itself absolute. And for this very reason, this harmony contains cheerfulness, but within limits; its light shines so brightly because it shines forth from the shadows; it has a sweetness that is also sharp, and therefore is not cloying; it has a life that does not fear death, but knows it very well. *Et lux perpetua lucet (sic!) eis:*[3] even the dead of Lisbon. Mozart saw this light as little as any of us; but he *heard* the entire world of creation that is encompassed by this light. And it was fundamentally right that he did not hear a middle, neutral tone, but heard the *positive* tone *stronger* than the negative. He heard the latter only in and with the former. But in this inequality he nevertheless heard both together (one example, among many: the Symphony in G Minor of 1788!) He never heard abstractly only the one side. He heard *concretely*, and therefore his compositions were and are *total* music. And insofar as he heard the created world entirely without resentment or bias, what he brought forth was not his, but creation's own music: its dual, but nevertheless harmonious praise of God. He really never had to or wished to express himself in his works: neither his vitality nor his sorrow nor his piety, nor any program at all. He was wonderfully free from the constriction of needing or wanting to say something himself in his music. Rather, he simply offered himself to be to some extent the opportunity through which a bit of wood, metal, or cat gut could let themselves be heard and played as the voices of creation: the *instruments*—from the piano and violin, through the horn and clarinet, down to the venerable bassoon, and somewhere in their midst, without any special pretension, and precisely for that reason distinguished, the *human* voice—sometimes leading, sometimes accompanying, sometimes in harmony, each giving its particular contribution. He made music from each of them, using human emotions as well in the service of that music, and not vice versa! He was himself only an ear for that music, and its mediator for other ears. And he died when his life's work, according to the clever people, was just ripening to reach its true fulfillment. But after *The Magic Flute*; after the *Clarinet Concerto* of October 1791; after the *Requiem*; who can say that the fulfillment was not *already reached*? And was it not already there in what has been preserved from the very young Mozart? He died in misery as a kind of "unknown soldier," and has this in common with Calvin and with Moses in the Bible: that no one knows where he was buried. But what difference does that make? What is a grave, when a life was permitted to perform this service: in simplicity and unpretentiously, and therefore in such serenity, credibility, and urgency, to bring the good creation of God—to which the limitations and the end of humanity also belong—into language?

This had to be inserted here—before we turn toward chaos!—because we find in the music of Mozart—and I wonder whether one can find it so strongly in any of those who came before or after him—a shining and (I might say) a convincing proof that it is a *slander* on creation to ascribe to it a share in chaos because it includes in itself a "Yes" and a "No," because it has a side turned toward God but also a side turned toward nothingness. Mozart allows us to hear that even in this second side, and therefore in its totality, creation praises its Master, and thus is perfect. On this threshold of our problem—and this is no small thing—through Mozart order is created for those who have ears to hear: and better than any scientific deduction could have done it.[4]

The Problem of Theology and Aesthetics

Let us begin by reiterating Barth's question: why and in what sense can one say that Mozart has a place specifically in *theology*? There can, of course, be no question about Mozart's place in the history of Western culture, to which Christianity also belongs. And no one who has "ears to hear"—no one who has been moved to exaltation or peace or joy by the sublimity of Mozart's music—could deny that it can perform a "spiritual" function analogous to religious experience, and in this sense belongs to the history of Western "spirituality" along with many other works of art, great and small. But—unless we regard Barth's claim as merely a rhetorical flourish, a justifiable hyperbole—is this enough to merit Mozart a position within theology? Can we really ascribe to him a place in the process of *fides quaerens intellectum*—that is, in the quest for precisely the *understanding* of faith?

Gerardus van der Leeuw makes a similarly striking statement about Bach: in him, "the artist is priest, is himself a theologian."[5] But van der Leeuw is referring specifically to Bach's sacred music, his ability to combine "his service to the congregation with his service to art, the liturgical structure of his work with its aesthetic structure."[6] In this context it is understandable that "here art has become in truth a holy action":[7] the church musician is a minister, and the composer who sets sacred texts has not only the pastoral function of communicating the Word but also—if the task is undertaken in earnest—the implicitly theological one of understanding it and illuminating it for contemporary hearers. (That van der Leeuw considers Bach's accomplishment a "miracle" testifies to the rarity of a successful integration of the theological and artistic functions of the church musician; nevertheless, their connection is clear.)

But Barth seems to go further: it is not a question of Mozart's success as a liturgical musician (indeed, it might be argued that the spiritual qualities of Mozart's sacred works have little to do with their intended church settings and are entirely separable from the latter). Rather, it is Mozart's music itself, according to Barth, that conveys an insight that must be called "theological."

If we ask how this can be—in what sense an insight that is neither expressed as *logos* nor directly concerned with *theos* can nevertheless belong to "theology"—then we come to the heart of the question of the possibility of theological aesthetics. Is the place of a Mozart or a Bach exceptional, or does all art, precisely as art, have an intrinsic relationship to the object of theology? If so, what is the nature of that relationship?

This first chapter will inquire whether there can be an integration of these two endeavors—art and theology—within theology itself. Before attempting to discuss what such an integration would entail, however, our first step will be an attempt to clarify the meanings of the terms "aesthetics" and "theology" and to discern the boundaries and dimensions of their intersection.

The Notion of Theological Aesthetics

Hans-Georg Gadamer remarks on the importance of engaging in conceptual history,[8] since many of the concepts that we take for granted, like art, history, beauty, or science, have a history and are conditioned by epochal concerns and biases. A thorough historical study of all the terms involved in the interaction of theology and aesthetics is beyond the scope of the present work; but it is necessary at least to indicate briefly some of the different meanings given to our principal terms, and the consequent ambiguity of the notion of a "theological aesthetics."

The Concept of Aesthetics

The term "aesthetics" (derived from the Greek αἴσθησις, meaning "perception by the senses") was apparently coined by Alexander Gottlieb Baumgarten, whose 1750 tract *Aesthetica* was concerned with the study of the sensible (as contrasted with supra-sensible) mode of knowledge.[9] Already in Baumgarten several elements are present in the notion. He first speaks of "aesthetics" as the "science of cognition by the senses" (*scientia cognitionis sensitivae*). As such, it is the preliminary or "lower" part of cognitional theory or epistemology—"*gnoseologia inferior*." However, Baumgarten also calls aesthetics the "art of thinking beautifully" (*ars pulchre cogitandi*) and the "art of forming taste" (*ars formandi gustum*),[10] and he identifies its goal as the attainment of "beauty": "The end of aesthetics is the perfection of sensitive cognition, as such. But this perfection is beauty."[11] In Baumgarten's usage, then, "aesthetics" is the study dealing with the "lower" faculties of the mind, imagination and intuition, as well as with their products, art and poetry.[12] Baumgarten thus raises to the level of a "science" the examination of a level of cognition that rationalist philosophy had neglected as being "obscure" and inferior to the realm of clear ideas.[13]

The Enlightenment's adoption of Baumgarten's designation of a special "science" of aesthetics had far-reaching consequences. Hans Urs von Balthasar points out that the attainment of independent status for aesthetics also had the negative consequence of insulating it from logic and ethics. This would provide the background of the exclusion of the aesthetic from theology by Kierkegaard and his followers.[14] Vienna University philosopher Augustinus Wucherer-Huldenfeld makes a related criticism: aesthetics as developed from the Enlightenment definition presupposed a Cartesian division between mind (spirit) and body. It confined aesthetics to the latter sphere, and defined beauty as the object of such aesthetics. This led to the "scientific" (*wissenschaftlich*) canonization of the "vulgar misunderstanding of the beautiful," with the concurrent loss of the ontological sense of beauty and its eventual reduction to a product to be "consumed."[15] Contemporary thought, as we shall see through the course of this study, largely reacts against such consequences, and attempts to restore the aesthetic to its larger life context—including the religious and theological dimensions.

Kant, in his *Critique of Pure Reason* (1781), protests against the "misuse" of the word "aesthetics," and restricts its application to the etymological sense: the science of sense perception and its conditions (although in the *Critique of Judgment* of 1790 he allows a wider usage).[16] Hegel, on the other hand, limits the term in his *Lectures on Aesthetics* to the study of the beautiful, and more specifically to the "Philosophy of Fine Art" (explicitly excluding the consideration of the beauty of nature, which he considered inferior). He immediately acknowledges, however, that this use is etymologically incorrect:

> The name "aesthetics" in its natural sense is not quite appropriate to this subject. "Aesthetics" means more precisely the science of sensation or feeling. Thus understood, it arose as a new science, or rather as something that was to become a branch of philosophy for the first time, in the school of Wolff, at the epoch when works of art were being considered in Germany in the light of the feelings which they were supposed to evoke. . . . The name was so inappropriate, or, strictly speaking, so superficial, that for this reason it was attempted to form other names, e.g. "Kallistic." But this name, again, is unsatisfactory, for the science to be designated does not treat of beauty in general, but merely of *artistic* beauty. We shall, therefore, permit the name Aesthetics to stand, because it is nothing but a name, and so is indifferent to us, and moreover, has up to a certain point passed into common language.[17]

A notable expansion of the meaning of this "so frequently misused" term occurs in Schiller's celebrated series of "Aesthetic Letters."[18] Although he identifies the object of his inquiries as "the beautiful and art,"[19] he understands these terms in the widest possible context. The "aesthetic" is the area of integration of the human faculties: it designates the condition of spirit (*das Gemüt*) in which sensation and reason are active at the same time.

> All things that can in any way appear to us can be thought of under four different aspects. A thing can be related directly to our sensible condition (our being [*Dasein*] and well-being [*Wohlsein*]): that is its *physical* character. Or, it can be related to the intellect [*Verstand*] and create knowledge in us: that is its *logical* character. Or it can be related to our will, and be treated as an object of choice for a rational being: that is its *moral* character. Or, finally, it can be related to the totality of our different powers, without being a definite object for any single one of them: that is its *aesthetic* character.[20]

Hence Schiller's notion of an "aesthetic" education toward "taste and beauty" is in fact aimed at "the development of the whole complex of our sensual and spiritual powers in the greatest possible harmony."[21]

On the basis of this brief survey we may already distinguish several interconnected but distinct centers of interest within "aesthetics":

1. The general study of sensation and imagination and/or of "feeling" in the wider sense of nonconceptual or nondiscursive (but nevertheless "intellectual") knowledge.
2. The study of beauty and/or of "taste."
3. The study of art in general and/or of the fine arts in particular. (I use the word "study" rather than "theory" in order to include empirical, phe-

nomenological, historical, and other such approaches besides the philosophical or systematic.)

In each of these, either the receptive or the creative aspect may be emphasized: the aesthetic as a mode of apprehending reality, or as a mode of articulating or constituting the real.[22] The three will coincide or diverge to varying degrees, depending on the way in which terms are defined, on the relative weight given to each, and on the positions one takes regarding their relationships. The center of interest will also depend on the degree to which one's approach is subject- or object-oriented. In an object-centered approach, the emphasis is on a class of "aesthetica," whether these be defined by a relationship to beauty or to art. In a completely subject-oriented approach, on the other hand, the study of aesthetics would not concern any particular class of things or qualities: the determining factor would be an "aesthetic frame of mind," or (in Lonergan's terminology) an "aesthetic pattern of experience" on the part of the experiencing subject. The result is that virtually anything can be an aesthetic object, given the right subjective conditions. (It should be noted, however, that the "subjective" approach is compatible with an aesthetics that takes "beauty" as its proper object, when "the beautiful" is regarded as a transcendental quality of being. See chapter 4.)

It may be assumed that the study of sensation and imagination will always be presupposed (although not necessarily explicitly treated) as the theoretical underpinning for any "aesthetics;" but the relation between the other two senses is debatable.

It might be argued, for example, that the third division, the study of art, is simply a subset of the second, the study of the beautiful—or perhaps vice versa. Yet we find that neither the meaning of "beauty" and "art" nor their relationship one to another is entirely straightforward.[23] Is "the beautiful" an objective and universal quality toward which all art must strive; or is it purely relative to subjective or cultural perceptions? Does "ontological beauty" determine art's goal— or do artists determine what we perceive as beautiful?

That the latter can sometimes be the case seems incontestable. As Gadamer remarks, "a verdict on the beauty of a landscape undoubtedly depends on the artistic taste of the time. One has only to think of the description of the ugliness of Alpine landscape which we still find in the eighteenth century—the effect, as we know, of the spirit of artificial symmetry that dominates the century of absolutism."[24] Oscar Wilde makes the point more audaciously by having one of his characters argue the position that Nature itself imitates Art:

> For what is Nature? She is no great mother who has borne us. She is our creation. It is in our brain that she quickens to life. Things are because we see them, and what we see, and how we see it, depends on the Arts that have influenced us. . . . Nobody of any real culture, for instance, ever talks nowadays about the beauty of a sunset. Sunsets are quite old-fashioned. They belong to the time when Turner was the last note in art. . . . Yesterday Mrs. Arundel insisted on my going to the window, and looking at the glorious sky, as she called it . . . And what was it? It was simply a very second-rate

Turner, a Turner of a bad period, with all the painter's worst faults exaggerated and over-emphasized. . . .

Where, if not from the impressionists, do we get those wonderful brown fogs that come creeping down our streets, blurring the gas-lamps and changing the houses into monstrous shadows? To whom, if not to them and their master, do we owe the lovely silver mists that brood over our river, and turn to faint forms of fading grace, curved bridge and swaying barge? The extraordinary change that has taken place in the climate of London during the last ten years is entirely due to this particular school of Art. . . . To look at a thing is very different from seeing a thing. One does not see anything until one sees its beauty. Then, and then only, does it come into existence. At present, people see fogs, not because there are fogs, but because poets and painters have taught them the mysteriousness of such effects. There may have been fogs for centuries in London. I daresay there were. But no one saw them, and so we do not know anything about them. They did not exist until Art invented them. Now, it must be admitted, fogs are carried to excess. They have become the mere mannerism of a clique, and the exaggerated realism of their method gives dull people bronchitis.[25]

We shall return in a later chapter to a closer examination of the idea of "the beautiful" and its ontological status. For present purposes it will suffice to note that at least one major current of thought regards the beautiful as the object of "disinterested" pleasure. As Gadamer makes clear, much of Western aesthetics (in the second sense) follows the Greeks, for whom "the beautiful" (τὸ καλόν) is identified with things whose value is self-evident: one cannot ask what they are for.[26] Similarly for Kant, the object of aesthetic pleasure can neither be employed as useful nor desired as good; moreover, "real existence" (*Dasein*) adds nothing to aesthetic content, which consists entirely in self-presentation (*Sichdarstellen*).[27]

It is not at all clear, however, that "art" always pursues such an end. It may first of all be questioned whether the different activities designated as "art"— painting, sculpture, theater, dance, architecture, music, poetry, narration, literature, photography, cinema, and so on—can actually be subsumed under a single category at all.[28] Even if we presume that there is, if not a common "essence," at least a certain "family resemblance" between the various arts, we nevertheless must recognize in them a wide variety of both forms and purposes. As Mikel Dufrenne points out in his introduction to a UNESCO study on aesthetics,

> art does not have, always and everywhere, the same status, content, and function. . . . Today the world 'art' is highly suspect and the extent of the concept is very vague. . . . It is not only the "theories" of art which hesitate to determine its essence, it is also the practice of artists, who continually give the lie to any definition.[29]

Maritain reminds us that τεχνη is "art" as well as ποιησις.[30] Aristotle defines art as the ordination of reason by which acts reach a determined end by determined means,[31] and in his spirit Maritain sees the "useful" arts—or the practical "crafts"—not only as the origin of all art but also as the embodiment of its most typical characteristics as a "virtue of the practical intellect."[32]

Even if we make a distinction between useful and "fine" arts, it is not apparent that the latter must necessarily be defined by their having "beauty" as their goal.[33] Although some theories of fine art see the pursuit of beauty as its intrinsic nature, others argue convincingly for different meanings: play, representation, communication, emotional expression, and so forth. (These goals, of course, need not necessarily be mutually exclusive, and some may be combined with the idea of "beauty" as an end of art. This is particularly true of theories of art as representation. Kant, for example, defines art as "the beautiful representation [*Vorstellung*] of a thing." In this way even what is ugly may become beautiful through its representation in art.)[34] Among the Greeks, it was frequently assumed that mimesis was the sole intent of art.[35] Some art seems to aim at the production of emotions—not necessarily positive ones—for their own sake.[36] Even negative psychic states may be "enjoyed" because of the "aesthetic distance" that allows us to feel them while recognizing that their cause is not "real." (As an example one might think of the Japanese Butoh dance form, which purposely creates a sense of eeriness and revulsion in the viewer.) Art may even be self-defining; it may be "the ingenious manipulation of fixed forms and modes of treatment which makes the work of art a work of art"[37] rather than a relation to some end (be it "beauty" or any other).

On the other hand, art may be seen (as in Dewey) primarily as a mode of communication.[38] At least some forms of the fine arts can be didactic. This is especially true in the religious sphere. Here art (in the form of ritual, symbol, dance, images, gestures) is employed to convey a message (although not necessarily a verbal one). Although religious art sometimes attains to sublime heights of beauty (one may think of the frescoes of the Sistine Chapel, or the stained glass windows at Chartres), it may be questioned whether this is intrinsic to its purpose—or even whether it may at times impede its primary religious function.[39] (This theme will recur throughout our study, and will be explored thematically in the final chapter.)

The presumed connection between art and beauty becomes even more questionable when we look outside the Western tradition. Maritain writes that "the dynamism of Indian art itself tends, I would say, to a supreme end which is not beauty, but praxis, practical use, especially spiritual experience."[40] James Martin briefly summarizes the views of several Hindu aestheticians who confirm Maritain's view. Ananda K. Coomaraswamy, for example, insists that "all art is essentially iconographic, and that authentic art forms and objects embody and transmit 'spiritual' meanings."[41] True art is ideational; modern (Western) aesthetics errs in placing its goal in the life of feeling. "Aesthetic" satisfaction for its own sake is a form of idolatry or of dehumanization.[42]

It would seem, then, that we should avoid attempting to formulate an a priori definition of the connection between the "beautiful" and the arts. We will instead admit, with Gadamer, that there can be different criteria for what constitutes "art"[43] and with David Tracy that we need a "critical pluralism of methods of understanding and explaining" the experience of art.[44] In that case, we will be justified in seeing "art" and "beauty" as two interrelated but distinct centers of interest for "aesthetics" in our inquiry into its relationship to theology.

The Object(s) of Theology and the Object(s) of Aesthetics

Just as several different objects or centers of interest are possible for "aesthetics," so likewise for "theology." Hans Küng and others have examined in a schematic way theology's move through a number of paradigm changes that can be seen in the light of a shift in "point of view" toward progressive interiority.[45] Changes in theology's method naturally imply different conceptions of its object as well. In a very general and schematic way we may discern three interconnected objects of theology's attention that emerge in the progression: God, faith (or religious experience), and (in extension of the second) theology itself.

In its classical and "objective" phase, theology is conceived as a body of knowledge (*scientia*) concerning God: *"Deus est subiectum huius scientiae."*[46] (Naturally other things—indeed, ultimately all things—are treated by theology as well; but they are a proper study for theology only insofar as they are considered in relation to God.)[47] As theology turns increasingly to the human subject, its object is reconceived in terms of reflection on faith or religious experience or simply "religion."[48] Theology becomes a *Glaubensverständnis.*[49] Finally, theology may turn to reflection on its own methods, hermeneutical principles, and conditions of possibility; it becomes "the theology of theology."[50]

Dimensions of Theological Aesthetics

On the basis of the foregoing, what is meant by "theological aesthetics" in its wide sense is the practice of theology, conceived in terms of any of these three objects, in relation to any of the three senses of "aesthetics" outlined above; that is, theological aesthetics will consider God, religion, and theology in relation to sensible knowledge (sensation, imagination, and feeling), the beautiful, and the arts. The nature of the relations can be varied. Here I will briefly outline several interconnected themes. My treatment is meant to be suggestive rather than exhaustive. I will, for example, advert only in passing to literary studies and their methods, which have in recent years increasingly been integrated into scriptural, hermeneutical, doctrinal, and methodological studies. I shall instead concentrate on the nonliterary embodiments of beauty, feeling, and art in their connections with theology.

Theological Aesthetics as Practice: The Aesthetic Dimension of Theological Discourse

Karl Barth wrote concerning theology:

> if its task is correctly seen and grasped, theology as a whole, in its parts and
> in their interconnexion, in its content and method, is, apart from anything

else, a peculiarly beautiful science. Indeed, we can confidently say that it is the most beautiful of all the sciences. To find the sciences distasteful is the mark of the Philistine. It is an extreme form of Philistinism to find, or to be able to find, theology distasteful. The theologian who has no joy in his work is not a theologian at all. Sulky faces, morose thoughts and boring ways of speaking are intolerable in this science. May God deliver us from what the Catholic Church reckons one of the seven sins of the monk—*taedium*—in respect of the great spiritual truths with which theology has to do.[51]

It is notable that for Barth, theology is beautiful precisely as a "science." But many think that theology's pursuit of "scientific" status has also led to negative consequences. Hans Urs von Balthasar contends that it is theology's attempt to imitate the method of the exact sciences that has undermined the beauty of theology.[52] Not only has modern theology neglected beauty as an object of inquiry, but also it has largely lost its connection with living religion and spirituality—that is, with the pursuit and communication of "great spiritual truths." Already at the beginning of the nineteenth century, Alois Gügler, a representative of early Catholic Romanticism, commented on theology's lack of spirit: "How many manuals of dogmatic and moral theology could we pick up without finding in them any inkling of religion?"[53] The modern technological world, according to Balthasar, has lost its sense of knowledge as wonder and contemplative receptivity; instead, the ideal of knowledge has become *Bewältigung*: mastery, domination, exploitation.[54] The academic world largely reflects this ideal of abstract, objectivizing rationalism; and academic theology has to a large degree allowed itself to be seduced by it.[55] In this way it stands in danger of losing its inherent spirituality, and with it its inherent poetry and beauty. In a world that is without beauty—or at least that "can no longer see it or reckon with it"—Balthasar warns, "the good also loses its attractiveness, the self-evidence of why it must be carried out."[56] Likewise theology, if it neglects its connection with spiritual beauty, loses its ability to convince.

Many other commentators echo Balthasar's concerns. Bruce Lawrence notes that theology "privileges reason not feeling, and religious academics, even those not allied explicitly with theology, tend to mirror its emphasis: though many may have had the experience of spirituality, they feel peer pressure to discount or hide the impact of some inner force motivating and perhaps guiding their life's work."[57] Karl Rahner reformulates Balthasar's comment that modern times lack a *kniende Theologie* (theology "on its knees" in worship) by saying that we are lacking a mystagogical and "poetic" theology. As a consequence, Rahner joins in calling for a return of the aesthetic dimension to theology.[58] This means not only that theology should take account of feeling, beauty, and art as aspects of religion and of primary religious language,[59] but also that theology itself should speak "with feeling" and in images, integrating the religious and poetic elements into its mode of discourse. Theology cannot be a merely "abstract" science, since its goal is to guide us beyond all concepts to the experience of God's mystery.

Rahner's writings have powerfully reintroduced into academic theology the notion that the very heart of its method must be a *"reductio in mysterium."*[60] This methodological principle is based on the insistence that the concern of theology can be nothing but God, and that the reality of God is missed if it remains for us merely an idea. Theology aims at an existential encounter with God. But:

> God, and what is meant by God, can only be grasped when we surrender our own conceptual understanding to the ineffable and holy mystery which lays hold on us as the mystery which is near to us and which embraces us in love.
>
> The theologian is not the purely intellectual expositor but the one who thrusts all duly explained earthly realities into the incomprehensible mystery of God. The theologian is the one who shows that no human proposition . . . is ultimately really understood unless it is released into the blessed incomprehensibility of God.[61]

The intrinsically mystagogical and supra-rational dynamism of theology implies that in its exercise it must also have a "poetic" element:

> we must admit that it is a consequence as well as a defect of a theology that is rationalistic and proceeds only "scientifically" that the poetic touch is missing. Nowadays we demand from theology something which, although not new, has been neglected during the last few centuries: theology must somehow be "mystagogical," that is, it should not merely speak about objects in abstract concepts, but it must encourage people really to experience that which is expressed in such concepts. To that extent we might understand poetic theology as one method of a mystagogical theology.[62]

To achieve the goal of incorporating such a poetic element, theology must have the courage to overcome the fear (albeit sometimes well-founded) of aestheticism. It "must abandon the conviction that the only legitimate interest of students of religion in art is or should be an explication of the allegedly religious or theological significance of specified artworks,"[63] and must be willing to see its own task as including an aesthetic element. The need for an "aesthetic theology"[64] comprising both a "theopoiesis" and a "theopoetics" is particularly evident in the attempt to reintegrate pastoral and spiritual theology with systematics, as well as in the study of the Scriptures. But there is also room for the poetic within the more abstract areas of theology. As Amos Wilder points out, the works of many of the greatest and most "intellectual" theologians of the past have been shot through with imagination.[65] Contemporary theologians should be willing to follow their example.

At the same time, the recognition that theology should speak with and to the "aesthetic" dimension should not imply a loss of the distinction between conceptual thought and feeling, or the abandonment of the former in favor of a theology conceived as a purely "poetic" or "rhetorical" enterprise. Frank Burch Brown, while arguing for the necessity of aesthetic sensitivity in theology, nevertheless cautions that "theology cannot satisfactorily appropriate aesthetic truth simply by becoming aesthetic itself or by failing to exercise its own rational capacities."[66] If systematic theological language is usually not of the same kind as the language of originating religious experience, this is because it performs a special function with regard to the latter: it is a second-order language that distances itself in order to reflect critically on experience.[67] As Rahner writes:

> There is also a theology that, holding its breath, as it were, patiently and rightly undertakes long conceptual explorations from which we cannot expect immediate religious or mystical experiences. We have to leave it to individual theologians to decide to what extent they appeal or do not appeal to religious experience in their theology.[68]

Nor should we deny the power of abstract conceptual thought about God to be deeply beautiful in its own way. When it genuinely mediates personal insight, it can be attractive, elevating, personal, and spiritually engaged—as anyone knows who has been draw into wonder and prayer by "abstract" theology. Heidegger's remark in *Identität und Differenz* on the metaphysical conception of God is well known: "the first cause as *'Causa sui'* [self-caused]: this is the accurate name for God in philosophy." For Heidegger, real religion can have nothing to do with God so conceived: "before this God one can neither fall on one's knees in awe, nor can one play music and dance before this God."[69] Nevertheless, the *qawwali* singers of the Sufi tradition praise God in exstatic song under the title *Al-Qayyūm* ["the Self-Subsisting"]; the highly emotive *bhajans* of north India in their expression of love for Krishna can also refer to God as the Absolute of nondualist Vedanta; Olivier Messiaen composed haunting and disquieting meditations based on St. Thomas's ontology of the divine subsistence.[70] Aquinas and Śaṅkara were both metaphysicians as well as mystics and poets. Could we not find many other examples of living religion mediated by metaphysical thought that contradict Heidegger's assertion? Or rather, should we not take the important truth in Heidegger's critique of "ontotheology"—like that of Pascal's distinction between the "God of the philosophers and savants" and the "God of Abraham, Isaac, and Jacob"[71]—as a warning against a certain objectivizing and conceptualist kind of thinking that has little to do with genuine metaphysics or theology?

As Lonergan says, the primary differentiation of consciousness in the history of humanity is that between "common sense" (including the mythical, symbolic, and artistic realms) and transcendence, not that between "theory" and transcendence. This means that most religious experience will have a symbolic mediation, rather than a conceptual one. Nevertheless, the latter is not excluded.[72] Naturally, the extent to which abstract thinking can mediate spiritual experience will depend largely upon the individual mind involved: not only on the presence or absence of "intellectual conversion" but also on one's degree of familiarity with the conceptual language, one's temperament, and one's background. But is this not true of art as well? "For those who have ears to hear," as Barth says, Mozart's music is sublimely spiritual; but not all have such "ears to hear." And some music (one might think of twelve-tone compositions, for example, or Messaien's musical "grammar") is "difficult" and even inaccessible to the listener who is not disciplined in its aesthetic language.

Moreover, while insisting on the need for an "aesthetic" theology, we must also admit that on the practical level there are perhaps others who can speak to faith with feeling better than academic theologians, who cannot all be poets and artists. Although there is need for a more profound engagement of theology in general with the aesthetic realm, each still retains its own independent validity, and a certain functional differentiation is both valid and fruitful. Theology, after all, is not all-sufficient; as Lonergan says, it "illumines only certain aspects of human reality" and therefore must "unite itself with all other relevant branches of human studies."[73] Within theology, a special point of contact is found in those operations outlined by Lonergan as the "functional specialty" of "communications," which deals with the process of leading others to share in "one's cognitive, constitutive, effective meaning."[74]

Without retracting what has been said about the legitimacy and desirability of an "aesthetic theology," therefore, we must also admit that theology will remain primarily in the "intellectual" rather than the "aesthetic" pattern of experience. Hence the desired union of theology with other branches of study implies collaboration, rather than a fruitless attempt to subsume every aspect of human endeavor into theology as such. Frank Burch Brown characterizes the normal relationship of conceptual theology to the arts as complementarity and dialectic. Having asked the question whether theology itself can be an "art" (in the sense in which he defines the word), Brown replies that

> insofar as the means and ends of theology are largely intellectual and conceptual (as they characteristically are) then its constructive, imaginative work is not basically or even mediately aesthetic. Here there is making, but without aesthetically embodied meaning. This explains why theology in its intellectual forms cannot in itself fully succeed in its goal of "bringing all of life and the world into relation with God" and why it must exist in complementarity and dialectical relation not only with praxis but also with those richly aesthetic arts that can bring these relations imaginatively to life.[75]

The Aesthetic as a Source for Theology

The realm of aesthetic experience (or the aesthetic level of experience) may serve as a source for both historical theology and systematic theological reflection in at least two ways. First, it is a locus of explicitly religious (and theological) experience, expression, and discourse; second, it is a locus of secular human experience that is either (a) "implicitly" religious or (b) susceptible to correlation with the sacred. That is, the aesthetic realm provides theology with "data" concerning its three objects (God, religion, and theology itself), as well as with knowledge of the cultural matrix to which these are related in reflection.

AS A LOCUS OF EXPLICITLY RELIGIOUS EXPERIENCE

First of all, the realms of imagination, feeling, symbol, and art are a locus of the Christian faith and tradition on which theology reflects. The history of Western art provides the most obvious example. John Ruskin remarked that every civilization records its history in three books: those of its words, its deeds, and its art; and that of these three, the last is the truest. An analogous statement may be made concerning religion.[76] In their origins, religion and art formed a unity,[77] and even in the subsequent differentiation of consciousness a great proportion of religious consciousness remains embodied in nonconceptual symbolic form. Moreover, art remains in many ways the closest "analogue" to religion.[78] Hence the history of art constitutes a frequently neglected "text" that reveals a dimension of faith that is necessarily missed if theology attends solely to doctrine and abstract conceptualizations.

Apart from literature, the monuments of "high" ecclesiastical art—the catacomb frescoes, the mosaics of the basilicas, Gregorian chant, the Gothic cathedrals, Renaissance religious painting, Baroque oratorio, and the like[79]—are perhaps the most evident (and most accessible) locus of the Christian tradition in the "aesthetic" realm. But theology must also attend to the wider sphere of popular culture as the embodiment of religious experience. As Karl Rahner remarks, "if scientific theology is to be true to its own nature, it will have to reflect on the religion of the people much more than it usually does."[80] Such popular religion, according to Rahner, is not only a constitutive moment of the church's existence;[81] it is also superior to conceptual theology insofar as it is closer to God's original revelation and its invitation to divinization, precisely because it has not gone through the narrowing process of systematic thought.[82] To reflect theologically on this source will mean attending not only to the popular and "mythic" dimension in Scripture but also to "the entire symbolic religious life" of the church,[83] including "piety, myth, ritual, liturgy, religious orders and movements, symbols of popular culture and elite cultures alike"[84]—a task, David Tracy remarks, that has hardly begun.[85]

Margaret Miles argues that this dimension of "theological aesthetics" should serve as a corrective to an overly conceptual account of religion. Most of our accounts of Christian history are based on verbal texts. These tended to be written about, by, and for the upper classes in society. "These texts, almost exclusively the product of culturally privileged, highly educated, male, and most frequently monastic authors, constitute the bulk of the literary products of Christianity before the modern period."[86] Such a history, being linguistic, favors language users:— that is, those for whom spoken and written language are the dominant mode of expression. But this "renders inaudible and invisible those whose primary mode of understanding and relating to the world is not verbal."[87] The latter, however, are arguably the larger part of the human race in most periods. (This would especially apply to the poorer classes and to women of all classes, who have largely been excluded from literacy and from the kind of education and culture that emphasize verbal skills.) Hence in "literary" history the masses of people are largely left out of view. From a theological point of view, such a history is seriously lacking: "it is inadequate, to say the least, to attempt to understand a historic community entirely from the study of the writings of a few of its most uncharacteristic members"[88]—in particular if one's interest is in the community's faith or religious consciousness. Hence the consideration of the symbolic and artistic dimensions of religion—which are far more universal than the literary—is relevant to theology.

Art and symbolic behavior objectify aspects of consciousness that are nonverbal, but are not for that reason pre-rational or pre-spiritual: they are (or can be) a way of thinking, and not merely a translation or illustration of verbal, conceptual thought. (We shall return to this idea in greater detail in the next chapter.) In Patrick O'Brian's popular novel *Post Captain*, his hero Dr. Maturin is at a concert when he suddenly becomes aware of the scent of the perfume of the woman he loves. He reflects:

> A foolish German had said that man thought in words. It was totally false; a pernicious doctrine; the thought flashed into being in a hundred simultaneous forms, with a thousand associations, and the speaking mind selected one, forming it grossly into the inadequate symbols of words, inadequate because common to disparate situations—admitted to be inadequate for vast regions of expression, since for them there were the parallel languages of music and painting. Words were not called for in many or indeed most forms of thought: Mozart certainly thought in terms of music. He himself at this moment was thinking in terms of scent.[89]

In contemporary philosophy, Gadamer is preeminent in attempting to retrieve the Romantic insight that "art is knowledge and the experience of the work of art is a sharing of this knowledge."[90] Karl Rahner agrees: although we can certainly attempt to "translate" from one symbolic thought-form to another, the nonliterary arts "can be considered autonomous ways of human self-expression that cannot be adequately translated into words."[91] Religion is especially related to such modes of thought because it is (among other things) a way of "seeing" and "feeling" the world, as well as a way of conceiving it, in relation to God. Calvin compared the Scriptures to a lens through which we see the world. I am suggesting that the "lens" of religion is also constituted by its nonverbal dimensions—although of course these are related to the intellectual and specifically to the scriptural "lens." The kinetic images embodied in sacramental acts can be rendered fully intelligible only in performance, not in speaking about them.[92] (Naturally, this does not exclude subsequent theological reflection on the performance, but it means that this reflection can never be total, and must always refer back to the lived act.)

Moreover, because they relate to a transcendent object, many of religion's expressions are appropriately nonverbal, and a "negative" hermeneutic must be applied even to its verbal expressions. The latter are more related to the metaphorical speech of poetry, which addresses the existential human condition, than to the abstract concepts of science.[93]

The "priority of poetry" in the existential and religious realm[94] means that even "scientific" or metaphysical theological concepts and judgments are more adequately understood, from a historical point of view, when placed in the fuller context provided by the "aesthetic" dimension of religion. Thus, theology may achieve insight into its own context and method through parallels in the history of the arts; it can use that history as a source for the knowledge of concrete religion; and it can find there (particularly in liturgy and art) an "illustration" of its own meanings.

Naturally, a complex hermeneutical task is implied in the use of symbol and art as a theological source. The historical theologian must engage not only in the history of art but also in the history of looking at or listening to or participating in art.[95] We cannot presume that others saw and heard the same things we do in the works and rituals we have inherited: one must develop a "period point of view," attending to the cultural context of the work.[96] By the same token, it may be precisely what was not conscious to the artist or the artist's contemporaries—the imaginative presuppositions of the work, its religious and cultural "language"—that are most revealing to us.

Likewise, there are limitations to the use of the arts as a theological locus. Historically a great deal of religious art, especially that which has become classical, was, like literature, the product a minority educated class. Although art was frequently aimed at the masses as a means of edification and education, its production was often directed by ecclesiastical patrons, so that it reflects conceptual theology. This enhances its use as an "illustration" of theology, but at the same time limits its use as a separate "source" of data on religious experience. "Official" religious art tends to be hierarchically controlled, conservative, and traditional; hence a good deal of religious art is imitative and conventional. There are also the limitations of art technique and of the artist: "The artist, too, is a particular self with a particular history in a particular culture. The artist, too, is a finite, social, historical self employing a language that carries the entire history of the effects and influence of the tradition."[97] In short, *"l'artiste parle dans une matière don't il n'est pas complètement le maître, une langue don't il n'est pas l'inventeur que dans une faible mesure."*[98] Nevertheless, because its possibilities and limitations are different from those of verbal religion and theology, the symbolic and artistic level of religion provides an important complementary source for theological reflection on the tradition.

AS A LOCUS OF GENERAL HUMAN EXPERIENCE

The aesthetic realm may serve as a source for theological reflection also in a second way: not merely as a locus of explicitly religious experience but also as an expression of human spiritual being that implicitly embodies transcendence. This applies to the entire realm of "feeling" and imagination, to the pursuit of beauty, and in a particular way to the arts. Rahner writes: "Whatever is expressed in art is a product of human transcendentality by which, as spiritual and free beings, we strive for the totality of all reality . . . It is only because we are transcendental beings that art and theology can really exist."[99] It should perhaps immediately be added, however, that not all art is good art; and although human transcendentality is the condition of possibility for art's existence, individual works of art may be the expression of "lower" or truncated forms of subjectivity as well as of transcendence toward God. (This ambiguity of art with regard to transcendence will be further explored in chapter 6.)

In any case, according to Rahner, art *can* be truly inspired, in the properly theological sense: it can be the bearer of a divine revelation, apart from the "special" revelation embodied in the Scriptures:

> We might then argue that the self-expression contained in a Rembrandt painting or a Bruckner symphony is so strongly inspired and bourne by

divine revelation, by grace, and by the self-communication of God that it tells us, in a way that cannot be translated adequately in a verbal theology, what persons really are in the sight of God.[100]

These assertions presuppose Rahner's view that "revelation" cannot be completely distinguished from the "faith" that accepts it, and that the primary recipient of revelation is humanity as a whole, in its various cultural, linguistic, and conceptual embodiments.[101] This view will be explored in a later chapter. If we accept it, however, it becomes clear that even in the absence of any explicitly "sacred" content, "religious phenomena in the arts themselves would be constituent elements of an adequate theology."[102] In this way we could understand Barth's statement that Mozart's music "belongs to theology": in art we may find not only non-verbal formulations of the religious tradition but also a locus of revelation—that is, of God's self-communication, accepted in human consciousness and freedom.

Finally, the aesthetic realm (in all its dimensions) is of relevance to theology insofar as the latter is seen as being (at least in one of its functions) "correlational." In Paul Tillich's classical formulation, "Theology moves back and forth between two poles, the eternal truth of its foundation and the temporal situation in which the eternal truth must be received."[103] "The 'situation' to which theology must respond," for Tillich, is "the totality" of human "creative self-interpretation in a special period."[104] This includes the artistic as well as the scientific, economic, political, and ethical forms of existence.[105]

Theology as Metaphor and as Metaphysics

"Aesthetic theology" as described above designates a form of theology that (to varying degrees) depends on the aesthetic realm for its language, content, method, and theory: the conjunction of theology with the practice of imaginative and/or beautiful discourse ("theopoiesis") and with the theories thereof ("theopoetics"). The latter includes the application of literary and artistic theories either to theology's sources, in particular to the Scriptures, or to theology in general, conceived as an essentially hermeneutical enterprise.[106] When the two aspects are combined, one has a type of theology that not only attends to and examines the aesthetic embodiment of religious experience but also adopts narrative, metaphorical discourse as its own primary mode of communication or basic structure emphasizing the way in which stories and images have the power to shape communities of experience and practice.[107]

Such an "aesthetic" theology[108] remains close to the primary form of Christian religion, which is inextricably tied to the narratives about Christ. The understanding of these narratives as art emerged as a result of the separation of science and philosophy from theology in the Enlightenment, at the same time that aesthetics took form as an independent field. The insight was developed through the hermeneutics of the Romantic period.[109] Scheeben calls the Scriptures "a painting and a drama of divine wisdom."[110] This does not imply that the Bible is "fictional" in the sense of being untrue; but it means that its truth can only be grasped and reconstructed as a world of images.[111] One way in which theology engages in the "understanding" of faith is by (re-)presentation of the Bible's world-picture(s) and the further elaboration of its narrative, metaphorical understanding of God and salvation.

Such a method has the advantage not only of being in close accord with the Scriptures but also of having an immediate "spiritual" relevance. As Bruce Lawrence remarks, "spirituality eschews argument. It resists discourse. Instead, it couches all truth as narrative, relying on stories that suggest an implicit link to readers/listeners."[112] It aims at a "dramatic" apprehension of truth, "truth manifest in dialogue, in a narratively-structured interaction which resists theoretical reduction and premature or facile resolution."[113]

Roman Catholic academic theology in the post-Tridentine period was largely dominated by a philosophical and conceptual approach. Paul Tillich was correct, however, in seeing in such "philosophical" theology a secondary and derivative specialization: the primary language of theology (like that of religion) is symbolic or (in the senses defined above) "aesthetic."[114]

Nevertheless, there are several reasons theology (including theological aesthetics) also requires a critical metaphysical or ontological dimension. Lonergan has discussed at length how the operation of the intellect on the level of symbol, metaphor, and narrative raises questions that cannot be answered on that level, but need the further development of cognitional theory and metaphysics.[115] Nicholas Lash pursues the same idea specifically in regard to theology in his discussion of the necessity for its narrative forms to relate to metaphysics: "To suppose that narrative is an alternative to metaphysics, metaphor an alternative to analogy, is to overlook the fact that 'Metaphor . . . raises questions that only analogy . . . can answer, while conversely analogy can only answer questions that are raised in a metaphorical form.' "[116]

Lash acknowledges the validity of Gadamer's retrieval of the cognitive status of literary and artistic modes of experience and expression, but he introduces a note of caution: art *may* be knowledge; however, in the use of metaphorical language there is also a constant danger of self-indulgence and dishonesty.[117] (We shall return to this important theme in chapter 6.) A story-teller uses metaphor to help an audience "shape" its experience. "But the attempt to 'make sense' of the world elides with dangerous ease into the attempt to make the world, in our imagination, conform to how we would have it be."[118] As Balthasar remarks against Hamann's romantic glorification of feeling over against reason, "What we are used to calling 'aesthetic' is as tinged with the vanity and unreality of original sin as is (enlightened) reason."[119]

Furthermore, Lash continues, Jewish and Christian religious discourse is not only narrative but also "autobiographical," in two senses: they are both self-involving, and they locate the speaker in a particular cultural, historical tradition. This means that our religious narrative is always influenced "more deeply than we know" by the circumstances of its production,[120] and lacks "that aspiration to universality and timelessness of expression which is characteristic of 'theoretical' or 'scientific' discourse."[121] At the same time, "Christian religious discourse, as autobiographical, tends to attribute an unwarranted universality to the particular forms in which, in particular circumstances, it finds expression."[122] For the same reason, the use of narrative is always subject to ideological distortion.[123] We have learned from Marx, Freud, and Nietzsche that not only conceptual thought but also "all the expressions of consciousness possess not only their manifest meanings but conceal and distort a series of latent, overdetermined meanings that demand new modes of analysis."[124] Therefore, Lash concludes, the dynamic of Christian love itself, in order to be responsible, demands "continual submission to a process of verification, of the correlative purification of illusion."[125]

Several considerations may be added to Lash's remarks. The metaphorical level of speech is particularly—although not uniquely—vulnerable to what Wittgenstein called *"die Verhexung der Sprache"*: the "bewitchment" that language exercises over its speakers, making us mistake our words for real states of being. Hence a purely narrative approach stands in danger of unconsciously fostering a certain literalism or fundamentalism, especially on the popular level of religion. When this occurs there is the danger of a chasm, if not a conflict, between religion and secular experience, especially empirical science and the mentality that stems from its influences on life.[126] Religion stands in danger of becoming—or at least of seeming to become—the expression of a naive and anthropocentric world view, opposed to the larger and more humble cosmic perspective corresponding to the world revealed by modern science. Humbert Wolfe's poem "Betelgeuse" (which is now best known in the musical setting by Gustav Holst) illustrates such a view: "God" is seen as a single, small leaf in the forests of the red giant star:

> On Betelgeuse
> the gold leaves hang in golden aisles
> for twice a hundred million miles,
> and twice a hundred million years
> they golden hang and nothing stirs,
>   on Betelgeuse.
>
> Space is a wind that does
> not blow on Betelgeuse,
> and time—oh time—is a bird,
> whose wings have never stirred
> the golden avenues
> of leaves on Betelgeuse.
>
>   On Betelgeuse
> there is nothing that joys or grieves
> the unstirred multitude of leaves,
> nor ghost of evil or good
> haunts the gold multitude
>   on Betelgeuse.
>
> And birth they do not use
> nor death on Betelgeuse,
> and the God, of whom we are
> infinite dust, is there
> a single leaf of those
> gold leaves on Betelgeuse.[127]

The poem tells us symbolically that the geocentric world view to which the religious idea of "God" corresponds is dwarfed and rendered insignificant by scientific knowledge of the cosmos. Religion that uses "mythic" narrative language as its unique mode of discourse is in danger of being—or of being perceived as—mythological.

On the other hand, there is also the opposite danger: that the "mythological" and conditioned character of religious narrative be acknowledged, and religious truth consequently be devalued or totally subjectivized. In that case, religion is relegated to the realm of "mere" poetry and made a matter of individual "taste."

There is a need, therefore, for a form of theological discourse that mediates between the realm of narrative and the claims of empirical science and critical reason. Such a theology must be able to deal with the various differentiations of human meaning and discourse, and evaluate the truth claims of each in its proper context.

Moreover, narrative and metaphor stand in need of interpretation, as well as critical assessment and verification. Symbolic discourse in the realm of undifferentiated consciousness can accommodate internal tensions and even contradictions.[128] But when consciousness is differentiated, the question arises: "what do we do when our stories conflict"[129]—either with each other, or with the claims of other traditions, or with nonreligious differentiations of consciousness? How do we deal with different interpretations of the same story, or with different practical and moral imperatives drawn from the same narratives?[130]

Such considerations point to the need for a level of theological reflection that stands at a critical distance from religious narrative and metaphor. Empirical science seeks formulations that are "impervious to linguistic manipulation" through the "quest of scientific discourse for a formal purity as little 'infected' as possible by the anthropomorphism of the metaphorical."[131] Religious metaphorical discourse attempts to preserve God's transcendence by appealing to a *"coincidentia oppositorum"* and by employing a dialectic of affirmation and denial, whereby the metaphorical meaning is affirmed through the negation of the literal sense.[132] Metaphysical theology attempts to formulate a theory of religious meaning and to counter the dangers of bias and anthropomorphism by applying to religious discourse what Nicholas Lash calls "that branch of philosophy the logic of whose procedures focuses on analogical usage of unrestricted generality."[133]

Lash notes that some theologians consider the way of metaphysical analogy to be closed, and/or assimilate the logic of analogy to metaphor. "If this were the case," he comments

> then there would be no way past the Feuerbachian critique, because we would be unable to discriminate between the "models" of God that we fashion in metaphor and the discovered mystery signified by such constructions. All that we say of God, affirmatively, is indeed "projected" from our human experience, is anthropomorphic in character, and we would have no way of showing the sense of such language to be other than "merely" projective.[134]

To the objection that Kant destroyed the possibility of analogous metaphysical language, Lash replies that Kant's critique only affects a certain inadequate conception of analogy—one which was not that of Aquinas, for example, or of his contemporary followers.[135]

Lash therefore points out the need of narrative religious discourse to integrate "correctives" on several levels, theoretical and practical. As discourse, it demands "grammatical" or philosophical consideration; as narrative, it demands literary-critical consideration; as autobiographical, it demands historical consideration. There are also certain practical religious correctives to anthropomorphism: the history of religious silence, simplicity, and iconoclasm, and the history of suffering (which, however, can also corrupt and disfigure).[136]

There is need, then, for a theological discipline that mediates between narrative discourse and empirical science, as well as between the realms of "common sense" and theoretical language, showing the warrants of the truth claims of each and their relationship to each other.

The nature of the relation between metaphorical and metaphysical speech about God will be explored in the next chapter. For the moment my purpose is only to stress that theology, as conceived here, includes both an "aesthetic" and a metaphysical component. Naturally, the latter occurs at a secondary level of reflection. As Paul Lauritzen says, Christianity is to be seen essentially as a life-giving and life-transforming story, not as a primitive metaphysics that is to be demythologized and surpassed in a "higher" realm of rationality.[137] In Ricoeur's words, "The symbol gives rise to thought, but thought always returns to and is informed by the symbol."[138] Naturally as well, a metaphysical or ontological theology today must take into account not only the Kantian critique but also the warnings of Heidegger and his followers concerning "ontotheology." In Lonergan's terms, it must be a metaphysics that has made the shift to "interiority" as its starting point. Nevertheless, it must be stressed that the logical and metaphysical understanding that arises from the lived experience of faith is not alien to the latter, but is an aspect of its effective presence in human life, including that of the mind, by which it is enriched.

Theological Aesthetics as Theory

"Theological aesthetics," then, as I conceive it, includes both narrative/metaphorical and metaphysical approaches. It comprises both an "aesthetic theology" that interprets the objects of theology—God, faith, and theology itself—through the methods of aesthetic studies, and a more narrowly defined "theological aesthetics" that interprets the objects of aesthetics—sensation, the beautiful, and art—from the properly theological starting point of religious conversion and in the light of theological methods. Hence "theological aesthetics" in the second, narrower sense will include the following elements:

1. A theological account of human knowledge on the level of feeling and imagination ("aesthetics" in the sense of Schiller and Kant). The treatment of God and imagination involves the question of metaphor and analogy mentioned briefly above: how can the transcendent God be thought by a human mind that is tied to sensation? A related area is the theology of revelation and its relation to symbolic consciousness. Finally, there is a reflection on theological method: the development of a theological theory of interpretation (both of the Scriptures and of religious experience) that appeals to imagination and art,[139] and the relationship

of this hermeneutical task to systematic thought. This "epistemological" form of theological aesthetics explores the relations of symbolic and theoretical consciousness, of hermeneutics to metaphysics, of religious experience to secular reason, of feeling to logical discourse, of beauty to truth.

2. A theology of beauty. This will reflect on the nature of the beautiful in relationship to God and to the "transcendental"; the way in which beauty is a quality of revelation; and the place of "beauty" as a criterion of theological judgment.

3. A theological reflection on art and on the individual arts. This reflection will attempt to understand how the arts can communicate concerning the divine; how they can mediate revelation and conversion; and what formal similarities they show to the practice of theology. (The last will include the theory of the "theopoiesis" alluded to above.)

A final methodological consideration concerns the place of "theological aesthetics" as here described in relation to theology as a whole and to the particular divisions of theology. Before approaching this question, however, it will be advantageous to turn briefly to concrete examples of how "theological aesthetics" may actually be done. Two theologians who have explicitly described a section of their work as "theological aesthetics" are Gerardus Van der Leeuw and Hans Urs von Balthasar.[140] The two exemplify very different approaches, each emphasizing a distinct aspect of "aesthetics." I will first briefly summarize the work of Van der Leeuw, who has written a "theological aesthetics" in the third sense described above. I will then examine in greater detail the project of Hans Urs von Balthasar, whose notion of theological aesthetics encompasses much of the first two elements I have discussed.

The Phenomenology of Art and Its Connection to Revelation: The Theological Aesthetics of Gerardus Van der Leeuw

The Dutch theologian, philosopher, religious historian, musician, and statesman Gerardus Van der Leeuw is best known for his volumes on the phenomenology of religion.[141] In his study of the holy in art,[142] he employs the same method, but with the addition of a Christian theological perspective.

Van der Leeuw takes "aesthetics" in the Hegelian sense: the study of art, particularly the fine arts. His "theological aesthetics"—or "aesthetical theology," a term he uses interchangeably[143]—seeks the "path from art to theology and from theology to art."[144] His first task is to discern the historical relation between the arts and the sacred, and subsequently to outline a theological synthesis based on these data. He divides his treatment into sections dealing with individual forms of art: dance, drama, word, picture, architecture, and music. He proposes no metaphysics of art,[145] but attempts to arrive at a phenomenological description of each art form,[146] concentrating particularly on its "comprehensible associations" with the sacred.[147] He includes in each chapter a description of these associations, analyzing examples of diverse works of art through a broad range of religions. Much of the work consists of "aesthetic theology" (in my sense of the term): the use of poetry and art to evoke religious associations and/or to explain them. Each chapter contains as well a section on the historical conflicts or "enmity" between the particular art and religion.

Each of Van der Leeuw's chapters ends with a preliminary "theological aesthetic," which attempts to connect "the essential core of the art in question" with God's revelation in Christ.[148] He attempts to indicate the "theological significance" of each form of art—that is, how it conveys religious (not necessarily theological) meaning, and what "points of access" it provides to the holy.[149] Van der Leeuw's concise summary of these relations lacks the richness provided by his many examples, but gives a sense of the direction of his thought: "The dance reflects the movement of God, which also moves us upon the earth. The drama presupposes the holy play between God and man. Verbal art is the hymn of praise in which the Eternal and his works are represented. Architecture reveals to us the lines of the well-built city of God's creation. Music is the echo of the eternal Gloria. In the pictoral arts, we found images."[150]

Only at the end of the book does Van der Leeuw propose a comprehensive "theology of the arts" or "general theological aesthetic." He begins by giving a theory of the relation of the arts to each other: their unity, specific differences, and interdependence. He then asks what all the arts have in common from a theological point of view, and how the "*intelletto*" of the artist is related to God's creative Spirit.[151] He suggests that the theological understanding of the arts must begin with soteriology: specifically, with the notion of Christ as the image of God: "The doctrine of the image of God includes the entire theological aesthetics or aesthetical theology."[152] It is the fact that God has represented God's self in history that gives art and religion their common essence as answers to God's call. Both share in the task of "representation" that is made possible and necessary by God's self-revelation.

Since my purpose here is merely to exemplify one way of understanding the project of "theological aesthetics," for the moment I will not pursue the content of Van der Leeuw's theology beyond this brief summary. I shall return in later chapters both to the notion of the image of God in Christ and to Van der Leeuw's analyses of the theological meaning of the individual arts.

From the Beauty of Theology to the Theology of Beauty: The Theological Aesthetics of Hans Urs von Balthasar

If the notion of "theological aesthetics" has gained some currency in contemporary theology, it is largely due to the work of Hans Urs von Balthasar, whose magistral work *Herrlichkeit* (*The Glory of the Lord*) signified the opening of a new approach in twentieth-century Catholic thought.

It has been remarked that *Herrlichkeit* is in some ways a rewriting of Karl Barth's *Church Dogmatics*.[153] There is no doubt, in any case, of the influence of Barth on Balthasar's thought as an inspiration and a "dialogue partner." Hence Balthasar's notion of theological aesthetics will be more clearly understandable if we look at it in comparison to Barth's remarks on God, beauty, and theology.

Karl Barth on the Beauty of Theology and Its Object

Barth's principal comments on the subject occur in the context of his treatment of the divine glory [*"Herrlichkeit"*].[154] This concept is defined, on the basis of the scriptural ideas of פָּבוֹד (*kabod*) and δόξα (*doxa*), as God's "dignity and right" to manifest the divine being in various ways, making it apparent as the One that God is, creating recognition of it, "imposing" it so that God "is not mistaken for another or forgotten."[155] In summary, "God's glory is God Himself in the truth and capacity and act in which He makes Himself known as God." At its core, "glory" refers to God's freedom to love:[156] it is "the truth and power and act of His self-demonstration and therefore of His love . . . the self-revealing sum of all divine perfections. It is the fullness of God's deity, the emerging, self-expressing and self-manifesting reality of all that God is. It is God's being in so far as this is itself a being which declares itself."[157]

God's "glory," then, is not only the divine self-sufficiency, God's essential freedom as "the One who is not conditioned or controlled by any higher authority"[158] or goal, but also God's sufficiency for all other beings, so that if we have God, we "lack nothing" (Ps. 23)—even if, in our sinfulness, we may desire something other.[159] In this sense, God's glory can also be described, in accord with biblical thinking, as God's "radiance" and "light." These symbols signify that God's self-manifestation as the all-sufficient One does not operate in vain, but efficaciously reach God's creatures in truth and power, turning them to God.[160] For this reason, God's glory also includes the response of worship that is evoked in creatures.

God's all-sufficiency means that God is joyous in essence, and that in God creatures find their fulfillment and joy. Barth's theology here echoes the Patristic and Scholastic idea of creation "for the glory of God." The being of creatures is essentially "ecstatic," centered outside themselves.

> God wills them and loves them because, far from having their existence of themselves and their meaning in themselves, they have their being and existence in the movement of the divine self-glorification, in the transition to them of His immanent joyfulness. It is their destiny to offer a true if inadequate response in the temporal sphere to the jubilation with which the Godhead is filled from eternity to eternity.[161]

God's glory is therefore also "the indwelling joy of His divine being which as such shines out from Him, which overflows in its richness, which in its superabundance is not satisfied with itself but communicates itself."[162] Because of this intrinsic connection with joy, the idea of "power" is insufficient to describe God's glory; it must be complemented by the notion of the divine "beauty."

Although the concept of "beauty" does not play an important or autonomous part in the Scriptures, it is essential to the theological explanation of God's glory because it allows us to understand why this glory is not a mere fact, or a fact that is effective solely through power. "It is effective because and as it is beautiful. . . . In and with this quality it speaks and conquers, persuades and convinces. It does not merely assume this quality. It is proper to it."[164] Because it refers to God's "overflowing self-communicating joy," which by its nature gives joy, God's glory cannot be thought of as something neutral, "something which excludes the ideas of the pleasant, desirable, and enjoyable and therefore of the beautiful."[164] Rather, God's glory can be recognized as "worthy" of love because of "its peculiar power and characteristic of giving pleasure, awakening desire, and creating enjoyment."[165] In speaking of the divine beauty, then, Barth refers to the "form and manner" of God's glory, "the specifically persuasive and convincing element in His revelation."[166]

> If we can and must say that God is beautiful, to say this is to say how He enlightens and convinces and persuades us. It is to describe not merely the naked fact of His revelation or its power, but the shape and form in which it is a fact and is power. It is to say that God has this superior force, this power of attraction, which speaks for itself, which wins and conquers, in the fact that He is beautiful, divinely beautiful, beautiful in His own way, in a way that is His alone, beautiful as the unattainable primal beauty, yet really beautiful. He does not have it, therefore, merely as a fact or a power. Or rather, He has it as a fact and a power in such a way that He acts as the One who gives pleasure, creates desire and rewards with enjoyment. And He does it because He is pleasant, desirable, full of enjoyment, because He is the One who is pleasant, desirable, full of enjoyment, because first and last He alone is that which is pleasant, desirable and full of enjoyment. God loves us as the One who is worthy of love as God. This is what we mean when we say that God is beautiful.[167]
>
> . . . only the form of the divine being has divine beauty. . . . And where it is recognized as the form of the divine being it will necessarily be felt as beauty. Inevitably when the perfect divine being declares itself, it also radiates joy in the dignity and power of its divinity, and thus releases the pleasure, desire and enjoyment of which we have spoken, and is in this way, by means of this form, persuasive and convincing. And this persuasive and convincing form must necessarily be called the beauty of God.[168]

Our knowledge of God's beauty, according to Barth, stems uniquely from revelation, and is therefore centered in Jesus, the image of God's glory. "We should not know anything about that which attracts us as the beauty of God's being. . . . if this life had not been presented to us in the distinction in which it arouses joy, in the self-representation of God which consists in the fact that He becomes flesh." What evokes joy in the creature is the revelation that God is One and yet also "another," a fact made present in the incarnation.[169] The other two examples that Barth gives of the beauty of God encountered in revelation—the unity of the divine attributes and the Trinity—are for him intrinsically connected to the incarnation. The "form or way or manner in which God is perfect is also itself perfect, the perfect form." This means that God's being is a unity of identity and nonidentity, simplicity and multiplicity, and therefore includes the creature. The doctrine of the Trinity expands this idea: God's being is not self-enclosed and "pure divine being," but reaches out in self-sharing. As the triunity—

> and by this we mean in the strict and most proper sense, God Himself—is the basis of the power and dignity of the divine being . . . so this triune being

and life ... is the basis for what makes this power and dignity enlightening, persuasive and convincing. For this is the particular function of this form. It is radiant, and what it radiates is joy. It attracts and therefore it conquers. It is, therefore, beautiful.[170]

Because of the beauty of its object and method, theology is a beautiful science. Barth cites Anselm of Canterbury's dictum that the *ratio* sought by faith is not only *utilitas* but also *pulchritudo* that is *speciosa super intellectum hominum*[171] (*Cur Deus Homo*, I, i). Not only is it delightful [*delectabile quiddam*] (*Monologion*, 6), but this delight is its first purpose.[172]

Barth writes that the theologian who misses this beauty "has good cause for repentance."[173] Nevertheless, he insists that this beauty is to be perceived rather than discussed: "however much we may try to illustrate it in detail, this insight depends too much on the presence of the necessary feeling to allow of theoretical development. But again, and above all, reflection and discussion of the aesthetics of theology can hardly be counted a legitimate and certainly not a necessary task of theology."[174] Although the theologian cannot overlook the fact that God is "also" beautiful,[175] since it is demanded by biblical truth itself,[176] it would be a mistake to see beauty as the "essence" of God's glory.[177] Indeed, "While the statement that God is beautiful must not be neglected, since it is instructive in its own place, it cannot claim to have any independent significance."[178] It is a "parenthesis" to the treatment of the divine glory,[179] a "subordinate and auxiliary idea":[180]

> we cannot include the concept of beauty with the main concepts of the doc-trine of God, with the divine perfections which are the divine essence itself. In view of what the biblical testimony says about God it would be an un-justified risk to try to bring the knowledge of God under the denominator of the beautiful even in the same way as we have done in our consideration of these leading concepts. It is not a leading concept. Not even in passing can we make it a primary motif in our understanding of the whole being of God as we did in the case of these other concepts.[181]

Barth's reservations about theological attention to the beautiful stem from a fear of religious "aestheticism." Theology must not become occupied with its own beauty, nor with the beauty of its object; this would be contrary to the "Church attitude" that must determine theology's exercise.[182] The creature must be occupied with the glory of God, not with itself or its own fulfillment (even though that fulfillment in fact results).[183]

> The Church attitude precludes ... the possibility of a dogmatics which thinks and speaks aesthetically. It is true, of course, that the object with which it has to do has its characteristic and quite distinctive beauty which it would be unpardonable, because ungrateful, to overlook or to fail to find pleasing. But the moment dogmatics even temporarily surrenders to and loses itself in the contemplation of this beauty as such, instead of letting itself be held by the object, this beauty becomes the beauty of an idol. ... It [theology] must not turn its attention and give itself to that which edifies in general (however sweet or bitter). When it is orderly in this respect, and only then, it will be

continually struck by the beauty of its object, and moved, willy-nilly, to genuine and grateful contemplation.[184]

Despite his insistence that the category of the beautiful is necessary to a theological explanation of God's glory, Barth acknowledges a certain "danger" in its use:

> Owing to its connexion with the idea of pleasure, desire and enjoyment (quite apart from its historical connexion with Greek thought), the concept of the beautiful seems to be a particularly secular one, not at all adapted for introduction into the language of theology, and indeed extremely dangerous. If we say now that God is beautiful, and make this statement the final explanation of the assertion that God is glorious, do we not jeopardize or even deny the majesty and holiness and righteousness of God's love? Do we not bring God in a sinister because in a sense intimate way into the sphere of man's oversight and control, into proximity to the ideal of all human striving? Do we not bring the contemplation of God into suspicious proximity to that contemplation of the world which in the last resort is the self-contemplation of an urge for life which does not recognise its limits? Certainly we have every reason to be cautious here.[185]

Even while admitting the need for theology to advert to God's beauty, therefore, Barth is critical of metaphysical attempts to bring God under the category of the beautiful. "To do this is an act of philosophical willfulness of which Pseudo-Dionysius is guilty" and which "lurks behind" the celebrated passage on God's beauty in Augustine's *Confessions* (X, 27). "The Bible neither requires nor permits us, because God is beautiful, to expound the beauty of God as the ultimate cause producing and moving all things, in the way in which we can and must do this in regard to God's grace or holiness or eternity, or His omnipotent knowledge and will."[186] The theology of Pseudo-Dionysius, according to Barth, is "hardly veiled Platonism," and for good reason the Church in general did not follow its direction. Even the idea of the beauty of Christ, popular in medieval piety, "was always an alien element, not accepted with a very good conscience, and always looked on and treated with a certain mistrust. Theology at any rate hardly knew what to make of the idea and would have nothing to do with it."[187]

On the other hand, says Barth, aestheticism should not be regarded as a worse danger than any other "ism." "There is no reason to take up a particularly tragic attitude to the danger that threatens from the side of aesthetics—which is what Protestantism has done according to our historical review."[188] And there is equally a danger from the theological neglect of beauty: for "where this element is not appreciated— ... what becomes of the evangelical content of the evangel?"[189] Without attention to its beauty, there is the danger that the "good news" should lose its persuasive power, the appreciation of its joy and goodness.

Balthasar's Theology of God's Beauty

Barth's comments and reservations about the notion of the beautiful in theology are a good starting point for understanding Balthasar's project. First, what Balthasar means by "theological aesthetics" is very much in the spirit of Barth: a theology of revelation centered on God's "glory" ("*Herrlichkeit*," the title of the work) revealed in Christ. Second, however, Balthasar's work is also intended as a "correction" of Barth. Balthasar sees Protestant theology's rejection of aesthetics as the result of its refusal of the analogy of being. This refusal is consistent with a dialectical rather than an analogical conception of the relation between grace and nature.[190] The rejection of the analogy of being and the emphasis on the gratuity of grace lead Protestant theology to conceive of beauty solely in terms of event, and to mistrust any ideas of inherent qualities in which humans might repose or which they could manipulate.[191] But the complete rejection of aesthetics (as Barth already saw to some degree) results in a truncated conception of faith. It removes from faith the "*incohatio visionis*"; it separates "seeing" the glory of God's revelation from "hearing" its message, and hence signifies the elimination of God's glory from the present age.[192]

In contrast to Barth, Balthasar places aesthetics in the context of the Platonic-Aristotelian metaphysical tradition of the analogy of being. This permits him to develop a Christian theology in the light of beauty as "the third transcendental" (accompanying "Being" and "the Good"). Through this "confrontation of beauty and revelation in dogmatic theology" aesthetics can be restored to theology as a main artery that had been abandoned.[193]

Balthasar envisions two ways of restoring the aesthetic dimension to theology: like Barth, to remain with the "inner beauty of theology and revelation itself"; or to go beyond this and "probe the possibility of there being a genuine relationship between theological beauty and the beauty of the world." Balthasar opts for the second, although he echoes Barth's sentiments concerning its "dangers."[194] "Man's habit of calling beautiful only what strikes *him* as such appears insurmountable, at least on earth." Hence there is a risk that a "theology that makes use of such concepts will sooner or later cease to be a 'theological aesthetics'—that is, the attempt to do aesthetics at the level and with the methods of theology—and deteriorate into an 'aesthetic theology' by betraying and selling our theological substance to the current viewpoints of an inner-worldly theory of beauty."[195]

Balthasar's remedy for this danger is twofold: first, to apply aesthetic categories in an analogous and transcendental way; second, to conceive theological aesthetics not as a self-standing theology but as a part of the larger theological project.

To begin with the latter: Balthasar's theological aesthetics is meant to be read as the first part of a triad that is completed by theo-dramatics and theo-logic. Balthasar insists already at the beginning of his work that the restoration of aesthetics to theology "is in no sense to imply that the aesthetic perspective ought now to dominate theology in the place of the logical and the ethical."[196] Only in the larger context of ethics and dogmatics is a theological aesthetics justified in the economy of Christian theology.[197] Balthasar complains about the misunderstanding of his theological aesthetics that results from its separation from the entire project: "to call the *Theological Aesthetics* the masterpiece, the work of my life (very often only the introductory volume has been read, and on the basis of that all the rest is presupposed), for which the author is famed as a 'theological aesthete,' to do this is to misunderstand my fundamental intention."[198]

Revelation calls for a further dimension of engagement that theological aesthetics indicates, but does not directly deal with: "the manifestation of God, theophany, is only the prelude to the central event: the encounter, in creation and in history, between infinite divine freedom and finite human freedom. This central issue is dealt with in the *Theo-dramatics*. . . . God does not want to be just 'contemplated' and 'perceived' by us . . . no, from the beginning he has provided for a play in which we must all share."[199] "Aesthetics remains on the plane of light, image, vision. That is only *one* dimension of theology. The next involves deed, event, drama. . . . God acts for man; man responds through decision and deed. The history of the world and of man is itself a great 'theatre of the world.' "[200] The necessary ethical dimension of theology is thus presented in a theo-"dramatics," in which the theater is used as an image for life itself.[201]

Finally, the triad is completed by a theo-logy: a methodical, a posteriori reflection on what has been done in the first two parts. This involves "reflection on the way in which the dramatic event can be transposed into human words and concepts for the purposes of comprehension, proclamation and contemplation."[202] Balthasar here asks about the nature of truth as presented by the Scriptures, its philosophical form, and how that philosophical form is open to the incarnate form of Christ's truth.[203]

The later parts of Balthasar's triad are crucial to understanding the context and limitations of his theological aesthetics. However, since the purpose here is simply to give an overview of the content and method of Balthasar's theological aesthetics, it is his first volumes that are of primary interest. Here we find a definition and outline of his project that will allow us to locate it within the different meanings of "theological aesthetics" described above. It will be helpful first to review Balthasar's outline of the work as a whole, and then to look more closely at his concepts.

The first volume of *The Glory of the Lord* comprises an introduction and a consideration of the nature of "theological aesthetics"; to this I shall return shortly. The second and third volumes are called "Studies in Theological Style." Balthasar presents "a series of monographs on those who have most characteristically moulded theology from Irenaeus to the present time, a series offering a typology of the relationship between beauty and revelation."[204] The twelve thinkers Balthasar chooses are meant to show that "truly epochal theology" is always illumined by God's glory.[205] The fourth and fifth volumes deal with "The Realm of Metaphysics." Balthasar examines the "splendor" of the divine in the world as seen in the sphere of myth and in the philosophy that comes out of it. These pose the alternative of human autonomy or divine revelation. In the light of the latter, Balthasar then asks: what does Christianity do with the καλόν of antiquity? He concludes with the need for Christianity today to confront metaphysics in order to proclaim God's glory.[206] Finally, the sixth and seventh volumes are dogmatic. They deal first with the biblical theme of "glory" in the Old and New Testaments, culminating in Johannine and Pauline theology, and then with the dogmatic themes of glory as: (1) epiphany: God's being with us; (2) justification: the divine "poiesis"; and (3) charis or grace.[207]

In the light of this outline, we may now return to Balthasar's first volume to examine why and how he considers these contents to constitute a "theological aesthetics." In terms of the three senses of "aesthetics" defined above, it is clear that Balthasar is interested primarily in the first two. He sees theological aesthetics as having two phases. First there is a "theory of vision," or fundamental theology. This is " 'aesthetics' in the Kantian sense as a theory about the perception of the form of God's self-revelation." Second is a "theory of rapture," which is dogmatic theology: " 'aesthetics' as a theory about the incarnation of God's glory and the consequent elevation of man to participate in that glory."[208] This moment is "aesthetics" in the second sense: a theory of beauty. It is to be noted, however, that its definition of "beauty" is strictly theological. Theological aesthetics is "a theology which does not primarily work with the extra-theological categories of a worldly philosophical aesthetics (above all poetry), but which develops its theory of beauty from the data of revelation itself with genuinely theological methods."[209] The third sense of "aesthetics"—a theory of art—is less present in Balthasar's project: "Only in a derivative way is the problem of Christian art to be treated: is it possible and, indeed, how is it possible for divine 'splendor' to be expressed by means of worldly 'beauty'?"[210]

If beauty is to be conceived transcendentally, its definition must begin from God.[211] But Balthasar agrees with Barth that we can never attain to God except through the incarnate Son. Hence we should never speak of God's beauty without reference to "the form and manner of appearing which he exhibits in salvation history."[212] Moreover, "what we know to be most proper to God—his self-revelation in history and the Incarnation—must now become for us the very apex and archetype of beauty in the world, whether men see it or not."[213] The paradox of the Incarnation "stands at the fountainhead of the Christian aesthetic, and therefore of all aesthetics."[214] For this reason, theology (which for Balthasar includes a philosophical element) "is the only science which can have transcendental beauty as its object."[215]

What Balthasar intends by "theological aesthetics," then, is essentially a Christologically centered theology of revelation. Balthasar's own description of the intent of his theological aesthetics shows its similarity to Barth's ideas: "What is involved is primarily not 'beauty' in the modern or even in the philosophical (transcendental) sense, but the surpassing of beauty in 'glory' in the sense of the splendor of the divinity of God himself as manifested in the life, death, and resurrection of Jesus and reflected, according to Paul, in Christians who look upon their Lord."[216]

> Why is the first part of this synthesis called *The Glory of the Lord* (*Herr-lichkeit*)? Because it is concerned, first, with learning to see God's revelation and because God can be known only in his Lordliness and sublimity (*Herr-heit* and *Hehr-heit*), in what Israel called *Kabod* and the New Testament *gloria*, something that can be recognised despite all the incognitos of human nature and the Cross. This means that God does not come primarily as a teacher for us ("true"), as a useful "redeemer" for us ("good"), but for *himself*,

to display and to radiate the splendour of his eternal triune love in that "disinterestedness" which true love has in common with true beauty. For the glory of God the world was created; through it and for its sake the world is also redeemed. And only the person who is touched by a ray of this glory and has an incipient sensibility for what disinterested love is, can learn to see the presence of divine life in Jesus Christ. *Aistheisis*, the act of perception, and *Aistheton*, the particular thing perceived (radiant love), together inform the object of theology. The "glorious" corresponds on the theological plane to what the transcendental "beautiful" is on the philosophical plane. But for the great thinkers of the West (from Homer and Plato via Augustine and Thomas down to Goethe and Hölderlin, Schelling and Heidegger), beauty is the last comprehensive attribute of all-embracing being as such, its last, mysterious radiance, which makes it loved as a whole despite the terrifying reality it may hide for the individual existent. Through the splendour of being, from within its primal depths, the strange signs of the biblical events (whose very contrariness to all human expectations reveals their supraworldly origin) shine out with that glory of God whose praise and recognition fills the Scriptures, the Church's liturgy, and the mottoes of the saintly founders of religious orders.[217]

Balthasar's notion of God's "glory" is clearly reminiscent of Barth's; but Balthasar differs in that he not only makes it a leading concept but also takes its perception (aesthetics) as the starting point for his entire theological synthesis. Indeed, since God's "glory" is the "most divine aspect of God," to begin with aesthetics is the "only appropriate stance" for theology:

> Only such a stance can perceive the divine as such, without obscuring it beforehand by a theological relationship to the cosmos (which, imperfect, calls for divine completion) or to man (who, still more imperfect and lost in sin, requires a savior). The first desideratum for seeing objectively is the "letting be" of God's self-revelation, even if the latter is also "his eternal love for me." This first step is not to master the materials of perception by imposing our own categories on them, but an attitude of service to the object. Theologically this means that the unspeakable mystery of God's love opens itself to reverence and adoration on the part of the subject (*timor filialis*). This means, too, that God's splendour (surpassing the transcendentality of "philosophical" beauty) reveals and authenticates itself precisely in its own apparent antithesis (in the *kenosis* of the descent into hell) as love selflessly serving out love. Thus *The Glory of the Lord* points not only to the proper center of theology, but also to the heart of the individual's existential situation.[218]

Balthasar, unlike Barth, connects the idea of God's "glory" with the metaphysical transcendental "beauty." The crucial issue between them is whether "beauty" is to be considered as applying only to the inner-worldly relation between matter and form and their appearance, or as a transcendental quality of being. The Fathers and Scholastics take the latter position. On the basis of creation and redemption they attribute "beauty" to God as the "eminent sum of all creation's values."[219] Balthasar follows their lead. Nevertheless, he explicitly agrees with Barth in distinguishing between the "transcendental beauty of revelation" in Christ and "inner-worldly natural beauty."[220] As Barth saw, the Christian idea of beauty must include

> even the Cross and everything else which a worldly aesthetics (even of a realistic kind) discards as no longer bearable. This inclusiveness is not only of the type proposed by a Platonic theory of beauty, which knows how to employ the shadows and the contradictions as stylistic elements of art;[221] it embraced the most abysmal ugliness of sin and hell by virtue of the conde-scension of divine love, which has brought even sin and hell into that divine art for which there is no human analogue.[222]

These considerations allow us to see more precisely the sense in which Balthasar's theology is "aesthetic": namely, in that "it consists in reflection on what it is that enables us to *perceive* the drama of the Cross and the *descensus* and the Resurrection as the revelation of the divine glory."[223] Moreover, unlike funda-mental theologies that concentrate on the conditions in the subject for the accep-tance of revelation, Balthasar's theological aesthetics is primarily concerned with what it is in the *object* of our perception that allows us to see it as revelation: "any thought about what it is that enables *us* to see the divine glory is intimately linked to questions about the object of such perceiving. What is it about *what* we see—the divine *Gestalt* of the incarnate, crucified Lord—that enables us to see in this figure, as nowhere else, that triune majesty?"[224] That quality is revelation's "beauty," which awakens a kind of "eros" within us.[225]

Balthasar follows St. Thomas in discerning in beauty the two elements of "form" and "splendor."[226] "Form" (*Gestalt*) itself is seen "as the splendor, as the glory of Being."[227] The form of things is the presence in them of "the depths" of being, and a pointing beyond themselves to those depths.[228] It is the intimation and presence of the goodness of ultimate reality in form that explains its attrac-tiveness, delightfulness, beauty:

> The form as it appears to us is beautiful only because the delight that it arouses in us is founded upon the fact that, in it, the truth and goodness of the depths of reality itself are manifested and bestowed, and this manifes-tation and bestowal reveal themselves to us as being something infinitely and inexhaustibly variable and fascinating.[229]

The center of Balthasar's theological aesthetics, therefore, is the contemplation and grasp of the "form" of God's revelation in Christ and the Scriptures. The legitimacy of the project lies in the analogy of beauty, and hence the analogy of the theological to the aesthetic: the contemplation of the form of Christ "exactly corresponds to the aesthetic contemplation that steadily and patiently beholds those forms which either nature or art offers to its view."[230]

For Balthasar, as for Barth, the beauty of revelation explains its power to convince and evoke a response of faith. What Balthasar calls the "splendor" of God's beauty in the world corresponds to the Thomistic idea of the "light of faith."[231] Those who are transported by a vision of beauty are "enraptured" and give themselves with enthusiasm to it.[232] It is crucial to Balthasar's theology that the transport of the soul by the form of Christ be understood "not as a merely psychological response to something beautiful in a worldly sense...but as the movement of man's whole being away from himself and towards God through Christ."[233]

The Place of Theological Aesthetics in Theology

Balthasar's theological synthesis provides a convenient starting point for a discussion of the place of theological aesthetics within the theological enterprise as a whole.

As was noted above, Balthasar's theological aesthetics is a union of fundamental and dogmatic theology. As such it is meant to be a corrective to the kind of abstract and rationalistic fundamental theology (in the guise of "apologetics") that frequently characterized post-Vatican I Catholic theology. Maurice Blondel had already started a new direction with his method of immanence, based on anthropological analysis. In the 1940s and '50s the Jesuit school at Lyon "expounded a *nouvelle théologie* which renounced apologetics altogether and instead sought to ground faith more firmly in the contemplation of the central Catholic mystery."[234] Balthasar was indebted to both these sources, and in his theological aesthetics attempts to bring their efforts to a new level.

Balthasar holds that fundamental theology and dogmatics are finally inseparable, because it is only in the light of grace that one can perceive the fact of revelation (which neo-Scholastic fundamental theology had tried to "demonstrate" by pure reason, abstracting from faith commitment to the content of revelation).[235] For Balthasar, however, the act of perceiving revelation cannot be separated from the object that is perceived: the enrapturing form of God's beauty as shown in Jesus Christ, and especially in Christ crucified.[236] Hence theology right from the beginning, including the aspect of fundamental theology, must be Christocentric.

For the same reason, the doctrine of beholding (fundamental theology) and the doctrine of the enrapturing power of the beautiful form (dogmatic theology) are complementary and inseparable in the same manner as faith and grace: "since no one can really behold who has not also already been enraptured, and no one can be enraptured who has not already perceived."[237] Hence there is a point "where the proofs for the truth contemplated necessarily bear the character of a ritual initiation."[238] Moreover, Balthasar insists upon the relationship between the medium and what it expresses: the "form" is exactly suited to the "splendor" that shines through it.[239] Apologetics can therefore be linked to the way in which we make aesthetic judgments of excellence or uniqueness:[240] through the perception of and being grasped by the beauty of a specific, unrepeatable form.

Balthasar's method thus envisions a form of apologetics intimately united with dogmatics. He enunciates his "fundamental conviction" that

> you do good apologetics if you do good, central theology; if you expound theology effectively, you have done the best kind of apologetics. The Word of God (which is also and always the activity of God) is self-authenticating

proof of its own truth and fecundity—and it is precisely in this way that the church and the believer are inserted into one another. The man who wants this Word to be heard in what he has to say . . . does not need to resort to another discipline (called Fundamental Theology) to gain a hearing for it.[241]

As John Riches puts it, in Balthasar's conception "Divine authority as *doxa* requires no other justification than itself; its rightness, like that of a work of art, has its own evidential force for those who see it."[242] Or, as Balthasar himself says of those who are "enraptured" by the form of Christ's beauty: "the world will attempt to explain their state in terms of psychological or even physiological laws (Acts 2:13). But *they* know what they have seen, and they care not one farthing what people may say."[243]

Balthasar's statements about the "self-authenticating" quality of God's self-revelation and of faith are on one level consistent with the teachings of the First Vatican Council[244] and with the Thomistic analysis of the act of faith. Nevertheless, the Catholic tradition in general rejects the notion that one may simply appeal to the "light of faith" in the *theological explication* of the motives for belief; faith must be in accord with "reason," which legitimately explores its intellectual "grounds of credibility."[245] Balthasar's conception of a "dogmatically" based apologetics is both legitimate and useful, particularly if theology is being envisaged from an intra-ecclesial viewpoint.[246] But if it were accepted as the *exclusive* form of fundamental theology, there would be danger of a certain "fideism," in the sense defined by Nicholas Lash: "an approach which, insisting that appropriate criteria of assessment are only available *within* particular patterns of experience, or 'ways of life,' refuses to submit the claims of faith to 'external' assessment, whether by the historian, the social scientist, or the philosopher."[247]

Some have pointed out that there is a particular danger in appealing to the "beauty" of revelation as a form of evidence. O'Donaghue argues that "it may be that for the leaping imagination of the poet, beauty is truth and truth beauty, but at a more grounded level it is possible to think of many beautiful conceptions and ideologies which have little relationship to truth. It is possible to be *splendide mendax*: it is possible to be deceived by fair appearances."[248] Hence Barth's identification of beauty with the "convincing" quality of revelation[249] is limited in its application: on the one hand, what is "really" and divinely beautiful (and for the Christian this must include the cross) does not necessarily convince; on the other hand, one can be enchanted and convinced by falsehood.

Moreover, there is a certain subjectivity in aesthetic judgments: "it may be argued that the Buddhist sage is more attractive than the Christian saint, that the death of Socrates outshines in beauty the death of Christ even when the Resurrection is brought within it."[250] Of course, Balthasar holds that Christian revelation brings its own criterion of beauty, which cannot be judged by "worldly" standards. But this merely moves the question to another level: "how do I judge the beauty of the form of Christ unless by way of my inner idea or sense of the beautiful? Either Christ shatters my conception of the beautiful or he fulfills it."[251] In either case, there arises the question of the criteria of theological-aesthetic judgments, the source of these criteria, their warrants, and their relationship to conflicting claims. I suggest that these topics might be the subject of a "theological aesthetics" within a fundamental theology conceived differently from Balthasar's, to which it would serve as a complement and (in some cases) a corrective.

David Tracy's proposal of a division of theology according to its different "publics" is helpful in locating Balthasar's theological aesthetics in relation to a more widely conceived fundamental theology. Tracy names three complementary points of view from which Christian theology may be approached: "foundational," "systematic," and "practical."[252]

Foundational (or "fundamental") theologies are directed to the academy. They provide arguments that all persons, whether religious or not, can recognize as reasonable. The primary value for this form of theology is honest, critical inquiry.[253] Its emphasis is on the transcendental "truth" as related to the religious or the holy. It operates through metaphysical thinking, and its major mode of discourse is argument or dialectic.[254]

Systematic theologies are directed to the church community *ad intra*. They re-present and reinterpret "what is assumed to be the ever-present disclosive and transformative power" of the tradition. Their primary concern is loyalty and/or creative and critical fidelity to that tradition.[255] This kind of theologizing emphasizes the transcendental "beauty" as the manifestation of the truth of the holy. It utilizes the disciplines of poetics and rhetoric, and discourses primarily through conversation with the religious classics.[256]

Finally, practical theologies are directed to society at large. For their operative norm they take praxis (practical action informed by and informing theory). Responsible commitment to this norm and/or involvement in the situation of praxis is the supreme value.[257] Such theologies emphasize "the good" in its relation to the holy or to religious experience. They involve the disciplines of ethics and politics, as related to transforming faith-praxis. Their theological discourse involves the critique of ideology and (at times) the proposal of a future ideal.[258]

It is easy to recognize the characteristics of Balthasar's theological aesthetics in Tracy's description of the "systematic" form of theology. I suggest that another dimension of theological aesthetics may form part of "foundational" (fundamental) theology as conceived by Tracy. Balthasar's and Van der Leeuw's versions of theological aesthetics begin "from above"—that is, they examine the arts, beauty, and perception from the perspective of the content of Christian revelation, accepted as God's word. The "foundational" aspect of theological aesthetics would begin "from below": it would inquire into the conditions of possibility in humanity for the reception and interpretation of a divine revelation in the forms of sensation, beauty, and art. It would inquire into the criteria for "beauty" and for relating the categorical experience "beauty" to the transcendent beauty of God, as well as to God's truth and goodness. It would also ask whether and in what sense we may speak of the beauty of the Christ; how it relates to what we otherwise consider beautiful; how and to what degree it can embody transcendental beauty; and how it compares with other experiences of sacred beauty and truth.[259] In short, it would formulate explicitly and examine the truth claims that are implicit in both the systematic (poetic-rhetorical) and the practical (ethical-political) forms of Christian discourse.[260]

Tracy has argued convincingly that a fundamental theology conceived on "transcendental" lines need be neither rationalist[261] nor "foundationalist."[262] Nor need it be seen as a rival to the more ecclesially oriented theological aesthetics of Balthasar; rather, it should provide the latter with a transcendental anthropological warrant that permits a wider conversation *ad extra*.[263] (It is notable that Balthasar himself does not deny the possibility of the "path of anthropological verification," but sees it as secondary and complementary to his approach).[264] At the same time, systematic theological aesthetics would add a needed concreteness to the necessarily heuristic and relatively indeterminate structures of transcendental method.

A theological aesthetics might also be conceived as an aspect of "practical" theology. "Praxis" is by its very nature intimately connected with "poiesis." A practical theological aesthetics would explore the place of imagination, beauty, and art in motivating Christian morality and action in the world.

THE PURPOSE OF THIS CHAPTER has been to clarify the notion of "theological aesthetics." We have seen—perhaps only too extensively—that the term can cover a number of diverse theological projects and concerns. Happily my conclusions to this conceptual exploration may be summarized briefly. In its wide sense, theological aesthetics includes "aesthetic theology"—that is, the use by theology of the language, methods, and contents of the aesthetic realm. The art of making theological discourse affecting and beautiful ("theopoesis") is appropriate to all branches and kinds of theology. The application of aesthetic theory (e.g., literary analysis) to theological contents is most pertinent to those "functional specialties" that Lonergan names research, interpretation, history, and communications. The remaining specialties—dialectics, foundations, doctrines, and systematics—are the principal field of theological aesthetics in its narrower sense: the use of properly theological starting points, categories, and methods to formulate an account of (1) perception (including sensation and imagination), (2) beauty, and (3) the arts. Such an account may be formulated from the point of view of what Tracy calls "systematic" theology (as in Balthasar and Van der Leeuw), or from the complementary perspectives of foundational and practical theology. It will be my intent in the following chapters to uncover some of the basic elements of a "foundational" type of theological aesthetics, applying the insights of a "transcendental" theology in the line of Rahner and Lonergan to the question of the relation of the divine to human imagination, to beauty, and to art.

CHAPTER 2

God in Thought and in Imagination:
Representing the Unimaginable

Prologue: Schoenberg's *Moses und Aron*

"Unique, eternal, omnipresent, invisible and unimaginable God!" These words, spoken by Moses at the beginning of Arnold Schoenberg's *Moses und Aron*, serve as a leitmotif that recurs not only through the entire opera but also through all of Schoenberg's religious works.[1]

Moses und Aron gives the clearest and deepest expression to the problem to which the mature Schoenberg kept returning: the conflict between the idea of a unique, transcendent God, beyond all thought and imagination, and the religious need for images. The former was for Schoenberg the central tenet of Jewish faith,[2] and its great historical contribution to humanity; the latter, the inevitable medium for the human response to God, and the wellspring of the artist's vocation.

Schoenberg takes his inspiration for the opera from the incident of Aaron's building of the idol of a golden calf for the Israelites in the desert (Exod. 32:2–6). Rather than using biblical texts, he wrote his own libretto, using the scriptural story as a loose framework for the exposition of his theme.[3] This unfolds principally in the dialogue and conflict between Moses and Aaron, the symbols and spokesmen respectively of Idea and Imagination in religion.

The opera begins immediately with "The Call of Moses" (act I, scene 1): Moses' encounter with God speaking through a voice in a burning thorn bush (Exod. 3:1–4.17). After a musical prelude of only five bars' duration, the first words of text are declaimed by Moses in the *Sprechgesang* that characterizes the role throughout the opera. This use of tonal speech rather than singing serves several purposes. First, it gives rhetorical force to Moses' words; Schoenberg frequently uses the device for this purpose in his choral works. Second, it symbolizes Moses' difficulty in speaking (Ex. 4.10: "If you please, Lord, I have never been eloquent . . . but I am slow of speech and tongue." Schoenberg's Moses declares, "My tongue is not supple; I can think, but not speak"). And, perhaps most important, it illustrates Schoenberg's theme of the tension between his two title characters and what they represent. Moses, symbolizing thought and word, speaks: his discourse is forceful but stark. Aaron's eloquence, representing the seductive beauty of imagination, is symbolized by song. Significantly, for the Voice of God Schoenberg combines *Sprechgesang*, spoken by a six-part chorus, with six voices singing the same text, at times simultaneously with the spoken word (forming a kind of musical "halo") and at times either anticipating or repeating it.

In the first scene, Schoenberg quickly establishes the three interconnected themes that unify the work: the unimaginability of God; the election of Israel; and the role of the prophet as leader of the people.[4] The opera's first words present the formula of Schoenberg's idea of God: One, eternal, omnipresent, unseeable, and unimaginable. It is this idea or thought (*Gedanke*) of God, newly awakened in Moses, that identifies the unique God:

> "God of my Fathers, God of Abraham, Isaac, and Jacob,
> you have reawakened their thought in me . . ."

It is knowledge and worship of the one, transcendent God signified by this idea that will make Israel God's chosen people.

> This people is chosen
> before all other people
> to be the people of the one God,
> that they may acknowledge him
> and consecrate themselves to him alone.

Because of faithfulness to this idea Israel must suffer; but it will be united with the Eternal, and thus a model for all peoples.

It is Moses' enlightenment, his wisdom, that will make him the leader of the people. It is the power of the God-idea—the "name" of God—that will be the only witness to the legitimacy of his mission:

> MOSES: What will convince the people of my mission?
>
> THE VOICE: The name of the Unique One!
> The Eternal will free them, so that they no longer serve what
> is transitory.

But because of Moses' complaint of his lack of eloquence, Aaron is given as his spokesman:

> I shall enlighten Aaron,
> he must be your mouth!
> Out of him should your voice speak,
> as Mine does out of you!

Thus the function of the leader is divided, giving rise to the central conflict of the opera.

The second scene of act I, "Moses meets Aaron in the Wilderness," presents in dramatic form the conflict of Moses' ideas with concrete religion, grounded in imagination. The biblical basis of the scene is brief:

> The Lord said to Aaron, "Go into the desert to meet Moses." So he went,
> and when they met at the mountain of God, Aaron kissed him. Moses in-

formed him of all the Lord had said in sending him, and of the various signs
he had enjoined upon him. (Exod. 4:27–28)

In Schoenberg's presentation, the encounter forms not so much a dialogue as two
parallel monologues: an uneven duet, in which Moses' speech overlaps with
Aaron's song. In Aaron's mouth, the ideas that Moses has been sent to proclaim
are given aesthetic form, both musically and conceptually. It is Aaron who for the
first time makes into a discernible melody the twelve-tone series on which the
opera's music is based.[5] Similarly, Aaron "beautifies" Moses' thought, transforming
it into religious ideas that will be understandable and attractive to the people.

Aaron presents himself in the image of a "vessel" from which God's grace
will be poured on the people; Moses, however, warns that grace is given through
knowledge (*Erkenntnis*). Aaron conceives the "uniqueness" of God as the possession of power that other gods cannot oppose; Moses, meanwhile, states that the
other "gods" do not exist at all, except in human imagination (*Vorstellung*), while
the true God, although omnipresent, has no "place" in imagination. Aaron conceives of God's revelation precisely as the inspiration of human creativity to produce worshipful images of the divine:

O creation (*Gebilde*) of highest fantasy, how much it
thanks Thee, that Thou dost charm it to form (*bilden*)
Thee!

As Aaron sings these words, Moses enunciates his central message: no image (*Bild*)
can give a picture of the unimaginable (*unvorstellbare*) God.

This contrast determines the difference in the two leaders' conceptions of
what it means for Israel to be the chosen people, and hence also of their own
function. For Moses, Israel's task is to be faithful to the idea of the utter transcendence of God:

People chosen to know the Invisible,
to think the Unimaginable.

For Aaron, on the other hand, this people is chosen to love God. But such love
needs a concrete object; therefore, "Never will love tire of creating images." In a
spirited passage (the score is marked *Schwungvoll*), he celebrates Israel's call to
love one sole God "a thousand times more than all the other nations love their
many gods." But Aaron has heard Moses' last words; his exalted song changes to
a slow and soft recitative (marked *langsam* and *molto piano*) as he voices his doubt
about the possibility of loving a God known only in negative ideas:

Invisible! Unimaginable!
People chosen for the only One, can you love what you
dare not imagine?

But for Moses it is not merely a matter of prohibition, of not "daring" to imagine
God:

Dare not? Unimaginable, because invisible;
because immeasurable,

because infinite;
because eternal;
because omnipresent;
because almighty.
Only He is almighty.

God is by nature beyond thought and picturing; this is for Schoenberg the profound meaning of the biblical injunction "Thou shalt not make for thyself any graven image" (Exod. 20:4). Already in 1925, during the early days of his gradual return to Judaism, Schoenberg had expressed the idea in the second of his *Four Pieces for Mixed Choir* (op. 27), entitled "Thou shalt not; thou must" ("*Du sollst nicht, du mußt*"):[6]

Thou shalt not make for thyself any image! For an
image reduces, delimits, grasps,
What should remain unlimited and unimaginable.
An image wants a name:
A name can only be taken from what is small;
You should not worship what is small!

You must believe in the spirit!
Immediate, unfeeling,
and selfless.
You must, Chosen One, you must, if you wish to remain
chosen!

Belief in the spirit, faithfulness to the idea of the inconceivable God, is the meaning of Israel's "election." Schoenberg reiterates this theme in the final speech of his play *The Biblical Way* (*Der Biblische Weg*): "The Jewish people lives for one idea: the idea of a single, immortal, eternal and inconceivable God."[7] And in his setting of the *Kol Nidre*, the Yom Kippur formula nullifying vows and promises that have been made contrary to the Jewish faith, Schoenberg stresses repentance for any commitments "that have removed us from our holy task, for which we were chosen"—namely, to be faithful to the revealed God, characterized once again as "the One, eternal, invisible, and unimaginable."

The difference between Moses' and Aaron's conceptions of God and of the nature of Israel's election is expanded in their contrasting views of God's relation to history. Even while adopting Moses' characterization of God as "unimaginable," Aaron imagines God anthropomorphically. He presents the biblical view of salvation history as a genuine dialogue between God and Israel, in which God responds to human acts, rewarding the good and punishing the evil:

Unimaginable God:
You punish the sins of the father on his children and
his children's children!
Righteous God:
You reward those who are obedient to Your
commandments!

But for Moses, God's transcendence cannot be determined by human acts; God is the cause of all, and is in no way caused by us. Moses replies to Aaron's declaration:

> Do you punish?
> Are we able to cause anything that determines Your
> action?
> Righteous God:
> You have ordained
> how all things must happen:
> Should a reward be given to one who would like to be
> able to act differently? or to one who cannot do
> otherwise?

For Aaron, God is "good" in that God responds to human need and virtue:

> You hear the prayers of the poor,
> You receive the offerings of the good!

But Moses rejects such notions:

> Almighty God,
> are You to be bought by the offerings of the poor,
> whom You yourself made poor?

Virtue and knowledge of the true God are their own reward, and there is no other. Rising to song for the only time in the opera, Moses exhorts Aaron and the listener:

> Purify your thinking,
> free it from what is worthless,
> vow it to the truth!
> no other reward is given to your offerings.

The duet ends with Aaron's vision of God's power manifesting itself in the miraculous liberation of Israel from Pharaoh's bondage, while Moses solemnly declares:

> The irresistible law of thought forces its
> accomplishment.

The third scene, entitled "Moses and Aaron preach God's message to the people," is continuous with the fourth. The two are based on Exod. 4:29–31:

> Then Moses and Aaron went and assembled all the elders of the Israelites.
> Aaron told them everything the Lord had said to Moses, and he performed
> the signs before the people. The people believed, and when they heard that
> the Lord was concerned about them and had seen their affliction, they bowed
> down in worship.

The Israelites, awaiting the coming of Moses and Aaron, speculate on the nature of the new god they will bring. It becomes clear that Aaron has correctly understood the mentality of the people. They desire a powerful god, one who will deliver them from Egyptian bondage; a lovable god who is revealed in beauty; a god they can love, obey, worship, and offer sacrifice to. When Moses arrives, he announces that God demands no sacrifice: "He does not want a part, but demands everything." Meanwhile, Aaron tells the people that God's entire favor will be poured out on them, and commands that they kneel in worship. But the people are confused; they see no object for their prayer. Aaron proclaims the doctrine of the invisible God:

> Close your eyes,
> stop up your ears!
> Only thus can you see and hear Him!
> No living person sees or hears Him otherwise!

The people and the priests reject the idea of an invisible, omnipresent God, who wants no sacrifice and gives no rewards:

> We neither fear nor love Him!
> For He neither rewards nor punishes us!

Moses despairs; his thought (*Gedanke*) is powerless in Aaron's words. Aaron seizes the initiative: "I am the word and the deed!" He will adapt the message to make it powerful and intelligible, bending Moses' rigid thought into supple imaginative form. Symbolically, he takes Moses' rod and turns it into a serpent:

> In Moses' hand, a rigid rod:
> the Law;
> in my hand, a supple serpent:
> prudence.

He performs a further miracle, showing Moses' hand first leprous and then healthy, and promises that God will perform a similar wonder for Israel, healing and strengthening their hearts to conquer Pharaoh. This message the people are willing to accept:

> thus this God becomes imaginable to us,
> the symbol is enlarged into an image;
> full of courage, the heart believes in a God
> Whom visible miracles attest.
> Through Aaron, Moses lets us see
> as he himself looked upon his God;
> so this God becomes imaginable to us,
> Whom visible miracles attest.

The people are incited to rebel against the Egyptians, and they set off for the desert. Moses, who has been silent in the background, now joins Aaron in the foreground and attempts to direct the people toward a spiritual purpose:

> In the desert, purity of thought will nurture you,
> sustain you, and develop you . . .

But even as he speaks, Aaron takes up the message, again transforming it into a less demanding and more material form:

and the Eternal One allows you to see
in those spiritual marvels
an image of your earthly happiness.
The All-knowing one knows that you are a nation of
children,
and does not expect from children
what is difficult even for adults.

He assures them of miraculous sustenance from God, exalts them as those whom God had chosen above all others, and promises them a land full of milk and honey. The first act ends with the people's acceptance of Aaron's message: they sing in a marchlike hymn that they are the chosen people, given the promise of freedom and prosperity to be won by God's power.

Schoenberg omits the entire story of the Exodus and of Moses' encounter with God on Mount Sinai. After a brief interlude, in which the people wonder where Moses and his God now are, the second act begins. The first two scenes, "Aaron and the elders before the mountain of revelation," expand on a single biblical verse:

When the people became aware of Moses' delay in coming down from the
mountain, they gathered around Aaron and said to him, "Come, make us a
god who will be our leader; as for the man Moses who brought us out of
the land of Egypt, we do not know what has happened to him." (Exod. 32:1)

Schoenberg portrays the Israelites in conflict with one another, impatient with waiting, desirous of the order that the old gods had given. To pacify them, Aaron consents to give them back their gods, and promises to form a golden image. The people rejoice to have gods that represent their inmost feelings for life, gods they can imagine and feel with, gods who assure the moral order by intervening in history, rewarding and punishing:

O gods, images of our eyes,
gods, lords of our senses . . .
gods, near to our feelings,
gods that we can totally comprehend:
may blessedness reward virtue,
may righteousness punish evildoing . . .

Scene 3, "The golden calf and the altar" (based on Exod. 32:2–6), shows the disastrous results of Aaron's accommodation to the peoples' desires. In his call to worship he recognizes what they are actually adoring in the golden idol he has formed:

This image attests
that in everything that exists, a god lives . . .
Worship yourselves in this symbol!

The people offer blood sacrifices, including human self-imolations. There follows an orgy of drunkenness and dancing. Schoenberg uses musical primitivism to portray the decadence that follows from the abandonment of the transcendent idea. The people engage in further human sacrifice, wanton destruction, and sexual frenzy. Finally, in a very brief fourth scene, Moses suddenly returns. At his word, the Golden Calf disappears:

> Begone, you idol, symbol of the impossibility
> of containing the Infinite in an image!

The people depart, and Moses is left alone with Aaron.

The fifth and final scene of the act corresponds to Exod. 32:21–25. Aaron's attempt to mediate God's transcendence by imagination and beauty, to translate the thought of the infinite into an understandable and attractive form, has ended in idolatry and dehumanization. It would seem to be the moment of complete vindication for Moses' aniconic ideal. Instead, however, Schoenberg brings the problem to a further level of development. Explaining his actions to Moses, Aaron claims that he had to provide an image (*Bild*) for the people. Moses in reply reasserts the primacy of idea and word, which do away with images. But Aaron explains that this show of the power of the word was simply another form of image:

> MOSES: Your image faded at my word!
>
> AARON: Otherwise your word would have been denied image and wondrous power, which you disdain. Nevertheless, the miracle of your word's destroying my image was nothing more than an image itself.

The problem, for Schoenberg, is not merely the inadequacy of "popular" and imaginative religion; Aaron's insight implies that every conception of God's activity in history, or of human dialogue with God, including the most abstract, is involved in imagemaking. The issue is not merely that of conceptual *versus* imaginative thought, but rather that the very "positivity" of biblical revelation reduces the divine to finite form, and in this sense necessarily occurs on the level of "representation" (*Vorstellung*) or image.

Moses, as yet unshaken, appeals to the Law, which was spoken directly by God and which is neither image nor miracle. He demands:

> Do you now sense the all-power of the Thought over
> word and image?

Aaron counters that he understands only that the people, whom he loves, must be preserved. But the people are incapable of grasping Moses' idea: they can only feel, and cannot believe in anything they do not feel. A people that lived for the idea of the transcendent would be a nation of martyrs (for Schoenberg, a prophetic statement about Israel's fate). Once again Aaron pleads the necessity of mediation of the idea of God through imaginative religion:

AARON: No people can grasp more than a part of the image, which expresses
the graspable part of the idea. So make yourself comprehensible to
the people in a way suited to their capacity.

MOSES: I should falsify the idea?

AARON: Let me explain it! . . .

Rejecting Aaron's suggestion, Moses again appeals to the Law, set forth on
the tablets. But these also, Aaron insists, are simply an image, a mere part of the
idea. Moses now begins to recognize the truth in Aaron's insight: his concepts, his
dialogue with God, his reception of revelation are themselves limitations of God,
"images" of the unimaginable. In frustration, he now smashes the tablets of the
law[8] and asks that God relieve him of his mission. For Aaron, this is lack of
courage. Moses has God's word, with or without the written tablets; and Aaron
rightly preserves the word when he speaks it, even in images: for they are images
of the idea; indeed, they *are* the idea, as is everything that emerges from it.

The pillar of fire and cloud appears. In Schoenberg's account, it is a wonder
produced by Aaron. Moses rejects it as an idolatrous image, while for Aaron it is
a God-sent sign.

In it the Eternal shows not Himself,
but the way to Him:
and the way to the promised land!

The scene ends with the despair of Moses:

Unimaginable God!
Inexpressible, many-faceted idea!
Do you permit this interpretation?
Ought Aaron, my mouth, to form this image?
So I too have formed an image for myself: false,
as an image can only be!
So I am stricken.
So all that I thought was madness,
and cannot and must not be spoken!
O word, thou word that I lack!

The music for the third and final act of the opera was never written. Shortly
before his death, Schoenberg suggested that in performances it should simply be
spoken. In this text, which has no biblical basis, Schoenberg comes to a partial
resolution of the work's central conflict. The single scene consists of a final interview between Moses and Aaron—the latter now a prisoner in chains. The dialogue
reveals a sudden shift in perspective. Aaron's contention that thought needs to be
interpreted in images now seems to be accepted. As Aaron puts it to Moses,

I was to speak in images,
while you spoke in ideas;

I speak to the heart,
while you speak to the mind.

Now the problem is no longer the use of images, but their misuse. Moses accuses Aaron of translating his spiritual message into a material one: of taking the symbols of spiritual freedom literally, transforming them into a political program of liberation for the people and power for himself.

Alienated from the source, the thought,
then neither word nor image suffices for you . . .
. . . but only the deed, action, could satisfy you.
Then you made the rod into a leader,
and my power into a liberator . . .
Then you desired actually, physically,
to tread with your own feet an unreal land,
where milk and honey flow . . .
Thus you won the people not for the Eternal,
but for yourself . . .
Here images govern thought,
instead of expressing it.

By his images, according to Moses, Aaron has used the God-idea, instead of serving it. But it now seems to be taken for granted that it is possible for both words and images to serve and express the idea, if they remain grounded in its transcendence. Aaron's fault is that he has lost that grounding. By proclaiming an anthropomorphic God who corresponds to human needs, he has restricted God's freedom and infinity and betrayed the true mission of Israel.

The Almighty—whatever else He may do-
is not obliged to do anything,
is not bound by anything.
He is not bound by the misdeeds of the wicked,
nor the prayer of the good,
nor the sacrifices of the penitent . . .
You have betrayed God to the gods,
thought to images,
this chosen people to the others,
the extraordinary to the ordinary . . .

Moses' final monologue, addressed to the people, tells them that they must use the talents given them to fight for the God-idea; if they misuse those talents to seek their own pleasure, they will return to the wilderness. Aaron, freed by Moses, stands up and immediately falls over dead.[9] The opera ends with Moses' confident prophecy:

But in the wasteland you will be invincible and will
reach the goal:
union with God.

Schoenberg ultimately presents a positive relation between thought and imagination in the human representation of God—not merely in the synthesis briefly implied in the third act of the opera, but above all by his attempts to embody it in his work as a composer. Schoenberg himself, after all, performs the functions of both Moses and Aaron:[10] he presents his "theology" not merely conceptually but also in dramatic and musical form: he engages the senses to challenge the mind. What at first seems a choice between mutually exclusive alternatives— "either imageless thought or the indeed suggestive, but misleading image"[11]— turns out to be capable of synthesis. But Schoenberg insists that the synthesis is not one of equal elements: it is the thought of God that must rule over all pictures, images, and manifestations.[12]

Clearly, Schoenberg's "thought" of God is not a rational-idealistic grasp of the divine by means of concepts. On the contrary; Schoenberg's notion of thought (*Gedanke*), based as it is on the philosophies of Kant and Schopenhauer, is that of an "empty" idea, pointing to a "noumenon" that remains in itself unknown.[13] The failure of words to express God (Moses: "O word that I lack!") is thus inevitable: inexpressibility is intrinsic to the God-idea.[14] The word, despite its primacy, is in the last analysis similar to the sensible image in its powerlessness to manifest God;[15] both pictures and concepts belong to the realm of *Vorstellung* or "imagination."

The inconceivability of God corresponds to Schoenberg's primary religious concern: to affirm the divinity of the biblical God in the face of the tendency, correctly pointed out by Feuerbach and Freud, to create ideas and images of God through the projection of human attributes and/or desires.[16] For Schoenberg, as for Martin Buber, revelation means the encounter with God as an absolutely free subject.[17] Our relation to God cannot make any claim on God's freedom, nor should it attempt to use God for our own earthly purposes. Schoenberg makes this plain in his "Modern Psalm, no. 1" (1950; like *Moses und Aron*, the piece was still uncompleted at the time of Schoenberg's death the following year).

O Thou my God: all peoples praise Thee and assure Thee
of their devotion.

But what can it mean to Thee whether I also do so or
not?
Who am I that I should believe that my prayer is a
necessity?

When I say "God," I know that I am speaking about the
Unique, Eternal, Almighty, Omniscient, and
Unimaginable One, of whom I neither can nor should
make for myself an image.

Against whom I may not and cannot make any claim,
the One who will fulfill or disregard my most fervent
prayer.

And nevertheless I pray, as every living being prays;
nevertheless, I ask for graces and miracles; for
answers.

Nevertheless I pray, for I do not wish to lose the
blessed feeling of unity, of union with Thee.

O Thou my God, Thy grace has granted us prayer, as a
bond, a beatifying bond with Thee. As a bliss that
gives us more than any answer.

The sarcastic emphasis that Schoenberg places on the words "graces" (*Gnaden*)
and "miracles" (*Wunder*) stresses his recognition that to have such hopes is to
misconceive God by locating the divine within the world, the human sphere of
operation. This is to "imagine" God falsely, and to that extent to deprive God of
real deity.

Like Rilke in his poem "The Contemplative," Schoenberg insists that the
genuine and beatifying encounter with God occurs when we abandon our attempts
to use God, and instead submit ourselves to God's transcendence:

... How small is that with which we wrestle;
what wrestles with us—how great it is!
if, more like things, we let ourselves
be bent, so, by the great storm—
we would become wide and beyond name.

What we conquer are the small things,
and our very successes make us small.[18]
The eternal and mysterious
will not be bent by us.
That is the angel who appeared
to the wrestlers of the Old Testament:
when the sinews of his opponents
stretch like metal in battle,
he feels them under his fingers
like the chords of deep melodies.

Whoever is defeated by this angel—
who so often renounces battle—
he goes forth erect and just
and great from that hard hand
which closed upon him, as though forming.
Victories do not tempt him.
His growth is this: to be
deeply defeated by the ever Greater.[19]

The genuine and beatifying encounter with God is possible only through grasping
the idea of God as beyond conception and imagination.

For Schoenberg, God is revealed in word and image insofar as these mediate
the enlightenment that comes from an encounter with the living God. In this
process, the figure of the leader of the people is vital.[20] The enlightened prophet
(Moses) attempts to communicate the ungraspable God through the medium of
word. But art can also share this function, since, for Schoenberg, it too is intrin-

sically oriented to the expression of what is conceptually ungraspable.[21] Schoenberg adopted his theory of aesthetics from Schopenhauer's *The World as Will and Representation* (*Die Welt als Wille und Vorstellung*). According to Schopenhauer, the "Platonic ideas" are objectifications of will. The artistic genius (Aaron) uses imagination or representation (*Vorstellung*) to bring about perception of these "ideas" or archetypes. Music has a special place among the arts: while the others objectify will indirectly, through the medium of the forms, music is a direct expression of will (i.e., reality) itself.[22]

In Schoenberg's theological application, the divine being is inconceivable and unimaginable (*unvorstellbar*); but imagination (*Vorstellung*), on both the verbal level (*Wort*) and the sensible (*Bild*), can evoke the "idea" of the ungraspable Eternal, and in this way can mediate union with God. But *Moses und Aron* is above all an expression of the tension between revelation and art, between the inspired God-idea and human "representation" or imagination. The latter, Schoenberg shows, is too easily made the expression not of selfless knowledge of God but of self-centered human desire. That desire may express a legitimate worldly goal, as in Aaron's love for Israel and his ambition to build it into a united and free people. But to use God for such purposes through appeal to miracles and divine interventions turns true religion into idolatry and magic,[23] and ends in the loss not only of the God-idea, but also of Israel's real mission in the world and of the genuine source of moral value.

Defining the Problem

Schoenberg's *Moses und Aron* raises a wealth of interconnected problems for theological reflection.

First there are questions regarding God and imagination: can God be imagined? can God be thought? what is the relation between "idea," "word," and "image"? between "feeling" and thinking?

Second, there are questions regarding the nature of our relationship to God—that is, religion: how is God's transcendence reconciled with the human need for images and affect? can human beings love a God who is truly transcendent? how is God's self-revelation related to human projection? how is "idolatry" differentiated from true worship? how is God's sovereign freedom related to human needs and desires, and hence to human hopes and prayers? does God indeed "act" in history? does God direct history according to a plan? does God reward and punish? how does religion as "idea" relate to religion as imagination?

Third, there are issues that concern the place of art and beauty in our relation to God. Is God beautiful as well as sublime? Does God correspond to human longing? What is the place of the artist, the creator of images, in the representation of God's revelation?

The first two sets of questions belong to the realm of theological "aesthetics" in the Kantian sense: the theory of perception, imagination, and feeling with regard to God and revelation. This will be the focus of the present chapter. We shall see that there are two levels to be considered: the relation of sensibility and imagination, on the one hand, to God's transcendence and, on the other, to historical revelation. On both levels there occur the religious problems of idolatry and projection.

The third set of questions concerns aesthetics in the narrower senses of the theory of beauty and of art; these will concern us in the next chapters. Finally, in the last chapter, we will return to the conflicts between the beautiful and the good and the different "agendas" of religion and art.

The Unpicturability of God: The Iconoclast Tradition and the Problem of Idolatry

> And God spoke all these words, saying, I am the Lord your God, who brought you out of the land of Egypt, out of the house of bondage. You shall have no other gods before me. You shall not make for yourself a graven image, or any likeness of anything that is in heaven above, or that is in the earth beneath, or that is in the water under the earth; you shall not bow down to them or serve them: for I the Lord your God am a jealous God, visiting the iniquity of the fathers upon the children to the third and fourth generation of those who hate me, but showing steadfast love to thousands of those who love me and keep my commandments. (Exod. 20:1–6)

In the Byzantine tradition of the church, the first Sunday of Lent celebrates the "Memorial of the Sacred Images"—honoring the icons that are such a salient feature of Byzantine church architecture and spirituality. The affirmation of devotion to images is thought to have theological significance; indeed, the feast it commemorates is called the "triumph of orthodoxy"—that is, of the "right teaching"—that was threatened by iconoclasm.[24] In the Eastern Christian view, "the victory over the iconoclast heresy is a victory over earlier Christological heresies."[25] This emphasis given to the vindication of the use of images not only reveals their theological importance in the Eastern church (to which we will return later) but also reminds us of the acerbity of the dispute of which they were once the subject.

What is now known as the "iconoclast controversy" was at least in part a particular manifestation of a more general problem in Christianity. "Iconoclasm" of one form or another has been a recurrent tendency of Christian thought, harking back to its very origins. Von Rad calls the prohibition of depictions of God "intrinsic" and "fundamental" to the Old Testament, despite the difficulty this posed for popular religion.[26] Not only were images of alien gods to be shunned but the God of Israel could also not be physically "portrayed."[27] Aidan Nichols cautions, however, that we should not oversimplify the situation of aniconism in ancient Israel. Nichols's careful sifting of the data leads him to several conclusions that point to a modification of the picture of strict aniconism that was prevalent in the last century: we cannot be sure that the religion of Moses was aniconic, although it is possible that the Second Commandment reflects his teaching against imitation of the cultic art of Egypt; the oldest stratum we possess of evidence for the ban on images is found in the book of Judges, and indicates the existence a premonarchical iconic Yahwism, which it contests; the priesthood of the official sanctuaries in Israel was certainly aniconic; by early in the Christian era there are evidences of Jewish representational art—(in addition to those mentioned below, Nichols cites mosaic-decorated synagogues at Beth Alpha and Ain-ed-Duk and sculptings in Galilean synagogues); the total prohibition of images is not part of the original intent of the law, but is an example of the construction of a "hedge" around the law by the rabbis.[28] Nevertheless, although we know that in the Jewish diaspora there was use of figurative as well as decorative art (the synagogue at Dura Europus and the Jewish catacombs in Rome provide striking examples), the pictorial representation of God was scrupulously avoided. As Kittel notes, there are at most symbolic representations of the disembodied hand of God in such scenes as the sacrifice of Isaac and the assumption of Ezekiel.[29]

Although there are questions about the degree and extent of aniconism, therefore, the prohibition of images of God seems to have been well established in Judaism. Moreover, in the early church the Jewish prohibition of images of God was reinforced by pagan philosophical objections to representing the divine. As Van der Leeuw points out, behind the Acts of the Apostles' account of Paul's condemnation of idolatry (Acts 17:29) stands not only the Old Testament but also the Stoa.[30] Already Heraclitus had complained that the ignorant "pray to these images as though they wanted to talk to buildings; they do not know the true nature of the gods and heroes."[31] By the Christian era a "pagan" philosophical tradition had developed that opposed idolatry and proclaimed a true God who is not visible or even conceivable. Early Christian apologists were at pains to insist that Christians worshiped this God of philosophy, not any anthropomorphic god of popular religion.[32]

As far as is now known, Christian art (in the form of catacomb paintings and the decoration of house-churches) did not begin to develop until after the New Testament period. Perhaps from the mid-second century, certainly by the early third century, images were painted on the walls of hypogea and baptisteries.[33] The nature of these images was symbolic and/or narrative, like the images in contemporaneous Jewish synagogues: they present the τεκμήρια θεοῦ—"tokens of God's works and deeds."[34] There were no representations of the divine as such. Stories from the Old Testament were followed by stories of Christ; and in the latest period of catacomb painting there appear hieratic representations of Christ as the divine-human—the image of God in the flesh.

Protests and cautions were heard already in the earliest period of the development of Christian iconography. Many of the Fathers (including Tertullian, Cyprian, Irenaeus, Clement of Alexandria, Justin, Tatian, Athenagoras, and Origen) spoke out against the dangers of pictorial art.[35] (The very vehemence of their protestations, however, testifies to the strength of the pictorial instinct—or temptation.)[36] The grounds of the Patristic objections were varied. The danger of superstition and idolatry was real; so was that of syncretism. Irenaeus mentions that the (Gnostic) heretics had images of Jesus set up among the philosophers, along with Plato and Pythagoras. It is reported that the Emperor Alexander Severus honored a figure of Jesus, along with Abraham and Orpheus, along with the household gods in his *lararium*. There was a particular opposition to statues: these were associated not only with idolatry but also with the Greek exaltation of the body and cult of humanity. Although some among the Fathers, in particular the Cappadocians, spoke in favor of images and defended their pedagogical usefulness,[37] a more or less strong anti-iconic stance is found in many others. Origen, for example, contrasted "static and dead" artistic images with the living image of Christ in his followers.[38] Eusebius of Caesarea rejected any representation of Christ on the basis of the impossibility of portraying his divinity: "How could anyone paint the image of a form so marvelous and incomprehensible—if one may still call a 'form' the divine and intelligible essence?"[39] The Synod of Elvira (Illiberis = modern Granada, Spain) in the year 306 issued a unanimous condemnation of use of images in churches. Significantly, its canon paraphrases the words of Exodus 20:4: "*Picturas in ecclesia esse non debere, ne quod colitur et adorabitur in parietibus depingantur.*"[40]

Opposition to images reached its apex in the iconoclast movements of the eighth and ninth centuries, initiated by the Byzantine emperors with the support of a majority of the bishops. The iconoclast council of 754 condemned "the ignorant artist who with a sacrilegious lust for gain depicts that which ought not to be depicted, and with defiled hands would bestow a form upon that which ought to be believed in the heart." Although the dispute was carried out largely on grounds that continued the Christological controversies of previous centuries, the issues at stake were complex, and included political and social factors.[41] The theological question centered not on the possibility of representing the invisible Godhead *in se* (which was generally admitted to be excluded), but on representations of Christ as the divine-human. An important corollary issue involved the reverence or "adoration" that was given to images of Christ, his mother, and the apostles and saints.[42] The iconodule position was based on a Platonic notion that the image "participates in the reality of the exemplar—brings about the real presence of the exemplar which dwells in the image";[43] the veneration of the image was therefore considered a legitimate way of honoring the person represented. Because of the participated presence of the exemplar, icons were further considered a quasi-incarnational, pneumatophoric locus of supernatural "energy," which could be the source of miracles. Added to this was the argument—an "especially unconvincing" one, according to Balthasar—that the icons (or more exactly, their prototypes) were "not made by hands,"[44] but were themselves supernaturally produced.

The Second Council of Nicaea (787) in principle established the acceptance of images and their veneration.[45] Nevertheless, the West remained largely unconvinced: the Council of Frankfurt (794) rejected both the iconoclast council of 754 and the iconodule Second Nicaea.[46] Carolingian theology was ready to admit a pedagogical value to sacred imagery (the use of which was already well established in the Western church), but not a mystical presence. (In this it is followed by the Council of Trent, which even while reaffirming the decrees of Nicaea II denies that images have any indwelling presence or power.)[47]

The Protestant Reformation was the occasion of a new outbreak of iconomachy. Although Luther took a positive attitude toward sacred images, Karlstadt, Zwingli, and Calvin rejected them. Van der Leeuw summarizes the various mo-

tivations at work in the iconoclasm of the Reformation: "The Humanistic Enlightenment, with its view that God is too exalted to be represented; its fidelity
to the Bible, which values the respect paid to the letter of the Old Testament
prohibitions; its ecstatic personalization, which endures neither constraint for image nor sacrament; the protest of the poor against the riches of the Church—all
of this together has the effect first of destroying images and then shunning them
more or less rigorously."[48] To these may be added the danger of superstition and
an insistence on the primacy of the Word. Calvin, for example, explains that "there
is no difference whether they simply worship an idol, or God in the idol," because
"as soon as a visible form has been fashioned for God, his power is also bound to
it."[49] Moreover, he opposes the argument (classical from the time of Gregory the
Great) that images are the books of the uneducated:[50] this view for him not only
implies a class structure in religion but also assumes that pictures communicate
more readily than stories.[51]

But, as Schoenberg's Aaron brings home to Moses, recourse to the Word does
not resolve the problem. Van der Leeuw writes of iconoclasm:

> It destroys representations, those bibles of the ignorant, in order to impress
> upon them more emphatically the images of the Bible itself. To express the
> holy, one declares one's self free from line and color and turns to the spiri-
> tuality of the word. But this has by no means done away with the image.
> For no religion speaks in abstract concepts; religion speaks in myths, that is
> in the language of images. And no religion can get along without symbols.
> ... For even the bare walls and central position of the pulpit are "symbols."[52]

Protestant iconoclasm fled from images to the word, in Scripture and in theology.
But further questions arise. With regard to the scriptural word: how is the picture
thinking of the Bible—its "privileged anthropomorphism"—to be distinguished
from heathen myth?[53] Raimon Pannikar goes so far as to speak of the religion of
Israel as a kind of "iconolatry," because even though visual images are forbidden,
God is consistently portrayed in the Scriptures as having human characteristics.[54]
And the problem can be further extended to "word" in general: can even the
most abstract "word" capture the nature of the living God? and can any thought
of God, however removed from image, avoid the danger of idolatry?

From the Mysterious Other to the Mystery of Being:
From the "Unpicturability" to the "Inconceivability" of God

Balthasar notes that iconoclasm is not merely a phenomenon of the past, but is to
some extent a permanent feature of Christianity.[55] It tends to appear especially in
periods of reform. The reasons for the mistrust (or at the limit, the rejection) of
images reflect two primary concerns. On one level, there is what might be called
an "ascetical" objection to art: consciousness of a conflict between the goals of art
and those of spirituality, between the beautiful and the good, between sensual
pleasure and spiritual growth, between the material wealth associated with art
and the gospel blessing of the poor. (This objection will be examined at greater

length in the last chapter.) On another level, there is the "epistemological" objection already adverted to above, centered on the dangers of idolatry, false worship, and superstition. The development of this aspect leads to a further dimension of the problem of God and imagination: not merely whether and how God can be pictured in material form through paint or stone or clay, but whether and how the divinity can be known (or can make itself known) *as divine* through the mental images—or even the abstract concepts—of the human intellect and "heart."

In the biblical context, God is knowable and is "known" in the personal sense: God can be encountered, heard, responded to, related to, relied on. God is also revealed to have certain characteristics or ways of being. There is no constraint on verbal images; indeed, the Old Testament is full of anthropomorphic portrayals of God. But God is personal and free in a unique sense. God is faithful, not capricious; but God is not determined by anything outside God's self. God is mysterious because God is "holy." God's ways of being are "other" than humanity's ("My thoughts are not your thoughts, neither are your ways my ways"; Isa. 55:8) and are beyond our control: God is sovereign. This is essential to the meaning of the ban on images: "the reason for the prohibition is not the material or finite *nature* of the images per se but rather their religious *function* of allowing human worshipers to manipulate the deity to their own ends."[56] YHWH cannot be manipulated; hence God cannot be made into an idol, whose very meaning is availability to the worshiper's desires.

Metaphysical thinking adds a further dimension of insight into God's transcendence. Already pre-Socratic Greek philosophy had affirmed the qualitative difference between the One, or God, and everything else; on this basis Heraclitus and Xenophanes criticized the anthropomorphisms of Homer.[57] A decisive step occurred with Plato's contention that the first and highest reality, beyond all being, cannot be expressed in human *logos*.[58] Despite biblical anthropomorphism, the prohibition of images in Exodus already implied that YHWH is not "like" anything in the universe.[59] The combination of the scriptural idea of God's personal transcendence with Greek philosophical thought allows a profound expansion of the idea. Schoenberg expresses it powerfully through Moses' sharp correction of Aaron: it is not merely that God *must* not be imaged—that is, that representations are forbidden—rather, God *cannot* be imaged because of God's infinite nature.

But this insight implies a deeper problem: that of God's knowability in general. First of all, God is "spirit" and hence is intrinsically invisible—God is unlike anything that can occur in the realm of sensation and can be given sensible form. But even further, God's radical "otherness" is translated into an epistemological principle: the transcendent God can only be known (and, paradoxically, this is real knowledge) by the negation not only of materiality but also of all that we know as finite. Hence God is not merely "unpicturable," but is also strictly inconceivable: beyond every grasp of the finite mind, whether in image, word, or concept. (Hence Kant's remark concerning the command not to make images of God: "There is no more sublime passage in the Jewish law.")[60]

The identification of the biblical Creator with the absolute and infinite Being of metaphysics (already foreshadowed in the Septuagint rendering of God's name as ὁ ὤν) permeates the theology and spirituality of the Greek Fathers. God is (in the words of the Liturgy of St. John Chrysostom) "ineffable, inconceivable, invisible, incomprehensible." The famous hymn of Gregory of Nazianzen expresses the same insight with ecstatic wonder and adoration:

O Thou beyond all things!—for how else can I proclaim Thee?
What word can I use to sing of Thee? for no word can express Thee.
By what thought should I contemplate Thee? for no thought can apprehend
   Thee.
Thou alone art beyond speech; for Thou dost produce all things that speak.
Thou alone art beyond thought; for Thou dost produce all things that think.
All things—both those that speak and those that do not—proclaim Thee;
All things—both those that think and those that do not—glorify Thee.
The common yearnings and anguish of all things
Are for Thee. To Thee all things pray.
To Thee all thinking beings raise together a silent hymn.
In Thee alone all things remain; toward Thee all things together hasten.
Thou art the goal of all things; Thou art One, and All, and None;
Thou art neither one nor all. How shall I call Thee, Thou of all names,
Who alone cannot be limited? What heavenly mind can enter into
The veil beyond the clouds? Be gracious,
O Thou beyond all things; for how else can I proclaim Thee?[61]

The "incomprehensibility" of God became a major category for classical theology and entered into official statements of church doctrine. Already in the *Tomus Leonis* God's intrinsic incomprehensibility is presumed, and is contrasted with the revelatory incarnation: "*invisibilis in suis, visibilis est factus in nostris, incomprehensibilis voluit comprehendi*"[62] (*DS* 294). In the Lateran council of 649 (*DS* 501), it is enumerated among the attributes of the Trinity. The Council of Toledo (675) names the Father "*ineffabilis*" in essence (*DS* 525). The Fourth Lateran Council (1215) cites incomprehensibility and ineffability among the essential divine attributes that must be confessed: "*Firmiter credimus et simpliciter confitemur, quod unus solus est verus Deus, aeternus, immensus et incomutabilis, incomprehensibilis, omnipotens et ineffabilis*"[63] (*DS* 800); "*una quaedam summa res est, incomprehensibilis quidem et ineffabilis, quae veraciter est Pater, et Filius, et Spiritus Sanctus*"[64] (*DS* 804). The First Vatican Council includes incomprehensibility among the perfections of God, along with omnipotence, immeasurability, and infinity (*DS* 3001).

The use of this metaphysical (rather than descriptive) category is significant. God's nature is not merely "hidden": what is "hidden," although it may be kept from sight, in principle can be seen. Rather, God is intrinsically beyond our grasp: as Augustine says, "*si enim comprehendis, non est deus.*"[65] The highly influential treatises of Pseudo-Dionysius also make this point clearly: God can be grasped neither by sense perception nor by mind; the highest knowledge of God comes through "unknowing."[66] God's incomprehensibility "follows from the essential infinity of God which makes it impossible for a finite created intellect to exhaust the possibilities of knowledge and truth contained in this absolute fullness of being."[67] As Rahner points out, God's incomprehensibility does not mean that some things about God are known and others unknown (as might be the case with a finite being), but that the one and undivided being of God is both known and unknown:[68] God is known precisely as the finally ungraspable. Indeed, the height of human knowledge of God, according to Aquinas, is the insight that God exceeds all that we can understand.[69]

This idea has important implications. First, as Rahner emphasizes, it tells us something of the nature of human knowledge. Incomprehensibility is not an "attribute" of God alongside others like goodness, freedom, justice, and mercy; rather, it is the "attribute of [God's] attributes": all of God's "attributes" are finally incomprehensible.[70] This is to say that God's incomprehensibility is a doctrine about human finitude and the limitations of our knowledge.[71] However, these limitations are not to be thought of in a purely negative way. On the contrary, the fact that we can (and, according to Rahner, do) genuinely *know* the ultimate reality, precisely as the incomprehensible, shows that the essence of knowledge is not in the penetration and mastery of objects but, rather, in entering into the presence of the "mystery" of being: "Man as transcendent subject . . . does not experience himself as the dominant, absolute subject, but as the one whose being is bestowed upon him by the mystery. *This* is why, in forming any concept, he understands himself as the one who reaches out beyond the conceptual into the nameless and incomprehensible."[72] Moreover, this condition is not a transient phase: the essence of the final "beatific vision" of God, according to Rahner, is immediacy to God's mystery, so that God's incomprehensibility is not the limit, but the substance of our bliss and love.[73]

Second, the ontologically based notion of God's incomprehensibility reinforces the biblical affirmation of God's sovereign personal freedom. God's being is more than the "answer" to the meaning of human life. It follows that God can neither be used nor submitted to selfish human desires. God *is* the "answer" to human existence; but in order for this to be, human existence must be "ex-centric," centered outside itself, in God. "Recourse to God as answer to the question of meaning in man in his wholeness is right and indispensable. But it becomes the creation of a human idol if it does not bring man, forsaking himself, self-surrendering, and blessed only in that way, into the presence of the incomprehensibility of God."[74]

Third, a correlative insight is that the essence of "idolatry" consists not in the medium in which God is represented but in the way in which it is used: as a means of encounter with and "memory" of the living transcendent reality, or as a projection of human self-worship. (Recall Aaron's words about the golden calf in Schoenberg's drama: "Worship yourselves in this symbol!") Both defenders and attackers of images sometimes seem to gloss over this fact. Iconoclasts neglect the intrinsically symbolic nature of thought, and are tempted to fall into a fundamentalism of the word; iconodules are tempted to present perfectly valid theoretical justifications for images, while neglecting the uses to which they are actually put. As Paul Tillich was aware, every human representation of God—physical images, verbal images, metaphors, and concepts, including the concept of "God" itself—can become idolatrous. (Of course, this does not imply that every medium of representation is *equally* "dangerous" or equally suitable.) For this reason, the most radical critique of idolatry flees from both image and word, to seek mystical immediacy with God. It

> turns aside not only from the concrete image, but also from those that fill the soul. In all the mysticism which has invaded the West since Neoplatonism, from the Mohammedan Sufis to the German mystics of the Middle Ages, and from St. Theresa to the Quietists of the eighteenth century of the likes of Madame Guyon, ideas and images are systematically banished from the soul. Even the facts and forms of the Gospel have only temporary pedagogical value.[75]

The "Positivity" of Historical Revelation and the Problem of Mythology

The notion of God's "incomprehensibility" gives to theological aesthetics the problem of explaining the possibility of knowing and representing the infinite and immaterial God for an intellect that is both intrinsically finite and inherently tied to sensible presentations and to language. The question of religious imagination is thus included within the more general epistemological treatment of analogy.

The problem takes on a new dimension when (through the identification of knowledge with the objects of empirical science) the critique of metaphysics casts doubt on the analogical knowledge of God itself, while historical consciousness casts doubt on the facticity of Christian revelation. On the one hand, God becomes not simply ungraspable but altogether unknowable by reason; on the other hand, the claims of historical revelation are dismissed as unverifiable and mythological. A gap then arises between the "scientific" mode of consciousness, identified as rational understanding (*Begriff*), and religious consciousness, which is relegated to the level of "imagination" (*Vorstellung*) and "feeling." For some, this means that religious faith is revealed as irrational and illusory; for others, on the contrary, faith and the realm of feeling are affirmed as a needed alternative to the limits of "rationality."

Harmut Sierig sees Michelangelo's Sistine chapel painting of God the Father creating Adam as the unintentional symbol of the beginnings of a modern mentality that would reach its culmination in Feuerbach and Nietzsche: "from this point on people begin to see God in human terms: not as God-become-human who saves us in Christ, but rather God as the ideal picture of humanity. God is simply a metaphor for human perfection."[76] Jungel sees the epistemological dimension of the modern God problem as stemming from Descartes' separation of the divine being *in se*, an independent essence existing over against the human subject, from the mental concept of God, which (although it stems from God) is totally a function of the thinking subject.[77] (This in contrast to Patristic and early Scholastic theories that linked our ability to conceive God to a participation in the divine "light" itself. The loss of this perspective in fact predates Descartes, having begun already in late medieval Nominalism.)

Enlightenment rationalism not only distanced God's being *in se* from human conception but also stressed the separation of the rational from the sensible. Leibniz distinguished between the eternal truths of reason (*Vernunft-Wahrheiten*) and the truth of historical facts (*Tatsachenwahrheiten*). Balthasar and others see a seminal moment in Lessing's picturing of this distinction as a "nasty ditch" between the necessary, universal truths of reason and the accidental truths of history. The former are identified with the province of philosophy; the latter with religion and theology.[78] Moreover, adapting the schema of Joachim de Fiore, Lessing sees a progression: the Old Testament, representing the Law, was the age of the Father; the New Testament, centered on faith, was that of the Son; the age of the Spirit represents the overcoming of both law and faith by Reason.[79]

In Kant and his followers we find the continuation of these ideas: the valuation of "reason" over feeling and imagination, and the identification of historical religion with the latter. But in Kant a further and crucial element is added: the elimination of the knowledge of God from the sphere of "speculative reason"— in order, as Kant says, "to make room for belief."[80] The legitimate use of speculative reason, for Kant, cannot be pressed beyond the limits of (sensible) experience.[81] By examining the transcendental conditions for the unity of our experience of the world, speculative reason arrives at an idea of God.[82] However, by speculative reason we can know neither whether such a being actually exists nor what its nature is, although we can speak hypothetically of God's relation to the world by analogy to relations within the world:

> the transcendental and the only definite concept which purely speculative reason give us of God . . . [is] only the idea of something on which the highest and necessary unity of all empirical reality is founded, and which we cannot represent to ourselves except in analogy with a real substance. . . .
>
> I represent to myself that Supreme Being through concepts which, properly speaking, are applicable to the world of sense only. As, however, I make none but a relative use of that transcendental hypothesis . . . I may perfectly well represent a Being which I distinguish from the world, by qualities which belong to the world of sense only. For I demand by no means . . . that I should know that object of my idea, according to what it may be by itself. I have no concept whatever for it, and even the concepts of reality, substance, causality, ay, of the necessity in existence, lose all their meaning, and become mere titles of concepts, void of contents, as soon as I venture with them outside the field of the senses. I only present to myself the relation of a Being, utterly unknown to me as existing by itself, to the greatest possible systematical unity of the universe.[83]

At the same time, Kant insists that the rational idea (*Begriff*) of God must serve as the "proof stone" of every representation (*Vorstellung*) of God, including those of religious revelation.[84] Otherwise, we are in grave danger of creating an idolatrous God for ourselves.[85] Idolatry results in religion from giving the sensible power of imagination (*das sinnliche Vorstellungsvermögen*) equality or superiority to the intellectual Idea.[86] Although he does not develop an explicit theory of the relation of religion to reason, as Hegel would, Kant implies that ordinary religion occurs on the level of imagination (*Vorstellung*) and is (at its best) a less adequate form of the rational religion of morality.[87]

Fichte renounces every possibility of imagining or representing God, even conceptually. He extends the biblical injunction against idolatry to include metaphysical thought. God

> should not be thought at all, because this is impossible . . . in that something is grasped, it ceases to be God; and every alleged concept of God is necessarily that of an idol. Whoever says, Thou shalt not make a concept of God, is saying in other words: Thou shalt not make any graven images, and his commandment means intellectually the same thing as the sense of the old Mosaic commandment: "You shall not make for yourself a graven image, or any likeness."[88]

Hegel sets out to correct the errors of the "little enlightenment," as he disparagingly characterizes the thought of Kant, Fichte, and Jacobi.[89] Kant and his followers, Hegel writes, had attempted to defend faith against the claims of rationalism; but they could only do so by placing the Absolute in a "beyond" accessible only to faith. In so doing, they caused an even wider rift between faith and reason.[90] By contrast, Hegel intends to surpass "the old opposition between reason (*Vernunft*) and faith (*Glauben*), between philosophy and positive religion,"[91] by placing the question within a newly conceived philosophy of religion.[92]

Like Lessing, Hegel adopts Joachim de Fiore's tripartite schema, adapting it to the dialectical structure of consciousness. All of history is conceived as Absolute Spirit's self-alienation and return to self. In this process, Absolute Spirit or the divine nature manifests itself in human consciousness in three ways: in art, religion, and philosophy.[93] The three have the same "content," but manifest it in different forms. Art represents even the highest ideas in sensuous form, "thereby bringing them nearer to the character of natural phenomena, to the senses, and to feeling."[94] Religion presents the divine self-revelation on the level of imagination (*Vorstellung*). In the true and final philosophy, Spirit knows itself on the highest level, that of absolute Idea (*Begriff*).[95]

Rationalistic *Vernunfttheologie*, based on the Kantian "metaphysics of understanding" (*Verstandesmetaphysik*), undertook a rationalistic exegesis (*räsonnirende Exegese*) that effectively eliminated the positive content of religion, including the central doctrines of Christianity. In contrast, Hegel affirms the content of the Scriptures, the creeds, and the doctrines of the church, insisting that there can be no opposition between (true) philosophy and positive religion, because there is only one Spirit that is self-revealing in both.[96] The absolute Idea, realized on the level of reason, contains the determinate content of religious history as a moment within itself.[97]

However, because divine revelation is received in a human manner, it must be interpreted and explained when one reaches the final level of spirit. In philosophy the content of positive religion is *aufgehoben* or dialectically "sublated" into the truths of pure thought: religion's imaginative form is "canceled and transcended,"[98] and its truth affirmed at a new level. The discipline of the philosophy of religion concerns itself explicitly with the unity of the two.[99] From another point of view, one may say that religion mediates between consciousness of God through the senses (art) and through thought (philosophy): it "illustrates" thought in concrete, imaginative, metaphorical form.[100] In a letter to Von Baader, Hegel summarizes his views on the relation of philosophy to religion:

> As to the way in which I speak of the difference between religion and philosophy, I am really bringing everything down simply to a difference in the *Form* of knowledge and cognition, and in view of the fact that the *content* of the truth is not only common to but identical in both, to which the (Holy) Spirit bears witness, i.e., in view of the fact that the Reason is *in itself, free*, I prefer to indicate the form of the religious by the term *imagination* or *representation*, to show that this religious cognition and knowledge has to do with something *external*, something *given*, etc.; for religion is and should be for all men, not only for trained thinkers, and so its content should, so to speak, penetrate into the heart from the *imagination [Vorstellung]*, as does our habitual knowledge, without any intervening elaboration into a scientific concept; and it is *from this aspect* that I say that in such a content thinking Reason is not in itself, inasmuch as it is only imagined.[101]

Whether Hegel's thought should be interpreted as faithful Christian theology, as the epitome of rationalism, or even as disguised atheism[102] (a debate that raged already almost from the time of Hegel's death and D. F. Strauss's division of his followers into the Hegelian left, center, and right wings), there is no doubt that his distinction of philosophy from religion in terms of rational thought (*Begriff*) and imagination (*Vorstellung*) provided the context for the radical critique of positive religion that followed.

Hegel's follower David Friedrich Strauss raised the question of positive religion in a new way. While Hegel had taught that the positivity of religion is *aufgehoben* in philosophical system, Strauss held that what is essential to religion is precisely its positivity, which is irreducible to philosophical concepts. Moreover, having decided in his *Leben Jesu Kritisch Bearbeitet* that the gospels are not historical, but the mythical creation of the early Christian community, he concluded that they (and the Christianity flowing from them) are therefore not relevant to the level of *Begriff*, but only to imagination. The distinction between *Vorstellung* and *Begriff* becomes that between myth and history.[103]

Feuerbach, a member of the Young Hegelian movement that formed in Berlin in support of Strauss, moved the distinction a step further. In *Das Wesen des Christentums* (1841), Hegel's notion of "alienation" is applied to the projection of human attributes onto God, and the task of philosophy becomes the releasing of consciousness from religious illusions. The opposition between *Vorstellung* and *Begriff* is now not one between two levels of truth, but between mere imagination and real knowledge, between fantasy and reality. Religious imagination is now associated with the imaginary, with false projection.[104] Feuerbach thus sets the stage for Victorian positivism (including Marxism). Historical religion is associated with myth, and seen as part of a pre-scientific mentality that is to be overcome by the progress of empirically based reason. At least some of these ideas perdure as the background of the scientific and technological mentality that underlies the "common sense" of much of the contemporary Western world.

In this context, even if the idea of God is maintained, it becomes difficult to reconcile the divine transcendence with the positive aspects of religion, which appear arbitrary and mythological. Rahner summarizes:

> The world in which man lives today seems to him a closed system, sealed off to a certain extent from God, a universe of unthinkable extent and variety, largely impenetrable and fully determined by its own laws. If God is not actually depersonalized, his government of the world is less easily thought of than hitherto on the analogy of the action of someone in this world. God has become more transcendent, and his name simply stands for the unfathomable mystery which lies behind all accessible and definable reality . . . But if God is thus nameless and remote, and the world and everything within it profane, provisional, and replaceable, only at an immense remove the work of God's hand and the reflection of his being: then man's sense of his own existence sets him a strange and oppressive problem. It is no longer easy for him to see a definitely constituted religion, with its thousand and one truths, customs, prescriptions, and rules, as the concrete obligation of God's will and the necessary institution for his salvation. He finds all this so anthropomorphic and concrete that it is hard for him to realize that this multiplicity of details constitute[s] God's way, and indeed the necessary way, of communicating himself to man for man's salvation.[105]

Garrett Green points out that just as the Kantian proposition that statements about God cannot claim to be speculative knowledge need not lead to their rejection—for one can hold them to be true in another realm, which Kant calls that of "practical" reason[106]—so the relegation of positive religion to the sphere of myth and imagination need not mean its repudiation: "religion, in an age virtually defined by the paradigm of natural science, has generally been understood as the great alternative to science, as the chief example of the *other* way of thinking and acting."[107] Religious myth might be rejected as the enemy of "real" knowledge; but it might also be valued as the height of poetry, the embodiment of a human dimension of truth that complements (or even corrects) the merely objective-empirical type of rationality that leads to technological domination of the world.

This idea, associated today especially with Heidegger, is already adumbrated in thinkers like Coleridge and the German Romantics. Its explanation and justification will form part of the task of a "theological aesthetic." In this moment of defining the problem, however, it must also be pointed out that from a fundamental-theological point of view it contains several dangers, already alluded to briefly in the last chapter. The association of religion with myth, poetry, and art is a positive one as long as these are recognized as a real way of knowing. But in the absence of a philosophical justification for the possibility of the mind's reaching "ontological" truths, the recognition of the nonempirical character of religious discourse[108] may be expanded to a conscious acceptance of a chasm between religion and what we normally mean by "knowledge." Religious myth may

be "saved" from the critique of empirical history and science by an implicit abandonment of its claim to speak of any reality beyond that of internal feeling. (The
alternative to this, in the absence of any kind of "natural theology," would seem
to be pure fideism.)

Religion may then be seen as serving a valuable "aesthetic" role in life, but
only so long as it abandons its "supernaturalism." (Both Dewey and Santayana
exemplify this position in their philosophies of religion. Dewey thinks that traditional "supernaturalism" actually stultifies religious commitment because of its
emphasis on intellectual assent to the actual existence of values in a supernatural
realm.[109] Santayana likewise holds that loyalty to religious ideals need not and
should not be based on a conviction of their existence. This—the way of "traditional supernaturalism"—would make religion into illusion. When religious doctrine is not taken literally, but its myth and ritual are recognized as a way of
believing in and living by the "poetic universe"—which contains only those aspects
of reality selected by poetic imagination—then it "surrenders its illusion and ceases
to deceive."[110])

In this case, Christianity is in danger of being reduced to an aesthetic humanism[111]—or the relic of an aesthetic humanism, a living repository for the
poetic-religious tradition of the past. Its beauty, including the beauty of its doctrines, may be affirmed; but this beauty is disconnected from the intellectual
apprehension of reality. But, as Balthasar remarks, when beauty loses its connection with Being, "we have again entered an age of aestheticism, and realists will
then be right in objecting to this kind of beauty."[112]

Another aspect of this danger is that religion, if not simply rejected, might
be marginalized and privatized: that it may become, like art, a matter of individual
"taste." As Tracy remarks, when the technoeconomic realm defines what is valued
in society, then "what alone will count as truth in the public realm [is] the methodically controlled results of the technical realm in all its forms. The rest is
taste, or emotion, or 'art.' "[113] Since *de gustibus non est disputandum*, religious relativism must result. Religion thus loses the possibility of public relevance in a
pluralist society and theology lacks criteria for dialectical assessment of conflicting
religious truth claims.

The Historical Jesus and the Images of Christ

Another dimension of the problem of religious imagination arises from contemporary historical consciousness. In the iconoclast controversy, the difficulty concerning the portrayal of Christ arose primarily because of the doctrine of the
hypostatic union. That is, it was the problem of imaging the divine being that
underlay the disputes. The portrayal of Christ's humanity as such—or of Mary
or the apostles, or of events of salvation history—does not seem to have posed a
problem. The same uncomplicated attitude toward imagining and picturing salvation history and its characters seems to continue through most of Western religious art. Pictures, as we have seen, were considered to be the "scriptures" of

the illiterate. Even Karl Rahner, considering the relative functions of hearing and seeing in receiving the Christian message, writes:

> insofar as religious images represent events of salvation history that may be grasped by the senses, this question presents no special problem. Such images provide the experience of visible historical events.... One irreplaceable way of getting to know a person is to see and not just to hear that person; a portrait cannot be totally replaced by a biography. The same is true of salvation-historical events. They must also be seen, and seen in an image, if we are not actually present to them.[114]

But an unproblematic acceptance of the picturing of the past seems to overlook the historicity and situatedness of every event and of every language—including that of depiction. Every image is at the same time an interpretation, whether it attempts to be "realistic" in its portrayal of a historical context (like film versions of the life of Christ) or abstracts from that context and presents the figures and events of the past in a later historical situation (like much Western religious art) or in a conventionalized, quasi-symbolic setting (like canonical Byzantine icons) in order to show their trans-historical meaning. But if it is truly *historical* events and persons that have trans-historical religious significance, does not every such interpretation raise questions: to what extent does the portrayal "represent" the originating event, and to what extent are its content and context an unconscious projection of elements in the interpreter's world that may have a quite different source? Even if the central meaning evoked by a portrayal is consistent with the religious interpretation of historical events, does not the concreteness of every portrayal necessarily introduce elements extraneous to that meaning that nevertheless "color" the story—possibly adding another, unconsciously conveyed level of meaning that may be in some way at odds either with history or with other aspects of its significance? (So, for example, much Western religious painting portrays Christ with characteristics typical of the painter's society—beardless and in Roman clothing in the catacombs, for example, or with blond hair in Gothic representations. Such idealized representations make the idea of the incarnation "relevant" to a culture. But do they also allow the viewer to forget that the incarnation takes place not in a generalized "humanity" but in a Jewish man of a particular period? Does the frequent portrayal even of the pre-resurrection Christ as a majestic, "lordly" figure unconsciously reinforce patriarchal or feudal religious attitudes, rather than sentiments of equality and community? And so on.)

Karl Barth presents another side of the problem. On the basis of the absolute uniqueness of the Christ event, he censures any attempt to render Christ pictorially. He calls the history of such attempts a "sorry story." It is, of course, true that this history certainly includes a great deal of sentimental kitsch. But it also contains the catacomb frescoes, Byzantine icons, Giotto, Michelangelo, Rembrandt, and El Greco—to name only a few. Barth, however, explicitly includes the works of genius in his rejection:

No human art should try to represent—in their unity—the suffering God
and triumphant man, the beauty of God which is the beauty of Jesus Christ.
If at this point we have one urgent request to all Christian artists, however
well-intentioned, gifted or even possessed of genius, it is that they should
give up this unholy undertaking—for the sake of God's beauty. This picture,
the one true picture, both in object and representation, cannot be copied, for
the express reason that it speaks for itself, even in its beauty.[115]

Balthasar makes a more restrained but similarly directed comment on pictorial representations of Christ. Manifesting some sympathy for the motivations
of the iconoclasts, he remarks that

we are given much food for thought by the argument of the iconoclast Constantine V, which says that a merely human representation of Christ—unavoidable, since the divine side of his being remains irrepresentable—constitutes an assault on Christology and must eventually lead to Nestorianism.
Constantine's argument is valid at least by way of a permanent warning
against allowing the Image of himself that God made to appear in the
world—the Image that is his Son—to be extended without any critical distance whatever into other images which, regardless of all their religious relevance, nonetheless belong to the sphere of aesthetics.[116]

But the problem is deeper than implied by these passages from Barth and
Balthasar. If we take seriously the historicity of the Christ event, it becomes clear
that the root issue is not merely the limitations of pictorial art as compared with
the true historical "image" in the person of Christ. For the "one true picture" or
"image" of God in Christ is accessible to us only through Scriptures that are
themselves works of literary art and of interpretation. The New Testament itself
already gives different "pictures" of Christ; and its mediations of Christ are always
further interpreted within a community that unconsciously "sees" and understands
them within a certain imaginative framework.

As we have seen through Schoenberg's *Aron*, for all the difference between
word and image, when they refer to God they are in a radically similar situation.
Wolfhart Pannenberg rightly points out that the notion of the "word" of God is
itself mythico-magical in origin. Even when the biblical concept is to some extent
replaced by the Greek *Logos* and the latter is used to explain the incarnation, the
problem of mythology is not resolved: "the Christian idea of the incarnation of
divine Logos may even be described as a representation of the basic notion [*Grund-
vorstellung*] of the mythical word as a symbolic manifestation of the named object
in the sensible medium of sound—although on a more sophisticated level [*auf
einer Ebene höherer Differenzierung*]."[117]

Hence Rahner is no doubt right in affirming that the central theological
question is that of historical revelation itself: "how the first historical and visible
experience of salvation history could have a religious significance."[118] But a second
question immediately follows: how can the historical events themselves—events
that do not take place simply in "humanity" or in "the world," but in a particular
time, place, and culture—be transmitted to subsequent generations? How impor-

tant is it that they be transmitted in their original context? What is the relationship between that context and subsequent interpretations? In short, a theological aesthetics of the imagination must also face the question of the transmission of a truly historical revelation. In its central Christian form, this is the question of the relation between the Jesus of history and the Christ of faith.

One of the many stories of the Hindu tradition tells of "Krishna and the wrestlers." The evil king Kamsa had condemned Krishna (the avatar of the supreme God, Vishnu) to a gladiatorial contest meant to end in his death. When Krishna entered the arena to submit to his punishment, each person present saw a different figure. The gods in the heavens, looking down, recognized Vishnu, the Lord of the universe, and they bowed in worship. The spectators saw a gracious, playful, and lovely youth. The wrestlers, his would-be executioners, trembled in fear, for they saw a mighty warrior. And King Kamsa himself saw approaching him Māra, the god of death.

Somewhat similar stories are told of Jesus, especially in connection with the epiphany to the Magi. Marco Polo brought back from Persia the tale that when the Magi visited Jesus, each of them saw a different figure, corresponding to the age of each viewer.[119] John Damascene tells the same story, which appears in the Armenian Gospel of the Infancy, in a slightly different form. Here Jesus' appearance corresponds not to the ages of the Magi but to the symbolism of the three gifts: he is seen as a child, as the grown son of a King, and as dead and resurrected.

The theo-logic of such stories, if they are taken literally, has the flavor of Docetism. In Hinduism, this is not a problem. The common theological understanding of the avatar doctrine is, in fact, docetistic. Strictly speaking, an avatar is not an "incarnation" in the Christian sense: it is merely a transient appearance, and occurs in a body made of "heavenly" matter. Furthermore, many Hindu intellectuals based in the Vedantic tradition accept the myths in a purely spiritual, symbolic sense; the question of historicity is unimportant. (It will be recalled that Gandhi accepted both Krishna and Christ in this way.)[120] But Christianity, in its classical forms, insists on both the genuinely historical character of Jesus' humanity and its decisiveness for revelation. Edward Schillebeeckx puts the matter succinctly with regard to the New Testament:

> [R]eligious experience, the religious experience of God, has its focal point in the New Testament in its connection with the man Jesus Christ. Is Jesus here the symbolic point of reference of a kind of *mysticism of being*? Or is a *historical* event really the specific Christian access to God? The New Testament defends the latter point of view, sometimes with great stubbornness. Johannine theology, which most markedly demonstrates a degree of God-mysticism, nevertheless attacks any *lyein ton Iēsoun* (I John 4:3), that is, any attempt to do away with Jesus of Nazareth in favour of a heavenly or spiritual Christ principle."[121]

If we take this New Testament view seriously (which is not necessarily the same as taking it as definitive), we must ask ourselves what it means for the history of the Christian images of Christ. Jesus' real humanity means that he did not appear in different physical forms; he was radically "situated" in a spatio-temporal context, like all of us, and had particular personal characteristics rather than others. The same is true of the events of his life. Yet in the Christian imagination, the "historical" Jesus takes on a multiplicity of characters,[122] from the mystic to the social revolutionary to the model corporate manager.[123] (To take only a single example, compare several film portrayals: Zeffirelli's *Jesus of Nazareth*; Coppola's *The Last Temptation of Christ*; Pasolini's *The Gospel According to St. Matthew*).

Of course, many images make no pretension of representing "history" in the modern sense; they intend rather to present a religious *idea* with a more or less conscious theological content. (Look, for example, at Michelangelo's *Bruges Madonna*, with its Christ-child radiant in the serene consciousness of his divinity.) But such images do intend to tell us something true about the Jesus who actually lived, even when his life is now seen glorified and in the light of the resurrection. However, they always present their theological message in a form that is at least in part determined by nontheological factors. Hence one may question the validity of any image in relation to both its theology and its nontheological premises.

Two sorts of question therefore arise. First, how are these images and the theologies they embody related to the Jesus of history? Second, how are they related to the changing contexts in which they are produced and the subsequently changing contexts in which they are received? (For example, the New Testament presents Jesus as Messiah, the catacomb painters dress him in the imperial purple, the Middle Ages make him the feudal Lord. How do these images relate to the life of Jesus and his resurrected power? How do their explicit theological meanings relate to their implied [and sometimes also explicit] sociopolitical meanings in each period? How do any of these images of Jesus as "King" speak to the consciousness of a democratic and nonpatriarchal society?)

Such issues are perhaps most strikingly apparent in the sphere of visual images because of their concreteness, hence I have drawn my examples from that area. But physical images are only the clearest example of what is true of the entire sphere of imagination. The same kind of hermeneutical questions must be applied to all its manifestations, including narratives and imaginative paradigms.

If we accept the idea of a genuinely historical revelation, then the problem for theological aesthetics regards not merely the possibility of imagining the transcendent but also of imagining the historical past and of re-presenting that past to different mentalities. It includes the examination of theological criteria for a critical hermeneutics of images. It must also ask itself the significance for Christian imagination of the phrase about Christ in the first letter of Peter (1:8): "Without seeing him, you love him."

The Task of Fundamental Theological Aesthetics

One may react theologically to the problems raised in this section in several different ways. One might accept the total "deconstruction" of metaphysics—whether on Kantian or Nietzschean or Heideggerian or "postmodern" grounds. If a metaphysically conceived God is judged to be literally unthinkable, one might conclude,

FIGURE 1. *Michelangelo Buonarroti. Detail of Christ Child.* Bruges Madonna. *Notre Dame, Bruges, Belgium.*

like Jungel, that the only alternative is to renounce the traditional concept of God and construct a new one beginning from Jesus.[124] Jungel insists that theology must start from the content of revelation. The discussion of whether and how God is speakable "must take place with regard to very specific speech events which claim that God has spoken," and not abstractly. This might lead to a "theological aesthetics" that would overlap with Balthasar's, but with the significant omission of his ontological perspective. (Without which one might object, as Pannenberg does, that there are no criteria for determining whether it is *God* who has spoken.)

Alternatively, one might accept Whitehead's project of constructing a new kind of metaphysical doctrine that "finds the foundation of the world in the aesthetic experience, rather than—as with Kant—in the cognitive and conceptual experience."[125] This would make all theology "aesthetic" and would effectively eliminate the problem of God's inconceivability, since the divine transcendence is not absolute. Many Christians find the idea of a finite or bipolar God in "process" metaphysics attractive because of its apparent compatibility with the biblical image of God.

Finally, one may be convinced of the validity and necessity of an ontological approach to theological knowledge—one appropriately corrected and circum-scribed by the insights of critical cognitional theory, linguistic analysis, and decon-structive hermeneutics. One may attempt to formulate a transcendental cognitional theory that explains the revealability and knowability of God in terms of the created and engraced capacity of the human mind to participate in God's mystery. This corresponds to the task of the first part of what I have named fundamental-theological aesthetics: a transcendental theory of the perception of revelation.

In this case, further questions arise. If the mystery of God is in some way knowable to the human mind—precisely as the inconceivable mystery—what is the relation of the conceptual and the imaginative in that knowledge? How does it account for the historical nature of revelation, and how is it related to the transcendental? Should we, like Hegel, see religious imagination as a lower stage to be demythologized in rational thought; or with Heidegger, shall we conclude that silence in the realm of thought is closer to the "real" God, whose mystery is expressed only in symbol and myth? Or is there a way of preserving both theo-retical rationality and religious symbolism, without the elimination or "sublation" of either?

On the basis of an ontologically based notion of the inconceivability of God it would be possible to construct an essentially apophatic and mystical theology. Such a theology might be radically iconoclastic, yet affirm a positive historical revelation through the word (as in mystical forms of Islam); or, like Vedanta Hinduism, it might conclude that precisely because no image or concept can ad-equately represent the ineffable God in the finite mind, a multitude of images is permitted and required as temporary helps and guides on the way to final reali-zation, or as accommodations for those minds that are not capable of the higher way.

In the light of the foregoing, we may conceive three interconnected divisions of the task of a "fundamental" theological aesthetics as a study of the perception of revelation in sensible form. It will attempt through "transcendental deduction" to discern the anthropological "conditions of possibility" of:

1. Knowing God through a mind intrinsically tied to sensibility—in partic-ular in the light of the Kantian critique of knowing. This involves the recognition of the radical openness of the personal subject to the transcendent; in traditional theological language, the doctrine of the human person as "image" of God.

2. Receiving (or embodying) a historical revelation from God in personal and symbolic form. This involves understanding the notion of the "image" of God as extending to interpersonal relations, so that materially and linguistically located human history can be the embodiment of revelation.

3. Using "word" or language (in the widest sense, including verbal, pictorial, musical, and gestural symbols and images) to embody, formulate, interpret, and communicate the knowledge of God and of historical revelation. This implies the possibility of "analogous" discourse, on the level of both concept and image. This means the analogous use of concepts, imaginative paradigms, and symbols to represent: (a) the divine transcendence; (b) the human mind itself; (c) human revelatory events in their historical particularity and universal relevance.

(Clearly, these three dimensions are not separable from each other, but are aspects of the one reality of the human person as being "spiritually" existent in and through historical [linguistically, symbolically conditioned] existence in the world.)

Such an anthropology should serve a function in the theological specialties that Lonergan calls "dialectics" and "foundations." By incorporating the experience and category of "conversion," it allows us to formulate criteria for the recognition of revelation; to discern different levels of meaning to the notions of truth and beauty; to relate the beauty of religious ideas and images to their truth claims; and to dialectically compare different religious paradigms with each other and with our own performance as religious subjects and communities.

CHAPTER 3

꙳ᘛᘚ꙳

Divine Revelation and Human Perception

Prologue: Adam as the Image of God

The illustration on the following page shows the figures of God and Adam from the Creation sequence in the exterior arch of the north portal of Chartres cathedral. God is portrayed in the form of Christ, God's visible expression; Adam is shown as envisioned in the mind of God, before his physical fashioning. Several biblical themes are present: Christ is the perfect image of God; God creates the world through and for Christ (Col. 1:15–19; Heb. 1:1–3; Jn. 1:3, 10); Adam is created in God's image (Gen. 1:26–27); Christ is the new and perfect Adam (1 Cor. 15:45–49). These ideas are synthesized in the Patristic theological notion (ultimately derived from Plato's *Timaeus*, 29–30), that Christ as God's "Word" or Wisdom contains the "ideas" or "archetypes"[1] of all creatures, and is himself the exemplar for humanity in particular. Origen's *Commentary on the Gospel of John* provides an example of this "exemplarism" that had such profound effects on subsequent theology and art:

> . . . We call "principle" [or "beginning"—ἀρχή] that which makes a thing what it is, in accord with its archetype [ετδος]: for example, if the first-born of all creatures is the image of the invisible God, then the Father is his principle. And in the same way, Christ is the principle of all beings created in the image of God. If humanity exists in accord with the image [εἰκών], and the image is in accord with the Father, then the model for Christ is the Father, his principle, and the model for humans is Christ, since they are made not according to the One of whom Christ is the image, but according to the image [i.e., Christ]. . . .
>
> . . . We must therefore say that according to the nature of things, the principle of knowledge is Christ insofar as he is the Wisdom and power of God; but for us, "the Word was made flesh" to dwell among us, for we are not capable of receiving him at first except in this way.
>
> It is perhaps for this reason that he is not only the first-born of all creatures, but is also "Adam," which means "human being" [ἄνθρωπος]. For St. Paul says that he is Adam: "the last Adam [made into] a living spirit" [1 Cor. 15:45]. . . .

73

FIGURE 2. God and Adam. *Sculpture from Chartres cathedral.*

... See if we cannot interpret the text, "In the beginning (ἀρχῇ) was the Word" according to its spiritual sense: all things are created with Wisdom, according to a plan whose elements are contained in the Word.

In the same way that a house or a ship is built or constructed according to the plans of an architect, just as this house or this ship has as its principle the model and the mental plans [λόγοι] of the builder, in the same way, I believe, all things have been created according to the mental plans [λόγοι] predetermined by God in God's Wisdom for God's creatures, for "God created all things in Wisdom" [Ps. 103:24].

We must add that after having produced (if I may say it) a living Wisdom, God gave to her the task of giving form, shape, and perhaps even existence, to both beings and matter, according to the forms contained within herself....

... We cannot be silent about the fact that he [i.e., Christ] is rightly the Wisdom of God, and that he is so called for this reason. For God's Wisdom does not subsist only in the mental images of the God and Father of the universe, analogously to the way mental images are in human minds. But if one can conceive of an incorporeal substance, consisting of all kinds of ideas, and containing the rational principles [λόγοι] of the universe, a living and as it were animated substance, then one will know the Wisdom of God, which is above every creature, and which rightly says of itself: "God established me as the beginning of His ways for his works" [Prov. 8:22]. It is because God thus established Wisdom that every creature is able to exist, for each participates in the divine Wisdom, according to which all were made. For according to the prophet David, God made all things in Wisdom [Cf. Ps. 103:24]. There exists a great number of creatures thanks to participation in this Wisdom, but without their grasping the one by whom they have been established in being; very few understand Wisdom, not only in what concerns themselves, but also insofar as it concerns other things, for Christ is complete Wisdom.[2]

General Epistemological Considerations

The purpose of this section is to outline the most basic epistemological presuppositions of a fundamental theology of the imagination that would respond to the questions raised in the preceding chapter. I shall utilize a transcendental examination of the acting subject to provide the anthropological conditions of possibility for the knowledge of God and the reception of a divine revelation. It will be shown that among these conditions of "transcendent" knowledge are sensibility and the exercise of imagination. These will be the particular focus of our attention.

A few methodological considerations are in order before engaging in the projected analysis. My intention here is the construction of what Garrett Green calls a "natural theology of the imagination." As Green outlines it, such a project would attempt to show that imagination is crucial to the process of knowing, and hence forms part of the religious a priori. It would then analyze the structure of *Homo imaginans* to provide an anthropological base with which the truths of revelation can be correlated. Imagination would then be seen as an implicit revelation of the divine and a precondition for supernatural faith.[3]

Green, however, rejects such a project on the grounds that "the 'positivity' of Christian revelation—its dependence on certain concrete paradigms—precludes the possibility of a 'natural theology of revelation.'"[4] I would say rather that Christianity's "positivity" excludes the deduction of its particular historical content from any a priori structures of the existential human subject. Nevertheless, from such structures one can heuristically "anticipate" certain characteristics that any revelation to the human subject must possess (e.g., historicity itself, although not the content of history).

Moreover, the positivity of Christianity (or of any religion) demands examination of the structure of imagination itself—that is, we cannot simply acknowledge the centrality of "paradigmatic imagination" in religion (as Green does); we also need some kind of epistemology of imagination. Green sees that the resolution of the 1934 conflict between Barth and Brunner on the *Anknüpfungspunkt* for revelation lies in an examination of human imagination as our "paradigmatic" ability.[5] But he wishes to avoid any connection with ontology or "foundationalism." Nevertheless, I think that what he means by paradigmatic "imagination" is one form of what Lonergan calls "insight," mediated by images. What I believe must be added to Green's affirmation of the human paradigmatic ability is precisely a properly epistemological/ontological dimension—that is, an explanation of why this kind of cognition is truly knowledge, how it reaches "being."

Green acknowledges that philosophy can be a "'descriptive grammar,' an analytical tool for investigating the logic of various human endeavors and a therapy for conceptual conundrums resulting from 'grammatical' confusions."[6] I consider this task part of the function of the cognitional theory that underlies what Green calls a "natural theology" of the imagination. I would add, however, that a philosophical theology must confront not merely logical and grammatical issues but also the question of the criteria for making judgments of truth through the use of both imagination and thought. Whether one calls such a study a "natural theology" or not (the term is ambiguous and easily leads to misunderstanding), it is logically independent of the specific content of the Christian paradigm, even though it may be undertaken with the latter in view. (However, this does not mean that the accomplishment of such a study is separable from "grace" or from God's self-revelation.)

Moreover, I believe that a philosophical theology of this kind is necessary if one is to avoid the intellectual danger of a fideistic "positivism of revelation." Pannenberg's critique of the use of "speech-act" theory in theology is relevant to Barthian forms of theology in which an ontological-epistemological component is eliminated:

> The gospel, for example, is then presented as a performative linguistic act which by its nature establishes the truth of what it says in the area that is opened up only by these words. In this approach the truth of the propositions proclaimed is supposedly not bound to answer the human question of verification or falsification. The apologetic concern to render the proclamation

immune against critical reflection is understandable, but the price paid for such immunity is a high one. We are supposedly dealing with a linguistic action of God, and yet this evidently [*offenbar*] comes to us [only] in the form of a human proclamation. If the latter is interpreted as a linguistic action, there is simply no way of distinguishing it from the object to which it is related and then, possibly, to understand it as also legitimated by that object. As a result, the claim that the words embody a divine linguistic action collapses into an anthropomorphic projection on the part of a linguistically active human being.[7]

In short, if religious imaginative paradigms are to be related to truth claims, and if the latter are thought to be compatible with (although not reducible to) reasonable, responsible, and critical human thought, then a "fundamental theology" of the imagination seems necessary.

Intellectual Knowledge Through the Sensible Symbol

Karl Rahner succinctly summarizes the centrality of sensibility in human knowing, including the knowledge of God. For Christian anthropology, he writes, persons "are beings of an a posteriori, historical, and sensory experience. This holds also for that dimension of their existence in which they face God in their religion." This insistence is tied to the conviction of the intrinsic unity of spirit and matter in the human person. Rahner points out that for St. Thomas, for example, the human being is a unity of spirit and "prime matter," not of spirit and body: the body is the concrete result of the "informing" of the material principle (which is not an existent thing, but an abstract intelligibility) by spirit. In this sense, the body is the visibility of the soul. Therefore, "There is no coming to oneself except by way of exit into the bodily reality into which the spirit first reaches out and finds itself, forming itself and going out of itself."[8]

Hence, "against all attempts to safeguard religious knowledge by detaching it from other kinds of knowledge, traditional Christian anthropology has always clearly insisted that sense knowledge and spiritual knowledge constitute a unity, that all spiritual knowledge, however sublime it may be, is initiated and filled with content by sense experience."[9] The cognitional theory of Aquinas, based on Aristotle's empiricism, holds that "even the most spiritual, most 'transcendental,' most sublime concept can be reached by human beings on this earth only through a '*conversio ad phantasmata*,' that is (in Kantian language) that every concept without sense intuition is empty, that is, nonexistent. This statement applies also to religious knowledge."[10] The entirety of Rahner's *Spirit in the World* is an explanation of the text from St. Thomas's *Summa Theologiae*, I, q. 84, a. 7, on the question, "Whether the intellect can actually know anything through the intelligible species that it has, without turning itself to sensible images [*phantasmata*]." Thomas concludes that "incorporeal things, of which there are no sensible images, are known by us through comparison with sensible bodies, of which we have images. . . . We know God, as Dionysius says, as cause, and by eminence and negation. In the present state of earthly life, we can also know other incorporeal substances only by way of negation or comparison with corporeal things. And therefore, if we know anything of this sort, we must turn to corporeal images, although there are no images of these incorporeal things themselves."[11]

For our purposes here it is not essential (or possible) to examine at length the bases of the assertions of transcendental Thomist theory of knowledge, as found, for example, in the phenomenology of knowing, cognitional theory, and epistemology that Lonergan proposes in *Insight*, or in the metaphysics of knowledge contained, for example, in Rahner's *Spirit in the World* or in Lotz's *Die Identität von Geist und Sein*. It will suffice to point out briefly how a critically realist account of knowledge insists upon the connection of intellectual insight with sensible data and gives a central place to imagination as the mediating moment between the two.[12]

What is meant in this context by "imagination" corresponds to both the "*Phantasie*" and the "productive *Einbildungskraft*" of Kant's philosophy. "Imagination" designates first of all the faculty through which the presentations of the different senses—which are dispersed over time and are of different kinds (pictorial images, sounds, scents, kinetic feelings, etc.)—are "represented" in the mind in a synthetic way.[13] But imagination's field is not restricted to the synthesis of present experiences or of past sensations, recalled in memory: it can also create new conjunctions that have never been experienced.

Lonergan describes at length how "insight," or the act of understanding, arises out of imaginative constructs based on sensible data. Its occurrence is dependent upon the process of abstraction, which Lonergan describes thus:

> [a]bstraction in all its essential moments is enriching. Its first moment is an enriching anticipation of an intelligibility to be added to sensible presentations; there is something to be known by insight. Its second moment is the erection of heuristic structures and the attainment of insight to reveal in the data what is variously named as the significant, the relevant, the important, the essential, the idea, the form. Its third moment is the formulation of the intelligibility that insight has revealed.[14]

Abstraction is therefore also an "illumination" of sensible data by the mind[15]— that is, it is the mind's explication of the coherence between its own intrinsically "intelligible" nature and the world.[16] The last step in this process is what Lonergan calls "formulation"—that is, the symbolic (or "linguistic," in the wide sense) embodiment of insight, through which the known is present for the knower.

In the light of contemporary linguistic consciousness, it should be noted that normally neither perception nor the construction of the sensible "image" that permits understanding nor the necessary symbolic "formulation" of understanding is purely dependent on each individual subject's mind: all are conditioned by the subject's social and linguistic situation.[17] (Hence, as Gómez Caffarena remarks, the consideration of language becomes the point of insertion of aesthetics into metaphysics.)[18] The "image" that mediates sensible data for intelligence may be a word, a linguistic construct, or a conventionalized symbol; and these are normally not invented, but learned. Pannenberg summarizes nicely:

Reason does not produce the universal only through abstraction or—in the nominalist explanation—through the generalization effected by linguistic labeling. Since rational reflection presupposes both the sensorimotor life of perception and the life of language [*Sprache*] and imagination [*Phantasie*], it already operates at every point within the tension of Gestalt and field, part and whole, particular and universal. It is true, of course, that both sides acquire their clear contours only in rational [*vernünftige*] reflection.... Ernst Cassirer correctly emphasized the point that "the original and decisive achievement of the concept [*Begriff*]" is not to compare and group representations [*Vorstellungen*] already at hand but, rather, "to form impressions [*Eindrücke*] into representations [*Vorstellungen*]." This operation is one that at every point has already been carried out by language, which identifies representations by means of words, thus rendering them repeatable and therefore available in an identical form and also making it possible to raise the question of their interrelationships, the distinctions between them, and the traits they have in common.[19]

Pannenberg's statement should be understood with the qualification that the operation of forming impressions into representations has *normally* been carried out already by our language: the case of a person who is only learning a language (the young child, for example) is different (Pannenberg's references to Piaget show that he is aware of this). Even in the case of one who already has a language, there may be instances in which a linguistic representation for a particular new experience is not available (this may be the case with the creative artist or scientist, for example). It is possible for us to experience "more" in a particular circumstance than our words are adequate to: we may experience something as being (thus far) without a name, as a question, as a feeling of wonderment. Moreover, although it is probably true to say that in discursive, conceptual thinking the image that normally mediates insight is the word, in the intellectual process as a whole one must understand the notion of "language" in a wide sense—one that includes also nonverbal symbols.

The acknowledgment of the place of language in the formation of concepts reveals the naiveté of the identification of *Begriff* with universal reason (which is contrasted with the "positivity" of religion on the level of *Vorstellung*). As Pannenberg remarks, the contemporary philosophy of language reverses what Plato says at the end of the Cratylus (438d-g) about the knowledge of essences being independent of the ambiguities of words.[20] It must be recognized that the language of a particular culture implies a view of the world (*Weltansicht*) and both opens up and limits the horizons of thought and being.[21] As Rahner writes:

> Our word is more than a thought: it is thought become incarnate.... [T]he word is more than a mere externalization in sound, a signaling of a thought which could equally well exist without the accompaniment of this animal noise.... No, the word is rather the corporeal state in which what we now experience and think first begins to exist by fashioning itself into this its word-body.... For this reason no language can substitute for another....

Men speaking different languages can understand one another and one language can be translated into another, just as the most diverse men can live together and even be born from one another. But this does not make languages into a row of external façades, behind all of which dwells simply one and the same thought. The *noche* of a John of the Cross and the *Nacht* of a Novalis or a Nietzsche are not the same; the *agape* of the hymn in the thirteenth chapter of the First Letter to the Corinthians and the "love" of European peoples differ not merely in their "application."[22]

Indeed, language in a sense mediates and "constitutes" the world of human meaning.[23] On the other hand, this insight need not lead to linguistic determinism or linguistic relativism, "according to which the different languages are so many different images of the world and perspectives on the world, and none can escape that particular image and that particular schematization within which he is imprisoned."[24] The processes of the mind are not separable from the need for symbolic mediation of some kind; but they are separable from any particular language inherited by the subject. As Pannenberg says,

> The mother tongue of individuals does not impose a certain direction on their thinking in the sense of channeling it, although it must be admitted that the structure and vocabulary of a language do embody certain emphases in the linguistic community's experience of the world and that these suggest certain modes of representation rather than others to the individuals using the language. But a much greater influence along these lines is exerted by the convictions that dominate in certain phases of a culture's development. These convictions are not explicable in the light of the structure and vocabulary of the language; they do, however, themselves lead to shifts in the meanings of words and thus in the associations linked with such words. The linguistic relativists greatly underestimate this influence of ideas on the development of language.[25]

More fundamentally, even while affirming the necessity of symbolic mediation for thought, we may nevertheless recognize that the activity of intellection is in a certain radical sense "prior" to language.[26] Language is the "primordial" invention of the human mind; it therefore has priority not over intellect itself but over all other intellectual exercises.[27]

Pannenberg cites Chomsky's views that there are universal structures of intellect that determine all languages and that we can think without words. (Cf. *ST*, I, q. 93, a. 7., where Aquinas speaks of the "interior word" that belongs to no spoken language.) Pannenberg also quotes the conclusion of Eric H. Lenneberg's study of the biological bases of language—namely, "that cognitive function is a more basic and primary process than language, and that the dependence-relationship of language on cognition is incomparably stronger than vice versa."[28] Pannenberg also appeals to Piaget's studies of the ontogenetic conditions for a child's learning a language, as well as to Konrad Lorenz's writings on the phylogenetic conditions for human language to come into existence, as evidence against linguistic behaviorism (like that of the later Wittgenstein) and relativism.[29]

Gadamer, like Pannenberg, recognizes that when we use a particular language, we are fixed in a direction of thought that comes from beyond ourselves. Nevertheless, he insists that "our specific human possibilities do not subsist solely in language" and that "there is a pre-linguistic experience of the world, as Habermas, drawing on Piaget's researches, reminds us."

Tracy likewise acknowledges that "Tradition is inevitably present through the language we use," whose effects on us and our understanding can never be fully brought to awareness. But the recognition of our linguistic and cultural conditioning "can also occasion a recognition that every tradition is both pluralistic and ambiguous (i.e., enriching, liberating, and distorting)." Hence there is both the possibility and the need of the rational critique of our inherited language to uncover its distortions.[30]

Because of the "linguistic virtuality" of reason, such a critique is possible. The relativity imposed by language "is not one which holds us in unbreakable shackles, as those of us who can think to some extent in different languages know very well."[31] Neurologist Antonio Damasio points out that contemporary studies of the brain lead to the conclusion that knowledge, "which exists in memory under dispositional representation form, can be made accessible to consciousness . . . virtually simultaneously" in both verbal and nonverbal versions.[32] Hence the coexistence in individual minds of different kinds of symbolic mediations of thought— heuristic and conceptual, pictorial and verbal, felt and formulated—allows for comparison and dialectic between our various symbolic "languages," so that no one of them can be absolutely determinative of our interpretation of experience.

The Preapprehension of the Total Horizon

The ultimate reason for the "priority" of intellection over language is that the conditions of human knowing include not only the acquired a priori of language and the innate a priori of sensibility (spatio-temporality), but also an a priori of being corresponding to the act of judgment.

In his phenomenological description of the working of imagination, Pannenberg shows how its inspirations emerge in the setting of some particular, momentary field of attention, which is in turn related to one's life-project as a whole. The latter is experienced in a feeling (*Gefühl*) that expresses an anticipation (*Vorgriff*) of the whole of life.[33] The identification of any particular object presupposes our ability to reflect on the field in which it appears as *this* particular thing; such a horizon is always present, at least unthematically. Hence "the universal is also at every point simply given to reflection as symbiotic unity of life and as field of movement, objective space, and world. It thus forms the unexpressed, unthematic horizon within which phenomena, whether of perception or of imagination, make their appearance."[34]

Pannenberg explicitly states that this description is a more phenomenological treatment of the theory Rahner presents in *Spirit in the World*.[35] The latter is Thomistic in its more explicitly intellectualist focus. In the language of Thomism, there is in the process of knowing an implicit, unthematic "*excessus*." When the mind grasps an object through understanding and judgment, in the very process it transcends that grasp: it is tacitly aware that the object is more than what is grasped, and at the same time it recognizes the provisional character of its own insights.[36] This *excessus* points to the a priori condition of possibility for the mind's knowing sensible objects *as* objects and of differentiating them from itself— namely, the pre-apprehension (*Vorgriff*) of "being" as such: the total horizon of knowledge and its dynamism[37] (which is tied, as Pannenberg says, to the entirety of our life-project). (Rahner notes that the "transcendental deduction" of the *Vorgriff* overcomes both Kant's separation of the intellectual from the sensible and his exclusion of genuine ontological knowledge. For Kant the transcendence of understanding and of its formal a priori "does not in principle extend beyond the basis provided by the power of the imagination, of sensory perception"; the formal object of the human spirit is *ens materiale, ens principium numeri*. In the Thomistic understanding, on the other hand, the "transcendence which is the enabling condition of judgments upon, and a priori knowledge of, objects of the world of perception must necessarily be a transcendence extending beyond the world, and hence is accepted to be such in every kind of knowledge belonging to this world. Once this transcendental deduction is carried through, then that condition is fulfilled under which even Kant is prepared to recognize a metaphysic as valid.")[38]

The total horizon and goal (*Woraufhin*) of the mind's and person's dynamism is normally present to us not as an object but as the unthematically known condition of possibility for knowing or loving any other. "It can never be approached directly or experienced immediately. It is there only by referring us to something else, something finite, which is the object of direct regard."[39] Hence it is "pre-apprehended" as transcending every content of mind, and thus as a "mystery": "because we possess a primordial reference to the incomprehensible mystery, *therefore* we are able to set ourselves at a critical distance from every individual object and item of knowledge: we can distinguish and arrange particular objects of experience; we are capable of recognizing each individual piece of knowledge as provisional, ideologically suspect or open to improvement."[40] Likewise, because of this horizon the imagination is not completely determined by the previous symbolic patterns and linguistic forms in which the individual has been inculturated and socialized, but is in principle free to respond to new questions leading to new images, insights, judgments, and self-determinations.

In summary, the application of transcendental method to human knowing arrives at the conclusion that, on the one hand, the knowledge of sensible reality takes place within the horizon of a nonobjective pre-apprehension of being; on the other hand, that any knowledge of "spiritual" realities (including the knowledge of the self as spirit that is the basis for ontology)[41] is necessarily mediated, both in its arising and in its formulation, by symbols that arise in connection with sensible experience, synthesized by imagination.

Thinking in Concepts and Images

On the basis of the foregoing schema, one must reject the rationalist and positivist presentation of the relation between conceptual thought and imagination. Rationalism of the Hegelian type, as we have seen, considers the realm of imagination

(*Vorstellung*) to be a lower (although legitimate) level that comes to fullness of truth only through sublation (*Aufhebung*) into the concept (*Begriff*). Positivism goes further: it limits the range of valid "thought" to the world of mesocosmic empirical objects and relegates discourse about the nonempirical—the metaphysical as well as the artistic and religious—to the realm of the merely imaginary.

Although it is perhaps overly optimistic to speak with Garrett Green of the "demise" of positivism,[42] it is clearly the case that contemporary science and philosophy reveal the presuppositions of positivistic thought to be epistemologically naive. Green notes that the advances of contemporary science allow us to recognize the limitations and relativity of "that middle-sized world that modern science had taught us to call 'reality.'" Science now recognizes that there are "realities"— subatomic particles, for example—that cannot be seen or pictured. Hence our idea of "knowing" is expanded beyond the limitations imposed by positivism.

> One of the most debilitating consequences of the bondage of the modern imagination to the mesocosmic paradigms of modern science has been a narrowing of attention to those aspects of reality that can be visualized in terms of Newtonian space and time, and the corresponding illusion that anything requiring imagination must be imaginary. . . . As soon as one probes beyond the middle-sized world of familiar objects, whether in natural science, in poetry, or in theology, imagination becomes increasingly indispensable.[43]

Quantum theory and post-Einsteinian astrophysics teach us that there are things that are "real" that cannot be seen or sensed or pictured. Contemporary science supports the epistemological position that "the real" is not identical with the bodies we encounter in the world of sensible experience—what Lonergan calls the "already out there now real."[44] Rather, "the real" is the verified:[45] what is known by insight into data and judgment based on sufficient evidence. Science cannot justify either its conclusions or (more significantly) its purposes and methods without appeal to criteria that go beyond the sensible and that are rooted in the mind's experience of itself as a dynamism toward the intelligible. In this perspective there is no intrinsic conflict, but rather a complementarity between scientific thought and the pursuit of an ontological level of truth.

At the same time, contemporary science and philosophy evince a renewed appreciation of the place of imagination, not as a "lower" level to be replaced by conceptual thinking, but as both an intrinsic component in the latter and a complementary approach to reality.[46] We may distinguish three ways in which imagination functions in thought: first, as a necessary stage in the development and use of abstract theoretical concepts; second, as an independent way of knowing the dimension of "meaning"; third, as a necessary means of personal integration of the different realms of knowing and an intrinsic element within all conceptual thought that is not purely abstract.

First, imagination has a distinct and limited but crucial function in the generative process of all thinking, including the abstract/conceptual thought of which science and mathematics are the prime examples. The objects of quantum physics, for example, can be expressed directly only through theoretical explanatory categories and mathematical relations that, as Lonergan says, offer no foothold for sensible images.[47] (To this extent there is a parallel between the objects and methods of the natural sciences and those of metaphysics and theology.)[48] This fact reveals the difference between two ways of thinking. For, as Lonergan makes clear, the impossibility of "picturing" the objects of theoretical reason does not apply only to physically invisible realities, but to any thing whatsoever when considered "in itself":

> no thing itself, no thing as explained, can be imagined. . . . Once one enters upon the way of explanation by relating things to one another, one has stepped out of the path that yields valid representative images . . . if I . . . prescind from all observers, then I also prescind from all observables. As the electron, so also the tree, in so far as it is considered a thing itself, stands within a pattern of intelligible relations and offers no foothold for imagination. The difference between the tree and the electron is simply that the tree, besides being explained, also can be observed and described, while the electron, though it can be explained, cannot be directly observed and can be described adequately only in terms of observables that involve other things as well.[49]

However, the impossibility of valid representational or descriptive images for the content of theoretical, explanatory categories does not imply the exclusion or the devaluation of "imagination," even on this level of thinking. For even the most abstract thought arises from "phantasms" or images. Contemporary neurology seems to confirm this observation of Scholastic cognitional theory. According to neurologist Antonio Damasio, "thought" includes both words and arbitrary symbols. These are based on topographically organized representations in the brain, which give rise to images: "Most of the words we use in our inner speech, before speaking or writing a sentence, exist as auditory or visual images in our consciousness. If they did not become images, however fleetingly, they would not be anything we could know."[50]

Second, there is also a wider sense of the term "imagination." Its function in this sense is not restricted to the reproduction of absent sensations but includes the insightful discovery and construction of analogies, metaphors, and paradigms; it can employ verbal as well as sensible and abstract symbols.[51] Albert Einstein, describing his own thinking process, attributed the major role to visual imagery, and considered that words had to be sought only at a later stage.[52] Damasio also quotes physicist and biologist Leo Szilard: "The creative scientist has much in common with the artist and the poet. Logical thinking and an analytical ability are necessary attributes to a scientist, but they are far from sufficient for creative work. Those insights in science that have led to a breakthrough were not logically derived from preexisting knowledge."[53] Garrett Green calls imagination in this sense "the paradigmatic faculty, the ability of human beings to recognize in accessible exemplars the constitutive organizing patterns of other, less accessible and more complex objects of cognition."[54] As Green points out, contemporary philosophy of science accords a primary role to "imaginative" thinking not only in the origin of scientific thought but also in its exercise.[55] The use of models and paradigms becomes increasingly important precisely because the objects of contemporary science transcend what can be visualized in terms of Newtonian space and time[56] (as, for example, the imaginative models of "particle" and "wave" are used to generate insights about subatomic particles that are neither the one nor the other).

Third, imagination in both the "representational" and analogical/paradigmatic senses is crucial to the kind of knowledge that deals not merely with objects but also with the world mediated and constituted by meaning, the world of persons and historical events. Philosophy, religion, art, music, and poetry, including verbal images and metaphors, can embody this level of meaning: first, by evoking the fundamental sense of admiration or "wonder" that inspires the search for meaning in all its realms and that permits the attainment of that intensification of consciousness essential to one's ontological self-appropriation;[57] second, by mediating a form of intelligence that eludes (but also complements) discursive, conceptual rationality; third, by providing a means of symbolizing truths that transcend the objective/empirical level.

The importance of imagination (in all its senses) for thinking is particularly evident when we consider other modes of intelligence than the rational/conceptual/discursive. It is frequently pointed out that the rationalist conception of reason, concentrating almost exclusively on idea (*Begriff*) and the connection of ideas by thematic logic, is overly restricted. A number of contemporary philosophers and theologians have revindicated the place of the dimension variously called "feeling" (*Gefühl*) or "affect" or "the heart" (*das Gemüt*) in human intentionality (or "rationality," in the widest sense of the term).[58] The higher feelings or affects (as distinguished from merely biologically determined dispositions) are the embodiment (in the literal sense)[59] of a latent, habitual actualization of intentionality (i.e., the subject's unity with the other in knowledge and love)—the "attunement" of the practical, acting self to truths and values.[60] As such, they represent a genuine form of rationality (insight, evaluation, affirmation, responsible self-disposition), but one that does not proceed through the conceptualization and reflexive logical operation generally associated with "reasoning." In Scholastic terminology, they are a form of knowing by "connaturality"—a "felt resonance of the *being* (*nature*) of the agent, a nature attuned by responsible action."[61]

Affect per se is nonconceptual and nonrepresentational (i.e., of objects);[62] but it is intimately related to imagination in several ways. Like all modes of human cognition, it depends for its origin (at least ultimately) on representations of sensible experience. Moreover, images and imaginative constructs speak *to* affect, as the synthesis of one's personal being, in an immediate way, evoking a habitual or connatural knowledge;[63] they can be used as symbols *of* affect, as its language or mode of communication;[64] and they can mediate paradigmatic associations *among* affects (as well as between affects and conceptual, discursive thought). Such an imaginative and "aesthetic"[65] mode of rationality is familiar in our everyday intellectual operation and decision making; thematically reflexive, discursive thought is the exceptional mode of rationality—one to which we refer when doubt is introduced, when critical control is needed, or when system is desired. In Tallon's words:

> affective connaturality is the normal . . . way the good person . . . exists and
> acts. Connatural knowing and loving are not the exceptions, the backup

system, as it were, for when discursive, conceptual knowledge and delib-
erative freedom fail... but just the opposite: it is when discernment of
spirits by affective connaturality in one's personal situation fails... that you
then must fall back by default on reasoning discursively from general principles.[66]

Although a full treatment of the subject is impossible here, a few words may
be said at this point on the connection of between our more general epistemological
principles and the objects of the narrower "aesthetics," art and the beautiful. Art
may be seen as a specialization in the aesthetic kind of intellection that occurs
through feeling. As a medium of communication, art reproduces in intensified
form the experiences of life expressed in action, symbol, image, gesture, and text,[67]
and invites us to a perception of truth perceived in the affective/intellectual mode;[68]
as a quest for beauty, art presents the object of positive affect and reinforces our
dynamism toward it.

Paul Tillich sees the cognitive and the aesthetic as two poles of reason's
"grasping" or receptive side (as distinguished from its "shaping" function).[69]
"*Theoria*" for Tillich is the act of looking at the encountered world to take something of it into "the centered self" as a "meaningful, structured whole."[70] "Every
aesthetic image or cognitive concept is such a structured whole."[71] Although both
kinds of *theoria* are rational and both have an emotional component, in the aesthetic mode the emotional element is more decisive. Moreover, within each pole
there is a continuum: "Music is further removed from the cognitive function than
the novel, and technical science is further removed from the aesthetic realm than
biography or ontology."[72] Each mode, moreover, has its own rational structures.
This for Tillich is the meaning of Pascal's famous phrase about "reasons of the
heart which reason cannot comprehend" (*Pensées*, 277): "Here 'reason' is used in
a double sense. The 'reasons of the heart' are the structures of aesthetic and
communal experience (beauty and love); the reason 'which cannot comprehend
them' is technical reason."[73]

Gadamer also argues that "art is knowledge [*Erkenntnis*] and the experience
of art is a sharing of this knowledge."[74] The experience of art contains a claim to
truth

> which is certainly different from that of science, but equally certainly is not
> inferior to it.... [A]rtistic experience is a mode of knowledge of a unique
> kind, certainly different from the sensory knowledge which provides science
> with the data from which it constructs knowledge of nature, and certainly
> different from all moral rational knowledge and indeed from all conceptual
> knowledge, but still knowledge, i.e. the transmission of truth ... [75]

As "representation," the work of art (like the word) is an ontological event: it is
the "being there [*Dasein*] of what is represented."

Tracy sees the function of art in a similar way: "when anyone of us is caught
unawares by a genuine work of art, we find ourselves in the grip of an event, a
happening, a disclosure, a claim to truth which we cannot deny and can only

eliminate by our later controlled reflection."[76] The "classic" work of art is one that mediates such disclosures:[77]

> We find ourselves "caught up" in its world. We are shocked, surprised, challenged by its startling beauty *and* its recognizable truth, its instinct for the essential. In the actual experience of art we do not experience the artist *behind* the work of art. Rather we recognize the truth of the work's disclosure of a world of reality transforming, if only of a moment, ourselves: our lives, our sense for possibilities and actuality, our destiny.[78]

For Gadamer, philosophy, art, and history (to which we must add religion and theology) "are all modes of experience in which a truth is communicated that cannot be verified by the methodological means proper to science"[79]—precisely because the latter methodically prescinds from the subjective and trans-empirical element involved in such truth.[80] Subjective and intersubjective meaning involves realities that cannot be expressed "literally" in categories taken from the empirical world. Since the latter are basic to thought and language,[81] they must inevitably be employed to embody nonempirical insight—but in an analogical and/or metaphorical way.[82] Hence, in contrast to the classical view that sees metaphor as a mere rhetorical or artistic flourish,[83] we must recognize that there are aspects of the human encounter with reality that cannot be expressed without it.[84]

The faculty of imagination is therefore involved in the perception of meaning on multiple levels: in the representation of sensations and/or feelings that evoke or embody insights (which may or may not also be expressed conceptually); in the metaphorical use of words; in the paradigmatic use of historical events as models;[85] and in the analogous application of concepts.

Moreover, the use of analogical imagination, in combination with inverse insight,[86] allows us to use the mode of understanding proper to one realm to attain insight in another. Lonergan makes a critical distinction between different kinds or "realms" of understanding (all of which are valid): "common sense" describes things as they relate to our sensible mode of perception; "theory" attempts to explain things "in themselves" or as related to other things, prescinding from the way we perceive them; "interiority" relates these two prior realms to each other by relating them and their objects to the subject's conditions and modes of knowing. As Lonergan's phenomenology of mind in *Insight* shows, "imagination" in the wider sense is crucial to the attainment of understanding in each of these realms. It is also crucial in the ability to move from one realm to another that distinguishes explicitly differentiated consciousness.

We know and communicate as persons, not purely as scientists or people of common sense or cognitional theorists; and analogous imagination is necessary to the personal integration (while preserving the distinction) of the different realms of knowledge.[87] Explanatory categories themselves must be explained; and imagination occupies a critical role in the learning even of technical theoretical language.[88] (Naturally, when images simply replace abstractions, there arises the danger of the sort of misunderstanding Lonergan so vehemently warns against; the generation of abstract insight from images involves an inverse as well as a positive insight, insofar as, in grasping an abstract intelligibility, one also grasps the irrelevance of what belongs to the "empirical residue.")[89]

In short, there is both an interpenetration and a complementarity between abstract conceptual thought and imaginative thinking. As Green says, "The clearest way to represent the relation of image to concept . . . is not as a dichotomy but [as] a spectrum, extending from the pregnant image, full of implicit or potential application, to the developed concept, in which the underlying analogy has been articulated and delimited."[90]

At the extremes of the spectrum are mutually exclusive, complementary specializations of knowing: purely biological interaction with environment as the "already out there now real" and purely theoretical explanatory or heuristic concepts (Lonergan's realm of "theory").[91] But most human thinking takes place in a complex interaction between the various differentiations of consciousness. Already in perception and sensible imagination there is a degree of abstraction present because of the cultural and linguistic a priori that directs or even constitutes our sensible representations; and explanatory theory, even of the most abstract kind, arises out of imagination and has human content and connection with the world of experience only through imagination's paradigmatic and analogical functioning.

The most explicit mediation between the sensible/imaginative and the theoretical realms takes place in philosophy, which may express itself in both realms. Consciousness of the various differentiations of knowledge and the need to relate them to one another leads to a philosophy that takes its methodological stance not from the realm of scientific theory, nor from common sense, but from human interiority. It finds its data in intentional consciousness and relates the different realms of meaning to one another through the subject's self-appropriation as a knower.[92] Such a transcendental philosophy (and by extension the fundamental theology derived from it) sees both imagination and concept in the dual context of (1) the preapprehended but incomprehensible final object of the mind's dynamism, and (2) the conditions of knowing inherent in a finite, material, historical, and social being. In this perspective the relation of imagination to concept is not that of false to true nor lower to higher, but one of mutual interpenetration and complementarity in the polymorphism of human knowing of the transcendent "real."

Finally, the above should shed some light on the conflict and the similarity between word and image that is so central to Schoenberg's *Moses und Aron*. Here again, we are faced with a spectrum and an overlapping of functions rather than a total disjunction. Words (as Aaron points out) can form "pictures"; and, on the other hand, pictures, gestures, and other sensible images can serve as hieroglyphs or ideograms that symbolize abstract ideas,[93] and can constitute a "language" to communicate complex nonempirical meanings. Moreover, as we have seen, the process of intellection ("reasoning," in its wide sense) can take place through symbolic structures other than verbal language. Furthermore, word and image alike are rooted in sensation. Against any fundamentalism or idolatry of the word we must recognize that words, like images, are incapable of grasping the transcendent.

This having been said, it must be recognized that spoken and written language not only is the primary means of human communication but also has a particular aptitude for the expression of the world mediated and constituted by meaning. As Ricoeur says, "the word has the admirable property of making its sonority transparent, of fading away bodily in giving rise to the act that confers the sense."[94] The word can generally represent absent realities, abstract ideas, analogies, and judgments in a more clear and direct way than spatial images. While its symbolic quality extends its range to poetry, the capacity of word to express judgments of being and of doing make it the normal (although not exclusive) medium of ontological and ethical thought. Above all, word's unique ability to express negation directly makes it capable of expressing inverse insight and transcendence. It is possible for physical images to evoke these dimensions of thought—one might think, for example, of Zen painting or Christian icons, which use conventionalized styles to tell the viewer that the meaning of the image is not to be found simply in the act of seeing. But there is a directness and economy in the word "not" that images cannot approach. Moreover, while the physical image may symbolically represent what is immaterial, it always contains the danger of being reduced to its material content. Although spoken words are also material, their material form is (generally) not identical with what they represent, but is a conventional sign; hence the form cannot be mistaken for the meaning. And the spoken word's invisibility and lack of extended physical duration give it a similarity to the act of thought (so that Scholastic rational psychology referred to the act of understanding as a *verbum internum*, even though this was not identified with the linguistic word, which was conceived as being logically—although not necessarily chronologically—subsequent to it).

Furthermore, although spoken and written language are not the only media of rationality, the word has an irreplaceable position in the specifically explanatory, systematic, and critical functions of reason. Rahner points out that "Rationality *as such* is not directed in the first instance to the particular content of a proposition: rather, it is ordered, in a constantly new way, to the methods and validity of the connection of propositions to one another."[95] That is, "rationality" aims not merely at understanding but also at building "systems." Images may indeed be used to form a systematic context; but the economy, universal availability and "portability" of the word—its ability to communicate over vast reaches of space and time with minimal effort—make it the normal medium of reason that seeks systematic control over meanings and poses the question of verification.

At the same time, it should not be forgotten that all language—and not merely language in its artistic and mythic uses—is inherently "anthropomorphic" and carries an unconscious "projection" of the acquired and inborn a priori structures of the mind into our perception of reality. This is not to say that such a prioris prevent our reaching reality; on the contrary, they are the condition for our doing so. But it means that all human knowledge is "relative" to our way of knowing.

Conceiving and Imagining the Divine Self-revelation

On the basis of the foregoing general epistemological principles, we may now undertake to construct the outline of the first part of a "fundamental" theological aesthetics—that is, the discernment of the conditions of possibility for the communication and perception of revelation in sensible form. The central concern is to examine how words and images can be used to mediate the knowledge of God's self-revelation. As we have seen above, this will involve confronting two other more basic issues: how God is knowable to a mind intrinsically tied to sense perception, and how God can be revealed through human history.

Humanity as God's "Image"

The essence of the answer to the central question can be formulated in a theological thesis that corresponds to what is expressed symbolically in the "prologue" to this chapter: God is knowable through word and image *because* and *insofar as* the human being is itself the "image" of God.[96] Of course, to speak of humanity as God's "image" is itself to use an image. Hence the examination of the conditions for the validity of using *this* image—that of the "image of God" itself—should provide a paradigmatic case for understanding the theological use of words and images in general.

The statement that the human being is "in God's image" tells us that the relation between God and humanity is something like what occurs when we see a reflection in a mirror or a representation in a painting or a sculpture:[97] the form and being of the original reality are manifested or revealed in another. Pannenberg, following contemporary exegesis, notes that the affirmation of humanity's creation "in the image and likeness of God" in Gen. 1:26f. serves as the justification of humanity's function in sharing God's creativity and "rule" over the earth. But what the likeness to God really consists of, "Gen. 1:26f. does not tell us and does not need to tell us, since the point of the statement is to provide a basis for the function."[98] It is left to subsequent theological reflection to explain more precisely the nature of the similarity of humanity to God implied by the image of God's "image."[99]

Although the philosophical contexts and theological emphases of such explanations vary, what is constant is the recognition that our likeness to God consists above all in what we may today call our "personal" nature: our "openness" to being, our capacity for dialogue with God and with others—in the epitomizing categories of traditional philosophical language, our ability to know and love. St. Thomas Aquinas, for example, states that finite things can be said to be "like" God in several ways and at different levels: first, insofar as they exist; second, insofar as they are alive; third, insofar as they are rational, that is, can know or understand. The last is what constitutes for Thomas the "specific" human similarity to God that makes us God's "image."[100]

The human capacity to know and love constitutes an image of God because it participates in being on the level of self-consciousness, self-constitution, and freedom. This in turn means that its horizon is in principle unrestricted: we can affirm and value the self as self and the other as other only in the light of the pre-apprehension of being and goodness as a totality. In this, the structure of the mind is open to and reflects the divine. The primary "object" of God's knowledge and love is the divine being itself: God knows and loves all things in God's self, and as participations of God's being. This statement of course depends upon the notion of God as an infinite and perfect act of consciousness, or what Lonergan calls the "Idea of Being."[101]

This conception of God underlies the Trinitarian application of the idea of the human mind as God's image, an analogy formulated classically by St. Augustine and given further precision by St. Thomas. Without going into either the history of the "psychological analogy" or its contemporary interpretations, we may express its central insight in the following formulation: because it is of God's very nature that God can and does express and know God's self in what is other than God (that is, because God is "Word"), and because God is loving unity with that other (that is, because God is "Spirit" or "proceeding" love), therefore God is revealed or imaged in the human mind that comes to self-actualization through understanding and love. (In this formulation, the "immanent" Trinity is seen as the condition of possibility for the "economic" Trinity of history.)

Another formulation of the same insight might begin with the fact that God is not simply "a" being alongside others (which would make God finite), but "includes" all beings within God's self-conscious self. Hence the distinction between God and God's creation cannot be conceived on the model of distinctions between finite beings, but is, as Rahner says, a distinction "within" God; or, as Rahner also puts it, God *is* the distinction of the world from God's self.[102] That is, God's creative "act," by which God creates, knows, and loves the finite "other," is identical with God, as is also God's self-communication by "grace." Because God is, in short, a conscious unity that includes what is differentiated from itself (by creative and self-revealing knowledge and love), therefore human knowing and loving, which aim at a unity in difference, are the image of God.

For the human mind to be "like" God's universal knowledge and love, it must be open to all that can be known and loved, including God.[103] Indeed, since the knowledge and love of God must include all that is "in" God—that is, all that God knows and loves—we may say with St. Thomas that the human person is the "image" of God in (1) the capacity for and (2) the accomplishment of the knowledge and love of God[104]—understanding, however, that the latter takes place only in and through the world, especially the world constituted by human meaning, so that the "image" of God is not merely "spiritual" and personal but also interpersonal and historical in character.

The Theology of Revelation

The justification and explication of these affirmations involves an anthropologically based theory of revelation. This in turn will explain why, how, and to what extent the "image" of God, as understood above, grounds the use of words and images to represent the divine being. I shall refer primarily to Rahner's transcendental theology as the basis for the outline of such a theory.

The underlying premise of Rahner's theology of revelation is the inseparable connection of the knowledge and love of God with our engagement with the world. It is because our knowledge and love of God and of the world are intrinsically linked that human history is the possible locus and medium for God's self-revealing action. That is, it is because our access to God is always mediated by the world, and because our relations to the world always take place within the horizon of a dynamism toward God, that events, persons, thoughts, words, and images are able to serve as God's revelation.

The primal presence of God to the human spirit—the *notitia Dei insita*[105]— is not in the mode of an object or an idea, but occurs as the co-affirmed condition of possibility for the knowing and loving of objects.[106] This presence is at the same time the implicit "goal" (*Woraufhin*) of and reason for the dynamism to know and love. As we have seen, this means that God is known in a unique manner, as the transcendent "mystery" that can never be adequately "grasped" or conceptually delimited, because it is itself the condition of possibility for all delimitation; since it is the horizon within which all distinction takes place, it can never itself be defined. Every attempt to name or understand God must again resort to the pre-apprehension of the infinite:[107]

> The Whither [*Woraufhin*] of transcendental experience is always there as the nameless, the indefinable, the unattainable. For a name distinguishes and demarcates, pins down something by giving it a name chosen among many other names. But the infinite horizon, the Whither of transcendence cannot be so defined. We may reflect upon it, objectivate it, conceive of it so to speak as one object among others, delimit it conceptually: this set of concepts is only true, and a correct and intelligible expression of the content, when this expression and description is once more conditioned by a transcendent act directed to the Whither of this transcendence.[108]

The mystery of being that is pre-apprehended in this way is identified with God only by subsequent reflection on religious experience. Once this identification is made, the nonobjective pre-apprehension—which arises only in connection with the knowledge of finite objects and is only subsequently thematized as a distinct aspect of experience—becomes the point of reference and the hermeneutical key to all thematic knowledge of God. To know what "God" means, we must continually return to the experience of the unlimited horizon of our finite spiritual acts: "since merely to remove the limits of finitude as such is not enough to bring about an understanding of what the absolutely and positively infinite means."[109] There is, then, a positive as well as a negative aspect to our most fundamental and nonconceptual knowledge of God. It consists, not in a grasp of the divine essence, but in the grasp of our own movement toward it in the "excess" that we experience in knowing the being[110] of finite objects.[111]

The pre-apprehension of God that constitutes the human openness to being is the condition of possibility for God's self-revelation. Existentially, the pre-apprehension of the totality is not adequately distinguishable from God's self-offer and self-gift; on the level of transcendental reflection, the distinction between the two—which corresponds to the classical distinction between "natural" and "supernatural" revelation—is theologically needed for the sake of explaining the "point of insertion" (*Anknüpfungspunkt*) and the gratuity of grace. For Rahner, revelation is essentially personal and relational rather than merely propositional— that is, it consists essentially, not in the reception of certain "information" concerning God, but in God's communicating God's own self.[112] Revelation does not eliminate God's essential mystery, but invites us into it.[113] God's self-communication "is and remains the immediate coming into the presence of God's incomprehensibility"[114]—but in such a way that (1) we are invited to intimate communion with that mystery as our ultimate beatitude: "This radical process [of our transformation by grace] no longer leaves God at a distance, approached but never attained, the far off mover of the impulses of the human spirit acting through knowledge and freedom; it makes God in himself an attainable goal, though he still remains an abiding mystery, even in the beatific vision"[115]; and (2) we are enabled to accept that mystery in love: "The act in which man can allow for and accept God's incomprehensibility . . . without being broken by it . . . is the act of self-surrendering love trusting entirely in this very incomprehensibility."[116]

Once again, the key to Rahner's theology of revelation lies in understanding material and interpersonal existence as the intrinsic condition for human spiritual being.[117] *Quidquid recipitur, secundum modum recipientis recipitur:*[118] God's self-gift, in order to come to us as humans (which also means to create us as humans on a new level), must be freely accepted by us in the manner that human knowledge and freedom operate[119]—that is, mediated by the world,[120] beginning with our biologically, socially, and linguistically formed subjectivity. There is for human beings no purely transcendental experience: the transcendent is co-experienced as the transcendental condition of possibility of spatio-temporal things and events, and (by the same token) as immanent and operative within them. God's personal self-revelation, therefore, cannot be a purely internal and transcendental event; its transcendental "aspect" is realized only through categorical mediation. Revelation must therefore "also" have external form,[121] through God's "words" and "acts" of self-manifestation in history.

It is true that one might say, in Rahner's theology, that the interior presence of "grace" is already God's "word." But

> if the verbal communication of God was already complete in the inner word of grace, in the "illumination" by interior grace alone, then man would always and essentially accomplish his salvation only in the non-reflective, unobjectivated transcendence of his being, while the dimension of worldly objects and categories remained outside the scope of salutary acts, and man would be claimed by God only in the "fine point" of his soul, in his secret profundities, but not in the whole width of his being with all its dimensions. . . . Further, if things were so man would not be claimed by the event of salvation in his social dimension. But if man is essentially and primordially a being in a community, even in the dimension of the individual salutary decision, then knowledge of his grace cannot be adequately given by his inner experience of grace alone: it must also come to him from without, though not exclusively, from the world, from the community, from the history of salvation which is a social event historically transmitted. But this means that the proclamation of the word of God, that is, the word in so far as it is conveyed by the *historical*, external salvific act of God as an intrinsic moment of this act and by the community of believers, belongs necessarily to the inner

moments of God's salvific *action* on man. At the same time, the external revelation must depend upon the internal "word" (i.e., the experienced "excess" resulting from God's ungraspable immediate presence as the goal of our spiritual dynamism) in order for it to be a revelation *of God*.[122]

The immanence/transcendence of God,[123] as known from God's primal self-revelation as the horizon of totality, prevents us from thinking (i.e., on the theoretical level) of God's words and acts as distinct "divine" events occurring alongside worldly history or inserted into it "from without" (although the image of divine "intervention" may yet remain a legitimate one to describe their gratuitous and supernatural character).[124] Rahner enunciates the principle that God's causality is in direct and not inverse proportion to inner-worldly causality. Hence the highest level of God's causality[125] occurs in and through human rationality and responsibility; and revelation, while always God's free and supernatural gift, is also the human accomplishment of freely accepting that gift,[126] being created and formed by it, and actualizing it through embodiment in performance and formulation:

> [The] history of revelation is the history of human rationality, in as much as through the Holy Spirit. . . . [R]ationality is laid open in its inherent being to the immediate reality of the incomprehensible mystery and comes to full self-realization through history. The history of revelation is the history of rationality under the influence of grace.[127]

Therefore some events and persons are more revelatory than others; the more the actions and thoughts of a creature reflects its groundedness in the absolute source and goal of existence—that is, the more human acts and relations are free, intelligible, loving, good—the more God can be said to act and to communicate God's self in them.[128]

Revelation is the communication of the living mystery of God's self, of God's way of being. The gratuitous sharing of God's being with humanity is an act of love. Therefore the revelation of God's self to us is necessarily at the same time the constitution and revelation of God's relationship to us: what we are because of God's love and what that love is in history (these realities are referred to by such categories as "salvation," "divinization," and "revelation" itself). Revelation therefore consists not merely in knowing about that way of being but also in our assimilation to it. Hence revelation is gift and accomplishment; its primary moment, on our part, is in the acts through which humans are assimilated to God's way of being, and that may therefore be said to be the "symbol" or image of God. This takes place on both the individual and the social levels: insofar as human beings and their interrelationships are "converted," they become the embodiment or "expression" of God's life shared with humanity and "paradigms" or "images" of how God acts and what God is for us.[129]

But human activity, precisely as spiritual activity, necessarily involves a further degree of symbolization, through language (in its widest sense, including gesture, word, and image), for humans live not merely in the material world but also in the world mediated and constituted by meaning. We may therefore speak of revelation as God's "Word," insofar as God's self-communication requires linguistic or symbolic form in order to be humanly realized and communicated.[130] God is "speakable" through such symbols because of the correspondence with God's being that God's acts of creation and self-giving establish in us[131] (presupposing, of course, that God's acts are concretely realized through human "reception"). Symbols that in themselves can refer only to the world can be used in speaking of God because God constitutes a "real symbol" of God's self in the material/spiritual history of people; and this history is mediated and constituted on the level of meaning by linguistic signs.

The "speech event" through which God's relation to us is established and communicated historically[132] is also a human product and achievement, at various levels of success. We attain to assimilation to God's way of being (the "image" of God) to different degrees, and know it within available symbol systems that have diverse degrees of development and expressive potentialities. As Whitehead remarks, "A language is not a universal mode of expressing all ideas whatsoever. It is a limited mode of expressing such ideas as have been frequently entertained, and urgently needed, by the group of beings who developed that mode of speech."[133] At the same time, the encounter with God as the source of the "excess" beyond every content of thought also implies breakthroughs in which the available languages are expanded or transformed or reinterpreted and our way of life is opened to further conversion.[134]

Rahner's explanation of revelation as a "mediated immediacy" to God,[135] consisting of inseparably united transcendental and categorical aspects, allows us to formulate a theological understanding of *Moses und Aron*'s resolution of the problem of historical revelation as God's "deeds" and "word." In the thesis enunciated at the beginning of this section, God is knowable through history (including human deeds, words, and images) not only because but also (and only) *insofar as* the human being is itself the "image" of God.[136] But human assimilation to God is incomplete, subject to both development and decline, and is conditioned and produced (on the categorical level) by factors that are extrinsic to grace or even opposed to it. The failures of human acceptance of God's self-gift can distort the revelation of God, transforming images into idols based upon the projection of the self and its needs: *quia ipsi nolunt converti in melius, Deum convertunt in peius.*[137]

Hence "salvation history" in its general form is ambiguous: it is the revelation but also the veiling of God, the sign of salvation and an anti-sign:

> The history of religion is at the same time the most explicit part of the history of revelation and the intellectual region in which historical misinterpretations of the transcendental experience of God occur most plainly and with the most serious consequences, and where superstition most clearly flourishes. But it is always a case of both, and always in an ambiguity which is for us inextricable.[138]

This ambiguity naturally extends as well to the words and images that mediate religious meaning. To paraphrase Pannenberg, God can "speak" to us through words and images to the extent that our hearts are converted and open to the "totality," the ground and goal of existence; but to the extent that our lives are occupied with self or with objects in such a way that these make a total claim on us, our words and images, which always refer in the first instance to the world, are in danger of becoming distorted, mythological, or idolatrous.[139]

The Christian conviction is that in Jesus, God's self-gift has been freely appropriated, realized, and (therefore) incarnated in an absolute, victorious, eschatological way. This implies that in Jesus' historical person and mission, a definitive "sign" or "word" or "image" of God has occurred.[140] Therefore Jesus' life and teachings provide a paradigm for speech about God, about our relation to God, and about the human community called into being by God's love.

However, this does not entirely remove the problem of thinking and imagining God. A problem remains, first, because, as Pannenberg insists, Jesus is God's definitive revelation only in the light of the resurrection, which is a proleptic presence of God's eschatological triumph.[141] Jesus' life and teachings are revelatory, not by escaping from historical conditioning and limitation (including the limitations of Jesus' available language and culture), but because of their openness to that transcendence that becomes radically present in the Easter event.[142] Hence the final meaning of Jesus as revelation transcends (although it also depends upon) the content of his earthly existence and teachings.

Second, as we have seen above, there is the problem of the verbal and imaginative transmission of the history of Jesus and its meaning, both in their originating context and in relation to subsequent "worlds" of meaning. Hence for those who receive faith in Christ "by hearing" and in Christ's Spirit, there remains the task of correlating the received word of the message: with the transcendent Word; with the incarnate word in the historical Jesus, so far as he can be known to us; with the various words and images that have interpreted and mediated the meaning of Jesus to other cultures and generations, beginning with the New Testament itself; and with multiple words in which God's self-gift is embodied in other religions and cultures.[143]

If we summarize the conclusions of this presentation in a schema beginning "from above," we will see a parallel to the themes of Balthasar and Van der Leeuw, for whom theological aesthetics must begin with Christ as the image of God in the world.[144]

God's essential ability to express God's self *ad extra* is what is meant by saying that God is eternally Logos and Spirit.[145] In Jesus, the incarnate Word and the man of the Spirit, God "speaks" or manifests the divine being in history in a definitive way: Christ is the "image" of the invisible God (Col. 1:15; 2 Cor. 4:4; Phil. 2:5ff.; cf. Gen. 1:26–27)—in Rahner's language, God's "real symbol"[146] or "sacrament." In Jesus, the "form" of God is made manifest in human form. Because Jesus shares the nature of humanity, that nature is capable of becoming and actually becomes the medium for incarnating the form of God. Hence humanity as such has the potential for imaging God; and we do so to the extent that we live according to the paradigm of Jesus' life and in the same Spirit. Thus human ways of life, thoughts, words, and imagination can give sensible/spiritual form to God's presence in history, or become images of God, insofar as they reflect or reflect upon God's primal word and image revealed in Christ, or are the ontological precondition for doing so.[147]

I have conceived the task of the first part of a fundamental theological aesthetics as the formulation of a theory of the anthropological conditions for the reception of revelation through sensible perception. Such a theory involves discerning the conditions of possibility for: knowing God through a mind intrinsically tied to sensibility; receiving a revelation from God in personal and symbolic form; using symbols and images to communicate the knowledge of God and of historical revelation.

The discussion of these issues has been framed in terms of God's "image" in humanity. For the sake of theoretical clarity, we may make an abstract division between two dimensions of this "image:" (1) the permanent "structural" qualities of human being (human "nature") that make possible, and (2) the actual reception of God's self-revelation and assimilation to God's way of being. The former is the abstract "condition of possibility" for the latter.[148] Each of these has been treated schematically in the previous section. In what follows I shall outline—with no pretense at completeness or total systematization—some of the implications of this theory for the concrete use of thought and imagination in the realm of religion and theology.

The "structural" image of God consists of the intrinsic openness of the mind to the absolute—that is to the mystery of God as such. This openness is seen in the pre-apprehension of the totality that unthematically accompanies every act of objective knowing and loving. In the interests of perceiving and explaining the intrinsic rationality of religious consciousness, we may also thematize this dimension of experience by subsequent reflection (as we have done in speaking of the pre-apprehension of the totality and the "excess" experienced in knowing and loving things).

This thematization serves several functions. First, it is the basis for addressing two of the three concerns named above. The mind's intrinsic openness to the transcendent constitutes our ability to know God and our potency for receiving a supernatural revelation. Moreover, by adverting to the "excess" experienced as the condition of possibility for understanding, judgment, and love, it notifies us of the transcendent quality of being and indicates the limitations of our positive knowledge of God as transcendent. In this sense, it is the basis of the "negative" knowledge of God: our ability to say what is not God,[149] to distinguish God (but, as we have seen, by a unique differentiation) from finite objects of knowledge and from our way of knowing them. At the same time, and by the same token, it provides a basis for the heuristic and analogical knowledge of God.

What is meant by "analogy" is essentially, in Tracy's phrase, "a language of ordered relationships articulating similarity-in-difference."[150] In its theological use, it constitutes the "grammar" for the application of language—whose first point of reference is what is known through the mediation of sensation[151]—to the transcendent. As we have seen, in the Thomistic theory of cognition, even the most abstract concepts remain always inseparable from sensible experience, from which they are derived.[152] No such concept can contain or "represent" God's essence. Nevertheless, there is a relation between God and creatures;[153] and by virtue of this relation creatures (at various levels) participate in God's being, and are "similar" to God.[154] Moreover, in the human there is a presence and likeness of God in the mind's openness to the infinite, its pre-apprehension of the totality, which is the basis for its ability to make judgments of being and value. In the positive nonobjective presence and nonthematic knowledge of God in the unlimited intentionality of mind, the unique distinction of God from creation—that is, God's "immanence" and "transcendence," and the created "participation" of beings in God—is implicit. We are therefore able to discern the similarity-in-difference between God and creatures. Analogy is the systematic series of judgments in which we affirm the real relation of the creature to God, while at the same time denying the limitations of the creature when its qualities are affirmed (in an "eminent" way) of the creator.[155]

St. Thomas distinguishes between terms that can be analogously predicated of God *in se* (like "being" and "goodness") and those that refer to God's relation to us and the created similarities that arise from it. The latter are "metaphors"— terms that are applied to God as the creator and paradigm of qualities or relationships that are strictly speaking found only in creatures.[156] This distinction, Nicholas Lash observes, "stems from [the] recognition that, if we are to apprehend the truth which metaphor expresses, we must first deny its literal truth. There are, however, some expressions of which this denial is unnecessary, because we do not know and cannot specify the limits of their literal applicability."[157] That is, there are certain terms that, although they arise out of sensible experience, do not refer to particular objects, but rather thematize the dynamism of our mind itself. Such terms anticipate the total horizon of knowledge and love. In this sense they can be said to "intend" God; but only in a heuristic manner, as the mystery of being, the known unknown.

Most of our language, however, names objects and relations in the world that are intrinsically limited; they do not refer directly to the totality (being) as such, but to some instance or quality of being. They can therefore be applied to God only metaphorically, through the (at least implicit) denial of their limitations. Nevertheless, such metaphors and images, to the extent that they designate positive qualities or relations, can give us genuine knowledge of God. Their ability to do so has the same basis as that of abstract transcendental concepts:[158]

> The possibility of such religious language [*scl.* the use of metaphors and images] is ultimately based on the analogy of being, meaning that all realities have an inner connection, refer to each other, are in some way related, and can in the final analysis be understood only when we transcend them, as individual things, in the direction of the whole of reality.[159]

When we speak of the "actual" image of God revealed in the historical existence of humanity, we are primarily in the linguistic sphere of images and metaphors. The human person, because it participates in God's being, can manifest similarity to God not merely in its structure but also in its concrete achievements and relations—when and to the extent that these embody in some particular form God's creativity and/or self-communication to us. These embodiments are not originally conceptual, but lived; and their primary mental expression is in "feeling" and in what Otto called "ideograms": "illustrative substitutes for concepts."[160] Hence, as Balthasar emphasizes, they must be grasped as a *Gestalt*, in the "form" manifested by ways of living, acting, feeling, and relating; and they must be understood and communicated primarily by means of narrative images and paradigms, "pictures" of human life transformed by God. In this perspective we may concur with Sierig's designation of the Bible as a "book of pictures,"[161] and with Green's statement that its unity lies in its ability to "render a coherent Gestalt, a normative pattern for the faithful imagination."[162] (We may further agree with Green—as long as the statements are not taken reductively—that Christ is the "image" of God through the narrative shape of his life,[163] and that the "restored" image of God in humanity is the narrative shape of life conformed to the "image" of Christ, that is, the pattern of his story.[164])

In the communication of historical revelation analogy again comes into play, on two levels, for not only can we understand human history as the revelatory act and human thought as the revelatory "word" of God only by analogy, but we can understand history itself only by analogy. "Each of us understands each other through analogies to our own experience or not at all."[165] When such analogies are perceived, religious classics are able to evoke and shape our own primary religious experiences of trust, wonder, giftedness, and so on.[166] By the same token, however, there is an intrinsic ambiguity in historical revelation, both in the limitations of the revelatory events themselves and in their interpretive transmission. The material conditions that underlie the production and reception of religious classics may introduce ideological factors that conflict with their theological intent;[167] every language bears pre-conscious values and biases;[168] the imaginative transfer of classical symbols into new situations and languages can bring about distortion as well as expansion of meaning; and the plurality of religious classics themselves challenges the adequacy of each.[169]

Hence, in place of the rationalist contrast between *Vorstellung* and *Begriff*, or Lessing's "great ditch" between the particularity of history and the universality of reason, there is a complex and multileveled dialectic and complementarity operative between the various forms of religious thought and imagination. First, there is the interplay between the transcendental and categorical aspects of revelation. Second, within the latter, there is the complementarity between the personal achievement of converted existence and its formulation in various symbolic media; between historical events (insofar as they can be known to us) and their religious interpretations; within the latter between conceptual, narrative and poetic presentations; and between different systems of concepts and families of images.[170]

Within theology, I have suggested a complementarity between "aesthetic" and conceptual forms. The latter's task is not to replace either the aesthetic form or prereflexive sacred symbols, but to develop "a properly reflective language of critique and participation by means of the articulation of theological *concepts* that are neither mere categories nor simple replacements of the originating tensive religious language."[171] Theology formulates the theory of analogy that underlies discourse about God in general: this allows the "retrieval" of religious experience in a "second level" language of reflection, for the sake of returning to the symbol in an enriched way.[172]

Fundamental theology in particular has the task of discerning the implications of the "primordial" revelation in the pre-apprehension of God as ungraspable mystery. From the thematization of the latter are derived the basic "attributes" of God, which, as St. Thomas saw, are fundamentally expressions of what God is *not*.[173] That is, they essentially function as a linguistic rule for understanding the limits of all positive affirmations, analogies, and images. This limitation by "negative" theology (which, as we have seen, is correlative to the positive presence of God as "excess" of meaning) assures that it is *God* that is spoken of in our analogies, metaphors, and images as the origin of paradigmatic persons and events, and not a mere projection of our nature or desires.[174] It prevents our analogical references to God from becoming "mere categories of easy likeness slipping quietly from their status as similarities-in-difference to mere likenesses."[175]

This chapter has attempted to come to terms with the problem of thinking, imagining, and speaking of the incomprehensible God. On the basis of the epistemological and theological premises set forth, this section has dealt briefly with some of the forms in which the revelation of God takes place. The preapprehension of God, in conjunction with concrete religious experience, serves as a basis for formulating a basic notion of "divinity" and for justifying the analogous use of words and concepts. Historical persons and events, in the achievement of transcendence (by God's gift) embody a similarity to God's way of being—culminating, for Christian faith, in the person of Jesus as the "incarnation" of God's word. The events of salvation history serve as paradigms for human imagination. Transmitted in various forms, from the factual to the mythical, they provide "images" of God's way of acting with and in humanity, and hence of God's way of being. By a movement from the action to the actor, representative images of God's life in humans or in historical events may then be extended to become metaphorical images of God's self; then we have the anthropomorphism of the Bible and of other sacred scriptures.[176]

Finally, to conclude the present discussion, we may return briefly to the subject of the "icon," the visual image of God.[177] Lonergan discerns three levels on which images can function. They can correspond to a sensible content; or they can be signs, corresponding to an activity on the intellectual level that explains the import of the image; or—provided it is recognized that "the real" is the object of judgment and not merely what is known through sensation—they can be symbols linked to a known unknown, having a heuristic rather than a representational value.[178] Religious images can function on all three levels. They may representatively portray the persons or events of salvation history. (In this case, like narrative "pictures," they may have an ambiguous relation to history.) They may also serve as signs or ideograms, linked by convention to a certain meaning. Or they may be symbols of what is in itself not picturable. (This function may be combined with the first, as in icons of Christ as the incarnate God.)

The "picturing" of the invisible God—or of Christ as God—is in general a kind of metaphorical use of imagination. For example, the positive qualities of a human ruler can be seen as reflecting (or embodying, in the case of an actually or putatively "good" ruler—e.g., David) a quality of God or of God's relation to us. By extension, we may metaphorically speak of God as king. To physically portray God in the form of a king—or a shepherd, or a mother—is a means of conveying the metaphor in nonverbal form. Of course, such images in their visual concreteness are a step removed from verbal metaphors: they are, as it were, images of an image. Obviously, "pictures," as they are used in religion, are not generally to be understood as intending to be "representational." Their legitimacy will depend upon their ability to partake of the quality of "word"[179] in that they incorporate a moment of negation, "enabling them . . . to transcend beyond the finite object toward the absolute God."[180] As we saw in the first chapter, in most art (a fortiori in religious art) the purpose of a picture is not to show what a thing "looks like" but to re-present its being and/or to tell a "story" about it. Pictures communicate what God "is" by showing what God is "like" (or, more accurately, what is "like" God). Religious art must be understood theologically as analogical, not as "mimetic" in the usual sense. In this way, pictures are a special case of what Green calls imaginative "paradigms."[181]

Pictures can be of different kinds, and have different functions. One important form of religious art is representation precisely of the religious stories that embody imaginative paradigms. Another form is symbolic. The latter do give physical form to nonsensible realities; in this way, they are a step removed from paradigms taken directly from human relations. Pictures are, as the Greek Fathers said, representations of the imagination: images of what is imagined paradigmatically. The defense of icons was, of course, based on this symbolic understanding. A picture *when comprehended by the mind* is not simply physical: it becomes intelligible. In the spiritual mind it becomes spiritual. "For those given to contemplation, visible objects take on a deeper significance as disclosures of invisible realities. For the symbolic contemplation of intelligible realities through the medium of sensible objects is nothing more than the comprehension of the spiritual thought of visible objects by means of the invisible."[182]

The next chapter will examine the basis of this ability of sensible objects and symbols to evoke the transcendent directly, apart from the portrayal of historical revelation. In chapter 5, we will turn to a more specific examination of art as mediating revealed religion. Finally, chapter 6 will return to a recurrent set of problems posed for Christianity by the aesthetic realm. We have already adverted several times to the potential tensions between word and picture, conceptual thought and imagination. Not only the "icon" but also every exercise of paradigmatic imagination is in danger of "idolatry" when its analogical nature is forgotten and it becomes mythological—or when its aesthetic function of pleasing takes precedence over its theological function of mediating higher realities and values. Our conclusion will attempt to face these problems and suggest a resolution. First, however, we turn to the foundations of the positive relation of the aesthetic to religion: the nature of God as transcendent Beauty.

CHAPTER 4

❧❧

God and the Beautiful:
Beauty as a Way to God

Prelude: Mahler's Symphony no. 3, Fourth Movement,
"Misterioso," "O Mensch, gib Acht"

> O Man! Take heed!
> What says the deep midnight?
> "I slept, I slept—
> from a deep dream have I been awakened—
> The world is deep,
> and more deeply thought than day.
> Deep is its pain—
> Joy—deeper still than heartache.[1]
> Pain says: Die!
> but all joy desires eternity—
> desires deep, deep eternity!"

—Nietzsche, *Mitternachtslied*[2]

In the previous chapter we engaged in theological aesthetics in the first sense of the term: the epistemology of perception of the transcendent. In this chapter and the next, we will pursue the second senses: theological aesthetics as the consideration of beauty and of art in relation to the divine. What follows is far from a complete theory. I intend only to make a few suggestions on the topic of beauty as revelation. The present chapter explores the connection of beauty with "natural theology." It examines the possibility of seeing the beautiful as a "way" to God through a process parallel to the "transcendental" arguments of Rahner and Lonergan: God as the "condition of possibility" not only of thought and love but also of the apprehension of beauty. In examining this theme in connection with the traditional and modern arguments for God's existence, it is not my purpose to demonstrate or convince. (The reader is no doubt well beyond the need or desire for such an effort.) The "proofs" for God are relevant to a theology of revelation because they attempt to discern its primary condition of possibility: the structure of mind insofar as it is implicitly capable of knowing infinite being and can hence assign meaning to the term God and can affirm, if not the reality, at least the debatability of its referent.

"Natural Theology" and Aesthetics: The Beautiful as an Approach to God?

In the course of a broadcast interview, the violinist Yehudi Menuhin recalled a concert early in his career at which the physicist Albert Einstein was present. Menuhin recounted that after the concert Einstein came backstage to greet him, and complimented him with the words: "Thank you, Mr. Menuhin; you have once again proved to me that there is a God in heaven."

No doubt there are many who would cringe at the use of the word "proved" in this context; and it would certainly be legitimate to ask whether what Einstein meant by the word "God" corresponded with the meaning affirmed by most religious theists. Nevertheless, the point of Einstein's declaration in the anecdote probably resonates for most believers: we have experienced moments in which our faith in God—or our conviction that there is a God—was confirmed, strengthened, or validated through our being touched by beauty, whether encountered in nature, in works of art, or in the character of persons.

There seems to be no doubt that experiences of beauty can lead the spirit to God and confirm people in devotion, and that therefore the aesthetic dimension is one that must have a place in the communication of religious truths. After the long period of neglect that Balthasar documents in the introduction to his theological aesthetics,[3] there has of late been a resurgence of interest in the aesthetic in a number of theological areas: hermeneutics, theory of symbol, sacramental theology, liturgy, history of religions, to name only a few prominent fields. Balthasar himself, as we have seen, intended his "aesthetics" to function as a new kind of fundamental theology. My purpose in this chapter is also to relate aesthetics to fundamental theology, but in a somewhat different context from Balthasar's—one that is more closely related to the field that has been traditionally referred to as "natural theology"[4] or apologetics. As Einstein's comment to Menuhin intimates, aesthetic experience seems to play a major role—at least for some people—in the exercise of the practical judgment for belief in God—perhaps a great deal more so than the traditional "proofs" for God's existence set forth in apologetic theology. The question I wish to pose here is whether that role can and should be recognized as an aspect of the human mind's "primordial" knowledge of God—the *cognitio Dei insita* of which we spoke in the previous chapters.

The question may be posed in the following form: do those aesthetic experiences that raise the mind and spirit to God already *presuppose* a conviction of God's existence and add to that established conviction an affective component; or, on the other hand, can Einstein's statement be taken in a more literal sense— namely, that such experiences themselves provide a sort of "evidence" that can serve in the rational "grounding" of our conviction? (This formulation of the question should not be taken in the sense of a Cartesian "foundationalism." The "grounding" envisaged here is not that of a presuppositionless or neutral standpoint outside of every historical and social context. The metaphor of the "ground" or foundation refers here to the possibility of providing critically examined warrants for one's judgments.) My purpose, then, is to ask whether the role of beauty in leading the mind to God can be formulated and shown to be valid in the sphere of critical reason; that is, whether aesthetic experience—prior to its religious and theological uses—can provide a way for the mind to come to the judgment of God's existence.[5]

The "Ascent" of the Mind to God in the Western Tradition

The Origins

The idea of as "ascent" of the mind to God from the beauty encountered in the physical world is an ancient one that recurs frequently in the Western and Christian traditions. It must suffice here to mention only a few of its major representatives and variations.

The notion of "beauty" plays little part in Hebrew thought or in the New Testament. Von Rad notes that what we mean by "beauty" was appreciated by Israel primarily in the realm of happening: the Scriptures delight in God's creation and God's acts in history. For this reason, "Israel's artistic *charisma* lay in the realm of narrative and poetry. . . . [A]s far as we can see, Israel lacked all critical reflection on the phenomenon of beauty and on artistic reproduction as such."[6] Both Barth and Balthasar show, however, that the theologically significant content of the idea of "beauty" is found in the Scriptures, primarily under the category of "glory."[7]

Although there is no systematic approach to the "ascent" of the mind to God through beauty in the Scriptures, there are a few openings toward such a line of thought. As Balthasar points out, the Wisdom tradition sees the splendor of creation as a motive for the praise of God, in addition to God's historical deeds (see Wis. 13; Sir. 42:14–43, Ps. 8:104, etc.; Job 38f.).[8] The classical Pauline text Romans 1:19–20 states that God can be known from creation; and Wisdom 13:5 even connects the knowledge of God with the beauty of creation: "From the greatness and beauty of created things, their author, by analogy, is seen. . . ."

However, it was Greek philosophy, with its identification of the beautiful (τὸ καλόν) and the good (τὸ ἀγαθόν) that introduced reflective and critical thinking on the topic. The classic formulation of the "ascent" from the beautiful to the divine, and one that had a profound influence on later thinkers, is found in Plato's *Symposium*:

> He who has been instructed thus far in the things of love, and who has learned to see the beautiful in due order and succession, when he comes toward the end will suddenly perceive a nature of wondrous beauty . . . beauty absolute, separate, simple, and everlasting, which without diminution and without increase or any change, is imparted to the ever-growing and perishing beauties of all other things. He who from this ascending under the influence of true love, begins to perceive that beauty, is not far from the end.

And the true order of going, or being led by another, to the things of love, is to begin from the beauties of earth and mount upwards for the sake of that other beauty, using these as steps only, and from one going on to two, and from two to all fair forms, and from fair forms to fair practices, and from fair practices to fair notions, until from fair notions he arrives at the notion of absolute beauty, and at last knows what the essence of beauty is.

In contrast to the Stoics, the Christian tradition generally gave a positive evaluation to the affects in the spiritual life,[9] and fairly early took up the Platonic idea of transcendental beauty drawing all things to itself through the stages of physical, moral, and spiritual beauty.[10] This line of thinking found a major exponent in Christian thought in the writings of Pseudo-Dionysius, who presents God as the Beautiful and the universe as the irradiation of God's beauty:

the Superessential Beautiful is called "Beauty" because of that quality which it imparts to all things severally according to their nature, and because it is the Cause of the harmony and splendor in all things, flashing forth upon them all, like light, the beautifying communications of Its originating ray; and because it summons all things to fare unto Itself (from whence it hath the name of 'Fairness'),[11] and because It draws all things together in a state of mutual interpenetration.[12]

It is well known that the "aesthetic" dimension of spirituality—beauty and affective desire—played a large part in the personal life of Augustine. In his youth, he was much attracted to the literary classics and the theater; by profession he was a teacher of the art of rhetoric; and his conversion owed much to the homiletic skill of Ambrose and the sweetness he experienced in the church's hymnody.[13] His theology emphasizes the beauty of God and the role of desire for the beautiful in drawing us to God—but also the danger that it may keep us from God. He spoke of the affects as the "feet" that carry us to or away from God; there is a danger that they may be misdirected, but without them we cannot travel at all.[14]

Augustine had asked whether things are beautiful because they give delight, or *vice versa*;[15] in opting for the latter, he gave to Beauty an "objective" and ontological status, through which it could ultimately be associated with the divine. In one of the most celebrated passages of the *Confessions*, he addresses God as primal Beauty:

Late have I loved You, Beauty so ancient and so new, late have I loved You! and behold, You were within me, and I was outside, and I sought you there, and threw myself, deformed, upon the beautiful things which You made. You were with me; but I was not with you. Those things held me far from You; things which would not even exist unless they were in You. You called and cried out and broke open my deafness; You shone forth and glowed and chased away my blindness; You blew fragrantly on me, and I drew breath and I pant for You; I tasted You, and I hunger and thirst for You; You touched me, and I was inflamed with desire for your peace.[16]

Augustine's meditations on the beautiful provided later Western thought with a number of its major inspirations. He follows the idea of a hierarchy of satisfactions, attributing the perception of "beauty" (*pulchritudo*) only to the "higher" and more "cognitive" realm of sensation (i.e., vision) and to moral judgment; while the pleasure experienced in hearing and the "lower" senses is of the lower order of "sweetness" (*suavitas*).[17] To him is attributed the classical definition of beauty as "*splendor ordinis*,"[18] and he makes the distinction, important in the Middle Ages, between "beauty" and "aptness":[19]

> These things I as then knew not, and I fell in love with these inferior beauties, and I was sinking even to the very bottom; and unto my friends I said: Do we love anything that is not beautiful? Then what is fair, and what is beauty? What is it that inveigles us thus, and that draws our affections to the things we love? For unless there were a gracefulness and a beauty in them, they could by no means draw us unto them. And I marked narrowly and perceived that in the bodies themselves there was one thing as it were the whole, which in that respect was beautiful, and another thing that was therefore becoming, because it was aptly fitted to some thing, as some part of the body, in respect of the whole body, or a shoe in respect of the foot, and the like. And this consideration sprang up in my mind even out of the innermost of my heart, and I composed certain books on the Beautiful and the Fitting, two or three as I think. For I have them not now by me, but lost they are, and I know not how.[20]

Combining the Platonic tradition with a Christian awareness of creation, Augustine holds—in line with the author of the Wisdom of Solomon (13:3–5)—that the beauty of creation reveals its Maker: "When you consider all the beauties of this world, does not that beautiful order itself, as though with a single voice, call out to you, saying, 'I did not make myself, but God did'?"[21]

Augustine argues for the necessity of God from the incompleteness of the intelligibility that the mind finds in itself; and he explicitly connects this reasoning with the steps of the Platonic "ascent": from external beauty to the beauty of the soul, and finally to the supreme source of all beauty, which is also the ultimate truth:

> The human mind, in making judgments about visible things, is able to recognize that it is itself of a higher order than all visible things. However, because of its own defects and its ability to progress in wisdom, the mind itself is revealed as incomplete and changeable, and finds above itself the existence of a changeless and perfect truth. By devoting itself to this truth, the mind is made happy, finding within itself the creator and lord not only of itself, but of all visible things as well. . . . From the beauty of those things which are external, we discover the maker, who is internal to us, and who creates beauty in a superior way in the soul, and then, in an inferior way, creates beauty in the body.

Augustine affirms that not only the beauties of the world but also those sought by human art are ultimately derived from the divine beauty and its desirability. Nevertheless, he is constantly aware that they may be misused and become an obstacle instead of a means to God:

But I, O my God and my Beauty, from hence I also sing a hymn to You, and make a sacrifice of praise to my Sanctifier; because those beauties which are conveyed through the soul into cunning hands, all descend from that beauty which is above our souls, for which my soul sighs day and night. But those who fashion and seek external beauties derive thence [i.e., from the ultimate Beauty] their affirmation of these things, but not the correct way of using them. Yet there It is, although they do not perceive It, so that they might not wander too far, but might preserve their strength only for You, and not waste it on pleasurable exhaustions.[22]

Early Medieval Developments

The Neoplatonic current, mediated by Augustine and Pseudo-Dionysius, runs through the Middle Ages to the great scholastics.[23] The essential theme of Pseudo-Dionysius's theological aesthetics—the idea of a celestial and earthly hierarchy of ordered beauties proceeding from God and leading back from matter through the human spirit to God—became one of the fundamental and leading motifs of medieval theology. Crucial to medieval aesthetics is the idea that all human perception of beauty is ultimately aimed at spiritual beauty,[24] which is present to the mind as intelligible form. Hence the Victorines taught that there is a continuity between all levels: physical pleasure is extended into the affective joy felt in the experience of sensuous harmony; and this is grounded in the ontological correspondence between the structure of the mind and matter.[25]

Because of the unity of the world through its participation in the divine existence and beauty, all things could be seen as a vast work of art manifesting God's ineffable beauty.[26] And because of their common origin, existence, and finality in God, the world could be seen as a series of multidimensional symbols or allegories referring both to God and to other levels of existence. Hence Hugh of St. Victor writes that "All things visible, when they obviously speak to us symbolically, that is when they are interpreted figuratively, are referable to invisible significations and statements. . . . For since their beauty consists in the visible forms of things . . . visible beauty is an image of invisible beauty."[27] The interior life is in continuity with the physical order of the universe. St. Bernard writes that "The body is an image of the mind,"[28] and, by the same token, morality is analogous to physical beauty; for, as William of Auvergne explains, sensuous beauty is what gives pleasure to sight; interior beauty gives pleasure to the soul that perceives it, and "entices the soul to love it." Hence goodness "is called *pulchritudo* or *decor* because of the comparison with external and visible beauty."[29]

Boethius's influential teaching held that the entire cosmos is subject to the same laws of proportion that rule music, so that from the inaudible music of the spheres to the proportions of the human body (which is reflected in architecture and art) and the logic of the human spirit, all things form a great harmony. William of Auvergne expresses a common medieval idea (which perdured well into early modern times) when he writes: "When you consider the order and magnificence of the universe . . . you will find it to be like a most beautiful canticle . . . and the wondrous variety of its creatures to be a symphony of joy and harmony to very excess."[30] (The same idea could be expressed in the visual image of degrees of "light," visible and intelligible.)

A most interesting example of the combination of this theology with aesthetic practice is found in the memoirs of the great twelfth-century abbot Suger, who made the church at St. Denis the first great work of the Gothic style in northern France. Suger has left us an unusual record of both the Platonic theology of art and his spiritual experience of finding God in the aesthetic. In the verses inscribed on the gilded cast bronze doors of the basilica, representing the passion and resurrection of Christ, he gives to the viewer this message concerning the purpose of the artwork:

> Whoever you may be who wish to extol the glory of these doors,
> Do not wonder at the gold or their costliness, but at the skill of the work.
> The brightness of the noble work shines forth; but let the work that brightly shines
> enlighten the minds [of the beholders], so that they may travel through true lights
> To the True Light, where Christ is the true door.
> The golden door defines what is inherent in these [worldly] things:
> the dull mind rises to the truth through material things,
> and, being at first submerged, having seen this light it rises.[31]

The mind is meant to travel, in Platonic fashion, from the physical splendor of the materials to the more spiritual beauty of the work of art; then from the art to the mind beholding, and finally to the "light" of Christ. Significantly, Suger sees this process as being parallel to the allegorical interpretation of the Hebrew scriptures in the light of the gospel, for here also the mind is urged "from the material to the immaterial."[32] For example, one of the stained-glass windows of the basilica shows the apostle Paul turning a mill, to which the Old Testament prophets carry sacks of grain. The meaning is revealed in the verses:

> By working the mill, thou, Paul, takest the flour out of the bran.
> Thou makest known the inmost meaning of the Law of Moses,
> From so many grains is made the true bread without bran,
> Our and the angels' perpetual food.[33]

Suger was no doubt aware of the criticisms against the excessive richness of church decoration levied by followers of the Cistercian reform movement, and he gives several further theoretical justifications for his artistic program, in addition to the basic contention that the dull human mind needs a material stimulus to rise to spiritual contemplation. First, the liturgical service of God demands the finest that the world has (as Suger argues *a fortiori* from Old Testament practice, adapting the text of Heb. 9:12–14 to his purposes).

> To me, I confess, one thing has always seemed preeminently fitting: that every costlier or costliest thing should serve, first and foremost, for the administration of the Holy Eucharist: *If* golden pouring vessels, golden vials, golden little mortars used to serve, by the word of God or the command of

the Prophet, to collect the *blood of goats or of calves or the red heifer: how much more* must golden vessels, precious stones, and whatever is most valued among all created things, be laid out, with continual reverence and full devotion, for the reception of the *blood of Christ*! Surely neither we nor our possessions suffice for this service. If, by a new creation, our substance were re-formed from that of the holy Cherubim and Seraphim, it would still offer an insufficient and unworthy service for so great and ineffable a victim; and yet we have so great a propitiation for our sins.[34]

Even more profoundly, Suger reinforces the Platonic notion of "ascent" from the material to the spiritual by appealing to the doctrine of the incarnation, which implies that God is to be served in a "universal" way, uniting the bodily not only with the mental, but with the divine itself:

The detractors also object that a saintly mind, a pure heart, a faithful intention ought to suffice for this sacred function; and we, too, explicitly affirm that it is these that principally matter. [But] we profess that we must do homage also through the outward ornaments of sacred vessels, and to nothing in the world in an equal degree as to the service of the Holy Sacrifice, with all inner purity and with all outward splendor. For it behooves us most becomingly to serve Our Savior in all things in a universal way—Him Who has not refused to provide for us in all things in a universal way and without exception; Who has fused our nature into His into one admirable individuality; Who *setting us on His right hand*, has promised us in truth *to possess His Kingdom;* our Lord Who *liveth and reigneth for ever and ever*.[35]

In a more personal passage, Suger records his own spiritual progress through beauty to God:

Thus, when—out of my delight in the beauty of the house of God—the loveliness of the many-colored gems has called me away from external cares, and worthy meditation has induced me to reflect, transferring that which is material to that which is immaterial, on the diversity of the sacred virtues: then it seems to me that I see myself dwelling, as it were, in some strange region of the universe which neither exists entirely in the slime of the earth nor entirely in the purity of Heaven; and that, by the grace of God, I can be transported from this inferior to that higher world in an anagogical manner.[36]

On a theoretical level, a great deal of early scholastic thinking centered on the relationship of beauty to the good. The tradition received from Aristotle, the Stoics, Cicero, and Augustine presumed the identity of the two,[37] and earlier writers make no distinction: "the goodness of a substance, and its beauty, are the same thing," writes William of Auxerre.[38] Only in the thirteenth century was there an effort to surpass the descriptive and metaphorical categories of "common sense" and to construct a systematic theoretical explanation.[39] This development was inspired, in part, by a need to respond to the Manichaeism of the Cathari and Albigensians, who held that the material world was evil, and not God's creation.[40]

The metaphysical theory of the transcendental qualities of being was meant to show that being is intrinsically one, true, and good, and that these positive qualities are directly from God—indeed, are a "participation" in the divine being.

The definitive move into the realm of theory was first achieved by Philip the Chancellor, at the beginning of the thirteenth century.[41] In his *Summa de Bono*, the first systematic treatment of the transcendentals, he explains that the good is convertible with being, but differs rationally (*secundum rationem*).[42] Philip himself did not broach the question of beauty, but some of his contemporaries did. Robert Grosseteste affirms in his commentary on Pseudo-Dionysius (written prior to 1243) that the Beautiful (*Pulchritudo*) is one of the names of God. "If everything desires the good and the beautiful together, the good and the beautiful are the same." However, applying Philip's technique of dealing with the transcendentals, he goes on to explain that they are rationally different (*diversa sunt ratione*): "God is called good because He confers being on everything, and being is good, and He increases and perfects and preserves [it]. But He is called beautiful in that all things, both in themselves and together, produce a concordance in their identity with Him."[43]

The *Summa* of Alexander of Hales (1245)[44] makes a major step forward. It is presumed that goodness and beauty are *in se*, or "really," the same. But they differ with respect to the intentionality of the perceiver. "For beauty is a disposition of the good insofar as it pleases the apprehension, whereas the good strictly speaking has to do with the disposition in which it pleases our affections." Hence "the good" has to do with final causality, and beauty with formal causality.[45] Albertus Magnus follows in the same line. In his commentary on the fourth chapter of Pseudo-Dionysius's *De Divinis Nominibus* (formerly attributed to Aquinas, under the title *De Pulchro et Bono*) he defines beauty: "The nature of the beautiful consists in general in a resplendence of form, whether in the duly ordered parts of material objects, or in men, or in actions."[46] It is an objective quality that exists independently of its perception.[47] Hence Albertus rejects Cicero's subjectivist contention that beauty should be defined by people's conception of it (*De Officiis*, I, 27). Virtue, for example, is beautiful, even if it remains unknown.[48] Beauty is a transcendental quality of being: "everything that exists participates in the beautiful and the good;" and goodness and beauty are distinguished by the intentionality of the subject (*intentione*).[49]

Bonaventure and Thomas Aquinas

The Scholastic exposition of beauty as a transcendental finds explicit connection with the knowledge of God and with "natural theology" in the writings of St. Bonaventure. In his *Itinerarium Mentis in Deum*, Bonaventure outlines the levels of knowledge of God, proceeding through seven degrees that correspond to the days of creation. The human mind, according to Bonaventure, has three principal aspects: the animal or sensual intelligence is directed to external, bodily reality (*ad corpora exteriora*); spirit is oriented to and within the self (*intra se et in se*): and mind proper (*mens*) intends what is above the human self (*supra se*).[50] Progressing through these Bonaventure discerns six "grades" of knowledge of God prior to the sabbath rest of mystical vision: sensation (*sensus*), imagination (*imaginatio*), reason (*ratio*), understanding (*intellectus*), intelligence (*intelligentia*), and the apex of the mind or spark of synderesis (*apex mentis seu synderesis scintilla*).[51] As in Dionysius, the movement is from the external to the internal, from the temporal to the eternal.[52]

Of primary interest for our theme is Bonaventure's exposition of the knowledge of God on the first level, the "sensible mirror" of God. Here God is known both in the created "vestiges" of divine life that constitute the being of corporeal things and also as actively present in them;[53] for God is interior to all things that are perceived or known.[54] In sensible knowledge, apprehension is followed by delectation, then by judgment.[55] Bonaventure explicitly refers to beauty as a transcendental quality of all things that makes them capable of producing delight;[56] and this quality has its primary exemplar in God.[57] Moreover, the beauty of creatures is an image of divinity, and can lead to the knowledge of God, as Paul says in Romans 1:20:

> all the creatures of this sensible world lead the soul of the wise and contemplative person to the eternal God, since they are the shadows, echoes, and pictures, the vestiges, images, and visible showing of that most powerful, most wise, and best first principle, of that eternal origin, light, and fullness, of that productive, exemplary and order-giving Art; they are put before us for the sake of our knowing God, and are divinely given signs . . . For every creature is by its very nature a kind of portrayal and likeness of that eternal Wisdom.[58]

After the mind has come to the knowledge of God outside itself, in the divine "vestiges" in creation, it is led to the knowledge of God through itself and present in itself as God's image.[59] As in Augustine, this is the principal locus of the knowledge of God: the "vestiges" of the divinity in the external world turn the mind to reflection on its own spiritual and intelligible nature, in which God's existence is present and known (at least implicitly and dimly). That knowledge can be explicated and clarified by reflection on the mind's discernment of being, which is seen primarily in the act of judgment. Bonaventure argues elsewhere that every positive affirmation implies God: for every affirmation posits a truth, and every such positing presupposes the existence of Truth itself, the cause of all that is true.[60]

In a text that recalls Augustine, the *Itinerarium* also makes it clear that judgment would be impossible unless there were implicitly present to the mind an absolute norm of being, which is God. True judgments are possible, Bonaventure argues, because of the self-evident and indubitable first principles of knowledge, which are the basis for all judgments. But these principles are nothing other than the presence of the eternal light of God, the ultimate intelligibility and beauty, shining in our intellects. Therefore, an implicit knowledge of absolute being (which is also identically absolute goodness and beauty) is the condition for our knowing any particular beings, as well as for our ability to know the limitations of finite being. For, Bonaventure asks, "how could our intellect know that this being is defective and incomplete, unless it had a knowledge of a being without any defect?"[61] Since the mind also knows itself as finite, the light or intelligibility that grounds all judgments can only be that of the absolute being, God, enlightening our minds by the participation in the divine eternal truth: "Our mind itself is formed immediately by Truth itself."[62]

> Judgment occurs through our reason's abstracting from place, time and mutability, and thus from dimension, succession and change, through reason which is unchangeable, unlimited, and endless. But nothing is absolutely unchangeable, unlimited and endless unless it is eternal. Everything that is eternal is either God or is in God. If, then, everything that we judge with certitude we judge by such reason, it is clear that God's own self is the reason of all things and the infallible rule and light of truth, in which all things shine forth infallibly, indelibly, indubitably, irrefutably, indisputably, unchangeably, boundlessly, endlessly, indivisibly, and intellectually. Therefore those laws by which we judge with certitude about all sensible things that come under our consideration—since they are infallible and cannot be doubted by the intellect of the one who apprehends them, since they are as if ever present and cannot be erased from the memory of the one who recalls them, since they cannot be refuted or judged by the intellect of the one who judges because, as Augustine says, "no one passes judgment on them, but rather by means of them"—so these laws must be unchangeable and incorruptible since they are necessary; boundless since they are without limits; and endless since they are eternal—and for this reason they must be indivisible since they are intellectual and incorporeal, not made, but uncreated, existing eternally in the Eternal Art, by which, through which and according to which all beautiful things are formed. Therefore we cannot judge with certainty except in view of the Eternal Art which is the form that not only produces all things but also conserves and distinguishes all things, as the being which sustains the form in all things and the rule which directs all things. Through it our mind judges all things that enter it through the senses.[63]

It is notable that Bonaventure explicitly connects this intellectualist argument with God's giving of form to all that is beautiful (which includes truth). In his *Reductio Artium in Theologiam* he makes it particularly clear that what is critical to this line of thought is the Pseudo-Dionysian notion of a hierarchy of beauty: from corporeal and sensible beauty the mind is drawn upward to contemplation of itself as their perceiver, and to its own spiritual beauty and the beauty of intelligible form; and these, finally, are seen as dependent on and participating in a highest Beauty, which is also the highest Art, interior to mind and also above it, the cause of all beauty.

The "natural" image of God in the mind is reformed by grace, especially by the theological virtues. Bonaventure notes that at this level the contemplation of God is more through affective experience than by reason,[64] for by grace the mind recovers its "interior senses" so that it can be exalted beyond itself and can, according to the symbolism of the Canticle of Canticles, "see the highest beauty, hear the highest harmony, smell the most pleasant fragrance, taste the sweetest flavor, apprehend what is most delightful."[65]

Finally, God is known "above" the mind, in God's own being that cannot be contained in any creature, through the similitude of the divine light that shines upon the mind and constitutes the innate a priori knowledge of being and the good.[66] At this level God is mirrored in the mind in the primary divine name, "Being," which is known to the intellect before individual beings,[67] and in the name "Goodness," which designates God as the source and finality of desire.[68] Beyond all these grades, the mind enters into the mystical "excess" for which the theological virtues prepare it, and contemplates God beyond both the world and itself.[69]

It is clear that Bonaventure's thought, including his treatment of the knowledge of God's existence, has strong affinities with the Pseudo-Dionysian "ascent" from the beautiful to God. Moreover, unlike most medieval writers, Bonaventure explicitly adds "beauty" to the list of the transcendentals. In an *opusculum* of 1250, he speaks of the "four conditions of being, namely that it be one, true, good, and beautiful." These are distinguished, he explains, by the different forms of causality to which they correspond. Unity regards efficient causality; the true, formal causality; the good, final causality. But beauty "encompasses every cause and is common to each. . . . It has to do equally with every cause."[70] Hence it might be said that every argument from creation to God as first cause is at least implicitly an argument from beauty.

The thought of Aquinas offers less direct support to the notion of a "way" of the mind to God through beauty; yet here as well such a way is implicitly present.

Like many medieval writers, St. Thomas produced a commentary on the *De Divinis Nominibus*.[71] Although the concern here is primarily to explain the thought of Pseudo-Dionysius, rather than to construct an original theology, we find in this text certain background ideas that are significant to Aquinas's thought. All beauty stems from God as First Cause; for the beauty of any creature is nothing else but a likeness of and participation in the divine beauty.[72] Beauty consists of the possession of two properties: the "clarity" or "light" proper to a particular kind of being, whether spiritual or physical; and correct proportion.[73] God gives things beauty insofar as God is the cause of consonance (or proportion) and clarity in all things.[74] God, whose being is uncreated Light, causes the "clarity" in things by illuminating them; that is, by creating in them a participated similarity to the divine being. (Their "form.") It will be recalled that "light" or "luminosity" for medieval thought symbolizes the nature of being an "intelligible" and—at its higher levels—self-conscious. "Form," in turn, is the intelligible quality that gives actual existence to a substance. This scholastic idea, in combination with the biblical symbolism of light, accounts for the enormous importance of light in Gothic art and architecture.) God creates consonance or proportion in two ways: insofar as all things are ordered to God as their end; and insofar as they are ordered to each other. The latter is explained in the Platonic view by the fact that the higher levels of being are in the lower by participation, and lower are in the higher by a kind of eminence: so that all things exist in each other, and are ordered to each other.[75]

God is said to be beautiful by eminence (*secundum excessum*) and because of the divine causality (*per causam*), which implies a participation in the divine being. But God is perfectly beautiful, since the unity and simplicity of the divine nature do not permit the twofold defect that beauty in creatures suffers; namely, that it is variable and partial (*aliquo modo particulatam pulchritudinem*).[76] All that is beautiful "preexists" in God's uniform and perfect beauty, in the way that multiple effects preexist in their single cause.[77] God's beauty is the source of all existence; for "light" ("clarity") is of the nature of beauty, and "form," through which things have their proper intelligibility (*ratio*)[78] and their actual existence (*esse*), is a participation in or "irradiation" by the divine light.[79] Similarly, God's beauty is the source of all things' proportion or "consonance" (Aquinas here gives this term the sense of "agreement" or "union"), since it is the common goal of all.[80]

God creates the world in order to share the divine beauty: anyone who possesses beauty wishes to expand it as much as possible.[81] Like an artist, God creates for the sake of beauty. All things are made, therefore, to be beautiful, so that they imitate in various degrees their exemplary cause.[82] There is nothing that does not participate in beauty and goodness, since every thing is both good and beautiful in its intelligible substantial "form."

Dionysius says that beauty and "the good" are the same. In commenting on this text, Aquinas follows Philip the Chancellor and Albert the Great in admitting their real identity (since the defining qualities of beauty, "clarity" and "consonance" are both values, or "goods") but making a rational distinction. For Aquinas, this distinction consists in the fact that beauty adds to the notion of "goodness" an ordering toward the intellectual faculty.[83] In the *Summa*, he elaborates:

> For good (being what all things desire) has to do properly with desire and so involves the idea of end (since desire is a kind of movement toward something). Beauty, on the other hand, has to do with knowledge, and we call a thing beautiful when it pleases the eye of the beholder. This is why beauty is a matter of right proportion, for the senses delight in rightly proportioned things as similar to themselves, the sense faculty being a sort of proportion itself, like all other knowing faculties. Now since knowing proceeds by imagining, and images have to do with form, beauty properly involves the notion of form.[84]

It is in this context that we should understand Aquinas's definition of beauty: "what pleases by its very apprehension."[85] What is involved for Aquinas, Umberto Eco insists, is not merely the sensual perception of the external qualities of things but also the apprehension of properties and qualities organized according to the immanent structure of substantial form. *Visio* in this context is a kind of knowledge: "an intellectual, conceptual act of comprehension."[86] "For Aquinas, the intellect cannot know sensible particulars, and it is only after the abstraction, in the *reflexio ad phantasmata*, that it comes to know sense objects." Hence in Thomas "aesthetic knowledge has the same kind of complexity as intellectual knowledge, because it has the same object, namely the substantial reality of something informed by an entelechy."[87] (However, since Thomas implicitly acknowledges that beauty is a transcendental quality, it will have diverse levels; hence there can be a distinction between what is beautiful merely in appearance, and intelligible beauty.[88])

St. Thomas does not provide an explicit approach to God's existence from beauty; but the influence of Pseudo-Dionysius is obvious throughout his work, and the Dionysian schema of *exitus-reditus* underlies the very structure of the *Summa*. In this light, we can see that the fourth of Aquinas's "ways" of the mind to the affirmation of God's existence—the argument from the "degrees" in things—is in fact a generalization of the "Platonic" raising of the mind through the degrees of beauty to God. He argues:

> Among beings there are some more and some less good, true, noble, and the like. But "more" and "less" are predicated of things according as they resemble in their different ways something that is the maximum, as something is more hot which more nearly resembles that which is hottest. Therefore there is something that is truest, best, noblest, and, consequently, something that is most in being; for those things that are greatest in truth are greatest in being, as it is written in *Metaph*. ii. Now the maximum in any genus is the cause of all within that genus, just as fire, which is the maximum of heat, is the cause of all hot things, as is said in the same book. Therefore there must be something which is to all beings the cause of their being, goodness, and every other perfection; and this we call God.[89]

Thomas's version of the "ascent" of the mind to God centers on the recognition that the values we perceive in finite beings are not self-explanatory or self-justifying (although Aquinas does not explicitly name beauty as one of these values, he mentions both "goodness" and "nobility"; from his other writings we may presume that beauty falls into the same category). Such values are, instead, incomplete realizations of some anticipated supreme measure of the quality. This is clear from the degrees of perfection in things of our experience, none of which exhaust the values they embody. If the degrees of value, beauty, and so on, are real, and not merely arbitrary and subjective designations invented by our minds, then there must exist some source or ground of their existence; that is, there must be some reality to which they can be compared. This reality cannot be a finite being because, although they might be the maximum of some particular genus (as the sun is of fire, according to ancient physics), they are by their nature incomplete with regard to existence, goodness, beauty, and so on. They participate in such ontological values, but cannot exhaust them. Therefore things do not provide the explanation or grounds of their own degree of value, or of the reality of value at all; such an explanation must be sought outside the finite world. It can only consist in the affirmation of the existence of something that is *in se* (not by virtue of any other) the supreme degree of goodness, beauty, truth, and so on; and this is what is meant by God. As Avicenna says, God is the "cause that gives [degrees of] perfection": as such, God is that from which and for which things exist, that which gives meaning to the values they have or are.[90]

Thomas's formulation also exposes the problem that the modern mind finds with this mode of reasoning, and with the Dionysian "ascent" in general. To the modern mind, of course, it is not at all obvious that "more" and "less" demand the existence of a "most" that is the cause of all other realities in the genus. That some things are hotter than others does not imply for us (as it did for Thomas's Aristotelian physics) that there is some supremely hot thing. If there is de facto something in the universe that is hotter than anything else, this is a mere matter of fact and does not imply that nothing hotter is possible; nor, *a fortiori*, can one infer that this "hottest" is somehow the source or cause of all other heat. At best, one might formulate an abstract idea of what constitutes the quality of "heat"; but one certainly could not argue from that idea to the existence of some reality possessing the quality in pure and perfect form.

Naturally, one can separate St. Thomas's essential reasoning from the physical examples he uses.[91] One may draw a distinction between transcendental and generic qualities, and insist that only the former—qualities of being, predicated by analogy—imply an absolute instance, so that there need not be a maximum in each genus, but only in the ontological sphere. (Once one draws this distinction, the similarity of this argument to the previous "ways" from causality becomes apparent. The structure of the argument is the same; but the fourth way begins not with being or act, but rather with other transcendental qualities that are really identical with it. These demand an ultimate metaphysical principle—a first cause—to explain their existence, just as contingent being does.) But for post-Kantian thought, this strategy in itself is not sufficient, for Kant argues that while being and goodness may indeed imply a transcendental *idea* of their absolute perfection, one cannot reason from such an idea to the actual existence of a supreme Being or Good without resort to an illegitimate ontological argument.

For modern thinking, the obstacle to a rational ascent of the mind to God from the beautiful—at least as this process is traditionally presented—seems to lie ultimately in the inaccessibility of the very basis of the reasoning: the underlying notion of "being by participation." The Platonic "way" to God as reiterated by the Pseudo-Dionysian tradition, and as formulated scientifically by Bonaventure and Aquinas, can envision an "ascent" of the mind from the apprehension of lower degrees of beauty (or of being or goodness or intelligibility) to the affirmation of a highest instance precisely because it presumes that the positive qualities of all beings can be explained only as participation in a perfect instance and grounding source. But this metaphysical supposition, and the ordered "hierarchy" of being that it supports, can no longer be taken as self-evident. Hence the approach to God from the beautiful, despite its attractiveness, when formulated as it is by Augustine, Bonaventure, or Aquinas, becomes intellectually alien to the contemporary mind. As Paul Ricoeur has written, for the generation that has passed through Nietzsche, Heidegger, Derrida, and Blanchot, "what is forever excluded . . . is a pure and simple repetition of the philosophers of participation and presence."[92]

The Contemporary Approach of Jean-Dominique Robert

In this context the French Dominican Jean-Dominique Robert has attempted to formulate a contemporary approach to God's existence from the philosophical implications of aesthetic experience.[93] An overview of Robert's method will be helpful as a point of contrast and comparison for the "transcendental" approach that I will suggest in the following section.

Explicitly renouncing any attempt to begin with the "strictly metaphysical" Platonic type of ascent, as represented especially by St. Thomas's fourth "way,"

Robert proposes two different "ways" to God. They are (in inverse order to his own presentation): (1) from the creative act and its inspiration, both of which imply a dependence on an Other; and (2) from works of art, which are a kind of witness to an encounter with ineffable mystery.

Robert's approach to God through the act of artistic creation parallels the argument he had formulated twenty years earlier, based on the philosophical implications of the act of scientific knowing.[94] He summarizes the shape of the primary argument as follows: "science is possible because the world is thinkable and, in a certain sense, is already thought, prior to any scientific act taking place. It seemed to me, then, that one could discover an Act of Thought [*Pensée*] that is at work in the universe."[95] (This reasoning has obvious affinities with Aquinas's fifth "way" and with other versions of the "cosmological" argument from the order or intelligibility of the world to a supreme Mind.)

Robert sees, however, that this argument is open to objection from those who conceive science in what he calls an "idealist" (i.e., Kantian) way: as a network of intelligible relations invented by the human mind and projected onto the chaos that is "nature." In such a conception of scientific thinking, the "thinkability" of the world would have no implications beyond itself. An argument to a supreme act of (creative) thinking on the basis of scientific knowledge would be (as Kant held) of an invalid "ontological" nature. In the light of this objection, Robert develops another line of argument, based on the internal necessity of intelligibility and of noncontradiction in science. He attempts to demonstrate that these fundamental structures and principles of the act of knowing cannot be founded upon either the contingent real or the contingent and multiple human minds that perform science. In order to explain them it is therefore necessary to affirm a grounding or creative Thought (*Pensée Fondatrice*) that transcends both the world and human minds.

Robert believes that the same reasoning can be transposed to the act of artistic creation.[96] Every such act has a dual relationship: on the one hand, to the sensible world; and on the other, to the creative artist. The artist in working refers at one level to the sensible world, which gives material structure to his or her work; at another level, however, the artist responds to a different kind of reality, commonly referred to as artistic "inspiration," which provides as it were the "laws" or a priori structures of creativity.[97] These are experienced by the mind and heart as certain imperatives regarding beauty and spirit, in a way parallel to the way in which logical or mathematical structures impose themselves on scientific understanding. Like the latter, they are constants, not dependent on particular historical or social contexts.[98] (Robert's distinction of this level from that of the "material" structures of art nevertheless allows the preservation of the culturally conditioned nature of concrete artistic creation.)

Artists thus know that they are not the creators "out of nothing" of their works. The question then arises: what is the source or foundation of the basic a priori structures of aesthetic creation? Robert replies: if the world can be "translated" into art, if it can be "recreated," it is because the world is intrinsically suited to such operations. As Einstein and de Broglie maintained in the field of science, the "able" of "thinkable" or "visible" implies that the world in itself has an intrinsic relation to the thinking and seeing subject prior to the activity of thought or sight. Likewise, the world is "signifiable": before any art takes place, the universe lends itself to the artistic and creative function.[99] Does this not mean that the world itself is structured, that it possesses a prioris that are the basis of the order and beauty perceived both in science and art?

Artistic creativity, Robert holds, depends on an intrinsic relation between the a priori structures of nature as beautiful and a priori structures of the mind that perceives it as such. How is the correspondence of these two realities possible if each is independent and neither can be said to explain the other? As Descartes and Leibniz appealed to God as the guarantor of the correspondence of ideas and the real or as the giver of preestablished harmony, so Robert posits God as a "Third Reality" beyond nature or the mind to explain their coming together in the creation of artistic beauty.[100]

The idea of the Third Reality can be further specified, according to Robert. It is inadequate to think of it as being merely matter or nature, because it already implies spirit, since it "addresses" the artist on a spiritual level: it is the "voice" of inspiration. At the same time, Robert admits that the isomorphism between the mind and the world can in principle be explained on the basis of evolution: the mind naturally corresponds to and appreciates the structures of matter because it derives from them and is made by them precisely for their reception.[101] It is at least as rational, however, to choose a nonreductionist view and to see the foundation of artistic creation, as of knowledge in general, in an address to us by a personal Giver of meaning and beauty. In the last analysis, however, Robert holds that it is only by an act of free choice that we can espouse this position: it is reasonable, but not intellectually compelling.

Robert's second way to God, taking its starting point not in the act of creation but in the works of art, is unfortunately left as a mere "suggestion" whose development is sketched only briefly. There is, as St. Thomas says, a kind of knowledge that is born of love: we grasp the object to be known through first being conscious of the love that it excites in us. Great works of art bring the viewer or hearer to a feeling of joy, praise, and loss of self in love of Something: an ineffable reality that is manifest in the experience of beauty. Great art, in short, brings us to a disposition of adoration and love; in that state we already implicitly know the object of such acts, which can only be the supremely adorable Reality of God.[102] Once again, however, Robert holds that the acceptance of this explanation can only be the result of a free choice and personal engagement.

Robert offers a suggestive outline of the procedure that would have to be followed to complete his proposed approach. First, one would construct an "imaginary museum" of relevant works of art from all cultures. Second, one would have to discern the existential structures of lived experience that these works testify to, despite differences in culture, period, and so on. Robert believes that this examination would show that great art brings us to an experience of another world than that of sociobiological need and everyday life. There is a lived experience of unifying peace and joy that seems to originate outside the subject and that produces in the viewer or hearer a reaction of love and self-giving. The unnamed object of aesthetic experience is one of majesty and transcendence, and leads us to an attitude of adoration. While all of this could no doubt be explained on a purely psychological level, it is equally possible for the religiously engaged person to see it as evidence of the divine.

The third step in Robert's process would be to show that these lived experiences not only are a source of personal, affective knowledge of God but can, by reflection, become a source of theoretical knowledge. At this point it would be necessary to construct a metaphysical argument showing how the unity of the experience discerned, despite the multiplicity and radical contingency of the works themselves, gives one reason to posit a transcendent Beauty beyond the finite and contingent world.[103]

A Transcendental Approach Through Beauty?

Robert's approaches to God from beauty offer a number of fruitful suggestions and merit careful attention. At the same time, one may sense with regret that Robert has not fully carried through his project. In his way from artistic creativity, for example, he insists that the a prioris of mind and nature do not explain each other or depend on each other. But he does not really answer either the idealist (world depends upon mind) or the reductionist (mind is a function of matter) alternatives to his position. Rather, he appeals to an "option" without showing that this option is grounded, reasonable, and responsible.[104] There are also difficulties associated with the epistemological positions that seem to underpin Robert's approaches: he appears to accept a Cartesian mind-world dualism that is questionable on both philosophical and scientific grounds.

On the other hand, Robert's approach from aesthetic experience in general (although to some extent it shares the same problems mentioned above) offers the prospect of leading to a genuinely metaphysical argument. Unfortunately, Robert gives only an outline presentation of the tasks that such a procedure would have to accomplish. Furthermore, the metaphysical approach that he envisages seems to be a variant of the argument from the One and the Many. It is difficult to see how it would avoid the critical problems associated with the classical ways discussed earlier.

I would like to suggest that a more fruitful modern approach may be derived from the application to aesthetic experience of the transcendental method as developed by such thinkers as Coreth, Lotz, Rahner, and Lonergan. This method is able to take into account the critique of "philosophies of participation and presence" posed by modern thought and by its postmodern successors. It does not take for granted the principles of classical metaphysics and epistemology—for example, existence by participation and the analogy of being, which are the metaphysical correlates of the epistemological "principles" of sufficient reason and causality—but attempts rather to validate both metaphysics and epistemology in an "experiment" based first on the actual performance of the subject and then on the examination of its conditions of possibility.[105] Because it begins with a phenomenology of the subject in the act of knowing, this method avoids both positivistic reductionism, on the one hand, and the problems of Cartesian or Kantian dualism, on the other.

Transcendental Arguments for God

The efforts of theologians like Rahner and Lonergan to argue to the existence of God on this basis are well known. It may nevertheless be helpful to recapitulate the general structure of several arguments, emphasizing common points.

Rahner begins with the problematic nature of human being as "spirit in the world." The paradigm of being is not the kind of existence we observe in things, but what we know in ourselves: being as consciousness, self-presence, caring. But the human is not purely self-present being (spirit), in which there would be total identity of being and knowing; nor is it the defective form of being of mere material objects, which can be known, but lack knowledge and self-presence. It is a form of being that becomes itself through others, that reaches the level of spirit only through matter. As we have already seen, Rahner concludes that the condition of possibility for such a finite spirit—that is, a being that reaches the intelligible by abstraction from matter—is the pre-apprehension (*Vorgriff*) of the total horizon of being, the Absolute. Only in this perspective can we know ourselves and other finite beings, and know them precisely as having definite limits. This totality is unavoidably present to the mind and is implicitly known, albeit unthematically, because it is co-affirmed in every act of judgment and love.

From the thematic recognition of this flows the explicit knowledge of God. For the condition of possibility of the pre-apprehension of the totality of being is the existence of a being that corresponds to what is anticipated: unlimited (and therefore completely "luminous" or self-present) being. If such a being did not exist, the *Vorgriff* would anticipate "nothing." In fact, however, it anticipates a "more." In the act of making judgments of being and value we experience an excess (*excessus*) of meaning beyond every content we conceive. Hence it is not a matter of comparing the *ideas* of finite and infinite but of actively and unavoidably knowing the reality of the infinite as the condition for every finite reality.[106] This step of the argument is clearer in the writings of Rahner's contemporary, Johannes-Baptist Lotz. The "absolute being" (*das Absolute Sein*) that is anticipated as the horizon and condition of possibility of judgment is what the Scholastics called "common being"—not a subsistent reality, but a mental construct (what Lonergan calls a "heuristic notion"). But precisely because this absolute is not subsistent, in order to explain its absoluteness one must posit its condition of possibility; namely, the existence of a *subsistent* absolute (*das zweifach Absolute Sein*).[107] Such a being must be pure spirit (i.e., absolute identity of intelligibility and being, an absolute act of knowledge and love): what Rahner calls the ungraspable "Mystery of Being," or God.[108]

Lonergan's argument presupposes a detailed phenomenology and explanation of knowing, in the course of which it is shown that "the real" is what corresponds to intelligent and responsible judgment, rather than what is given in mere sense perception; that the working of the mind implies a dynamism toward complete intelligibility; and that (especially in scientific knowing) we employ heuristic structures to anticipate and discover what is yet unknown. Moreover, the act of judgment consists in the affirmation of something as "virtually unconditioned"; that is, as something whose reality depends on conditions that are in fact fulfilled. But every such affirmation presupposes the anticipation of a "formally unconditioned": that which simply and absolutely is. From this is derived the heuristic notion of "being" and the possibility of metaphysics.[109]

Lonergan formulates his argument for God's existence in a classical syllogism: "If the real is completely intelligible, then God exists. But the real is completely intelligible. Therefore, God exists."

Lonergan's reasoning is based on the premise that in every act of knowing, the mind implicitly intends (in the Scholastic sense of the term) the complete intelligibility of the real (i.e., what is known in correct judgments). Since the notion is so crucial to his argument, it may not be amiss here to attempt some clarification of Lonergan's position on "complete intelligibility." Lonergan does not say that we have complete intelligibility, or that we can grasp it, except as a heuristic notion (a notion intrinsic to all our knowledge); on the contrary, he insists that finite minds cannot attain such intelligibility. He does not say that the world or existence or life are completely intelligible; on the contrary, he points up the importance of inverse insights, which say we have encountered a point of no (further) intelligibility, and he insists on the presence of the "surd," the ultimately irrational, which exists materially and socially as well as intellectually. What Lonergan says is that inevitably, in all our knowing, we *intend* complete intelligibility (in the Scholastic sense: intellectually and/or affectively "go toward").

The mind therefore *knows* this intelligibility—not conceptually, but as implicitly and necessarily co-affirmed in the act of judgment. But such a complete intelligibility can only be if there exists the "Idea of Being," a spiritual act of intelligence that is total and infinite in its scope, understanding itself and, in itself, all other realities (Rahner's and Lotz's "complete identity of Spirit and being"). The Idea of Being must be spiritual and infinite because every material or finite spiritual intelligibility is of its nature incomplete. This complete spiritual Act of intelligibility is what is meant by God. God is thus seen as the interior ground of all that is knowable—that is, of all being: every act of knowing, actual or potential, exists or is possible because of this complete Act, and mediates Its presence.

J. L. Mackie puts an objection to Leibniz's argument from "sufficient reason" that is also relevant to Lonergan's argument from complete intelligibility:

> The principle of sufficient reason expresses a demand that things should be intelligible *through and through*. The simple reply to the argument which relies on it is that there is nothing that justifies this demand, and nothing that supports the belief that it is satisfiable even in principle.... If we reject this demand, we are not thereby committed to saying that things are utterly unintelligible. The sort of intelligibility that is achieved by successful causal inquiry and scientific explanation is not undermined by its inability to make things intelligible through and through. Any particular explanation starts with premises which state "brute facts," and although the brutally factual

starting-points of one explanation may themselves be further explained by another, the latter in turn will have to start with something that it does not explain, *and so on however far we go*. But there is no need to see this as unsatisfactory.[110]

But another skeptic, Leszek Kolakowski, recognizes and accepts the consequences of this "counterposition":

If the skeptics' arguments are valid, the idea of truth is indefensible, indeed meaningless. In order that something be true, a subject that cannot err has to exist. This subject has to be omniscient; we cannot conceive a subject that would possess a fragmentary knowledge but enjoy within this a perfect certitude. No partial truth can carry an absolute certitude unless it is related to the whole truth; otherwise the meaning of the partial truth must always remain in doubt: the owner of a partial truth can neither know how the truth beyond his reach might alter the sense of the truth he has taken possession of nor what the latter's scope of validity is. Thus, without the all-encompassing truth, there is no fragmentary one; and the all-encompassing truth presupposes an infinite omniscient intelligence.... I admit that the predicate "true" has no meaning unless referred to the all-encompassing truth, which is equivalent to an absolute mind ... either God or a cognitive nihilism, there is nothing in between.... [111]

... If he [the skeptic] is consistent, he has to get rid of the temptation to ascribe to his words any truth-value or cognitive meaning. His attitude is that no claims to truth are implied in speech acts.... Consequently, the skeptic's attitude is that we ought to stop worrying about how to justify the concept of truth and should instead abandon epistemological inquiry altogether, unless we can find access to an epistemological Absolute.[112]

But in Lonergan's view, one cannot abandon truth, either in practice or in theory. It can be shown that science and common sense inevitably make truth claims, and rightly do so; and thus their condition of possibility must also be real. But the recognition of this demands intellectual conversion concerning what knowledge is and what the real is. Moreover, Mackey's objection may hold against a rationalist position. But as we have seen, Lonergan's affirmation of "complete intelligibility" does not mean reality is intelligible "through and through," but that there is an ultimate intelligibility that grasps all that is, insofar as it is, and grounds the possibility of inverse (negative) as well as positive insight.

Lonergan warns that despite the simplicity of its syllogistic form, the "proof" of God's existence is difficult to grasp. There is "sufficient evidence" for the affirmation of the syllogism's minor premise, that the real is completely intelligible; but the grasp of that evidence presupposes not only intellectual "conversion" but also an arduous process of self-appropriation and philosophical formulation. Cognitional theory is difficult: it is hard for us to know what knowing is. It is particularly difficult to know what our knowledge of God is. Nevertheless, just as the act of knowing is prior to and easier than the analysis of knowledge, so our active knowledge of God is prior to and simpler than any philosophical efforts to formulate it. For even without any formulation of the heuristic notion of being, we are always in fact operating through it; and even without the explicit recognition of its implications, we implicitly and unthematically acknowledge the existence of God whenever we perform our higher cognitional operations.[113] The absolute is present to us as the co-affirmed condition of possibility of every act of self-transcendence in knowledge and love, even if we are not conceptually aware of its existence or explicitly deny it.[114]

Rahner's and Lonergan's approaches are based on an examination of the experience of knowing—for Lonergan, scientific knowing in particular. Rahner has more explicitly expanded the same line of thought to include the act of love. Hans Küng propounds a line of reasoning that, while not appealing explicitly to "transcendental method," applies a similar structure to our most basic stance toward existence.[115] Küng emphasizes that there is an element of option in the affirmation of God; hence he prefers to speak of "belief in" God[116] (although he also refers to this belief as a form of "knowledge" and "certainty").[117] In brief, Küng argues that only if God exists can we have a rationally grounded "fundamental trust" in reality. Every person must ultimately opt for such an act of trust, or must despair. If a positive option of trust is not only made but also affirmed as being rational and grounded in reality, then belief in God—an ultimate Truth and Goodness—is rationally justified. But finally one must affirm one's trust in meaning and value as grounded in reality, for otherwise one ends in self-contradiction and/or nihilism; there would be no reason for reasonableness itself. The intrinsic rationality of the positive option is experienced in the act of making it (although it cannot be demonstrated from "outside").[118] Hence the affirmation of God is rationally justified. Negatively, "denial of God implies an ultimately unjustified fundamental trust in reality. . . . If someone denies God, he does not know why he ultimately trusts in reality."[119] Atheism is not per se nihilism, but it has no defense against nihilism. Positively, "affirmation of God implies an ultimately justified fundamental trust in reality. As radical fundamental trust, belief in God can suggest the condition of possibility of uncertain reality. If someone affirms God, he knows why he can trust reality." By believing in God one does the absolutely most reasonable thing, and one experiences the reasonableness of one's trust.[120] (Although Küng does not do so, one could formulate his argument as an explicitly "transcendental" one: the real existence of God is the condition of possibility of a rationally justified fundamental trust in reality; i.e., the condition of possibility for the nonsubjective reality of intelligibility, meaning, and value. In the act of taking a positive stance toward existence, the reality of its transcendental condition of possibility is implicitly known and affirmed.)

The Ontology of Beauty: The Beautiful, the True, and the Good

In the light of these arguments we may now proceed to our question of a transcendental approach to God from the beautiful. If, as Coreth says, all the "proofs" for God's existence are simply explications of our fundamental "transcendental" experience, and can take as many forms as there are aspects to our finitude;[121] and if what we mean by "aesthetic experience" is more than a purely animal sensation of pleasure, but is (at least to some degree) the experience of the person as a whole, as a spiritual as well as a material being; then it should be possible to formulate a "transcendental" approach to God's existence that takes the fact of aesthetic experience as its starting point and finds God as the absolute and necessary condition of possibility of such experience.

To accomplish this, we should first attempt to determine, at least in a general way, the nature of beauty and its ontological meaning. That is, we shall ask what it is that connects beauty with the essence and/or with the perfection of being, so that it necessarily implies a relation to God. We may approach this topic by returning to the question of whether and in what sense beauty may be enumerated among the "transcendentals"; that is, the intelligible aspects of being expressed by notions that go beyond the "categories" used to designate particular beings or kinds of being, and that express what every being is, insofar as it exists;[122] that is, what all beings have in common by the very fact of their existence.

As we have seen, the transcendental status of beauty was generally accepted or presumed by medieval authors. But it was placed in question by later scholastic thinkers and was actively debated by neo-Thomists in the earlier part of the twentieth century. Some followed the aesthetics and philosophy of art stemming from German idealism (especially Schelling and Hegel),[123] and saw beauty in terms of the specifically sensible, material appearances of spirit; others saw it as an attribute of the finite world alone because it implies harmony, order, and hence diversity, as opposed to the unity and simplicity of God. Such perspectives naturally exclude the idea that beauty is a quality of being as such. Those who took this position included Cardinal Mercier; M. De Wulf; P. M. De Munnynck, O.P.; and E. De Bruyne. Others admitted beauty to transcendental status. Among these were A.-D. Sertillanges; V. Remer; J. Maritain; J. Wébert; J. Bittremieux.[124] A brief look at the positions of several representatives of Thomist thought will aid in clarifying the question concerning the metaphysical status of beauty.

A Thomist perspective that denies transcendental status to beauty is summarized by Jesús Iturrioz, S.J., in the summa of Scholastic philosophy published by the Jesuits of Spain.[125] Here beauty is seen not as a transcendental but as perfection of being.[126] That is, beauty is not an attribute of every being whatsoever, insofar as it exists (and therefore an attribute universally and analogously predicated), but is a quality that only some beings have, when certain qualities are present. Beings at a certain level of perfection acquire formal aesthetic value when they also possess the qualities of "splendor" and "light," by which they become actively able to be perceived by the normal person with aesthetic enjoyment.[127] The latter is defined as a kind of contemplation that brings a "superior" kind of satisfaction that differs from the pleasures of sense and the joy of attaining a goal or possessing a useful good. The aesthetic is a disinterested kind of joy, unconnected with concupiscence.[128] To be able to produce this effect, objects must have a degree of integrity and perfection, including truth and goodness, which above all confer "splendor."[129]

Modern Thomists who wished to enumerate "beauty" among the transcendentals were obliged to explain in what way it so functions, and how it is related to the usual triad. Suarez had held that if we speak exactly and avoid inventing any totally unnecessary distinctions, there are only three transcendentals: the one, the true, and the good.[130] In modern Thomism, the Louvain school attempted to heed Suarez's criticism of unnecessary conceptual distinctions by introducing a methodological consciousness to the derivation of the transcendental "properties" of being. Their procedure consisted of explaining the transcendentals in terms of how being must be conceived both in itself and in all possible relations. Using this method Louis De Raeymaeker enumerates the transcendentals according to the following schema:

A. Being considered absolutely (in itself):
  1. Negatively: every being is one or undivided (*indivisum*)
  2. Positively: every being is something (*res* or *essentia determinata*)
B. Being considered relatively:
  1. Negatively: every being is distinct from others ("*alius quid*" or *aliquid*)
  2. Positively: every being in relation to the soul, which by its faculties is open to knowledge and desire of everything,[131] is:
      a. In relation to intellect: true (*verum*)
      b. In relation to the will: good (*bonum*).[132]

Hence the transcendentals are five: *res, indivisum, aliquid, verum, bonum*. But the first three can be joined together and called "unity;" hence we arrive at Suarez's triad: the one, the true, and the good.[133]

Evidently, this schema does not name the beautiful as an intrinsic quality or relation of being. Nevertheless, De Raeymaeker considers beauty a transcendental and gives it separate treatment. Like Maritain, he sees beauty, not as an additional transcendental alongside the others, but as in some way designating their unity. The beautiful is "*bonum veri*": the goodness of truth. The definition of beauty is taken from St. Thomas: "*quod visum placet*" (that which pleases when it is seen).[134] But Thomas's "*visio*," according to De Raeymaeker, is to be taken metaphorically: it refers not to merely physical sight but to knowledge.[135] The sensible faculties (especially sight, hearing, and imagination) do indeed collaborate in the perception of beauty, but it is intellect that is essential.[136]

The beautiful differs from the transcendental "the true" in that "truth" designates simply the correspondence of the intellect with reality (*adaequatio rei et intellectus*). Beauty, on the other hand, designates this correspondence *qua delectabilis*: that is, insofar as it produces satisfaction or pleasure.[137] That is, beauty is truth considered under the aspect of its lovability or desirability: it is the goodness of the dynamism of the intellect (*bonum tendentiae intellectivae*).[138] Thus, like Cajetan, De Raeymaeker considers beauty to be a form of the good: "*Pulchrum est quaedam boni species.*" However, beauty differs from the transcendental "the good" insofar as it refers to a specific good—namely, the good of the intellect. As St. Thomas says, "the beautiful" adds to "goodness" an ordering toward knowledge.[139] But since the intelligible as the object of the mind is called "truth," beauty may be called "the goodness of truth" (*bonitas veri* or *bonum veri*);[140] that is, truth insofar as it is a good for the knower.[141] It follows that there is no special "faculty" for the perception of beauty: the intellect in knowing enjoys its own act.[142] If the term "good" is taken not transcendentally but rather psychologically, then we must say that "goodness," as the formal object of the will, is distinguished from beauty, which is an object of the intellect. De Raeymaeker quotes from St. Francis de Sales: "Beauty and goodness, although they have something in common, are nevertheless not the same thing: for the good is what pleases the appetite and the will, while beauty is what pleases understanding and knowledge. Or, in other terms, goodness is what delights us in our enjoyment of it, while beauty is what pleases us through our knowledge of it."[143] Beauty may also be described as the "splendor" or refulgence of order or of the truth (*splendor ordinis, splendor veritatis*), since the highest and most delightful act of intellection is synthetic comprehension, in which such order is contemplated.[144]

Fernand Van Steenberghen proposes a derivation of the transcendentals according to a schema similar to De Raeymaeker's, based on the "relations" of being:

A. In its relations of opposition, being is:
    1. Intrinsically: in opposition to any diversity or multiplicity it may contain; hence being is undivided, or internally one
    2. Extrinsically: in opposition to nothingness, and only to nothingness; hence being is distinct and determinate
B. In its relations of agreement, being is:
    1. Intrinsically: identical to itself (a purely logical relation)
    2. Extrinsically:
        a. In relation to all other beings: similar
        b. In relation to intellect: intelligible
        c. In relation to will: lovable[145]

Van Steenberghen notes that his attribute of distinctness or determination corresponds to the usual scholastic term *aliquid vel infinitum* ("something or the infinite"—with the latter term added in order to include God within "being" and yet not imply limitation). He eliminates the normal transcendental *"res vel essentia"* (a thing or essence) because he considers it to be identical with *ens* (being); and he adds "similarity" as a transcendental that St. Thomas did not notice.[146]

In confronting the question of whether beauty is an intrinsic attribute of being, Van Steenberghen disagrees with those who deny its transcendental status, making beauty an attribute of the finite world alone. For him, beauty is indeed a metaphysical quality and value. On the other hand, he thinks that Maritain and his followers are mistaken in attempting to confer on beauty a distinct conceptual status as a transcendental through the notion of *splendor veri*. Beauty is a transcendental quality because it is identical with the good; it is not another attribute of being distinct from its lovability.[147] The human appetite has many values, corresponding to the various dimensions of existence. To our biological needs correspond the goods needed for physical survival; to the desire for mastery over the world corresponds the value of *techné;* to the drive toward possession and well-being correspond material goods; to the desire to know corresponds the value of truth; to the finality of the person as such correspond moral values; and to the aesthetic dynamism corresponds the value of beauty, the harmony of things. But on the metaphysical level of discourse, all the distinctions between the various kinds of goods vanish. We are left with only two terms: the intellectual appetite (or "will") and its object, intelligible being (which, insofar as appetible, is called "the good"). Moreover, says Van Steenberghen, the desirability of being as being and the desirability of being as true coincide: there are not for the will as such two different ways of enjoyment of what is, but only one way—namely, through intellectual apprehension.[148] It is thus the desirability or lovability of being that is the foundation for all values whatsoever—that is, "the good" in all its forms as particular "goods." The moral good and the beautiful are the higher spiritual forms of the polymorphous "good."[149]

The Louvain school's concern for method and its turn to the subject as the foundation of metaphysics are echoed and further developed by the transcendental Thomist philosophers Lotz and Coreth. Conscious of Heidegger's "ontological difference," these insist on finding the character of being first in the subject's conscious performance of attaining self-identity (*Bei-sich-Sein*), rather than in the being of objects. Unity, truth, and goodness are seen as those determinations of being that are necessarily and unthematically co-posited as the conditions of possibility of the subject's attainment of self-identity and value through the performance of questioning, knowing, and willing. These "transcendentals" are identical with being as being: for those things that are not self-present have these qualities analogously insofar as they are able to be known and desired.[150]

Both Lotz and Coreth place beauty among the transcendentals, and like Maritain see it as in some way designating their unity. "Beauty, as the state of perfection and perfect harmony of unity, truth, and goodness, constitutes a transcendental along with these three," writes Lotz. "This description holds good for what is perceptible by the senses and still more for what can be contemplated spiritually."[151]

Coreth considers at greater length the sense in which beauty signifies the unity of truth and goodness, and hence occupies a unique place among the transcendentals. Beginning from St. Thomas's brief definitions ("*Pulchra . . . dicuntur, quae visa placent*"; "*pulchrum dicitur id, cuius ipsa apprehensio placet*"),[152] Coreth explains that the beautiful is a good—that is, something lovable and worth seeking, whose attainment brings satisfaction. But, differently from the notion of "the good" in general, as conceptually distinct from truth, the notion of beauty includes in itself an element proper to the latter. For beauty corresponds to a striving toward and finding satisfaction in the contemplation of an object. Hence, what brings completion to the dynamism toward beauty is something knowable, a "truth."

However, not every act of knowing is such that it mediates an experience of beauty. A purely conceptual, logical, discursively rational knowledge does not grasp the beauty of what is known, but only a contemplative vision that is absorbed in the object and takes pleasure in it. What characterizes the experience of beauty is not the mediation of thought but the immediacy of "vision" or intuition (*Anschauung*).[153] This does not mean, on the other hand, that the concept of beauty is restricted to the sphere of the sensible: a metaphysical or religious truth can also be experienced as "beautiful." A person can be immersed in such realities and find in them exaltation and inner satisfaction—not, indeed, though a purely ra-

tionally mediated knowledge of their truth, but through the immediacy of contemplative appreciation. Coreth holds that we may speak of spiritual as well as
sensible "intuition" (*Anschauung*). Indeed, every genuinely human sensible intuition
is carried out by spirit and is connected to a spiritual, intuitive (*intuitive*) act of
knowledge.[154] Expanding on Coreth's thought, we might say that such a spiritual
"vision" or "intuition" is possible to the extent that the subject's knowledge is not
merely conceptual ("notional") and objective, but is personal and includes a change
in the subject's own reality. In Lonergan's terminology, the subject "appropriates"
these realities and experiences a "connaturality" to them in him or herself. In this
way ethical goodness, virtue, and holiness can be experienced as "beautiful" in a
proper and not merely transferred sense. The spiritual "vision" of these realities
can produce in the subject the satisfaction, joy, exaltation, and sense of "giftedness"
that characterize beauty. Likewise, then, God may also be called properly "beautiful," the source and perfection of beauty.[155]

Coreth concludes that the conceptual distinction of the transcendental "the
beautiful" from "the true" and "the good" lies precisely in the fact that the notion
of beauty has no proper "content" of its own: its essence consists rather in the
unity of truth and goodness. Hence the beautiful is the true, insofar as in truth a
fulfilled striving comes to satisfaction; the beautiful is the good, insofar as the good
consists in the fulfillment of an act of contemplative knowledge. "The beautiful
is thus a truth, insofar as the latter is one with the good; it is a good, insofar as
the latter is one with the true. And in this sense beauty is the specific expression
of the unity of all the transcendentals: the unity of truth and goodness is beauty."[156]

Bernard Lonergan's account of the transcendentals reflects an even more radical methodological concern. Lonergan insists on the dependence of metaphysical
terms on a prior cognitional theory. Hence "being" is described in terms of knowing, rather than vice versa,[157] and the faculty psychology of the neo-Scholastics is
replaced by intentionality analysis. Accordingly, the transcendentals are derived
from the different levels of human intentionality.

Lonergan distinguishes between transcendental notions, transcendental precepts, and transcendental concepts. A "notion" in Lonergan's sense of the word is
a spontaneously operative heuristic anticipation.[158] The "transcendental notions,"
then, are identical with "the very dynamism of our conscious intending."[159] They
constitute the heuristic pre-apprehension of the totality that grounds our capacity
for self-transcendence by questioning and intending (in the Scholastic sense). They
direct the spirit to its goals and also "provide the criteria that reveal whether the
goals are being reached."[160] Their plurality corresponds to the different activities
that characterize the progressive levels of intentionality: understanding, reflection,
deliberation.[161]

These notions are the spontaneous structured dynamism of consciousness,
through which it is "open" to reality. They are operative in the imperatives that
are formulated as the "transcendental precepts": "Be attentive, Be intelligent, Be
reasonable, Be responsible."[162] And when the goals of these activities are objectified,
we arrive at the "transcendental concepts" (the "transcendentals" in the traditional
sense): "if we objectify the content of intelligent intending, we form the transcendental concept of the intelligible. If we objectify the content of reasonable intend-

ing, we form the transcendental concepts of the true and the real. If we objectify the content of responsible intending, we get the transcendental concept of value, of the truly good."[163] Since for Lonergan "the real" is equivalent to "being,"[164] his list of transcendental concepts (intelligibility, the true, the real, value or the truly good) corresponds exactly to the traditional transcendentals (the one, the true, being, the good). The difference in order is significant of Lonergan's conviction that cognitional theory must be methodologically prior to metaphysics (and hence the notion of intelligibility prior to that of being).

It is worthwhile once more to call attention to the difference in method between Lonergan and the neo-Scholastics treated earlier. While the latter presume a schema of metaphysical "faculties" (i.e., "intellect" and "will") to which "being" is related (giving the transcendentals of "truth" and "goodness"), Lonergan begins instead with a phenomenology of cognitional activities whose later levels presuppose and "sublate" the earlier, and sees the transcendentals as objectifications of the whole range of questions that can be asked on each level. For this reason the "unity" of being is seen in terms of "intelligibility"; what we mean by saying that being is "one" is that it is graspable as an intelligible whole.[165]

Lonergan does not deal with the relation of beauty to the transcendentals. We might, however, attempt to do so in the light of his method and categories. Beauty would seem to be a kind of value, corresponding to the fourth level of conscious intentionality, that of responsibility. Lonergan's description of this level—and hence of the concept of "the good"—concentrates on the active and ethical dimension: "There is the *responsible* level on which we are concerned with ourselves, our own operations, our goals, and so deliberate about possible courses of action, evaluate them, decide, and carry out our decisions."[166] But while the level of rational and responsible self-consciousness clearly involves a dimension of "doing,"[167] freedom is also a matter of determining our mode of being, our "stance" toward the world. On a deeper level than that of individual choices, we dispose of ourselves and determine our way of "being toward" the world, even if we do not act outwardly; we determine what it is we may responsibly love as well as what we will do because of that love.[168] The transcendental "notion" corresponding to "value" therefore implies more than the question, "what must I do?" It includes also the more basic question about the intrinsic "worth" or lovability of beings and of being: the quality that might be called their "beauty."

To speak of "beauty" in this connection is to introduce a perspective different from the primarily conceptual/ethical one of Lonergan's treatment. However, even here Lonergan's categories may be helpful. He recognizes that minds may act reasonably and responsibly in different "patterns of experience": diverse centers of attention, purpose, and interest.[169] He lists several such patterns: biological, dramatic, aesthetic, intellectual, practical, worshipful.[170] In each of these, all four levels of conscious intentionality—and hence all the transcendental "notions" and precepts that promote genuine self-transcendence—are operative, but in varying life contexts.

Lonergan's primary treatment of the aesthetic pattern is brief and fairly narrowly conceived.[171] Significantly, he identifies the focus of the aesthetic as delight, joy in existence.[172] He associates it primarily with art, which raises to a new and creative level the "spontaneous joy of conscious living."[173] But if the aesthetic pattern is post-biological, Lonergan nevertheless sees it as prescientific and pre-philosophical: "it may strain for truth and value without defining them."[174] For the present purpose, I suggest conceiving the aesthetic pattern more broadly: as a way of functioning intellectually and responsibly that centers on the contemplation, appropriation, and appreciation of the objects of the notions of intelligibility, truth, and value, rather than on the process of attaining them; and that therefore sees the fulfillment of these drives in terms of the joy and delight it brings rather than simply as an imperative or "precept." So conceived, the aesthetic pattern is complementary to Lonergan's "intellectual" pattern and "practical" patterns. In Lonergan's descriptions these center on "detached" scientific discursive reasoning and ethical activity, while what I am calling the "aesthetic" emphasizes the involvement of personal fulfillment, the joy that underlies even "pure" intellectual commitment; there is an aesthetic element even in the scientific and philosophical quests for truth and value.

In this perspective, "beauty" may be seen to have transcendental status: "the beautiful" is the name of the transcendental "value" when the latter is experienced in the aesthetic pattern. We judge something to be beautiful when we find it in accord with (the fulfillment of) some dynamism of our being: physical, cultural, spiritual. Objectively, beauty is the order of reason in things, their truth and goodness, their "rightness"[175]—that is, their intelligibility, their accord with the dynamism of the human person toward being and being-well. What characterizes it precisely as "beautiful" is the predominance of the note of fulfillment, and hence the stance of appreciation or complaisance. It should be noted that the terms used here do not imply total satisfaction, and are of a different order from merely physical enjoyment. As we have seen above, Iturrioz insists that the experience of beauty is a complacence of a "superior order" that has nothing in common with sensible pleasures like sweet odor, heat, comfort, nor with the joy of attaining a goal, nor with the satisfaction of possessing a useful good. Aesthetic appreciation is disinterested (cf. Kant) and without concupiscence.[176] In the broader view of beauty as a transcendental that I am exploring here, the disjunction of beauty from these other forms of good is not so absolute; there is an overlapping of values. Although the aesthetic pattern, as I conceive it here, is not necessarily totally "disinterested" experience, it is nevertheless in some way "ecstatic" or other centered. At the same time, there is "fulfillment" even in the most disinterested experience of beauty, because there is in the finite spirit an inherent dynamism toward the "other" as such. To that extent the human is "fulfilled" precisely in the loss of self in the other. Hence there is a dialectical quality to the enjoyment of beauty. As Gunther Pöltner notes, beauty as "presence" is satisfying; but as presence *of meaning*, it awakens further desire (*Sehnsucht*).[177]

The transcendental "notion" of beauty is the pre-apprehension of being insofar as it is lovable; the object of responsible decision, insofar as this is the fulfillment of existence. Beauty is distinguished conceptually from "value" seen as the moral good because of its contemplative and appreciative perspective. As Iturrioz, following Kant, puts it: the beautiful has the "form" of finality, without the representation of finality[178] (while virtue, or the moral good, explicitly represents finality; but having, as Gadamer says, no "light" of its own, it is easily confused with appearances).[179] To speak of the "beautiful" is to bring out a certain aspect of the good—namely, the joy of existence that is intrinsic to it. Beauty is value considered, not under the aspect of what is to be done, but simply regarded "in itself," which is also to say as the satisfaction of the dynamism of intentionality. "Beauty" is form, truth, and virtue seen in the perspective of their intrinsic relation to joy.

It should be noted again that in Lonergan's "intentionality analysis" the level of decision or rational self-consciousness presupposes and sublates the previous levels of experience, understanding, and judgment.[180] Hence "value" already includes the transcendentals of intelligibility and truth. Therefore this account of beauty, although methodologically different, is in fundamental agreement with Coreth's and Lotz's idea of beauty as the union of the true and the good, or the earlier neo-Scholastic conception of beauty as the "splendor" and "goodness" of the truth.

Similarly, philosopher Günter Pöltner of the University of Vienna speaks of beauty as "truth" in its self-presentation as freeing and as bestowing happiness. Hence beauty is not merely a quality of being but is that quality as capable of being experienced in the *Dasein* and *Sosein* of things, apart from their usefulness.[181] (In difference to Pöltner, however, I would include in the definition of beauty a certain kind of "usefulness," although at another, analogous level.) Moreover, the perception of beauty is intrinsic to the recognition of meaning: beauty signifies "that Being is not merely a neutral being-at-hand, but that Being and meaning are radically one."[182]

So conceived, the beautiful may also be related to the personalist category of "being in love" as it appears in Lonergan's later writings. Beauty is the quality of an object or person that calls us and permits us to be responsibly in love. Indeed, Viennese philosopher Augustinus Wucherer-Huldenfeld remarks that our *original* encounter with beauty is in the people we love and who love us: in love itself. Beauty perceived in nature and in art must ultimately be placed in the context of personal meaning and interpersonal encounter.[183]

In this perspective, "beauty" is what we call goodness or value (of various kinds) when its lovability becomes evident. "Beauty has the mode of being of light. . . . It makes itself manifest."[184] When its intrinsic worth is perceived, its value takes possession of us as worthy of commitment. In this sense beauty does not correspond to either of the "faculties" as traditionally conceived, but to the "heart."[185] As with value in general, beauty normally operates first on the implicit level, as "falling in love," and only subsequently (if at all) on the level of explicitly rational evaluation, judgment, and decision. As the Greeks held, the distinguishing characteristic of the beautiful is "that it draws directly to itself the desire of the human soul."[186] By extension, beauty as a transcendental may be seen as the "evidence" in the object (even prior to its actual perception) that can validate the implicit judgment of value that occurs in being in love, and that enables the latter to be a responsible stance.

This position is in agreement with the Thomist emphasis on beauty as splendor, clarity, and so on: beauty is not merely "the good" considered abstractly as existent *in se*, but the good as evident or perceivable. If we speak of beauty as a transcendental, then we must say that this "perceivability" and "enjoyability" is intrinsic to beings—in the same way as their knowability or intelligibility. Just as in the latter case, the actual perception of a particular beauty depends on conditions in the perceiver. On the other hand, it would also make perfect sense to restrict the meaning of the word "beauty" to what is perceivable and enjoyable precisely because it has particular qualities. Such qualities on the physical level might be, for example, characteristics that correspond to certain a priori structures of human bodiliness and psyche. For example, humans might be predisposed to find certain visual or auditory proportions "beautiful" because they correspond well to the way our senses work; or because they correspond to natural rhythms (e.g., the heart-beat) or to the proportions of the body; or because of genetically inherited psychic dispositions that may at some time have been connected with evolutionary advan-tage (for example, the sexual implications of the attributes generally associated with a beautiful male or female body, or the parental instinct evoked by the perception of vulnerability in children); or because of our preconditioning by cul-turally established norms; or because of a complex and ultimately indefinable com-bination of such factors.

The commitment mediated through beauty is seen not merely as a duty but also as somehow involved in our personal fulfillment through orientation to the other. As we have seen, this orientation has both an erotic and an ecstatic dimen-sion: the beautiful is what is perceived as lovable for its own sake; at the same time, the loving of it (for and in itself) satisfies a need in our being. (Naturally, these two elements may be present in very different proportions in any particular case of the judgment of beauty. Anticipating a theme of the final chapter, we may also remark that when this larger context of beauty is lost, then there appears the danger of an "aestheticism" that consists in experience or enjoyment without per-sonal commitment, hence divorced from the dynamism of morality and religion.)

To say that beauty is a transcendental notion and concept is to affirm that everything that exists is "objectively" lovable, to some degree: all being is worthy of our commitment, corresponds at some level to our dynamism toward value. Naturally, this does not mean that all things are equally beautiful, or are beautiful in the same regard, or that there is nothing that is (sensually or spiritually) banal or ugly, or the pursuit of a particular beauty is always morally good (indeed, I shall later argue that the pursuit of beauty may be an escape from or refusal of the good); but it means that "even the tedious and ugly contains a remnant of beauty, the complete extinction of which would be equivalent to the destruction of the being in question."[187]

Beauty is value, truth, and intelligibility insofar as they produce joy in their perception and/or contemplation. They do so because the perception of form, or intelligibility (which is also the condition for truth and value), fulfills the basic orientation of finite spirit, a condition of its well-being. In this sense, beauty is intrinsic to being: everything that exists has "form," in the sense of intelligibility and entelechy; and the perception of that form can produce satisfaction to the spirit at some level. (The sorting out of the kinds and levels of beauty leads to the formulation of "aesthetics" in the narrower sense, and also poses the problem of the relationship between beauty and the moral good: a topic to which we shall return in the last chapter.)

Beauty and the Joy of Existence

The preceding discussion makes it clear that there are two distinct ways of using the term "beauty": one that sees it as a transcendental, ontological concept and another that uses it as a categorical term designating certain definable characteristics (although exactly what these are may be debated). We may use "beauty" as a transcendental concept of universal extension, in which case it is ultimately identical with "goodness" and "truth." In that case, we must distinguish carefully between different kinds of beauty. Or, on the other hand, we may delimit the extension of the term "beauty," strictly distinguishing its referent from such other values as virtue, holiness, sublimity, and glory, and using another term (e.g., "the good") to designate what all of these have in common as realizations of the spiritual drives of the human person. From a philosophical point of view, the inclusion of beauty among the transcendentals serves as a corrective to the frequently objectivizing and/or exclusively ethical emphases of metaphysical treatments of "the good," especially under the influence of Kantian thought.[188] It is a reminder that our prime experience of being is that found in consciousness: being as "luminosity," self-presence. Such being is not affectively "neutral"; it comports an element of "being toward" and "being well," or complaisance in being. On the other hand, from the point of view of aesthetics as the study of art and its norms, the use of "beauty" as a metaphysical term may merely add confusion, for what art seeks as "beauty" is not a universally present good, but particular qualities that are distinct from and above the ordinary.

In the last analysis it is not necessary for present purposes to decide in favor of one or another of these semantic positions; it suffices to note their contrast. The two positions may be summarized briefly and schematically:

1. Beauty is a category naming a perfection of being—that is, it is a quality that only certain beings possess. Within this position there are subdistinctions based on the extension of the word. Beauty may be taken as a perfection:

   a. Only of things known through sensation.
   b. Only of finite realities, spiritual and moral as well as sensible.
   c. Of finite beings and of the infinite.

In the first two cases, the nature of beauty is found in the order and harmony of things and their agreement with the human spirit and senses. Since such qualities, even when not material, imply difference and thus finitude, beauty is neither a quality of being as such nor, strictly speaking, an attribute of God (although, like other finite qualities, it may be used metaphorically of God). In the third case, beauty is an attribute of God, but not of all beings, since it designates a certain degree of perfection in form or goodness.

2. Beauty is a transcendental:

   a. Identical with the good.
   b. Conceptually distinct from the good.

In either of these cases, beauty is analogously predicated of God and of all beings, in their varying degrees.

What is of interest to our discussion is that there are certain essential notes common to the idea of "the beautiful," whether it be conceived as a transcendental or as a perfection found only in certain beings. In these notes we must find the quality of "beauty" that makes it a perfection of being and that links it implicitly to a ground and goal of being, or God.

A key to what this quality is may be found in a statement in Pasternak's classic, *Doctor Zhivago*. The author writes of the novel's protagonist (who is significantly both a physician and a poet): "he once again verified and noted that art always serves beauty, and beauty is delight in the possession of form, and form is the organic key to life, [since] every living thing must possess form in order to exist; and in that way art, including tragedy, always recounts the joy of existence."[189]

As we have seen, aesthetic theory does not universally share Zhivago's conviction that art always serves beauty, but for the moment this is immaterial. Clearly there are experiences of beauty, at least in some art, as well as in nature. (It is not important whether we accept the Kantian distinction that would call nature "sublime" rather than "beautiful," as long as we recognize an analogy between the terms.) What is relevant in Zhivago's (and presumably Pasternak's) view is the conviction that what is crucial to such experiences is "delight in form"—and hence the conclusion that the essence of aesthetic experience is to be found in the affirmation of the joy of existence. We find here an echo—albeit probably an unconscious one—of St. Thomas, for whom the beautiful is that which has form (which is also *claritas*, luminosity: hence also intelligibility and being), insofar as it is apprehended with delight.[190]

Naturally, when we speak of the joy of existence we are immediately made aware of the various levels and kinds of aesthetic experience, from the purely sensuous to the deeply spiritual. If beauty can have a transcendental referent (either by analogy or by metaphor), then it—and the "joy" it inspires—will be predicated on the basis of similarities in difference. It is possible, of course, to experience a joyous apprehension on the level of simple sensible pleasure. To speak of "beauty," however, implies that there is also a dimension of aesthetic experience that goes beyond the sort of pleasure that we (apparently) share with the higher animals: a joy that is specifically human, like our ability to laugh and to cry (which are intimately associated with it). Such an experience involves a spiritual act of the person. Even if "beauty" is conceived narrowly as a characteristic of sensation, it implies finding in such experiences elements like harmony, order, and form, which are related to the transcendental values of unity, intelligibility, goodness. Beauty is, then, as in the Hegelian aesthetic, the material "expression" of spirit.[191] At this level we are dealing not merely with pleasure but also with the a priori dynamism toward that element of being we anticipate as "value," and subjectively experience as being-well.

This is to suggest that at least some kinds of aesthetic experience do not remain on a merely passive or merely sensible level. Such experience, although it begins in the senses, involves a spiritual reaction akin to the "wonder" that Aristotle claims is the beginning of philosophy;[192] and it invites the person to an intelligent and free act in which the self recognizes and is "given over" to the joy of existence, or allows itself to be "grasped" by it, in its universal extension. In this sort of aesthetic experience Balthasar's words quoted above would be true: "The form as it appears to us is beautiful only because the delight that it arouses in us is founded upon the fact that, in it, the truth and goodness of the depths of reality are manifested and bestowed, and this manifestation and bestowal reveal themselves to us as being something infinitely and inexhaustibly valuable and fascinating."[193]

Analysis of this kind of experience of the beautiful reveals that the rejoicing in existence (or in "form") that characterizes it is simultaneously tied to an acute awareness of finitude: the gratuitous joy of beauty and its delight in form arise precisely out of contrast with the abyss of nonbeing experienced in the fragile, threatened character of human existence, for which it is possible not to be. This contrast with a radical negation—even if present only implicitly—reveals why the potential object of delight in form is ultimately co-extensive with all existence—that is, with all that has "form" and being and is thus over against nothingness. It also explains why the experience of beauty, even if it is characterized as a "recounting" of the joy of existence,[194] can have many different emotional shadings (including sadness) and ethical/aesthetic modes (including tragedy).

This is why the "delight" of the beautiful can at the same time frequently be poignant, perhaps even to the point of bordering on pain: it is accompanied by the realization of finitude, with its threat of annihilation, and feels the spirit's rebellion in its acute, aching longing to be.[195] Maritain quotes a well-known passage from Baudelaire's *L'Art Romantique:*

> it is this immortal instinct for the beautiful which makes us consider the earth and its various spectacles as a sketch of, as a *correspondence* with, heaven. The insatiable thirst for all that is beyond, and which life reveals, is the most living proof of our immortality. It is at once through poetry and *across* poetry, through and *across* music, that the soul glimpses the splendors situated beyond the grave; and when an exquisite poem brings tears to the eyes, these tears are not proof of an excess of joy, they are rather the testimony of an irritated melancholy, a demand of the nerves, of a nature exiled in the imperfect and desiring to take possession immediately, even on this earth, of a revealed paradise.[196]

Much the same idea underlies this passage on aesthetic experience by J. W. N. Sullivan:

> At such moments one suddenly sees everything with new eyes; one feels on the brink of some great revelation. It is as if we caught a glimpse of some incredibly beautiful world that lies silently about us all the time. I remember vividly my first experience of the kind when, as a boy, I came suddenly upon the quiet miracle of an ivy-clad wall glistening under a London street-lamp. I wanted to weep and I wanted to pray; to weep for the Paradise from which I had been exiled, and to pray that I might yet be made worthy of it.[197]

Similarly, Friedrich von Schlegel associates the apprehension of beauty with our "fearful unsatisfied desire to soar into infinity."[198]

On the other hand, the beautiful puts us in contact not only with our deep desire to be and our attraction to the ultimate but also with our fear of what transcends our present horizon. Rilke writes in his first Duino elegy:

> Who, if I cried out, would hear me among the angelic orders? And even if one of them suddenly pressed me against his heart, I should fade in the strength of his stronger existence. For Beauty is nothing but the beginning of Terror we're still just able to bear, and why we are so in awe of it is because it serenely disdains to annihilate us. Every single angel is terrible.[199]

But even in the face of existential anxiety and suffering, beauty testifies to the more fundamental nature of joy. A striking testimony is found in the fourth movement of Mahler's Third Symphony, marked *misterioso*, in the setting of Nietzsche's *Mitternachtslied*, quoted at the beginning of this chapter. The same point is made by Pasternak when he writes of Zhivago: "Now, as never before, it was clear to him that art always and unceasingly is concerned with two things. It relentlessly meditates on death and thus relentlessly creates life. Great, genuine art is what is like the Apocalypse of St. John, and continues its revelation."[200] In a similar vein, but in more philosophical language, Paul Ricoeur writes of human "affective fragility":

> If being is that which beings are not, anguish is the feeling *par excellence* of ontological difference. But Joy attests that we have a part of us linked to this very lack of being in beings. That is why the Spiritual Joy, the Intellectual Love, and the Beatitude, spoken of by Descartes, Malebranche, Spinoza, and Bergson, designate, under different names and in different philosophic contexts, the only affective 'mood' worthy of being called *ontological*. Anguish is only its underside of absence and distance.
>
> If man is capable of Joy, of Joy in and through anguish, that is the radical principle of all "disproportion" in the dimension of feeling and the source of man's *affective fragility*.[201]

Ideally, we might attempt to illustrate these reflections by constructing Robert's "imaginary museum" or an "imaginary concert hall" and seeking to evoke and describe concrete instances of the effect of classic beauty on the mind.[202] In the next chapter, I shall in a modest way make some suggestions in this direction. But to cite further examples at this point would lead too far from the line of argument. I must instead appeal directly to the reader's personal experiences of beauty. The phenomenological moment of transcendental method can do no more than offer "signposts" that may aid in the subject's rational self-appropriation— in this case, as an aesthetic subject—through the heightening of experience. Do the reflections formulated in the preceding paragraphs correspond to experience? If these suggestions do evoke an experience of the beautiful that can be qualified as "spiritual," then it becomes possible to ask: what is the condition of possibility of this kind of experience—one in which the human subject affirms beauty and in doing so both rejoices in and feels the limits of his or her own finite being?

The Transcendental Condition of Beauty

My suggestion is that this question may make explicit another avenue of access to the "transcendental" way of affirmation of God's existence. I propose that the condition of possibility for the experience of beauty—in the sense of the joyous affirmation of the "form" or desirable intelligibility of existence, even in its finite limitation—is the implicit and unavoidable co-affirmation of ultimate Beauty, a reality the apprehension of which would be unmixed and unlimited joy in existence, and which in itself—that is, as self-apprehending—is self-conscious Beauty or infinite Bliss.

The idea that God is infinite bliss is, of course, a part of the classical Western tradition, yet it seems sometimes to be lost both in theology and in our imaginative representations of the Deity. Perhaps this is in part because, in order to underline its ethical imperative, Western religion has frequently emphasized God's justice and anger with the sinful world (an angry person is by definition not happy). This in turn is a natural result of the idea that God is engaged in a historical "dialogue" with the world, in which our responses "make a difference" to God. It would seem to follow (at least to projective imaginative thinking) that God, like us, cannot finally be happy until the eschaton. Thus God's "bliss" appears accidental: a state of being that God must attain, rather than an essential element in the meaning of the word "God." But my contention is that beauty points to the fact that being is in essence joyous: self-presence with delight. And the condition of possibility for finite beauty is the existence of the Beautiful as such.

This conclusion is revealed in the dialectic of fullness and longing in the spiritual experience of beauty: being is seen as capable of being apprehended with joy, worthy of giving oneself over to in affirmation and love. Yet this same being— both the being that is apprehended and the being of the one apprehending—is always limited, finite, marked with nonbeing and bearing the memory of death. In itself it appears incapable of supporting a total affirmation of the joy of existence. But the aesthetic act is possible and real because finite being in its apprehension by spirit is borne by its source and goal, which is "co-apprehended" with it—not in a separate act, alongside it, but rather as what is interior to categorical being and to the apprehending mind.

As in other forms of the "transcendental" argument, the critical point is that this ultimate reality is not conceived or projected as a transcendental idea, but is co-affirmed as actual in the very act of aesthetic joy.[203] The act of commitment to the reality of finite beauty is at the same time given implicitly and unavoidably to the reality of the Absolute. That reality may subsequently be explicated by reason as the condition of the reality of our factual experience, or it may be explicitly denied. In the latter case, the reality of our experience itself is undermined, and our joy becomes groundless and (to that extent) illusory. (It must be recalled at this point that the "joy" in question is distinct from simple sensible aesthetic "pleasure," which may as such remain unaffected by the existence of an ultimate "Ground" of beauty. On another level, the very existence of sensation—as of any being or act at all—calls for metaphysical explanation. This, however, involves a different set of categories than the aesthetic.) To phrase the argument in terms parallel to Hans Küng's: just as the affirmation of the existence of God is the only possible final ground for a fully rational act of fundamental trust in existence,[204] so it is likewise essential to an ultimately "grounded" apprehension of beauty, insofar as this implies the joy of existence.

It will be noted that each "transcendental" line of thinking arrives at God precisely as the fullness of the spiritual quality with which it begins and for which it seeks the condition of possibility. Thus Lonergan argues that if the real is completely intelligible, then God exists; he therefore arrives at God as the totally unconditioned act of intelligibility, or the "Idea of Being."[205] Kant argues (in the sphere of "practical reason") that if the good is an absolute "ought"—if there is a categorical imperative—then there exists an absolute Will. Similarly, the line of thinking I have pursued here argues that if finite existence can be apprehended with joy, it is because reality in its wholeness—in its various degrees of realization—can be and is to be apprehended with joy; and that this is possible only on the condition that there exists the absolute Act of such apprehension. It thus arrives at God as subsistent, self-conscious Beauty.

The reasoning in the last step of this process is similar, on the one hand, to Lonergan's argument leading to the subsistent Idea of Being, and, on the other hand, to the Platonic-Augustinian ascent of the mind. In higher aesthetic experience we pre-apprehend an unconditional beauty, a complete ground for joy in existence. But the finite beautiful cannot be unconditioned. Material beauty is merely potential, since it must be apprehended by mind. Spiritual beauty—the beauty of the apprehending mind itself, in the aesthetic act—cannot be total or unconditional: first, because it is (and feels itself) incomplete; second, because it depends upon material conditions outside itself; third, because, being spatio-temporal, it is impermanent and is concretely threatened by change and ultimately by death. The only possibility of a complete grounding of the reality of beauty is a subsistent act of apprehension of form that is at once subsistent Being, subsistent Consciousness, and subsistent Joy.[206] These three constitute the Hindu philosophical name for God, *Sat — Cit — Ananda*; and they are the supreme personal form of the three traditional transcendentals.[207]

God is thus self-subsistent Joy in God's own being and in all that participates in it, and the supreme goal and mover of human desire. To say this is not to overlook the fact that human desire can also be perverted. Barth writes: "it is true that the imagination of the heart of man is wicked from his youth (Gen. 8:21), that there is sinful and deadly desire, and that this is the desire natural to man." Nevertheless, he continues, God "is Himself supremely and most strictly an object of desire, joy, pleasure, yearning and enjoyment."[208] (Obviously, the vocabulary of the Roman Catholic tradition differs from Barth's regarding the meaning of "natural" desire, but the essential insight is common. We shall examine some of its implications—namely, the possible conflict between the beautiful and the good as objects of desire—in the last chapter.)

Does the above process of reasoning constitute a "proof," or, better, a "way" to the existence of God? It would perhaps be better to speak in the terms used by J-D Robert: *"Pas de démonstration, mais une 'monstration' qui est 'auto-monstration.'"*[209] As Coreth remarks, coming to the explicit knowledge of God is never a matter of discovering something completely unknown, but of explicating what is already present in the knowledge of being—and, I would add, in the perception of its beauty.

At the same time, it should be noted that any such "way" and "knowledge" is based on a pre-apprehension that is both intrinsic to humanity and existentially proleptic, for (as Barth noted in his comments on Mozart's music) the final beauty and joy of existence are for us eschatological realities. The affirmation of God as Beauty, like the affirmation of Absolute Being, Intelligibility, and Goodness, is thrown into question by our encounter with irrationality, evil, and pain. In this sense, the very existence of God—that is, of an ultimate Being, Truth, Value, Beauty—remains, as Pannenberg says, intrinsically "debatable" until the eschaton. From another point of view, this is a necessary consequence of the "infinity" and mystery of God, and again reminds us of the *sui generis* nature of God's relation to creation. In this sense, the arguments of "natural theology" are in fact existentially explications of hope, in its proper theological sense: they anticipate the "proof" of God's existence *by God*, through the final establishment of God's "reign" (the triumph of God's truth, goodness, beauty, joy) over all existence. Insofar as this eschatological reality is not merely future but also is active in the present world, working for the overcoming of evil, it constitutes the existential "horizon" of our spiritual being and allows us to discern the latter's implicit and inevitable ground and goal.[210] This point is crucial in the reconciliation of joy in the beautiful, on the one hand, and, on the other, a moral engagement that frequently requires self-sacrifice: a theme to which we shall return in chapter 6.

❧❧❧

CHAPTER 5

Art and the Sacred

Prologue

"The Ninth Elegy"

Why, when it is possible to accomplish this span of being so:
as a laurel, a little darker than every
other green, with tiny waves on the border
of every leaf (like the wind's smile)—: why, then,
have to be human—and, shunning destiny,
long for destiny? . . .

        Oh, *not* because happiness *exists*,
this too-hasty taking profit from an approaching loss.
Not out of curiosity, or as practice for the heart,
which *would* exist also in the laurel. . . .

But because being here is much, and because apparently
everything here needs us, this fleeting world, that
strangely fits us. Us, the most fleeting of all. *Once*
each thing, only *once*. *Once* and never more. And we also
once. Never again. But to have been this
once, even if only *once*:
to have been *earthly*, seems irrevocable.

And so we drag ourselves onward and want to fulfill it,
want to hold it in our simple hands,
in our overcrowded gaze and in our speechless heart.
We want to become it.—To whom can we give it? Preferably
to hold on to everything for ever . . . Ah, into that other state,
alas, what can we take with us? Not perception, that
we slowly learned here, and nothing that happened here. Nothing.
The sufferings, then. Then above all the heaviness,
then the long experience of love,—then
nothing but the unsayable. But later,

among the stars, what will this avail: *they* are *better* unsayable.
The traveler brings from the slopes of the mountainsides
down into the valley not a handful of earth, unsayable to others, but rather
an acquired word, pure: the yellow and blue
gentian. Are we perhaps *here*, in order to say: house,
bridge, fountains, gate, jug, fruit-tree, window,—
at most: pillar, tower? . . . but to *say*, understand,
oh to say them *so*, as never the things themselves
thought interiorly to exist. Is not the secret trick
of this silent earth, when it draws lovers together,
that in their emotion each thing should enjoy rapture?
Threshold: what does it mean for two
lovers, that they wear down a little
the ancient threshold of their own gate
—they too, after the many who went before
and before those yet to come . . . , lightly.

Here is the time of the *sayable, here* is its homeland.
Speak and bear testimony. More than ever
the things fall away, the things that can be experienced, for
what replaces them, displacing them, is an act without image.
An act under a crust, which easily cracks open as soon as
the action inside outgrows it and finds other limits.
Between the hammers our heart
exists, like the tongue
between the teeth; and yet,
nevertheless, it remains full of praise.

Praise the world to the angel, not what is unsayable: *him*
you cannot impress with glorious emotion; in the cosmos,
where he feels more feelingly, you are a novice. So show
him what is simple, what takes shape from generation to generation,
what lives as something of our own, near to hand and within sight.
Tell him about things. He will stand astonished; as you stood
by the rope-maker in Rome, or by the potter on the Nile.
Show him how happy a thing can be, how innocent and ours,
how even complaining sorrow purely resolves to take form,
serves as a thing, or dies into a thing—, and blissful
escapes beyond the violin.—And these things, which live
by perishing, understand that you praise them; fleeting,
they trust in us to rescue them, us, the most fleeting of all.
They want us to change them entirely in our invisible heart,
into—oh, endlessly—into us! Whoever we may finally be.

Earth, isn't this what you desire: *invisibly*
to arise in us?—Is it not your dream
to be one day invisible?—Earth! invisible!
What, if not transformation, is your urgent command?

Earth, you beloved, I will! Oh, believe me, your springtimes
are no longer needed to win me to you—, *one,*
yes, a single one is already too much for my blood.
Unspeakably I have been dedicated to you, long since.
You were always in the right, and your holy inspiration
is our intimate companion, death.

See, I live. On what? Neither childhood nor future
grows less . . . immeasurable existence
wells up in my heart.

—Rainer Maria Rilke

Dimensions of the Question of Art and the Sacred

The last chapter represented a certain narrowing of perspective in relation to the one preceding it: a turn from the theological consideration of aesthetics in its widest sense—the theory of perception, feeling, and affect in general—to the examination of transcendence as related specifically to the experience of beauty. The present consideration represents not a further narrowing of the latter perspective but, rather, a specification in a different direction. The purpose here is to examine ways in which art mediates the value of the sacred or "holy."

As we have seen earlier, it is difficult to give a definition to the term "art." It is not my purpose to attempt to resolve the disputes in this area of aesthetics. There is, of course, a kind of art that corresponds to what we described in the last chapter as the "aesthetic pattern of experience": art whose reason for being is the quest for beauty and the joy of existence. This is arguably its most significant form, and is frequently simply identified with the essence of art. Gadamer points out the derivation of this idea from Aristotle, who remarked that artistic representation makes even the unpleasant appear as pleasant (*Poetics* 4, 1448, b. 10). Following him, Kant defines art as the beautiful representation (*Vorstellung*) of something: it makes even the ugly appear beautiful (*Critique of Judgment*, no. 48).[1] But this view of art leads, as Gadamer says, to an "aesthetic differentiation" (*ästhetische Unterscheidung*) that produces an abstract state of consciousness, removing "art" from its connection to life and (most significantly for our interests) from its connection with the sacred:

> What we call a work of art and experience aesthetically depends on a process
> of abstraction. By disregarding everything in which a work is rooted (in its
> original context of life, and the religious or secular function which gave it
> its significance), it becomes visible as the "pure work of art...." It practically
> defines aesthetic consciousness to say that it performs this differentiation of
> what is aesthetically intended from everything that is outside the aesthetic
> sphere.[2]

Gadamer's projected restoration of art to its life-contexts would involve the relationship of the beauty presented in art to truth, goodness, and the sacred. On this basis one could certainly conceive a "theological aesthetic" corresponding to the Kantian definition of art.

Nevertheless, in discussing the mediation of the sacred, I think one cannot avoid referring as well to forms of art that are less explicitly (if at all) characterized by the "aesthetic consciousness" described by Gadamer. What is commonly called art, as we have seen, can be oriented to other purposes than the creation of beauty: art as the "craft" of representation, art as skillful communication, art as evocation or intensification of emotion, art as (self-) expression, art as ornamentation, and so on. For the present, then, while acknowledging the central importance of the pursuit of the beautiful in art, let us avoid an a priori definition of art through the "aesthetic differentiation" and admit that "art" is not necessarily a single thing and does not have a single goal. At the same time, the various pursuits that we look at as "art" do have what Wittgenstein calls a "family resemblance"; and perhaps we may characterize this as having to do with the heightening of experience by representation and/or performance.

Frank Burch Brown's work on religious aesthetics is helpful at this juncture.[3] Brown's explicit goal is to formulate a neo-aesthetics that can explain the factual complex involvement of religion with beauty and art in a way that seems impossible for the Kantian "purist" aesthetics that he (like Gadamer) rejects.

Brown tentatively defines "aesthetics" as "the basic theoretical reflection regarding all aesthetic phenomena, including their modes of significant interrelation with, and mediation of, what is not inherently aesthetic." "Aesthetic phenomena" or "aesthetica" are in turn defined as "all those things employing a medium in such a way that its perceptible form and 'felt' qualities become essential to what is appreciable and meaningful."[4] Brown makes a helpful distinction between primary and secondary aesthetica. The former are "objects that are made, displayed, or presented with the primary purpose of evoking aesthetic response." Secondary or unintentional aesthetica are "those objects that one at least temporarily considers specifically with respect to their capacity to evoke such a response, even though such a capacity is unintentional, incidental, or of secondary interest."[5] Included in this second category are natural processes and products. Brown notes that

> [an] object that in one context is seen primarily as aesthetic may in another context be responded to as aesthetic only in a secondary or unconscious way, if at all. Leaning on Michael Polanyi and gestalt psychology, we can say that in one context the perceptual gestalt is such that the purely aesthetic features of an object serve as the focus of one's awareness, although one has a subsidiary or tacit awareness of its other features; in another context the reverse may be true.[6]

The distinction is thus helpful in explaining the mixed functions of religious (e.g., liturgical) objects or acts that are also artful.

> If the context is such that one attends from (or looks through) those features of the object that could only be called aesthetic and attends to (or focuses on) those features that could only be called religious, then the object of perception normally is called religious. If the reverse is true, the object (or event or process) is called aesthetic.[7]

(It should be noted that the term "religious" here refers to *explicit* or thematic connection with the divine. If the perspective of the preceding chapter is valid, then the "aesthetic" as such—that is, without religious connections—can also implicitly mediate the presence of God in an independent way.)

Brown also notes that besides the immediately aesthetic, there are also "mediately" aesthetic effects: sensibly perceived data that, while not among the immediately perceptible elements of a work of art, are nevertheless aesthetically relevant; for example, the technical and stylistic features of an art work.[8] Furthermore, he points out that it is more helpful to speak of a "milieu" that is aesthetic rather than simply particular aesthetic objects. "The aesthetic milieu . . . comprises everything in focal or subsidiary awareness that, within a particular context, is either immediately or mediately aesthetic in effect."[9]

In the light of such distinctions, and in opposition to "purist" aesthetics, Brown insists that there is an "aesthetic continuum" extending from pure or "free" aesthetica (in the Kantian sense), where our interest in the object or experience is "virtually independent of any cognitive, utilitarian, religious, or moral benefits that also may accompany or accrue to the experience,"[10] to complex aesthetica, which are "integral and interdependent": "They integrate simpler kinds of aesthetic and nonaesthetic perceptions into a more complex gestalt. And their unique aesthetic effects are interdependent with, and mutually transformative of, perceptions that are religious, moral, social, and so forth."[11]

Unlike certain followers of Kant, Brown insists that the "conditioned" or "mixed" form of the aesthetic is not, therefore, to be considered "inferior" or aesthetically "impure." Drawing on Kant's statements about the "sublime" and developing his notion of "aesthetic ideas" that prompt us to "think more," Brown shows that, in fact, a complete dichotomy between "pure" and "impure" aesthetica does not hold up,[12] and that in general "the response we have to beauty and sublimity is in fact deeply conditioned by factors that are not themselves aesthetic."[13] Hence complex aesthetica are a legitimate concern of aesthetics, and a specifically religious and theological aesthetics is possible.

Brown also provides a working definition of "art" based on the "family resemblances" among the various practiced genres and theoretical concepts that are observable through history. What we mean by "art" is an activity that "entails knowledgeable, skillful, or inspirited making"; it always "exhibits intrinsically appreciable—that is, aesthetic—qualities not duplicated by the workings of sheerly abstract thought or exhausted by mere utility"; and it includes works that express the meaning of life.[14] Brown therefore defines "art" as "any and all of the creative skills, informed practices, and primary products manifest in the making of publicly recognizable aesthetica";[15] and a work of art is "anything that is at least partially artificial in origin, that reflects creativity, skill, or know-how, and that in large measure is, or could be, something appreciated by a public attentive to aesthetic factors such as form and style, and responsive to aesthetic effects such as those we regard as intrinsically interesting, expressive, or beautiful."[16]

If we take "art" in the very wide sense implied by Brown and other contemporary aestheticians,[17] my third form of "aesthetics," the study of art, will not be a subdivision of the second sense (aesthetics as a theory of beauty), but will overlap with it. Not all art is concerned with beauty, and not all beauty is mediated by art. Hence our field of inquiry will in some ways be wider than the study of beauty: art may mediate the sacred by embodying its beauty (in both the tran-

scendental and categorical senses), but also through the creation and communication of other heightened human experiences (e.g., fear, remorse, obligation,
desire), through skillful communication of the intellectual content of revelation,
or through the explicit evocation of "the holy." (Whether the last is indeed a
distinct form of experience is a question we will confront later in this chapter.)
On the other hand, the scope of this third type of aesthetics is in some ways
narrower than that of the second; for art includes only human creation, and not
the beauty of nature in itself,[18] nor the (transcendental) beauty of ethical goodness
and of truth in themselves (although all of these may be represented in art and
communicated through it, so forming the "complex" aesthetica of which Brown
speaks).

From the theological perspective also, our concern here represents not a narrowing but a concretization. The previous chapter was concerned with the relation
of beauty to the a priori structures of human spirit; its essential openness to the
transcendental, embodied in a "natural" knowledge of God that constitutes the
human capacity for revelation as "grace."[19] It would be possible to further this
discussion by speaking about the "beauty" of revelation in its transcendental dimension: the experience of the Spirit, producing the state of "being in love with
God in an absolute way"[20] and its accompanying affect of joy, "the peace the
world cannot give." But for the present I shall merely presume that the foundations for such notions have been established in the preceding chapter, and shall
turn to the ways in which revelation, grace, and "being in love with God" are
concretely manifested and communicated.

"Transcendental revelation" as conceived by Rahner and Lonergan is always
categorically mediated. In its widest sense, "general" categorical revelation comprises the whole of human history, insofar as it "embodies" God's self-
communication in human terms. The response to and formulation of God's self-
gift occur through intellectual, moral, and religious "conversion"; are realized in
historical acts of insight, ethical behavior, and love, and are formulated symbolically and intellectually in human cultures, most expressly in philosophies, systems
of ethics, and religions.

The purpose of this chapter is to examine the ways in which the arts may
embody or serve this categorical revelation of God. To recognize this function of
art is also to appreciate it as a dramatic illustration of the intrinsically "hermeneutical" nature of religion and theology. As with all existential insights and responses mediated by transmissions of past historical embodiments of inspiration,
we are dealing here with transcendence mediated by two categorical situations
and events: those of the artist and those of the viewer. In the first place, as Rahner
remarks, the production of art is the result of a particular and determinate historical spiritual event. Artists "announce what is eternal in a unique manner, in
which their historical peculiarity and their longing for eternity are combined in a
unity that constitutes the essence of the work of art."[21] At the same time, the
present revelation of concretized transcendence in any particular work depends
upon the viewer or hearer's interacting with the work (in its historical and existential contexts) in a way that is open to the spiritual horizon of the aesthetic
experience as such. This interaction is itself an "artistic" event: "I may understand

Dürer's hare as the most concrete aspect of a well-determined insignificant human experience, but when I look at it with the eyes of an artist, I am beholding, if I may say so, the infinity and incomprehensibility of God."[22]

Hence the theological-aesthetic appreciation of a work of art involves a complex hermeneutical interaction among the artist, the work, and the viewer or hearer, along with the life-context of each. These elements may be present to varying degrees and may interact in different ways in constituting art's mediation of transcendence. On the one hand, the grasp of the truth and meaning of a work may demand the adoption of what Baxendale calls the "period point of view" (i.e., insight arising from the work's original life context). On the other hand, as Van der Leeuw says, "works of art do possess their own life: they perhaps mean something very different to him who receives them than to him who created them."[23] The existential situation of the viewer or hearer may permit a new interpretation or appreciation of the work's revelatory power.

(A single example of this complex process will no doubt serve to call up many more in the reader's mind. John Tavener's "Akathist of Thanksgiving" evokes a religious context by its use of voice and harmony in a style consciously reminiscent of Russian church music. The poem he sets explicitly celebrates God's glory and invites participation in its thanksgiving by its evocation of experiences of beauty and glory in nature and in human interaction:

> O Lord, how good it is to be your guest:
> The wind-scented mountains, erect into the sky,
> Waters, as mirrors, unconfined,
> Reflecting rays of gold, light-footed clouds.
> All Nature secretly whispers, all full of caresses.
> And the birds and the beasts bear the stamp of your love.
> Blessed is Mother Earth: Her swift passing beauty, arousing the yearning for
> the eternal native land.[24]

The work operates on a first level through its musical and literary beauty and through the explicit invocation of religious feeling. But when one hears the poem with knowledge of its historical context—realizing that it was written by a Russian priest shortly before his death in a Siberian prison camp under Stalin—the words of glorification and the rejoicing in existence take on a new dimension, and challenge the listener to a different level of religious/aesthetic experience.)

Having defined the scope of investigation, we may now proceed to our theological question. The first part of this chapter will deal with art as the expression or mediation of "general" categorical revelation: the encounter with transcendence or with the sacred in human experience in general. Van der Leeuw claims that all "genuine" art—by which he means art that attains real beauty—is implicitly religious, because "the holy by its nature comprehends the beautiful."[25] I shall suggest that art may mediate transcendence in other ways as well, through what Tracy calls the "disclosure" of truths about the human condition.[26]

The second part of the chapter will consider art in its relation to the "special" categorical revelation that occurs in Christ and is transmitted through the Christian tradition. Balthasar has drawn attention and has written extensively on the beauty of the Christian message itself, and its realization in styles of living and spirituality. God's "art" is the whole of human life lived as the creation of moral and metaphysical beauty. "Such 'art' becomes visible in the Christian sphere in the life-forms of the chosen"—especially with "archetypal power" in the paradigms of Mary and the saints.[27] I acknowledge the validity and importance of a theological aesthetics of this kind; but my concern here will be more modest: I will consider some examples of how the arts in their ordinary sense, primarily musical and graphic, serve or intersect with the Christian message and tradition.

Art as the Direct Expression of Transcendence: "General Categorical Revelation"

A remarkable proportion of the world's music, painting, sculpture, and architecture is explicitly religious. These expressions and communications of religion as both idea and feeling are naturally the most obvious connection of the arts to "general categorical revelation": its embodiment in the world's religions. The scriptures of the great faiths are frequently among the masterworks of their respective languages; their architecture, images, and music are arguably the summit of human artistic achievement. However, because of the enormous extent and complexity of this topic, I will deal with explicitly religious art primarily only in the context of the "special" revelation of Christianity. This topic will occupy the second part of the present chapter.

Before considering explicitly religious art, however, I will be concerned with less explicit connections of art to the sacred. I will consider first Rudolph Otto's notion of a mediation of the holy through the "association of feelings." I will suggest that this theory may be deepened through connection with the theme of the last chapter: art can be a "word" of God (or, from the human side, an embodiment and formulation of "conversion") apart from bearing or evoking an explicitly religious consciousness, through the creation and representation of beauty, even when this beauty is not explicitly connected with a religious message. But, as I have insisted above, not all art aims at the attainment of beauty. Therefore I will also look at art's revelatory capacity as communicator of content: specifically, as a "language" that embodies experiences analogous to the religious, and as the bearer of a metaphysical heightening of consciousness pointing toward the divine. This will lead to the consideration of art in explicit connection with the religious "word" in the second part of the chapter.

Mediation of the Sacred Through Beauty and the "Association of Feelings"

Gerardus Van der Leeuw writes:

> All music that is absolute music, without additions, without anything counterfeit, is the servant of God: just as pure painting is, whether it treats religious subjects or not; and as true architecture is, apart from the churches it

builds; and as true science is, even when it has little to do with theology, but busies itself with gases, stars, or languages.[28]

Likewise, when Luther wrote that he considered music a *"predicatio sonora,"* he was regarding it not only as a vehicle for sacred texts but also as being in itself a mirror of God's beauty, and thus a means of reaching the soul directly with a message about God that is not entirely expressible in words. (Naturally, the different ways in which art mediates the sacred can also be combined: a creation of artistic beauty can also be the bearer of an explicitly religious message. As we have noted earlier and shall discuss in depth in the next chapter, there can also be a tension between these functions.)

I suggested in last chapter that the apprehension of beauty reveals as its ultimate horizon an absolute act of joy, of delectation in being. A recapitulation of the argument will lead into our present concern. The experience of beauty is a kind of delight, a joy in the experience of "form," the organizing principle that gives "shape" to things and to our knowledge of them. What distinguishes beautiful music from noise, for example, is precisely its patterns, which create a unity out of disparate elements. Analogously, "form" or organization is what makes biological life possible; and, on yet another level, "form" is what makes any existing thing into an identity, a whole that is differentiated from others; and "form" is what corresponds to the mind's quest for intelligibility.[29] In this sense, "form" is the key to existence itself, and delight in form—in what makes existence possible—is an implicit affirmation of the goodness and joy of existence, of being itself.

The affirmation of the joy of existence, however, can take place only in an intelligent and free being if existence is somehow—even if only implicitly—seen as worthwhile, as meaningful and having an ultimate intelligibility or purpose. To experience beauty is to experience a deep-seated "yes" to being—even in its finitude and its moments of tragedy; and such an affirmation is possible only if being is grounded, borne by a Reality that is absolute in value and meaning. In short, the experience of finite beauty in a spiritual being implies the unavoidable (although perhaps thematically unconscious) co-affirmation of an infinite Beauty: the reality that we call God.

The fact that God is the "horizon" of every experience of beauty explains why even the tragic emotions can be experienced in art as "beautiful," and why there is at the heart of every deep aesthetic experience—and perhaps particularly in music—an intense feeling of striving toward something beyond the moment. In Peter Schaffer's *Amadeus*, the aged Salieri says of Mozart's music: "This was a music . . . filled with such longing, such unfulfillable longing, that it seemed to me that I was hearing the voice of God." Such longing is intrinsic to the experience of finite beauty; for the joy of existence in any finite being can never be complete or ultimate, but must point beyond itself to a final and infinite goal. It is in this sense that philosophers from Plato onward have seen beauty as the manifestation of God to the mind through the senses, and have claimed that "the beauty of anything created is nothing else than a similitude of divine beauty participated in by things."[30]

Beauty is, therefore, an "attribute" of God. Beautiful art implicitly "speaks" of the divine exemplar, and at least raises the question of a transcendent human goal, eternal happiness in some kind of union with eternal Beauty. If that goal actually communicates itself as the gratuitously given sustaining dynamism of human existence, it is experienced precisely as lovable, desirable, beautiful. Hence beauty is a necessary attribute of grace and revelation, as it is of God's self that is communicated in these realities; and the beauty of art, like all beauty, not only tells us of the nature of our final horizon and goal but also evokes its gratuitous presence, drawing us to that goal and giving us already the taste of its reality.

Some preliminary ideas as to how beautiful art concretely mediates revelation are suggested by the example of music. In many religious traditions, music plays an important role not only as an embellishment of liturgical life but also as a symbol of the divine itself. One may think, for example, of the many and celebrated Hindu statues of Śiva. The god is frequently represented as the supernal veena player, who creates the world by his music, which also symbolizes knowledge and enlightenment. In another guise, he is Nataraja, the Lord of the Dance, who unfolds the universal order by his cosmic motion. In one of his four hands he holds a small drum, to whose rhythm he dances, creating the world; in the palm of another rests the fire with which all will be terminated; a third hand gives the gesture of peace, and the fourth bows downward like an elephant's trunk, symbolizing the grace that lifts the faithful to safety. One of his dancing feet crushes ignorance; the other is lifted in graceful motion to the music of creation and salvation.

In the West, from the time of Boethius, human music was regarded as an imperfect imitation of the "music of the spheres," the harmony of the celestial bodies moved in their orbits by the "prime Mover," God. In a heritage stemming ultimately from the Pythagoreans, both ancient and medieval thinkers developed the notion that the beautiful and harmonious motion of creation according to the laws of mathematics is the "music" with which it praises its maker and goal. The verse from the Wisdom of Solomon (11:20), "You have arranged all things by number and weight," was interpreted from Augustine onwards to refer to God's creation of "musical" order and harmony in the cosmos.[31] Isidore of Seville (d. 636) expresses the common medieval theology of music in his *Etymologiarum sive Originum libri XX*: "Without music no discipline can be perfect, for nothing is without it. Indeed the world itself seems to be composed by a certain harmony of sounds, and heaven itself revolves with an accompanying change of harmony."[32] What we normally call "music" is the sensible mirror of the deeper musical order expressed in both the harmony of the human body and soul and in the inaudible "music of the spheres" (*musica mundana*).[33]

The Pythagorean and Neoplatonic notion of creation as God's "music" is given further precision in Aristotle's idea that God "moves" the universe ὡς ἐρόμενον—as its beloved—that is, as its final cause or reason for being. Hence when Dante proclaims in the last lines of the *Paradiso* that his mind and will have been moved by the same love that moves the sun and all the heavenly bodies—

ma già volgeva il mio disio e il velle . . .
l'amor che move il sole e l'altre stelle[34]

—he is presupposing the commonly accepted medieval view that the stars and planets are moved in their spheres by heavenly intelligences that are caught up in the love of God,[35] and that praise God by the beauteous harmony of their motion, "heard" by Dante as the musical counterpart to the visible "laughter" of the universe:

> *"Al Padre, al Figlio, allo Spirito Santo,"*
>   *Cominciò "Gloria" tutto il Paradiso,*
>   *Si che m'inebbriava il dolce canto.*
> *Ciò ch'io vedeva mi sembiava un riso*
>   *Dell'universo; per che mia ebbrezza*
>   *Entrava per l'udire e per lo viso.*[36]

In short, the medieval West saw an "objective" connection of music and the arts with the sacred because they are concerned with re-creating or re-presenting the beautiful order given to the world by the Creator.

Another approach to this connection is suggested by Rudolf Otto in his theory of a "law of associations." Here the emphasis is not on music as reflecting the order or beauty of creation but on its communicative function. A few words must therefore be said about that function. It is generally assumed that musical sound per se (with the exception of music that consciously imitates sounds in nature) does not normally represent specific objects or concepts.[37] On the other hand, music does seem to function as a "language" or symbol system, representing not ideas but feelings. As Susanne K. Langer puts it, music is "a tonal analogue of emotive life."[38]

Various theories have been put forth to explain this "natural" capacity of music to symbolize and evoke emotion or states of mind.[39] On one level, there seems to be a connection between the elements of music and certain kinesthetic images or psychophysical states. Pitch (i.e., the frequency of sound waves), tempo, rhythm, timbre, and so on produce physical effects in the listener, who responds with varying degrees of sympathy, so that the music induces a certain "mood."[40] There may also be certain associations—both "natural" and culturally conditioned—of particular sounds with environmental or human sounds and rhythms.[41] Hence Leonard B. Meyer argues that because musical sounds are "continuous with and similar to our experience of other kinds of stimuli,"[42] for the sensitive and culturally attuned listener they will be related, consciously or unconsciously, to non-musical ideas, images, emotions, and frames of mind.

Similar ideas are at work in Otto's notion of the "law of associations."[43] For Otto the experience of the holy—the *mysterium tremendum et fascinans*—is completely *sui generis*. Nevertheless, the feelings generated by the experience are analogous to those produced in other areas of life: moral, aesthetic, intellectual. The presence of one set of feelings may stimulate the appearance of the analogous feelings from another sphere of experience. Thus the moods produced by certain kinds of music or art can arouse similar feelings that stem from the encounter with the Holy.

This theory explains, at least in part, why in particular cultures (in ancient Greece and China, for example) certain forms of music have been associated with immorality or corruption. It also explains the recurrence of certain characteristics and the absence of others in the sacred music of particular religions and perhaps even (to a limited extent) in the musical expressions of diverse religions in different cultural traditions. It may indicate, in other words, that while some few positive or negative characteristics of "sacred" music are virtually universally recognizable, at the same time particular theologies or spiritualities will tend to favor certain kinds of music.[44] Similar associations of feelings may take place with regard to shape, composition, coloration, and the spatial relation of objects; and to this extent, the visual arts as well may communicate meaning not only by their subject matter but also by their form or mode of representation.

It will be apparent from what has been said above concerning the "transcendentals" that I regard the experience of transcendence not as belonging to a distinct sphere, separate from the aesthetic, moral, intellectual, and interpersonal, but as the ultimate "dimension" of these. This does not, of course, prevent one from speaking of theoretically distinct "realms" of experience, differentiated by their principal operations, which correspond to their "formal" aspect. The realm of "the sacred," in my view, is differentiated, not by its object, but by the fact that here the "ultimacy" that is implicit in all human experience is recognized and spoken of explicitly. For this reason, I regard the experience of "the holy" (insofar as this term names the object of *explicitly* religious experience) as *sui generis* only in a qualified sense. That is, formally "religious" experience may be conceptually distinguished from other kinds; but concretely and existentially, it coincides with the experience of the transcendent/immanent divine implicit in every categorical mediation of the "transcendent."

Hence the "law of associations" in regard to the transcendent or the divine works both "vertically" and "horizontally." That is, not only is there an analogy between the feelings excited by (for example) a glorious sunrise or a trumpet voluntary and one aspect of the feelings appropriate to the "religious" experience of the "holy," but what is more, the basis of that analogy is the identity of the "holy" with the final object of human existence in all its positive modes of self-realization. In Lonergan's vocabulary, intellectual, moral, and religious self-transcendence or conversion interpenetrate and call for each other, because their ultimate finality coincides. This is why, as Van der Leeuw says in the quote that begins this section, all "pure" art (which Van der Leeuw presumes to be in the service of beauty) is implicitly "religious," even when it does not have an explicitly religious theme. Therefore the feelings and states of mind that it creates have an affinity both with their own highest forms (the "transcendental" dimension of the beautiful) and with the feelings, ideas, and concepts that mediate the explicitly religious encounter with God. For this reason, nonsacred art and music may also mediate the presence of the transcendent without evoking associations with the religious realm, but instead by revealing the "metaphysical" depths of secular human experience itself.

Art and Ontological Insight

As we have seen, the apprehension of beauty is already an ontological event. But art's capacity to reveal the "transcendental" is not limited to the presentation of beautiful form (which not all art in fact possesses, even if one accepts the debated proposition that beauty is its ideal goal). Art may also have a more or less explicitly ontological content. It may convey a message and/or evoke a metaphysical dimension of existence that constitutes a "revelation" of the divine self-communication, at least as the horizon of the experience: in the artistic evocation, for example, of inchoate desire, or joy, or longing, or wonder.

Hence God is not always revealed in art in what the Scholastics call the "splendor" of beauty, or in the "glory" of which Balthasar speaks. Art may pose the *question* of the ultimate goal of human love, rather than give an answer; to this extent, it may evade beauty, or may be beautiful in a painful or anxious or anguished way. But even such a question, arising from a desiring in darkness rather than from the "clarity" of divine beauty, may be the communication of God's love (and at the same time its limitation through the partial nature of human acceptance and realization, as is always the case in categorical revelation). In what follows, I will attempt some preliminary explorations into how this process may occur. It goes without saying that this treatment makes no pretense at completeness or systematic rigour; its purpose is merely to seek a few examples that may suggest some of the ways in which art may function in the metaphysical realm leading to the sacred.

As Van der Leeuw says, art by its nature reveals "the other."[45] Gadamer makes a similar observation: in the self-forgetfulness that characterizes a deep perception of art, we experience being wholly "with" something else.[46] The work of art as communication of another's experience or perspective may challenge the viewer or hearer through the "otherness" or "difference" disclosed in it—if it is allowed to engage the subject profoundly with its claim to truth. If it does not always work on us in the immediacy of perception, then it may do so in the subsequent reflection that it provokes:

> perhaps in the "tranquility" of that "recollection" which characterizes much reflection, I may consider how that disclosure [in the work of art] relates to my vision of the world. Are real affinities present? Is a confrontation, even destruction, of my present world demanded: Is a strange confirmation, even a "consolation without a cause," present? Is a recognition that "something else may be the case" at work?[47]

Naturally, the "other" revealed in art is not necessarily the "wholly other" of religion. What it manifests directly may be rather the latter's expression, or even the mere precondition for its expression.[48] But if, as Gadamer says, art is essentially an intensified form of the symbolic representation of life, toward which every experience tends,[49] then it has the power to evoke—at least as a question—the religious and moral dimension that are implicit in experience.[50] At least in its most profound moments, art relates us to the "ontological" dimension of existence by representing the being (*Dasein*) of things[51] in discontinuity from their "ordinary" context, and hence allowing the more ultimate context of both experience and the experienced to come to attention:

> [aesthetic experience] suddenly takes the person experiencing it out of the context of his life, by the power of the work of art, and yet relates him back to the whole of his existence. In the experience of art there is present a

fullness of meaning which belongs not only to this particular content or object but rather stands for the meaningful whole of life. An aesthetic experience always contains the experience of an infinite whole. Precisely because it does not combine with others to make one open experiential flow, but immediately represents the whole, its significance is infinite.[52]

In some art, this process becomes more or less explicit through the re-production and intensification of the experience of conscious being itself—human *Dasein*, in its ontological difference from the being of things. This experience arouses wonder. In the first place, it evokes the wonder of existence itself: "*das Mystische*," as Wittgenstein calls it; not how the world is, but *that* it is: the won-derment expressed in Leibniz's question, "why is there something rather than nothing?" Even more pointedly, it evokes the wonder of conscious being, being-toward, being self-present, having care for being (Heidegger's *Sorge*). Because art by its nature consists in various ways of *re*-production, it makes us aware or heightens our awareness of the *act* of experiencing, as well as of the particular content of that act: it provokes us not only to consciousness of the independent being of the other but also to reflexive consciousness of our own awareness,[53] and to wonder at its being. I am invited to encounter and respond to "that formidable, sometimes elating, sometimes sickening or maddening fact *I exist*."[54]

The kind of art that I have called "metaphysical" draws our attention to this process, which is implicit (to varying degrees) in all profound aesthetic experience. The poetry of Rilke, among others, is rich in examples. In the ninth Duino Elegy, quoted at the beginning of this chapter, Rilke reflects on what was for him a major function of the artist: expressing the existence of things, even the most ordinary, in their variety and uniqueness; appreciating and praising their forms of being, bringing them to name in human consciousness. This naming is a com-mon human function, even in utilitarian consciousness. But the poet heightens the experience and sees it as humanity's mission, its particular reason for existence: to bring the world to consciousness, give it the unity of awareness, extend its material being-there into invisibility, thought, spirit; and so to make the momentary eternal. There is, on the one hand, a sense of that unity with the whole of which Pasternak writes in describing the love of Zhivago and Lara: "Never, never, even in their moments of richest and wildest happiness, were they unaware of a sublime joy in the total design of the universe, a feeling that they themselves were a part of that whole, an element in the beauty of the cosmos."[55]

On the other hand, there is an acute awareness of the "ontological difference" between the laurel and the human consciousness that perceives and delights in it. It is this awareness that raises the question of the meaning of human existence, of mind. On one level, the poem proposes an answer: there is a certain necessity to spiritual being. We exist precisely to give spiritual being to the world, to matter, through our awareness of it. But this in turn raises a further question: what does this fleeting consciousness and naming signify in the light of death and eternity, of the unsayable? A clear and final answer is not forthcoming. But there is a conviction that even in the light of the eternal and nameless—even among the stars, and what is better left unsayable—human life on earth has beauty and meaning. Rilke's consciousness of existence faced with death leads, not to Sartre's "nausea," but to appreciation, praise, love, and unity with the whole.

This poem is not explicitly "religious"; but the felt conviction of the purposefulness of being, the mysterious joy in the facticity of *Dasein* ("immeasurable being wells up in my heart"), like Ignatius's "consolation without a cause," raises the question of God as the source and ultimate goal of existence and of its dynamism to unity.

In other poems of Rilke, this connection is more explicit. In the first part of *The Spanish Trilogy* the poet's desire for unity with all things is presented in the form of a prayer:

Out of this cloud—see!—that has so wildly covered over
the star that was just there—(and out of me),
out of this mountain-land over there, that now for a time
has night and the night winds—(and out of me),
out of this river in the valley that catches the form
of the sky's jagged light—(and out of me);
out of me and out of all of this to make
one single thing, Lord; out of me and out of the feeling
with which the flock, enclosed in the fold,
exhaling accepts
the great dark being-no-more of the world—, out of me and out of that light
in the dimness of the many houses, Lord:
to make one thing; out of the strangers, for
I know not one of them, Lord, and out of me and out of me
to make *one* thing; out of the sleepers,
out of the aged strange men in the old-age home,
who importantly cough in their beds, out of
children drunk with sleep on so strange a breast,
out of much that is uncertain and always out of me,
out of nothing but me and that which I do not know,
to make the thing, Lord Lord Lord, the thing
that cosmically-earthly like a meteor
gathers together in its heaviness
only the sum of flight: weighing nothing but arrival.[56]

Here we have, on one level, a strikingly evocative portrayal of an evening scene. The reader's memory and imagination are powerfully stirred by the concrete detail, the accuracy of description of things we have all experienced. But at the same time, these ordinary things are revealed in their mystery: there is an "otherness" that pervades them, even in their familiarity. That is, experiences reproduced or imagined are taken out of their normal context of a life-project; they are isolated, and therefore placed in the center of attention. We are aware of experiencing *them,* and of *experiencing* them (even if vicariously); and we are aware of the feelings subtly associated with the poetically isolated experience.

The poet expresses both an acute sense of self and a desire to merge the self with the other in a larger (yet always concrete and particular) reality. Underlying

156

all is the pressing drive to be "one thing" with everything experienced and portrayed. Is this merely a hyperbolic expression of the poet's vocation? A reflection
of the infinite scope and ambition of the soul—(*anima quodammodo omnia*)? Or
may this drive to unity signify supernatural love: the drive to share in the divine
omnipresence and God's infinite compassion toward all things—a foretaste of the
"communion of the saints" in its cosmic (but earthly, space-and-time-produced)
dimension?

In a poem from *The Book of Hours*, Rilke explicitly sees the world and his
love of it as revelations of God:

> I find you in all these things
> to which I am good, and as a brother;
> like a seed you sleep in what is small
> and in the great you give yourself forth greatly.[57]

Human consciousness itself, and especially artistic consciousness, is revelation: a
self-manifestation of God through the creature:

> . . . Denn im Manne
> will der Gott beraten sein.[58]

In an entirely different aesthetic, cultural, and religious context, Zen poetry
similarly exemplifies the "metaphysical" way of entry into the realm of the sacred.
Compare Rilke's long and linguistically complex verses with Bashō's 1686 poem,
which has become the most famous haiku in the Japanese language:

> Old pond:
> frog jump-in
> water-sound.[59]

Once again we have a portrayal of a scene that is absolutely concrete and
particular—one, moreover, that is entirely ordinary, natural, undramatic, and
seemingly insignificant. Here there is no explicit raising of the metaphysical question, no expression of wonder at being. Yet in its context, the poem is laden with
ontological significance coming to revelation in the hearer's mind.

The extreme economy of the haiku form, like the sparse brush strokes of Zen
sumi-e painting, focuses attention on a few details carefully selected out from sense
experience. These elements stand out in bold relief: they are *there*, present to the
mind, in stark facticity. At the same time, an entire context is merely suggested,
whose content and form must be supplied by the hearer's or viewer's imagination.
That context or horizon is both physical and meta-physical: the scene suggests a
life-context and also an ontological context. In Bashō's poem, the last line provides
a climax to the scene, like the conclusion of a syllogism. In our minds we hear
the sudden "plop" of the frog in the pond against a surrounding silence. Like the
purposeful clanging of the ladle against the kettle in the midst of the decorum of
the tea ceremony, or like the bell rung during meditation, the "water-sound"
represents *satori*, the sudden enlightenment or awakening that culminates Zen
practice. The humble and ordinary is revealed as having infinite significance; the
present moment touches on eternity.

The poem invites the hearer or reader to replicate the process: to reproduce in our minds not only the physical scene but also the poet's experience of it. In doing so, we are involved in levels of being and awareness. To appreciate the poem's meaning, the mind must act; and in being conscious of its action, it comes to heightened presence-to-self and presence-to the object and, most important, to heightened awareness of the "horizon" of both. As in Zen painting, more important than the lines are the empty spaces surrounding; more important than the sound is the silence out of which it comes and into which it recedes. In the context of Zen, this context is thought of not as "being" but as "nothingness," the "void" (*śūnya*). In continuity with Buddha's doctrine of *anitya*, which proclaims the insubstantiality of the world, the *Śūnyavāda* holds that all dharmas are empty of substance—are "void" of any self-subsistence or permanence of being. But expanding the doctrine, it proclaims that because their apparent substantiality and imperfection are illusory and they lack any real self-being, all dharmas are really identical with the perfection of being, with the great Void, the "no-thing-ness" of the Absolute. *Saṁsāra* is *nirvāna* and *nirvāna* is *saṁsāra:* form is emptiness, and emptiness is form. Hence all things are Buddhas—revealers of the absolute. That the means of revelation is no solemn event, but the funny sound of a frog jumping into a pond, is appropriate: for to attain the insight we must stand ironically aside from our "selves," put away our pretensions, and break with our ordinary way of thinking.

For a final example, let us examine the well-known Chinese poem entitled "Deer Fence," by the Tang writer and painter Wang Wei (ca. 700). In a modern poetic translation, it reads:

> In the empty mountains
> I see no one,
> But hear the sound
> Of someone's voice.
>
> Slanting sunlight
> Enters deep forest,
> And shines again
> On green moss.[60]

The scene is reminiscent of much Chinese ink painting of the style Wang Wei is credited with initiating, in which mountainous forms, looming out of cloud, enclose vast empty spaces, punctuated by tiny, highly detailed forest scenes. The explicit use of the word "empty" (*kung*) immediately suggests the great void of Taoism or the "emptiness" of Buddhism. (Wang Wei is known to have been a devout Buddhist). Here the full effect of the verses depends on the fact that the Chinese verb is unconjugated and can be used without pronouns—so that there is in the poem no indication of a subject or "voice." Literally, the four five-character lines translate:

> empty mountain(s) not see person
> only hear person speak sound
> return sunlight enter deep forest
> again shine green moss upon.

The absence of a personal voice here suggests the separability of experience from the subject—which, in Buddhist thought, is in fact a transient psychic phenomenon, lacking substantial being or independent "selfhood." Finitude and transitoriness (the precise moment of returning afternoon sun shining through the forest to light up patches of green moss against the surrounding shadow) are seen against the suggested horizon of the mysterious infinite and necessary reality, which can only be described negatively as "emptiness," which is symbolized by the vast mountainscape. The light entering the deep forest again suggests insight; the contentment in the beauty of the scene evokes the peace that comes with enlightenment; the poetic appreciation of the small patch of sunlit moss reflects the Zen recognition of the particular and transitory as the locus of infinity and is intimately linked with the Buddhist ideal of compassion toward all beings.

Clearly, the very nature of words makes literary art, in particular poetry, especially apt for expressing the "metaphysical" dimension of existence. Verbal language can directly express ideas, thoughts, and questions. By their abstract and symbolic character, words always implicitly present to consciousness the fact of the "ontological difference": the duality between the merely objective being of things experienced and the subject's self-present act of experiencing, naming, and understanding.

However, a similar process may also take place in other arts, including wordless music and pictures. Rahner speaks of a "sensory experience of transcendence" in images that helps to bring about the "properly religious experience of transcendence."[61] Rahner remarks similarly that nonverbal art "should probably be characterized, from the theological standpoint, by the fact that in different ways and by what is peculiar to it, it succeeds in making people aware of their original religious experience"—or, as we might say, of the "depth" dimension of experience in general.[62] Such images need not be explicitly religious in theme to mediate a relation to God's presence and self-gift, just as moral acts may be finalized to God's immediacy without any conceptualized reference to God.[63] The human senses cannot perceive God; but it is the whole person who, in a genuinely human act, sees or hears, therefore one can have "religious experience" through the senses.[64]

Rahner gives some initial indications of how the transcendent can be implicitly mediated to us in music and pictures because of the co-experienced "horizon" of every sensation:

> At first it may seem as though viewing stops at the finite object which is immediately seen, making it thus impossible to transcend it toward the absolute God. But we may reject this and say: every experience of an object, even though the object is always a single and finite one, is carried by an a priori pre-apprehension of the whole breadth of the formal object of the sense power. It is more than the grasping of the concrete single object that is being known. This is not true for hearing alone. It is not true only for the spirit as such with its unlimited transcendentality. It is true that the senses and the spirit differ from each other by the fact that the latter has an unlimited formal object, an unlimited a priori pre-apprehension, whereas this is

not true of the senses. Yet, even so, every act of the sense powers as such implies some experience of transcendence. Thus every time we hear a certain sound we also hear the stillness that surrounds it and constitutes the space in which a single sound may be heard. . . . Such an experience of transcendence, although a limited one, is also necessarily given in the act of seeing. Every time we see an object, we look, as it were, beyond it, into the expanse of all that may be seen. . . . Hence in seeing too, and not only in hearing, there is a kind of sensory experience of transcendence, that serves as a foundation and mediation in referring the sense-endowed spiritual subject to God.[65]

The "horizon" of sense activity considered per se is not the transcendental "being," much less the divine. In sensation we co-experience or pre-apprehend the a priori field of all possible sensible experience, that is, the spatio-temporal continuum as such.[66] But this pre-apprehension of space-time as such is relevant to metaphysical insight. First, it is parallel to the activity of co-experiencing the horizon of thought, to which sensation leads, and it may thus be used to evoke that more ultimate horizon by a kind of analogy. Furthermore, the experience of even the sensible horizon *as* a "horizon" can occur only in the sense experience of a conscious spiritual subject; that is, it depends upon the a priori openness of the subject to the entirety of being. In human acts it is precisely the person, embodied spirit and mind, not simply the sense faculty in itself, that experiences the sensible object and its horizon. Hence the limited spatio-temporal horizon, when it occurs in the context of higher mental activity, "refers" the subject to the more basic spiritual self-presence in which we pre-apprehend being, the true, the good, and the beautiful.

Leopardi's famous poem, "L'infinito" ("The Infinite") gives concrete shape to the process described philosophically by Rahner:

Ever dear to me was this solitary hill
and this hedge that so greatly limits
the view of the ultimate horizon.
But while I sit and look, endless
spaces beyond this, and super-human silence, and deepest quiet
I picture in my mind; where but for little, the heart would be
afraid. And as I hear the wind blow through these plants,
I compare that infinite silence to this voice;
and I remember eternity, and the dead seasons,
and the present living one, and its sound. And thus, within this
immensity, my thought is brought to naught:
and to drown is sweet in such a sea.

—Giacomo Leopardi, "L'infinito," 1819

The poet's immediate vision of a familiar scene leads him to imagine the farther visual horizon; and this in turn leads to the thought of the whole field of space (*interminati spazi di là da quella*). The visual image is complemented by an auditory one: endless space is also endless silence, the idea of which leads the heart to the brink of fear. (Compare Pascal's famous line in the *Pensées*: *le silence éternel de ces espaces infinies m'effraie*.)[67] The field of space leads by analogy to the field of time and its horizon: the poet not only adverts to the past and present but also "remembers" eternity (*e mi sovien l'eterno*). It would probably be reading too much into this phrase to hear in it an echo—except on a purely verbal level—of Plato's doctrine of ἀναμνησις. Leopardi's meaning is no doubt more simple: he is brought to a moment of reflection on life's limits and of the "eternal" beyond. (The idea of death is made explicit in the next line's phrase *le morte stagioni*.) Nevertheless, it is perhaps not inappropriate to connect Leopardi's process of thought with St. Augustine's notion of "memory" as that self-presence by which the mind is "available" to itself, the root of self-consciousness, through which we are aware of our finitude, and thus also of the horizon of being.[68]

Finally, the poet's sense of self is lost in the "immensity" he contemplates; and he rejoices in the loss, which is also bliss. This conclusion is, of course, not explicitly religious or "mystical" in the theological sense. It may be taken on a fairly innocuous level as a description of the repose of mind that comes after contemplative exposure to grandeur or vastness. But the poet's momentary ecstasy in nature may also become a symbol for unity with the "infinity" of the poem's title—however vague and undefined the latter may be on the level of thought; and the bliss experienced may evoke a deeper level of the paradox of losing the self in the "ever greater" in order to find its true reality.

Rahner's remarks quoted above concern sensible experience in general. Likewise, the experience Leopardi refers to is one of sensible experience of nature, not of art (although he conveys it to us artistically). Because art is sensible, it naturally shares the "ontological" characteristics of sense experience in general. But art may also heighten the "sensory experience of transcendence" and its implicit reference to the more ultimate horizon, and may be purposely used to do so. That is, art can be used to bring to light the sensory horizon and through it the transcendental horizon of the perceiving mind, the absolute.

For examples of the process in the realm of painting, we may once more refer to the many Chinese landscapes influenced by the aesthetics of Taoism and/or Zen. (A few notable examples from the Southern Sung and Yuan dynasties: *Mountain in Mist* by Ying Yu-chien; *Boat at Twilight* and *The Downpour* by Hsia Kuei; *Landscape with Willows* by Ma Yüan.) Here the empty spaces are integral to the compositions and their meaning; they evoke the absorption of the soul in nature, which in turn is the symbol of the immeasurable and eternal, the great Void. Other paintings present detailed and "naturalistic" portrayals of everyday and sometimes humorously observed objects, but against a background of emptiness that emphasizes the sheer facticity and contingency of their (and the viewer's) being (*Wild Goose*, by Mu Ch'i; *Fisherman on a Lake in Winter*, by Ma Yüan; *Bamboo in the Wind* by Wu Chien).[69]

The monk Mu Chi's painting *Persimmons*, like Bashō's haiku, makes the commonplace an occasion for enlightenment: here concrete objects and empty space operate like the contrasting sound and silence of the poem. The painting operates on several levels of irony or paradox. The six pieces of fruit are portrayed starkly and economically. On the one hand, the viewer feels them to be solidly

FIGURE 3. *Mu Ch'i.* Persimmons.

anchored, firmly sitting on a surface, which is in fact suggested by pale washes of ink below them, and the placing of one fruit in front of the others gives a sense of depth and "realism." On the other hand, no limit of the "surface" is portrayed, and hence no perspective is established; indeed, the vertical staining of the paper emphasizes its flatness. From this point of view, the fruit is floating in pure space. The colorful persimmons are rendered in black ink, while the surrounding space is subtly stained in shades of yellow and red. Yet the viewer "sees" the various shades of orange and red in the gradations of darkness of the ink. Two of the persimmons reverse the pattern, being pictured as empty circles. The placement of the objects is irregular, yet the whole has remarkable balance. The eye's focus wanders from the objects to their background and back again. At the same time, the mind's focus likewise shifts: we see persimmons, at the same time, we see the momentary and subjective acts of perceiving and portraying persimmons. Like a *koan*, the painting surprises us, throws us off guard, and reveals both the transitoriness of existence and its limitless horizon.

Such art, we might suggest, evokes the coincidence of the "immanence" and "transcendence" of the divine. It "represents" these precisely by the absence of any representation except that of things themselves, in their concrete particularity. Nor are these presented as the "symbol" of something "else": rather, their "suchness" (*Sosein*)[70] is itself what participates in the eternal and reveals it in both them and the viewer.[71] As Augustinus Wucherer-Huldenfeld remarks, such works of art—including abstractions—can serve as a "thickening" or "condensation" of being (*Verdichtung des Daseins*) and can, like all beings, bring to appearance the eternal "more" (*Je-Mehr*) of their depth, the ground of being itself.[72]

Certain forms of music seem to work in an analogous way. The meditative quality of some classical and modern Japanese music, for example, is based on a subtle interplay between sound and silence, between the progression of patterns and fleeting momentary tones and tone "colors," carrying Zen principles into the aesthetic realm. (One example among many: Toru Takemitsu's musical meditation for *gagaku* orchestra, "In an Autumn Garden.")[73] In the West, the music of Arvo Pärt works analogously (largely in explicitly sacred contexts) with purposely created silences, diminuendos approaching silence, and extended lines of pure tone. Does such music not sometimes produce an almost achingly intense consciousness of feeling and existence? Heard in their totality, they invite the listener to become present not merely to sound, rhythm, and tone but also to the horizon of hearing and of temporality itself, and finally to the horizon of the conscious existence perceiving its own temporal, contingent existence through the artistic intensification of being.

Of course, whether an artistic experience mediates the ontological depths of being, and whether those depths are connected with the "sacred" or not, depends largely on the context in which it is perceived—above all, the disposition, background, and concrete situation of the listener or viewer.[74]Moreover, certain forms of art may aim at a purely sensual level of perception. (Rahner cites impressionist art that seeks to produce merely color.) If this is indeed the only purpose and result of such art, Rahner says, then it does not mediate a relationship to God or even directly raise the question: "it moves in a dimension of humanity where the relationship to God is not yet present."[75] Nevertheless, even such works can be religiously significant for a particular person to whom they "accidentally" reveal the condition of possibility of their production or of their subject matter or of the perceiver's existential situation.

Art and the Christian Message: "Special" Categorical Revelation

Having looked briefly at some ways in which art may be a direct embodiment of "revelation"—through the quest for beauty, through the association of feelings, and through the heightening of the "ontological" dimension of experience—we turn now to explicitly religious art. Here art serves another form of categorical revelation: that embodied in a sacred tradition of thought and life. Our examples will be drawn primarily from the Christian tradition; at least some of the observations on the theological uses of art should be applicable to other traditions as well.

The mediation of a religious tradition and message through art poses special problems. Explicitly religious art may serve at least three different functions. First, religious works may express religious or theological content, either as the bearer or as the interpreter of words, especially the Scriptures (for example, liturgical chant). Second, they may serve as a nonverbal communication of ideas and feelings that are not directly derived from the message as "word," but are nevertheless intrinsically related to it (for example as an expression of its presuppositions or of concomitant affects; e.g., the sacred organ music of Bach). Or, third, they may create beauty in a religious context (for example, Mozart's charming but not especially "sacred" Epistle sonatas). (Of course, other goals may be involved as well—the self-expression of the artist, for example—but the above three seem to be the most significant for theological examination.) These three are not always clearly separable: they may intersect and combine, or they may each be present to varying degrees in particular works, with one or another of them in predominance.

Certain tensions frequently arise between these functions—that is, there is often a discrepancy of purpose between religious art *qua* religious and *qua* art. Van der Leeuw comments that "Nine-tenths of the 'religious works of art' which we know evidence no inner, essential continuity between holiness and beauty, having only a purely external connection, which admittedly can be very refined, violating neither art nor religion, but not proclaiming their unity."[76]

In a similar vein, Rahner notes that a great deal of explicitly religious art is not deeply religious, because it is "unable to evoke in those who see it a genuine and deep religious reaction. There exists what we call religious *Kitsch*." He illustrates the point with reference to certain artistic products of sentimental piety in the nineteenth century:

> We might perhaps say that basically the pictures in the nineteenth century of the Holy Family were painted with the best intentions by pious people, but nevertheless, they were not truly religious paintings, because they do not affect us deeply enough to elicit religious feelings. On the other hand, it is quite possible that a Rembrandt painting, which is not intended as religious, moves people so deeply, bringing up the question of life's ultimate meaning, that it is, strictly speaking, a religious painting.[77]

Certainly one can agree that there is a great deal of religious kitsch (although different critics might disagree about the application of the term to particular works). But Rahner seems to oversimplify the relation between artistic merit and religious significance by neglecting the highly subjective component in both aesthetic and religious reactions. Many pastors and practitioners of pastoral arts (musical, pictorial, architectural, homiletic) would probably agree with the observation that artistic works that are kitsch precisely *as art* (in the estimation of the professional) can nevertheless produce deep and genuine religious feelings in some people—perhaps even in a larger number than are so affected by "high" art.[78] On the other hand, attitudes that the theologian might judge to be kitsch (or worse) precisely *as religion*—for example, a superficial and merely sentimental piety, or a narrow and bigoted sanctimoniousness—might be embodied in art that is great in other ways: in its beauty, its technique, its communicative power, its ability to touch deep human (but not necessarily religious) feelings. (This description may fit some of the great Renaissance representations of the Madonna—Lippo Lippi's come to mind—that express very conventional piety, but convey a compelling vision of female beauty and/or speak eloquently about motherhood. The "sacred" music of Verdi and Rossini might also fit into this category.)

The relation between artistic expression and religious response is complex. A piece of art or music may evoke a strong and theologically valid religious reaction, not because of its beauty or its skill, but quite apart from these—or sometimes even because of their lack. It may be simply the content that moves the religiously disposed mind; or it may be that the work evokes associations (motherhood, family, love, tenderness) that lead indirectly toward the sacred; or it may be that a particular aesthetic medium, even if it is on an artistically "low" level, is able effectively to communicate the message because it speaks in the predominant cultural language. (Many ethnic or "folk" liturgies, for example, are aesthetically at a level that some would call kitsch, but those who have experienced them will testify that they often embody powerful faith and commitment.)

Two methodological consequences are suggested by the recognition of these complexities. First, it is necessary to begin with a somewhat closer and contextual examination of the different functions of religious art in their concrete interaction. Second, it will be important to select examples from those works of religious art that have attained the status of "classics": works that not only produce religious feeling in particular contexts but also have stood the test of time and speak to the wider Christian community.

A "Hierarchy" of the Arts?

As Rahner notes, there are many kinds of sense experience that may contribute to the mediation of the divine:

> Such are spatial features provided by architecture; experience of movement provided by liturgical gestures, walking in pilgrimages, or religious dance; olfactory experiences deriving from incense; experiences of touching or tasting in sacramental activities. All the sense powers may, in their mutually irreducible experiences, and in countless different ways and combinations, enter into the religious act.[79]

At various levels, these sense experiences may be "craftfully" or artistically ordered as different kinds of religious "art," each with a unique relation to sacred content.

Before proceeding to a closer examination of the methods by which art concretely mediates the holy, it may be profitable to consider briefly Gerardus Van der Leeuw's interesting proposal of a general theological schematization of the arts as an ordered "hierarchy." Van der Leeuw's leading idea is that from a theological point of view the arts do not all have the same relationship to the Christian message. The starting point for a Christian theology of the arts for Van der Leeuw must be the doctrine of the "image" of God; and from this point of reference the various arts may be seen as ordered "hierarchically" around a "midpoint" which is the production of the visual image. This does not imply that any one of the arts is superior to the others, only that each has a different relation to the central "point of intersection" of religion and art, where art turns to the absolute. [80]

All art, for Van der Leeuw, is "representational" in the broad sense of the term, but the pictorial is so in a special way because it is dominated by form and shape.[81] The centrality of the visual image, then, is specific to a theology that sees concrete "form," a historical mediation of transcendence, as the central and differentiating point of Christianity. Other religions and theologies will have different centers of gravity and different relations to art:

> That theology which places the impersonal, the spiritual (in the sense of the immaterial) in the central position will attempt to follow the movement of the arts from the fixed center to music. Such an immanent, pantheistic, mystical theology will understand music as the essence of all arts and leave the image behind. Schopenhauer did this in masterful fashion. A theology, on the other hand, which thinks historically and transcendentally, which places the incarnation of God at the center, will seek the mid-point of the arts in the image. It will find a strong analogy between the undifferentiated primitive religion and the equally undifferentiated art of the dance. It will ascertain a similar analogy between the mysticism which once more breaks through all forms and boundaries, and music, which knows neither content nor boundaries. But for itself it will find the connection between beauty and holiness in the image; and, since God created man in his own image and walked the earth in the form of a man, this theology will be convinced that it cannot be a sinful pride to search for God's image in these forms of his creation.[82]

On the basis of this insight, Van der Leeuw briefly suggests an intriguing Trinitarian schema of the arts. Dance, the original art, in which all the rest are found in undivided unity, with the allied art of drama, correspond to God as "Father," the primal and mysterious source. In images, art "stands still" and takes on concrete and permanent form. The arts of the word (literature), painting and sculpture, and building correspond to God's revelation in the Son, God's historical embodiment. In imageless music, art again becomes movement, expressing an invisible but felt dynamism in a progression through time: it represents the realm of the Spirit.[83]

The Sacred Word in Art and Music

We have already dealt at some length with the ways to God through beauty, metaphysical insight, and associations of feeling, in the context of art that is not explicitly religious. Specifically religious art can, of course, work in these ways as well. A great deal of Western art and music is "religious" only in its content or theme; its essential purpose as art is enrichment, decoration, or the creation of beauty (although I agree with Gadamer that the religious context in which that beauty or feeling functions cannot be ignored without losing something of the work's meaning).[84] The primary focus of the present section will be the more explicitly religious function of art as bearer of or accompaniment to sacred words, ideas, attitudes, and feelings. The latter must also be considered an aspect of the revelatory "word" in its wide sense. Hence our subject includes also art that aims not so much at communication of a specific message but, rather (like sacred architecture and much sacred music and painting), at the creation of a sacred "ambience" in space and time that is suitable to the message.

I will concentrate on music and pictorial art, attempting to discern the way in which their explicitly sacral function intersects with their nature as "art." In doing so, I will summarize and comment on Van der Leeuw's and Tillich's efforts to discern (from a theological point of view) some of the types and methods of religious art, with the goal of suggesting somewhat more concretely the ways in which various arts function in mediating the sacred. The discussion will necessarily be incomplete and limited in scope; it intends merely to indicate some directions for possible conversations with art historians and philosophers of aesthetics.

The Visual Arts

The relation between the revelatory word and the visual arts (here meaning primarily painting and sculpture) is complex.

Graphic design can, first of all, serve as a direct representation of words. Western writing takes place primarily in letters that, although they ultimately derive their forms from pictures, early became arbitrary and abstract signs for particular sounds. In contrast, Chinese calligraphy uses pictures as "ideograms"—although the modern form of most characters is so stylized that their original representational quality is not at all apparent, and many characters are formed in part by elements referring to sound rather than meaning. Even in the presence of alphabetic writing, however, pictures can serve a kind of hieroglyphic or ideographic purpose, directly representing words or ideas, either independently or in connection with writing.

We might call this use of art in its closest connection with word "ideographic symbolism": visual images are used as an alternative way of "writing" words or ideas.[85] In early Roman Christian catacomb frescoes and sepulchral inscriptions we find numerous examples: the fish, whose Greek name is an acronym for Christ as savior (ΙΧΘΥΣ = Ἰησοῦς Χριστός Θεοῦ Ὑιὸς Σωτήρ);[86] the anchor, representing "hope" (these two are combined in a fresco in the catacomb of Domitilla); a picture of fish and bread (the elements of the gospel miracle of the loaves) to represent simultaneously the miracle of the loaves and the eucharist (particularly beautiful in its economy and simplicity is an example found in the catacombs of Calixtus); "*Pax*" (in the sepulchral context meaning eternal rest) is written by a dove, sometimes with an olive branch (carved on many sarcophagi; a particularly lovely example in fresco is found in the Cubiculo Velatio in the catacombs of Priscilla); and so on. This "ideographic" and symbolic function continues as an internal element within other forms of art as well. For example, the apparently gratuitous presence of a dog in many medieval and renaissance religious paintings is perplexing unless the viewer recognizes it as a symbol of "*fides*" (among many examples, see Rosselli's painting of the Last Supper in the Sistine chapel).

Pictorial art or design, like musical decoration, can also be used for the illumination and illustration of texts. Early Christian and medieval manuscripts furnish many splendid examples of varied styles and degrees of integration with the written word. In the page from the Book of Durrow containing the beginning of the Gospel of Mark, the use of art is restrained: its purpose is simply to add beauty to the letters. But in the *Book of Kells* (fol. 130 r.), where a full page is given to the opening word of the Latin text of Mark ("*Initium*"), the illumination so predominates the writing that the word is illegible except to one who already knows what it is.

The illustration (rather than simple decoration) of written texts brings us into another sphere of religious art. The kind and degree of illustration used for texts can vary widely. We may distinguish two fundamental (and sometimes overlapping) types: the narrative and the iconic. The type that I call the "iconic" is distinguished by its representing the subject in abstraction from any particular historical narrative: the religious truth it presents is existential and trans-historical or eternal. The distinction should not be overly stressed, however, since even narrative religious pictures can have the iconic quality of presenting eternal and existentially relevant truths that invite the viewer into the narrative. Hence most early "narrative" frescos and mosaics present the action, not against a naturalistic background, but in the golden light of their true and eternal meaning. As an example of narrative painting, we might cite the magnificent Last Supper in the Rossano gospel in the Vatican Library. It is a realistic/symbolic (but not "historical") portrayal of the narration contained on the same page. The *Book of Kells*, on the other hand, gives us not so much textual illustrations as symbolic representations of the significance of gospel events (the crucifixion), as well as iconic portrayals of persons (Christ, the evangelists).

Such narrative and iconic pictures can also stand on their own, without accompanying written words, and in this form they are arguably the most important aspect of Western religious art. They also pose two special problems with regard to their relation to the sacred word. First, what is the relation and function of visual images vis-à-vis the sacred word? Second, by what means can the spiritual as such—that is, as a spiritual and hence invisible reality or quality—be indicated or represented in matter and given pictorial form?

The Relationship of Word and Image

As we have seen earlier in our brief overview of the iconoclast controversy, the West in general rejected the Eastern sacramental view of icons. It saw image making instead as serving an essentially didactic purpose. In this sense, artistic images are in theory subservient to the proclaimed word, in particular the sacred Scriptures. And, as we have seen, a great part of the tradition has justified religious images precisely as the *Biblia pauperum*, the presentation of the scriptural narratives in pictorial form for the sake of those who cannot read words.

However, this does not necessarily mean that art's religious function is limited to narration and illustration. On the other hand, as Rahner states, the mere fact that a picture represents salvation history does not suffice to make it "religious."

"A religious reality is truly such only when it helps us refer *directly* to the absolute God."[87]

How can the image do this (that is, apart from the mediation of God by beauty that we have spoken of above)? When it does so, what is its relation to the sacred message expressed in word?

We must first consider that the visual image (including even the photograph) necessarily interprets as well as portrays—all the more so when it is consciously used to present persons or events in a context different from that of the scriptural narratives (as is clearly the case of images of Christ as *pantocrator*, for example). Still, from the point of view that is especially strong in Protestant sensibilities, the word remains always the ultimate means of revelation and the criterion by which images must be evaluated. Garrett Green, for example, strongly emphasizes the role of "imagination" in revelation. But that imagination has itself a paradigmatic and irreplaceable source in the Scriptures. Green writes that "God is rendered authoritatively for the Christian imagination in scriptural narrative"; "proclamation . . . can be described as an appeal to the imagination of the hearers through the images of scripture."[88] Therefore "visual images can be judged according to their power to interpret scripture."[89]

In a somewhat similar vein, Pannenberg holds that the essence of the Christian religious image is to serve as a *Biblia pauperum*: its function is closely united with that of the word.[90] Writing against the Byzantine extension of the theology of the hypostatic union to icons, he insists that although images of Christ may be permitted, it is only through the act of faith that they can lead to God's dwelling in us—in the same way, that is, that the word operates. Pannenberg repeats Gadamer's observation that the purpose of representation (*Darstellung*) in art is to make the represented thing present (*gegenwärtig*) in the temporal existence (*Dasein*) of the human. For Pannenberg this implies that in general "performance art" better shows the purposes of representation than permanent images can. This is especially true in the case of mediating the presence of God, which has the nature of encounter and event. Precisely because it is permanent and timeless, the image cannot be more than a pointer to the God who is revealed in the humanity of Jesus; it cannot "actuate" God's presence, as Eastern iconodule theology would apparently have it.[91]

Rahner also notes that "word and image have complementary functions" in embodying and conveying revelation. Images that serve specifically as mediations of the Christian message for the community necessarily require verbal explanation: one cannot receive their full meaning simply from seeing them.[92] In this sense, Luther is right in saying that the ears are the organ of the Christian: faith comes from hearing (although not *exclusively* from hearing).[93]

This complementarity also implies that, as Gadamer says, the "true meaning" of the religious picture or the religious ritual cannot be uncovered by a purely "aesthetically differentiated" consciousness.[94] On the other hand, the recognition that for Christian art the meaning of the work depends upon the message must be qualified for, as we have seen, there can be in art varying levels of seriousness in fulfilling this ostensible purpose of Christian art. The content of the message is integral to the work to very varying degrees. Moreover, the truth of Rahner's observation does not contradict the fact that specifically Christian images may also be revelatory in the other, more universal ways discussed above—for example, through their beauty or metaphysical dimensions—or that, in given cases, these other functions may be so predominant that the specifically Christian meaning becomes secondary or even relatively unimportant to the viewer. Despite the gospel admonition, visual art, like music, frequently ends up attempting to serve more than one master.

In any case, because of the irreducibility of the different kinds of sense experience to one another, Rahner holds that visual mediations of revelation cannot simply be understood as illustrations adopted for pedagogical reasons: "images have a religious significance that cannot be replaced by the word."[95] This significance can, of course, be discussed in words. "Yet these words are no substitute for the viewing in itself."[96] Similarly, Gadamer's statements on the relation between language and understanding seem to imply that (verbal) language (*Sprache, Sprachlichkeit*) is the normal medium of hermeneutical experience (i.e., getting to the meaning of the object of conversation), although spoken language is not necessarily the medium of every experience itself.[97] Since works of art convey meaning and must be understood "like any other text,"[98] there must exist discourse about them; but such discourse does not exhaust the "meaning" of the aesthetic experience.

Furthermore, even when they serve as "interpretations" of the word, visual representations, like all interpretations, present not only a content but also a transcendental and historical horizon and a "pre-understanding" that serves as a hermeneutical principle. Any or all of these may be presented visually with a concreteness and an emphasis that frequently surpasses that of the concept or spoken word.[99]

The visual image, then, would seem to have a special place alongside the word as a conveyor of religious meaning. If the suggestions outlined in the previous chapters are correct, images not only correspond to a distinct sense faculty but also represent a different way of thinking: they can act as the medium for the production, embodiment, and communication of acts of perception, higher feeling, insight, desire, and love. Then the image is not simply an accompaniment to the word but also is itself a "word": the verbal message when expressed in visual form has been "translated" into an independent language, with its own mode of embodying meaning. And, like every translation, the visual image also transforms the message.

But "translation" is not an altogether sufficient metaphor for the function of visual religious art, since the latter also has its own direct link to religious experience.[100] It is certainly true, at least in Christianity, that the verbal "message" has a unique and central place. But, as we have seen, the scriptural word is often itself "pictorial" and imaginative; an actual picture may more effectively represent its meaning than literature can. Furthermore, the word is not the exclusive embodiment of Christian revelation. It is the most explicitly and conceptually communicative formulation of God's self-gift and the "religious conversion" it accomplishes. But existence in grace in its individual and communal dimensions is also expressed nonverbally in styles of life, actions, rituals, images, pictures. These are also workings of God's spirit and embodied "words" of God, whose specific content is at least implicitly allied to the verbal message, but also goes beyond it. In Christian trinitarian language, we may say that every such categorical revelation inspired by God's spirit is an element of the "incarnation" of God's "word," an incarnation whose earthly fullness is reached in the Christ event, which is itself the proleptic presence of the eschatological "pleroma."[101]

Hence the function of the picture, even in Christianity, is not simply subservient to that of the word but also is (at least in some cases) parallel to it. As Gadamer says, "the picture is an ontological event [*ein Seinsvorgang*]—in it being becomes meaningfully visible [*in ihm kommt Sein zur sinnvollsichtbaren Erscheinung*]."[102] Art "as a whole and in a universal sense brings an increase in 'pictoralness' [*Bildhaftigkeit*] to being. Words and pictures are not mere imitative illustrations, but allow what they represent to be for the first time [fully] what it is."[103] "Every picture is an increase of being [*Seinszuwachs*] and is essentially determined as representation, as coming-to-presentation [*Zur-Darstellung-Kommen*]."[104] A picture is a manifestation (*Manifestation*) of what it represents.[105] And the religious picture, along with the sacred word, is the fullest realization of the "epiphanic" nature of representation: "For it is really true of the appearance of the divine that it acquires its pictoral quality only through the word and the picture."[106]

But for the Christian, the ultimate meaning of "revelation" or of divine "epiphany" is to be found neither in the sensible nor in the conceptual realm, but in the personal: it is the person of Christ, encountered in the community's narratives, but also present in the living communion of the Spirit, that is its focal point. Behind the "epiphanic" quality of word and image referred to by Gadamer there lies a more ultimate reality. Hence it might be preferable to say, in accord with the Eastern Patristic tradition, that the divine acquires its pictoral quality because of the humanity of Christ: because Christ is God's *Logos* and *Eikon* in person, words and images of God are possible. (But we may also reverse the order: because God's spirit can be and is active in human words and images in general, it is also possible for it to achieve full presence in Jesus as the embodiment of God's message, the man of the Spirit.) Then it is possible that there are aspects of revelation that can be mediated in visual religious art in a way that cannot be expressed in other media. For persons are imaged visually in a unique way, one that symbolically summarizes a complex synthesis of ideas, feelings, emotions, and relations.

Pictures allow us to relate to the person of Christ (or to life "in" Christ) in ways that go beyond oral and written transmissions of the message about him and his meaning. Pannenberg is correct to oppose the quasi-hypostatic view of icons, and to assimilate the function of pictures to that of words. But because it "does not disappear behind its pointing function but, in its own being, shares in what it represents,"[107] the picture (like the word) can indeed be a kind of "sacrament" (or, in the technical language of Catholicism, a "sacramental.")

(It is beyond the scope of the present work to attempt a treatment of the specific symbolic acts that the church considers "sacraments" in the strict sense, even in their aesthetic connection. If we may be permitted a brief excursus, however, we may note that Gadamer provides some useful and provocative ideas toward such a reflection in his treatment of the difference between pictures and symbols. Pictures as such are not symbols; and symbols need not be pictorial. The picture, for Gadamer, stands between the sign (pure indication) and the symbol (pure representation). The sign simply points to something else; the symbol not only points to what it represents but also takes its place and makes it "immediately" present. The picture points, but also represents, "but through itself, through the extra significance that it brings." Symbols, on the other hand, of themselves "say nothing about what they symbolize. They must be known, in the way one must know a sign, if one is to understand what they indicate. Hence they do not mean an increase in being for what is represented . . . They are merely representatives [*Stellvertreter*]." On the other hand, the symbol, like the picture, means a share in the being of what is symbolized or represented. In the case of religious symbols, "what is to be symbolized is undoubtedly in need of representation [*Darstellung*], inasmuch as it is itself non-sensible, infinite, and unrepresentable [*undarstellbar*], but it is also capable of it. It is only because it is present itself that it can be present in the symbol."[108] The sacraments are a unique case of religious symbols, in that they are intimately tied to the Christian narrative as well as to specific signifiers. To the extent that they share the characteristics of "performance art" they are also "pictorial," in the wide sense of the word: they do not simply represent, as in Gadamer's understanding of symbol, but also signify, like words and pictures, and effect an increase in being for the participant ["grace"] precisely by signifying ["*sacramenta significando efficiunt gratiam*"]).

The material permanence of the image is not an obstacle to its "sacramental" functioning: as in the case of hearing the word, each looking at a picture—at least one that has artistic depth or profound religious associations—is an event. At the same time, the picture is implicitly associated with a communal history of such events—that is, the function that the image (especially the icon) has performed in the edification of the community.

It is in this perspective that Rahner sees the justification for the veneration of religious images. Aquinas, in considering this question, had repeated the traditional position that only persons may be "revered" *in se;* the "veneration" of images is an indirect way of honoring the person represented.[109] Asking whether images of Christ should be adored, Aquinas replies that there is a double movement of the soul inspired toward the image: insofar as it is a thing in itself, and insofar as it is a representation of another. Mere things are not deserving of reverence, which is proper only to rational beings. Hence images of Christ are revered only insofar as they are images, with the same reverence that is shown to what they represent—that is, Christ.[110] Because persons are owed a "reverence" for their own sake (i.e., as spiritual images of God), and material things are not, the later even have a certain advantage in mediating honor given to God: the medium cannot be mistaken for the end.[111] Rahner, on the other hand, makes the functioning of the image in the community the rationale for its veneration. We need not insist, he says, that veneration belongs only to the person or reality represented; a picture may be honored precisely because of the lasting religious meaning that it has had for many people.[112] Rahner's position keeps the personalist basis for "veneration," but changes the focus: veneration is given to the image, not primarily because of the person represented in the image, but because of those who use it and reach God through its mediation.

The two categories of religious pictures mentioned above—the narrative and the iconic—may be associated with two major (and frequently overlapping) religious functions of the image: the didactic and the sacramental (bearing in mind, of course, that "religious" art may also be used for primarily decorative and aesthetic purposes). The didactic function of art is oriented to the communication of a message. In form such art may be symbolic and ideographic, or it may be narrative; in the latter case, the narration may be historical and descriptive (e.g., Bruegel's *Der Bethlemischer Kindermord*), or allegorical (e.g., the Good Samaritan window at Chartres). Sacramental art, on the other hand, aims primarily at veneration, remembrance, and meditation; it intends to evoke in the viewer's mind and feeling the presence of what it represents.[113] It is most frequently iconic, and often takes the form of a religious "portrait" of Christ, Mary, or the saints—or even of the Triune God—outside any earthly historical context. (See, for example, Masaccio's fresco of the Trinity in Santa Maria Novella in Florence.)

In medieval Christian art, the two functions are often inseparably joined. In Giotto's portrayal of the crucifixion in the lower basilica at Assisi, for example, the pictorial narration of the event is combined with the symbolic representation of dogmatic truths (the angels collect the blood of Christ in chalices, evoking the new covenant), with a statement of the trans-historical significance of the event (at the foot of the cross are not only Christ's contemporaries but also St. Francis and his followers), and with an implicit appeal to the viewer to acknowledge and respond to the present reality of Christ's self-sacrificial love that consciously envisages the viewer him/herself. (Through most of Christian history the sense of "presence" to the events of Christ's life and death would have been augmented by the theological conviction that Christ enjoyed both the beatific vision and foreknowledge of the future, including personal knowledge of all future recipients of salvation. Hence the faithful of future ages were truly "present" to Christ during his earthly life. This idea is explicitly invoked in Pius XII's 1943 encyclical *Mystici Corporis*.[114])

Intrinsic to revelation—at least on the view I have adopted—is not only the unveiling of God as "other" but also and inseparably the transformation of the subject by God's self-gift: the human reception is constitutive, on the categorical level, of revelation itself. Because and insofar as human existence is converted, transformed by God's self-gift, it becomes the "image" of God. Pictorial art is particularly adapted to communicating this theological truth: the human form and human relations can be used to "represent" God precisely because (and to the extent that) they have become godly. As Green remarks, "The art historian would note the robust humanity of Michelangelo's God, but the theological point is just the reverse: not the anthropomorphic rendering of God but the theomorphic rendering of man."[115]

"Revelation" in its widest sense refers not only to the transmission of the originating message (contained in the privileged witness of the scriptures) but also to the community's reflection on it, explanation of it, recognition of its meaning in different circumstances, and formation of ideas and ways of living from it.

FIGURE 4. *Giotto di Bondone (1266–1336)*. Crucifixion. *Lower church, S. Francesco, Assisi, Italy.*

Christian art, therefore, is concerned not only with imaging the divine and the events of salvation history but also with providing images of life in the spirit and its consequences. Hence its function goes beyond what the great defender of icons, John Damascene, proposed: namely, furnishing our weak material minds with "corporeal models which provide a vague understanding of intangible things," giving form to what is intrinsically formless.[116] Rather, much of its subject matter is what falls properly within the field of the visual: earthly life—seen and known, however, in the light of spirit. Pictorial art frequently accomplishes this with great concreteness, embodying the ideal of transcendence in the forms significant to particular times and places. Hence not only images of the "saints" as exemplars but also images of the virtuous life, even if not explicitly connected to the Christian message, belong to the realm of sacred art.

The visual image has a particular relation to the object of religious hope. What Ricoeur says about imagination in general applies in a special way to the visual image:

> Desire is a lack *of* . . . a drive *toward.* . . . Human desire illuminates its aim through the representation of the absent thing, of how it may be reached, and the obstacles which block its attainment. These imaging forms direct desire upon the world; I take pleasure in them; in them I am out of myself. The image is even more: not only does it anticipate the perceptual outlines of gestural behavior, but it also anticipates pleasure and pain, the joy and

sadness of being joined to or separated from the desired object . . . The image informs desire, lays it open, and illuminates it. Through the image, desire enters into the field of motivation.[117]

Like music, visual art can show the object of hope as beautiful; but the visual can anticipate the spiritual or moral transformation of the subject because of that hope in a highly concrete way, taking its forms from contemporary experience. (So Christ is painted as the model of each ages's spirituality: as both the good shepherd and the imperial ruler in the catacombs; as the man of sorrows in the late Middle Ages; as a person transformed by interior light in Rembrandt and Velasquez; etc.)

Visual Symbols of the Transcendent

Having spoken of the theoretical relationship of word and image, we now turn to a second question, regarding concrete means: precisely how does the visual image function as "representational" in the sacred sphere—that is, in the sphere of what is in itself spiritual and invisible? We take for granted what has been said above about the evocation of the immanent divine by the portrayal of the simple "being there" (*Dasein*) and being such (*Sosein*) of things, so that pure artistic representation of finite objects may also evoke metaphysical and religious associations. The question here regards explicitly religious art: how does pictorial representation become at the same time the *explicit* symbol of the transcendent? How can it "speak" the message addressed to us by God in the dimension of categorical revelation embodied in the sacred word and in Christian life? This problem regards not only the representation of what is itself invisible but also the "narrative" function of art in the depiction of sacred history. Although the events that constitute it are historical and hence picturable, it is precisely their meaning for faith, their sacred significance, that must be conveyed by religious art. We inquire, therefore, about the concrete means by which visual art may indicate the sacred.

Van der Leeuw describes a number of artistic techniques and gives examples that are worth citing in detail, since they reflect the sensitivity of an artist as well as a theologian. He refers first to Otto's category of the "numinous," described as the *mysterium tremendum et fascinans*, to categorize ways in which pictorial art can mediate religious experience. It presents the fascination and attractiveness of the holy through color and light, and through the contrast of light and darkness[118] (as we shall see, these terms that are used literally in the case of visual art may also be applied metaphorically to sacred music). The awe-inspiring and fearful aspect of holiness is expressed primarily in sculpture and painting. Otto himself notes the monstrous form of many Indian deities. Van der Leeuw gives several examples from the Christian tradition. Christ in Byzantine art appears in "threatening majesty." Dürer's picture *Christ with the Crown of Thorns* brings to mind the gospel phrase, "Lord, depart from me, for I am a sinful man." In Michelangelo's portrayal of the damned in the Sistine chapel, we see faces reflecting the terror of the holy. In the Isenheim Altar, Grünewald presents the sacred as gruesome and "ghostly" (a nuance of the "awe-inspiring") through "the terrible glory of his colors and the

FIGURE 5. *Matthias Grünewald (1455–1528).* The Isenheim Altarpiece, Crucifixion, *1512. Musée Unterlinden, Colmar, France.*

demonic richness of his insanely impossible movements."[119] (It should be noted that in each of these cases an identification with "the holy" is possible only through a knowledge of the subject matter of the painting.)

Darkness and semidarkness are used to symbolize visually the encounter with "mystery": all earthly light and perceptible form disappear in the face of the holy, just as the mind finds itself in the presence of what cannot be reduced to conceptual intelligibility. We find examples in the semidarkness of Romanesque churches and in the art of *chiaroscuro*. (Van der Leeuw notes that in Eastern art the same effect is produced by the portrayal of "emptiness," as we have noted above.)[120] On the other hand, form, especially the human form, may also be used to express the superhuman and supernatural,[121] as in Michelangelo's Creation cycle. Here it is beauty and perfection that serve as the symbol of the divine.

Paul Tillich takes another route in analyzing the pictorial representation of the sacred.[122] In his essay "Art and Ultimate Reality," he analyzes visual religious art in terms of an original set of categories designating five "stylistic elements" that serve the expression of the sacred. Each of these elements (which are found in "innumerable mixtures" in the history of art) corresponds with a distinct "type" of religious experience.[123]

"Numinous realism" expresses the most universal and fundamental type, the "sacramental." It represents ordinary things "in a way which makes them strange, mysterious, laden with an ambiguous power," using spatial relations, stylization of forms, and "uncanny expressions" to do so.[124] The "mystical/pantheistic" element of style tries to evoke the kind of mysticism (more predominant in the Oriental religions than in Christianity) in which the ultimate is reached without the mediation of particular things.[125] The "prophetic-protesting" type of religion has descriptive and critical "realism" as its artistic medium. Descriptive realism has no directly "numinous" character; its object is simply the familiar "objective" world of everyday experience. But its function as art is to allow us to see and attend to what we frequently miss in our daily functional relation to our surroundings. This aesthetically mediated re-viewing of the ordinary can have religious power when the richness of the world is seen as "given" by and expressive of ultimate reality.[126] "Critical" realism, on the other hand, "shows ultimate reality by judging existing reality":[127] it depicts the evil and suffering in the world. By doing so in aesthetic form, however, it evokes hope for the reversal of evil.[128]

The attitude Tillich calls "religious humanism" appears in the stylistic element of "idealism." The present is seen as an anticipation of future perfection; hence objects are portrayed not realistically but in ideal form. (Tillich gives a special warning of the danger of this style, represented in "innumerable religious pictures." Because it represents the ideal "essence" apart from the reality of the existential human condition of estrangement, this approach is frequently guilty of "confusing idealism with a superficially and sentimentally beautifying realism" and hence producing art that is inferior both aesthetically and religiously.)[129] Finally, there is the "ecstatic-spiritual" type of religious experience. Tillich appears to favor this type, which "comes to its own within Christianity." It is "the religion of the New Testament," and Tillich identifies it in a particular way with Protestant movements. He presents it as a kind of dynamic synthesis that "appears in unity and conflict with the other religious types," and is realistic and mystical at the same time. This type produces the "expressionist" elements in art that "determine the art of the catacombs, the Byzantine, the Romanesque, most of the Gothic and the Baroque style, and the recent developments since Cézanne."[130]

It has been remarked that Tillich's conceptual framework would probably find favor with few art historians because it is theologically determined, rather than based on concrete analysis of works.[131] Nevertheless, I believe Tillich's approach can make a valuable contribution in the context of this section's restricted purpose—namely, to examine some of the major ways in which art can mediate revelation. Tillich goes beyond simple enumeration of techniques to suggest, in however incipient a fashion, intelligible groupings of art works of different periods in the light of similarities in their way of communicating religious ideas and feelings, and hence connecting them to a genuinely theological analysis of diverse and sometimes conflicting tendencies in the conception of and relation to the divine.

The Word in Music

By far the most usual and obvious case of music as the bearer of the sacred "word" is the setting of texts in chant and song. The purpose of such music is to create a sacred "ambience": to elevate the feelings, mind, and heart in the act of conveying the message, or a reflection on it, or a reaction to it.

In simple chant, the emphasis is on the text. The chanting of psalms permits a communal and uniform repetition of divine praise in a meditative setting; the chanting of the Scriptures and eucharistic prayers adds solemnity and grace to them.[132] To such chants one may add hymns intended for congregational singing. Examples of this singly focused kind of music abound, from the earliest pre-Gregorian chants to Luther's great hymn settings to contemporary liturgical pieces like Geoffrey Burgon's *Nunc Dimittis*. While such music may attain great beauty, its primary and original purpose is clearly the transmission of words.[133]

The great advantage of music among the sacred arts is that it can serve as the medium for verbal language (song) or can accompany it; it can therefore be used in the communication and/or reinforcement of a verbal religious message without the need of learning an auxiliary skill like reading letters or characters. Moreover, its artistic character lends a suitable aspect of pleasure to the hearing of the message. The Lutheran reformers defended the use of music in worship on precisely such grounds, giving four reasons why music is especially apt for the work of evangelization: because it can be combined with the Word; because it enters the senses pleasantly; because it moves the spirit directly; and because it aids in the memory's retention of the text.[134]

But nonverbal music can also be used as a means of religious communication, as another "language" for its expression. In that case, it can function in a way parallel to either the alphabetic or the ideographic modes of representing words and ideas. The contemporary composer Olivier Messiaen reflects on such uses of music for "linguistic" communication:

> The various known languages are, first and foremost, a means of communication. They are generally vocal in character. But is that the only way of

transmitting ideas? One can well imagine a language based on movement, images, colour, perfume, and everyone knows that the Braille alphabet uses touch. In each of these instances, one begins with a preliminary understanding: it is agreed that *this* explains *that*.

[Nonvocal] [m]usic, on the other hand, explains nothing directly. It can suggest, give rise to a feeling or state of mind, touch the subconscious, expand the faculty of dreaming, and these happen to be great powers: what it is absolutely unable to do is to "speak," in the sense of "inform with precision". Wagner tried to invent a communicable language with musical sounds. This is how he created the *Leitmotiv*.[135]

The musical leitmotiv functions in a way parallel to the ideogram: it serves as a nonverbal identification, representation, or evocation of a person or idea (in the manner of the "Grail" theme in Wagner's *Parsifal*, to cite a well-known example. A simpler and more ancient use of music as "ideophone" is referred to by St. Paul in I Corinthians: "if the trumpet's sound is uncertain, who will prepare for battle?" [14:8]. Since ancient times horns and drums have been used as "words" of command, signaling orders at long distance; a certain combination of notes signifies "alert" or "advance" or "retreat.") Even before Wagner's "invention" of the leitmotiv we may find instances of musical themes or types of sound being used in an "ideophonic" way; for example, Bach's use of different themes and musical forms to represent Father, Son, and Spirit in the "Saint Anne" fugue; or Cererol's use of three distinctly voiced choirs of instruments and singers for the same purpose in his *Missa de Batalla*. We may also include in this category the musical "halo" of strings that accompanies Christ's words (with the dramatic exception of his cry of desolation immediately before death) in Bach's *Matthäuspassion*.[136]

Not content with such "ideophonic" representations, Messiaen experimented with a more directly "linguistic" religious music, using nonverbal sounds in an "alphabetic" way to produce a kind of encoded expression of words. In his *Méditations sur le mystère de la Sainte Trinité*, he invents a "communicable musical language" in which he not only uses particular themes to represent the name and attributes of God and of the Trinitarian persons but also assigns musical notes to each letter of the alphabet and creates musical phrases that correspond to the Latin grammatical cases, so that he can literally "spell out" in music several texts from the *Summa Theologica*.

The relationship of music to word frequently becomes more complex and ambiguous as other functions of art come into play: decoration, the evocation of feelings, the creation of beauty. Music may be used to "illuminate" a text, as letters are illuminated in medieval manuscripts: from plain chant there develops elaborated chant with melismatic accents on significant words and syllables. Or music can become a sort of "illustration," in which its elements are used to portray or evoke feelings suitable to the text. Some forms of music seem more apt for use because they excite emotional states that complement the content. (As we have seen above, certain periods developed elaborate theories of the direct relation of musical forms to particular emotions.)

Van der Leeuw enumerates a number of techniques that music employs to convey the sense of the holy. Sublimity is evoked by slowness of tempo, suggesting the overpowering and inescapable character of the divine.[137] The effect of encounter with the holy on the mind is also suggested by sudden and unexpected transitions or surprising modulations. In Haydn's *Creation*, the modulation to C major, the sudden *fortissimo*, and the shift from slow to excited, quick tempo in the opening chorale provide an aural illustration of the word "light." In the final movement of Beethoven's Ninth Symphony, in the setting of the sixth quatrain of Schiller's "Ode to Joy," the concluding phrase, *"und der Cherub steht vor Gott,"* is sung twice by the chorus (without the *und* the second time); then *steht vor Gott* is repeated again; and finally, *vor Gott* is repeated twice more, with a dramatic change of key at the last repetition of the word *"Gott"*: "and only then does the word 'God' seem to receive its full significance; it is as though the doors of heaven were opened, as though we were truly standing before God, and the music of angels could reach our ears."[138] In the soprano recitative in the first chorus of Bach's *St. Matthew Passion* (*"Er hat uns allen wohlgetan"*), at the final words, *"Sonst hat mein Jesus nichts getan"* the key changes to C major and we perceive "the dawning day in the midst of death and woe."[139]

The musical analogy for darkness and semidarkness is silence and near silence. The musical "rest" is a kind of holding of the breath: "musical silence is thus by no means a 'rest,' but the greatest possible tension. . . . To be silent is not to be inactive, but is the greatest receptivity and highest activity."[140] The effect of *chiaroscuro* may be produced by the emergence of sound from quietness. For example, at the beginning of Beethoven's violin concerto, four soft beats of the timpani and the chord that follows constitute a musical semidarkness from which the light of melody then arises.[141]

There is a seemingly natural association of certain musical techniques with the evocation of the holy. To those mentioned by Van der Leeuw we might add several more. The use of dissonance and contrasting rhythms in Messiaen, for example, creates a "strangeness" whose effect is like that of Grünewald's use of color. Sustained purity of sound, very high or very low pitch, like barely audible notes (as, for example, in some of the sacred works of Pärt), touch on the limits of hearing, make us attend carefully, and by analogy suggest striving and transcendence. Harmony represents unity in multiplicity, communion in difference. Strictly marked tempo can be used to indicate solemnity (as in the priests' music in the last act of *Die Zauberflöte*). The "coloration" of music can also evoke aspects of the holy. For example, the voices of boy sopranos in English church music (and until the modern era, in virtually all Western church music) may be used to suggest purity and innocence, and evoke in the hearer the natural tenderness of adults toward children. Nevertheless, Van der Leeuw holds that there is no sacred "style" per se. He points out that during much of Christian history secular tunes were used to set sacred texts, and vice-versa: the melody of "O Sacred Head Surrounded" from Bach's *St. Matthew Passion* was originally a Minnelied; and many medieval masses were based on well-known songs[142] (we might cite, for example, the masses by Lassus, Ockeghem, Dufay, and others on the secular tune "l'homme armé").

Van der Leeuw is in basic agreement with Schopenhauer's view of music: it does not conjure up any specific ideas; it does not tell us about the world.[143] "Music is therefore by no means, like the other arts, the image of ideas, but is the image of the will itself."[144] The positive part of this statement agrees with Augustine's insight: music's attainment of wholeness only by movement, its lack of total self-possession in any moment, is itself an image of human existence. As time is the moving image of eternity, so music exemplifies the soul's time-bound character and its yearning for union with eternal and wholly self-present being.[145] In this sense, music is an intrinsic image of the "will."

However, I think we may perhaps legitimately ask whether the negative part of Schopenhauer's statement is not based on too narrow a conception of both "image" and "idea." Besides pictorial images there are also kinetic images, and music seems particularly apt at conveying them. They may not usually represent concepts directly (although in some cases they may do so, functioning as a learned symbolic language). But they are in any case associated with bodily states, emotions, and higher feelings (affects), and these in turn embody not simply pure "will" but also implied understandings and visions. With Gadamer, I think that even "absolute" music conveys meaning:

> Even if we hear absolute music we must "understand" it. . . . Thus, although absolute music is pure movement of form as such, a kind of auditory mathematics, where there is no content with an objective meaning that we can discern, to understand it nevertheless involves entering into a relation with what is meaningful. It is the indefiniteness of this relation that is the specific relation to meaning of this kind of music.[146]

Form, that is, has "meaning" simply as form. Hence I have suggested that like mathematics, with which music was identified in the ancient and medieval West, music of this kind can convey the sense of "ontological" wonder at the existence of form itself: the very fact of order or intelligible relations raises the mind to the question of the source of such order. But I am suggesting that such "contentless" music may also convey meaning in another way: not by reproducing images of particular objects, but by consciously or unconsciously representing kinesthetic images tied to certain objects, moods, states of mind, or feelings. In this sense, even "absolute" music may have "content." For this reason there is perhaps not an absolute dichotomy between the "symbolist" view that sees music as conveying ideas and values (Hegel, Schelling, Schopenhauer, Wagner) and the "autonomist" view that music does or should present an "aesthetic" message unconnected with any nonmusical ideas or values.[147]

Sacred opera, oratorios, and church cantatas frequently use music in the way I have suggested, uniting texts with emotionally or dramatically appropriate music. Rahner asks rhetorically: "when listening to a Bach oratorio, why would we not have the impression that, not only through its text but also through its music, we are in a very special way brought into a relationship with divine revelation about humanity?"[148] But the association of feelings may remain operative even in the absence of verbal component, so that an "ecclesial" form of purely instrumental music is also possible. (One might think, for example, of the sacred organ music of J. S. Bach.) As Van der Leeuw's observes: "Spiritual music is music which is not only a revelation of the beautiful, but also of the holy, not through the subject matter of the text or the occasion for which it was composed, but through the fact that holiness and beauty have mutually interpenetrated. Such music can be church music or have profane character."[149]

As we shall see in the next chapter, certain tensions can arise between musical and religious goals; or, as Van der Leeuw points out, the two can become parallel but disunited elements. On the other hand, in the greatest sacred music the working of the various levels together can create Luther's "sonorous preaching" of faith.

Art and the Holy: Affinities and Tensions

The first Vatican Council, after discussing the supernatural mysteries revelation and salvation, speaks of three ways in which the human mind can come to fruitful understanding of these mysteries: by exploring their analogical relation to our natural knowledge; by drawing out the relations of different aspects of the mysteries to each other; and by seeing their relation to the ultimate end or goal of human life.[150] Our considerations above show that art not only serves to communicate the message of revelation but also can pursue each of these theological ways of seeking understanding of it.

Art relates the message to our "natural" knowledge of God—that is, the intrinsic dynamism of our being—especially by connecting it with the beautiful and with the "metaphysical" question. It explores the relationships between the mysteries by symbolically indicating their connections, by picturing the moral life that results from them, and by interpreting their meaning by portraying them in the changing circumstances of different eras. (Of course, this concretization is not without its ambiguities, which can call for the application of a hermeneutic of suspicion. So, for example, the scriptural metaphor of King as applied to God or to Christ may evoke rather general ideas of power and rule—ideas that are themselves in need of explanation when applied to God. But when Christ is portrayed in the catacomb frescoes in the vesture of the Roman emperor, with accompanying apostles dressed as senators, there is an additional message implied about earthly rule: one that may very well be in conflict with the rational dynamism of human being in its sociopolitical dimension.) On another level, art relates our present life to the goal of our existence by providing images of hope, exciting desire for the transcendent horizon, and intimating the eternal as the source of meaning for the temporal.

As we have also seen, there are various ways in which art (especially verbal, musical, and visual arts) can accomplish these functions of "representing" or evoking revealed sacred reality and/or of reflecting on its meaning. A brief summary at this point may not be out of place. Art may re-present a content from ordinary life, calling attention to its transcendental horizon (*via* beauty or wonder). It may abstract from all objective content (as in nonrepresentational art, "pure" music, dance) to express feelings directly connected with spirit, joy, beauty, the intuition of existence. Or it may embody images, affects, thoughts that have an explicit religious content, with or without the accompaniment of a verbal message. Rarely (at least in the Western tradition) are there attempts to represent God or spiritual reality directly. More frequently, God's proper reality is presented symbolically and metaphorically; the message is presented through historical narration and portrayal; the working of revelation, grace, and salvation is shown in representations of transformed human life.

In becoming a medium for divine revelation, the arts may be said to open onto their ultimate spiritual possibility. As we have seen, this openness demands a transcending of what Gadamer calls the "purely aesthetic" consciousness. Kierkegaard has shown "the inner contradictions of aesthetic existence, so that it is forced to go beyond itself."[151] In the same way, Gadamer criticizes an "aesthetics" that separates the realm of art from existential and moral concerns: "In order to do justice to art, aesthetics must go beyond itself and surrender the 'purity' of the aesthetic."[152] "The experience of art must not be sidetracked into the uncommittedness of the aesthetic awareness."[153]

But even when art is open to the religious dimension, even when it is placed at the latter's service, a certain tension remains. As Van der Leeuw remarks, when religious art performs its function, it calls us to go not only beyond the limitations of its representation but also beyond itself: "the deepest, even the ultimate religious art, cannot exist before the face of God. In its highest forms of expression we feel a longing for a different image, a different song; some something which would no longer be 'art.' "[154] Indeed, all true art, whether it explicitly speaks of the sacred or not, invites us to "find the places where beauty passes over into holiness."[155]

> Thus we must tune our ears and sharpen our eyes for the beauty which confronts us with an absolute calm, for the beauty which appears in absolute majesty. We must listen to the word which is the Last Word, to the note which strives for the absoluteness of inaudibility; we must keep a lookout for the image which reminds us of the image and likeness of him whom we cannot see, for the movement which is conveyed by the rhythm of the stars, for the building which is the house of God. But we must also search within ourselves, to see whether we experience the beauty which is thus revealed to us as the wholly other. This we shall only know when beauty not only attracts us, but also repels us; not only enchants us, but also disturbs us in a way we never knew before. . . . At this point of intersection we seek, with the words of Rudolf Otto, that beauty which is both fascination and awe, which we approach with glad hope, but with trembling reverence.[156]

CHAPTER 6

꯾ꯗꯦꯖꯦꯗꯗꯗ

The Beautiful and the Good

Prelude

"Sonnet"

The journey of my life
in a fragile bark, through tempestuous seas,
has now already reached that common port,
where it goes to give account for every good and evil act.

There I now know how full of error
was the affectionate fantasy
that made art for me an idol and a king;
I know the value of what every one desires, against his will.

What shall become of amorous thoughts,
once welcome and joyous,
now that I approach a double death?
Of one I am certain, and the other threatens me.
Neither painting nor sculpting can any longer quiet
The soul, turned to that divine love
which opened its arms on the cross to take us.

—Michelangelo Buonarroti (1552–54)

The Tension Between the Aesthetic, the Ethical, and the Religious

Our concern in the last three chapters has centered on the positive side of the relation of the transcendent to human imagination, the beautiful, and the arts. We nevertheless saw in the second chapter that Christian theology from early on frequently found itself on uneasy terms with the realm of imagination. Iconoclasm was the epitome of the effort to protect the transcendence of God and God's self-revelation from the dangers of human projection and "idolatry." We have also had occasion to remark in passing that certain tensions have historically arisen between the quest for beauty and the quest for God; and we noted at the end of the last chapter that a tension frequently exists between the arts and the religious message they have been used to serve. At this point, at the end of our "fundamental" theological aesthetics, we turn our attention to a "dialectical" consideration in which our concerns overlap those of a more properly "systematic" theology. We shall first examine the negative aspects of the relationship we have been exploring, and then attempt a theological understanding of the way in which feeling, art, and beauty may be transformed in the light of Christian revelation.

Historical and Existential Context

Much of the historical conflict between Christianity and the arts, especially in the early church, can be ascribed to extrinsic factors. The arts in the Hellenistic world were closely linked with "pagan" religion and *mores*. Christian iconoclasm was explicitly tied to the First Commandment and the critique of idolatry that was voiced not only by the Jewish Scriptures but also by the pagan philosophers.[1] Drama in the ancient world exercised a religious or quasi-religious function, and was connected with the practice of magic.[2] The theater was also associated with loose morals and "salable love."[3] Dance was an integral part of theater, and also represented erotic exhibitionism.[4] Instrumental music likewise formed part of the ritual of pagan sacrifice, and certain instruments in particular were associated with orgiastic cults.[5]

However important these "extrinsic" factors were in the first centuries of the church, they do not suffice to explain completely the recurrent tensions between religion and art. It may be noted, for one thing, that similar tensions arose both in other religions[6] and in later periods of Christianity, when the dangerous pagan religious associations had long been forgotten. Some of the major periods of "iconoclasm" (of greater or lesser severity) have been mentioned above: the struggles that tore the Eastern church in the eighth and again in the ninth centuries; the Carolingian period in the West; the Cistercian reform; the Reformation. The use of music in the church was likewise severely restricted in the Patristic period and came under attack again at the time of the Protestant Reformation, especially in the Zwinglian and Calvinist traditions (this despite the facts that Zwingli was an accomplished musician and that both reformers appreciated music as a secular art). As Barth points out, the issue is not merely one of extrinsic associations: there is also a more fundamental and intrinsic difficulty, one that concerns not only the arts but also all aspects of earthly beauty and culture, including religion itself, insofar as it is a human product. ("Art, culture, and religion," declared Bonhoeffer: "the three great powers by which humanity contradicts the grace of God."[7])

Moreover, from the aesthetic side as well there are fundamental tensions between the arts and beauty, on the one hand, and the service of God, on the other. Art and beauty claim to be ends in themselves and resist being subjected to any other goal: "Art is neither the imitation of life nor empathy with life; it is a primary form of life, which thus receives its laws neither from religion nor from morality nor from science nor from the state, nor from other primary or secondary forms of life."[8] Religious values, on the other hand, claim not only ultimacy but also totality: they can recognize no others besides themselves precisely because by them we stand "before God"; hence they are ultimate and not conditional.[9]

For the attitude of faith, only God can be the ultimate consummation of human desire. But the aesthetic form of experience is also "consummatory." As Dewey remarks, "That which distinguishes an experience as aesthetic is a conversion of resistance and tensions . . . into a movement towards an inclusive and fulfilling close."[10] As we have seen in the last chapter, this is a problem for a religious attitude that sees its primal value in ongoing and never-terminated *encounter* with the living transcendent God, whose "reign," which brings about human completeness, must be expressed in the symbol of futurity. (This is why religious worship often prefers "rough and ugly" images to beautiful ones; their incompleteness as aesthetic objects allows them better to serve their religious end.[11]) Likewise, beautiful music is a danger for the sacred Word: "music which is real music does not illustrate the words, but exalts them, carries them along in order to annihilate them. Every text is destroyed by music in beautiful fashion. . . . Rhythm sweeps the word away and destroys it."[12]

The "aesthetic," then, whether experienced in art or in other forms of beauty, can be a distraction from the religious; at the extreme, it may become a sort of rival "religion," centered on experience in and of the world, offering not only a worldly object of "worship" but even a secular form of "salvation." Nicholas Wolterstorff quotes sociologist Max Weber:

> art takes over the function of a this-worldly salvation . . . It provides a *salvation* from the routines of everyday life, and especially from the increasing pressures of theoretical and practical rationalism. With this claim to a redemptory function, art begins to compete directly with salvation religion. Every rational religious ethic must turn against this inner-worldly, irrational salvation.[13]

Paul Tillich sees a deeper reason for the frequent substitution of aesthetics for religion. He notes that because of the real union of self and world accomplished through the aesthetic encounter, philosophers of Kantian and neo-Kantian schools "have seen in art the highest self-expression of life and the answer to the question implied in the limitations of all other functions [of mind]. And this is the reason that sophisticated cultures tend to replace the religious by the aesthetic function."[14]

The late biblical book of Wisdom, with more psychological insight than earlier prophetic condemnations of false worship, recognizes that it is the genuine value of earthly beauty that is the source of idolatry, and even expresses a certain sympathy for those who are so taken by nature's beauty that they miss its author:

> For all were by nature foolish who were in ignorance of God,
> and who from the good things seen did not succeed in knowing the
> One who Is,
> and from studying the works did not discern the artisan . . .
> For from the greatness and the beauty of created things
> their original author, by analogy, is seen.

But yet, for these the blame is less;
For they indeed have gone astray perhaps,
though they seek God and wish to find him.
For they search busily among his works,
but are distracted by what they see,
because the things seen are so fair.[15]

It is true that an aesthetic "religion" of "devotion to the world"[16] may already be a step beyond egotism toward a transcendent value; nevertheless, it is finally idolatrous because it stops short of the ultimately transcendent, the "wholly other" that is God.[17]

The "Platonic" Objection to the Arts

In short, there is an intrinsic tension between transcendent religion on the one side and beauty and the arts on the other. This tension is nothing other than the reverse side of the Platonic "ascent" from the world to God: one can become so enraptured precisely by the "godliness" of earthly beauty that one mistakes the image for its source, as in Plato's myth of the cave.

This "Platonic" objection to the aesthetic expresses a basic conflict that can manifest itself in various forms and be interpreted in different contexts: it may show itself as a contest between sacred and profane beauty, or between religion and art in general, or between spirit and matter, or reason and imagination, or philosophy and myth. Such conflicts lay behind many of the historical objections and/or reservations of Christians concerning feeling, the arts (including "mythic" expressions of religion), and natural (earthly) beauty. It will therefore be profitable to look more closely at its basis in the Platonic philosophy and mind-set that so influenced Christianity and Western thought in general; as Iris Murdoch says in her remarkable book on the topic, "although we may want to defend art against Plato's charges we may also recognize . . . how worthy of consideration some of these charges are."[18]

As we have noted earlier, Platonic philosophy accords to beauty a major—indeed, the central—position. But Murdoch notes that Plato defines beauty in such a way as to make it a "spiritual agent" that virtually excludes art.[19] To the scandal of many, Plato in both the *Republic* and the *Laws* proposes censorship (including the forbidding of certain modes of music),[20] and criticisms of artists are found throughout his works. In a celebrated passage in the *Republic* (398 A), he states that if a poet talented in evoking all kinds of emotions were to visit his ideal state, the citizens would honor him, but for the good of their souls would send him away to another city. The only poetry that should be admitted is that which inculcates virtue: hymns to the gods and praises of good people (*Republic* 607 A). In the continuation of the passage (607 B), Plato refers to the "old quarrel" between philosophy and poetry. In books III and X he makes explicit his complaint concerning art: it feeds the lower emotions, because it accepts and imitates appearances rather than engaging in the search for the real. When it imitates what is bad (as it frequently does, since evil is more varied and entertaining, and is easier to imitate), it actually augments evil: it is full of sensual images and it accepts the existence of evil with amusement, so that moral judgment is weakened.[21] Art's "images of wickedness and excess may lead even good people to indulge secretly through art feelings which they would be ashamed to entertain in real life."[22]

At the root of Plato's critique of the arts lies his anthropology. As is well known, Plato divides the human soul into three unequal and conflicting parts: the lowest is egotistical, irrational, and immersed in illusion; the central is aggressive and ambitious; the highest is rational and good. Art corresponds to the lowest level: "Art and the artist are condemned by Plato to exhibit the lowest and most irrational kind of awareness, *eikasia*, a state of vague image-ridden illusion."[23] Plato's philosophy, on the other hand, has as its goal the salvation of human existence from its immersion in passion and illusion.[24] Its "conversations" lead the mind beyond mere images to the level of "*logos*."[25] Hence it constitutes a crucial aid in the journey from appearance to reality, from uncritical acceptance of sense experience and egotistical conduct to understanding and moral enlightenment.[26]

The moving dynamism of this journey is "eros," which is active at all levels of the soul and connects desire with moral judgment.[27] Eros is moved by beauty, which the higher soul perceives as desirable, but not graspable; in this sense beauty is "transcendent" and leads the soul out of selfish pursuit of gratification onwards to the highest realm.[28] But eros can also be deceptive, and if not critically examined by reason can lead us into addiction to the lower passions.[29] The attainment of gratification is itself no guarantee of rightness: the wicked delight in false pleasures, the good in true ones (Philebus 40c 1ff).[30] The artist makes the better part of the soul become unwary; art is a means, as Freud also saw, of escaping from reality into a fantasy world.[31] Mimetic art is particularly blameworthy, for it allows us to stop at the level of appearances, when we should be seeking for intellectual vision of the "Forms."[32]

Murdoch argues that Freud and Plato mistrust art for the same reason: "because it caricatures their own therapeutic activity and could interfere with it. Art is pleasure-seeking self-satisfied pseudo-analysis and pseudo-enlightenment."[33] Using Freud as an interpretive aid, Murdoch summarizes the Platonic objections in a series of powerful passages:

> Form in art is for illusion, and hides the true cosmic beauty and the hard real forms of necessity and causality, and blurs with fantasy the thought-provoking paradox.... The pull of the transcendent as reality and good is confused and mimicked. The true sense of reality as a feeling of joy is deceitfully imitated by the "charm-joy" of art.[34]

Art proffers to the unwary a "pseudo spirituality and a plausible imitation of direct intuitive knowledge (vision, presence), a defeat of the discursive intelligence at the bottom of the scale of being, not at the top."[35] Art "obscures the nature of true *catharsis* (purification): by offering an easy emotional catharsis of its own.[36] "Art practices a false degenerate *anamnesis* where the veiled something which is sought and found is no more than a shadow out of the private store-room of the personal unconscious."

In short, art may cut short our spiritual journey by persuading us that we have already arrived.[37] Augustine, in a celebrated passage, says that our hearts are made for God, and are restless until they rest in God. In this sense, we are called to "use" (*uti*) finite goods, but complete "enjoyment" of the good (*frui*) must be reserved for the divine.[38] In contrast, art (and indeed earthly beauty in general) offers the heart at least momentary repose and a plausible fulfillment;[39] in this sense, to seek purely aesthetic delight can be a species of cupidity,[40] or even, at the worst, of idolatry. This danger is particularly present in specifically religious art:

> Art is dangerous chiefly because it apes the spiritual and subtly disguises and trivializes it. Artists play irresponsibly with religious imagery which, if it must exist, should be critically controlled by the internal, or external, authority of reason. . . .
>
> Art contributes, in a perhaps misleadingly "spiritual" way, to the material gear of religion; and what should be a mediating agency may become in effect a full-stop barrier. . . . Art fascinates religion at a high level and may provide the highest obstacle to the pursuit of the whole truth. A rigid pattern of integrated "spiritual" imagery arrests the mind, prevents the free movement of the spirit, and fills the language with unclear metaphor.[41]

"The abyss of faith," as Murdoch says, "lies beyond images and beyond *logoi* too."[42] But where theology—in the sense of the rational *logos* about God—stands mute and hesitant before the mystery, "art will eagerly try to explain . . . unless specifically prevented from doing so, art instinctively materializes God and the religious life."[43]

Plato's critique of art should not be reduced simply to his spirit-matter dualism. Also at work in his fear of art is a thoroughly practical and realistic recognition of the addictive and restricting power of pleasure. The same insight drove Aristotle to write in the *Nichomachean Ethics* that the wise person will have an attitude toward pleasure like that of the Trojan elders toward the lovely Helen: beauteous as she may be, let her depart, least she bring ruin on us and our children![44] And centuries later Freud would write, in the same vein: "Anyone who knows anything of the mental life of human beings is aware that hardly anything is more difficult for them than to give up a pleasure they have once tasted."[45]

In contemporary thought, Paul Ricoeur also reflects explicitly on the Platonic-Aristotelian theme of the danger of pleasure for the soul. Using Augustine's language, Ricoeur affirms that the "heart" (θυμός) is and ought to be "restless" in the quest for "happiness" or beatitude, the complete and lasting culmination that is the ultimate horizon of human existence and action.[46] Pleasure, like happiness, is complete and perfect; but unlike happiness, it does not correspond to our destiny as a whole, but only to a perishable moment.[47] Hence "repose in pleasure threatens to bring the dynamism of activity to a standstill and screen the horizon of happiness."[48] Pleasure binds us to bodily life. It "punctuates and ratifies my organic rootedness in the world. It magnifies the dilection with which I cherish the life that passes through me and this center of perspective that I am"——that is, the ego.[49]

Ricoeur notes that just as the finitude of knowledge is "recognized as such only in the truth-intention that transgresses it," so pleasure is revealed as *mere* pleasure only by one who has transcended it in the higher intention, toward beatitude.[50] The person who has not done so, who is in the grip of passion, puts his or her whole capacity for happiness into the objects by which the ego is constituted; hence what is experienced as "good" or "beautiful" on the sensual level becomes an idol, an obstacle to the attainment of the spiritually and "truly" beautiful that transcends the ego.[51]

These classical cautions about the dangers of pleasure, beauty, and art are apt in Christianity as well. Indeed, Murdoch remarks that the materializing effect of the arts has nowhere been felt more than in Christianity, which has been served by so many artistic geniuses. Some of the great Christian doctrines "have become so celebrated and beautified in great pictures that it almost seems as if the painters were the final authorities on the matter, as Plato said that the poets seemed to be about the Greek gods."[52] Murdoch uses the example of pictorial representations of the Trinity. Perhaps the point is even better illustrated by common Christian conceptions of heaven and hell (think of the influence of Dante, for example), or by popular Marian devotion, which has been so nourished by images derived from the apocryphal gospels and from various Marian "apparitions."

Even if we accept all this, however, the adage remains true: *abusus non tollit usum*. The danger of misuse does not vitiate the possibility of a proper use of art in the service of religion. Nicholas Wolterstorff comments:

> Of course sensory delight can be a threat to one's obedience to God. It can function as a distraction from one's other responsibilities. Worse, it can function as a surrogate God. . . . But the Christian's repudiation of this must not obscure from him the fact that the structure of this idolatry, as of every other, is that of a limited good's being treated as an ultimate good. Its structure is not that of something evil's being treated as good.[53]

The same may be said of finite beauty in general and of pleasure: although they may provide a premature halting place for the spirit, they need not do so; ideally, as we have already seen, they may be a foretaste and symbol that mediates the presence and attraction of the final Good and may therefore serve as a spur toward progress in the "ascent" toward true virtue and beatitude. As Ricoeur says, it is only when one forgets "the symbolic character of the bond between happiness and an object of desire" that the latter becomes an idol.[54] But the warning about precisely this idolatry takes on new power for the Christian in the perspective of the cross.

Beauty and Art in the Perspective of the Cross

As long as the question is posed in purely abstract and theoretical terms, art and beauty can clearly claim to belong to an integral and nondualistic vision of the human spirit and its relation to God. The true depth of the problem for Christianity appears only in the light of the cross of Christ as the revelation of God and of God's relation to our human condition.

The centrality of the cross in the Christian message is seen in the New Testament as a whole, and especially in the explicit Pauline theology of the cross.[55] A brief mention of some of the principal ideas will suffice to remind us of the significance of the symbol and what it represents.

In Christ crucified, God's power and wisdom are revealed to those who are called, although the cross is a stumbling block and a folly to those headed for perdition (1 Cor. 1:18, 23). The cross of Christ seems absurd in the light of the world's "wisdom"; but it is where God's mysterious wisdom is revealed (1 Cor. 1:17, 2:6–7). Those whose way of life is oriented to "the things of this world" show themselves to be enemies of the cross of Christ (Phil. 2:18–19). The celebrated hymn of Philippians[56] proclaims (in terms relevant to our concern for revelation) that Christ did not appear in divine form (μορφή), but in the form of a slave, obedient even to death on the cross (Phil. 2:6–8). Paul explicitly counsels the Philippians that this attitude should be a model for their own (Phil. 2:5).

The letter to the Hebrews reminds us that Christ, instead of joy, endured the cross[57] and proposes his conduct as a model for the believer (Heb. 12:2). The gospels not only relate the narrative of Jesus' passion as the culmination of his mission from the Father but also make an explicit connection between the cross and discipleship. The command to take up the cross and follow Jesus is found in the Synoptics five times, in different contexts (Mark 8:34 and parallels, Matt. 16:24, Luke 9:23; Matt. 10:38; Luke 14:27). In all of these texts, the idea of the cross is immediately associated with the necessity of "losing" or denying one's self; self-seeking, on the other hand, leads to ruin. The same association—in the context of the coming of Jesus' "hour" but without explicit reference to the cross—is made in John's gospel, as an expansion of the metaphor of the grain of wheat that must die to produce fruit (John 12:24–25).[58]

It seems clear, then, that the message of "the cross" is the symbolic epitome of the wider message of self-denial, "death" to self, in Christ, as the means of attaining new life (see, for example, the Pauline statement of the theme of being baptized into Christ's death in order to share his resurrection: Rom. 6:3ff.; cf. Col. 2:12). Moreover, the meaning of "death to self" is intimately connected with the agapic love of neighbor that is the sign of the new "resurrected" life in Christ's spirit.[59]

Without contradicting all that has been said in previous chapters about the positive relation of beauty to God, we must acknowledge in the message of the cross a reminder of the danger of a facile humanism.[60] The Christian practitioner or theoretician of art and beauty must continually reexamine the question already raised in the first chapter by Barth's and Balthasar's theologies: are we falling into the danger of deluding ourselves, as the aged and disillusioned Michelangelo says of himself, with "affectionate fantasy"—of making beauty and art an idolatrous self-gratifying substitute for the reality of the God who speaks to us in the cross of Christ?

It is not possible here to engage in a full "theology of the cross." I shall attempt, however, to succinctly summarize what I see as the essential elements of a theological/spiritual understanding of the symbol of "the cross" and of the New Testament imperative to self-denial, insofar as they affect the notion of Christian theological "aesthetics."

First, the symbols of the cross and of "death to self" speak to us, not of abstract human nature, but of our existential situation. They reveal and condemn the reality of sin, especially as the idolatry of the self. They remind us that the attainment of the good concretely involves not merely a "progression" but also a dialectic of conversion: not a straightforward growth of the spontaneous or "natural" self, but a death to self. There is, then, a permanent dialectic and an "ascent" in human existence, expressed in Jesus' call to conversion (μετανοῖα), in the Pauline contrast between life according to the spirit (πνεῦμα) and according to the "flesh" (σάρξ), and in the Johannine notion of triumph over "the world." But the terms of the dialectic are not to be understood in terms of an ontic opposition between two realms (spirit *vs.* matter)—as so frequently appears in the Platonic tradition, even within Christianity. Rather, the dialectic is ontological: it involves the direction of personal self-determination. This will consist either in seeking fulfillment through self-enclosure in a finite horizon or in anticipating happiness in self-transcendence and self-donation through love of the final good, the infinity of God (which includes within itself the total participated good of God's "other," creation).

For the Christian, then, the classical cautions about pleasure and beauty are seen in a new context: the doctrine of the "fallen" state of humanity. The doctrine of "original sin" is in its essence Christological and "staurological": it intends to explain the universal need for the salvation wrought through the cross of Christ. This doctrine allows the Christian to affirm both the essential goodness and godliness of beauty and earthly pleasure and, at the same time, their existential dangerousness. Created beauty can and should lead to God, the ultimate Beauty; the aesthetic pattern of experience should be valued as a partial perspective, to be integrated with the intellectual, moral, and religious in a higher and more total viewpoint of the existential subject. But, in fact, the human mind is concupiscent, divided; hence the *eros* of beauty can be separated from its ultimate ontological reason for being, and hence the aesthetic pattern of experience can be made an end in and for itself—that is, in and for the subject of the experience.

The idea of the cross is furthermore intrinsically linked with Jesus' teaching that the supreme occasion for the love of God, to which our lives must be ordered, is to be found in our needy neighbor (Luke 10:25ff.; John 13:34; 15:12–13; 1 John 4:7–8, 20–21, etc.). The cross tells us that love is indeed the ultimate act of freedom; but "love" itself is not to be defined simply in terms of a Platonic "eros" toward the beautiful and good that fulfill us. For the Christian, love is above all the "agapé" that is motivated, not by the other's beauty, but by his or her need[61]—as God first loved us in Christ (Rom. 5:6–8; 1 John 4:10).

Moreover, this love demands the sacrifice of self; that is, an absolute "claim" on us is made by the other, and by precisely that in him/her which is lacking in proper relation or proportion or attractiveness. We have spoken above of the "word" of God in beauty; the cross challenges us to see the "surd" of suffering and poverty in our neighbor as a word of God's self-revelation and an invitation to the response of love. In Shusaku Endo's novel *Silence*, the hero, a missionary priest who has entered Japan during the period of persecutions, reflects on this call after performing the secret baptism of a peasant child:

> As the water flowed over its tiny forehead the baby wrinkled its face and yelled aloud. Its head was tiny; its eyes were narrow, this was already a peasant face that would in time come to resemble that of Mokichi and Ichizo. This child also would grow up like its parents and grandparents to eke out a miserable existence face to face with the black sea in this cramped and desolate land; it, too, would live like a beast, and like a beast it would die. But Christ did not die for the good and beautiful. It is easy enough to die for the good and beautiful; the hard thing is to die for the miserable and corrupt—this is the realization that came home to me acutely at that time.[62]

And later, after hearing the confession of Kichijiro, the one-time Christian who has renounced his faith and betrayed the priest to the authorities:

> Could it be possible that Christ loved and searched after this dirtiest of men? In evil there remained that strength and beauty of evil; but this Kichijiro was not even worthy to be called evil. He was thin and dirty like the tattered rags he wore. Suppressing his disgust, the priest recited the final words of absolution, and then, following the established custom, he whispered, "Go in peace. . . ."
>
> No, no. Our Lord had searched out the ragged and the dirty. Thus he reflected as he lay in bed. Among the people who appeared in the pages of Scripture, those whom Christ had searched after in love were the woman of Capharnaum with the issue of blood, the woman taken in adultery whom men had wanted to stone—people with no attraction, no beauty. Anyone could be attracted by the beautiful and the charming. But could such attraction be called love? True love was to accept humanity when wasted like rags and tatters. . . . [63]

The message of the cross, then, challenges us to rethink and to expand our notion of the ascent to God through beauty, and indeed of the "beauty" of God itself. As we have seen earlier, Barth and Balthasar both insist that the Christian notion of divine beauty must be able to include even the cross, "and everything else which a worldly aesthetics . . . discards as no longer bearable."[64] The divine beauty seen in the cross gives a new sense to Rilke's phrase in the first Duino elegy, "beauty is nothing but the beginning of terror."[65]

From its earliest era, the church has applied to Christ in his passion the words of the fourth "Song of the Suffering Servant" from the book of Isaiah (Isa. 52: 13–53:12).[66] Here we read that "there was no beauty in him to make us look at him, nor appearance that would attract us to him" (Isa. 53:2–3). As Barth says, "Jesus Christ does present this aspect of Himself, and He always presents this aspect first. It is not self-evident that even—and precisely—under this aspect he has form and comeliness, that the beauty of God shines especially under this aspect. ... We cannot know this of ourselves. It can only be given to us."[67]

Yet to Christian faith, it *is* given that Christ is nevertheless—and precisely in the cross—the supreme revelation of God's being, God's "form," "glory," and "beauty." The transcendent "beauty" and "light" of God, then, must embrace also "the abysmal darkness into which the Crucified plunges."[68] This implies that the meaning of God's "beauty" is only finally known by God's self-revelation. It would be a misunderstanding of the "analogy" of beauty to make it the simple projection onto God of our "worldly" experience of the beautiful and desirable. In speaking of God's being,

> we must be careful not to start from any preconceived ideas, especially in this case a preconceived idea of the beautiful. Augustine was quite right when he said of the beautiful: *Non ideo pulchra sunt, quia delectant, sed ideo delectant, quia pulchra sunt (De vera rel.,* 32, 59).[69] What is beautiful produces pleasure. *Pulchra sunt, quae visa placent*[70] (Thomas Aquinas, *S. th.* I, *q.* 5, *art.* 4, *ad* 1). Yet it is not beautiful because it arouses pleasure. Because it is beautiful, it arouses pleasure. In our context Augustine's statement is to be expanded into: *Non ideo Deus Deus, quia pulcher est, sed ideo pulcher, quia Deus est.*[71] God is not beautiful in the sense that He shares in an idea of beauty superior to Him, so that to know it is to know Him as God. On the contrary, it is as He is God that He is also beautiful, so that He is the basis and standard of everything that is beautiful and all ideas of the beautiful.... [The Divine being] as such is beautiful. We have to learn from it what beauty is. Our creaturely conceptions of the beautiful, formed from what has been created, may rediscover or fail to rediscover themselves in it. If they do rediscover themselves in it, it will be with an absolutely unique application, to the extent that now, subsequently as it were, they have also to describe His being.[72]

Let it be clear that there is no question of retracting here anything we have said above concerning the genuinely "analogous" quality of beauty, or concerning the revelation of God in beauty as order, rationality, the attractiveness of the good, the font of desire. But God in Christ is revealed as also "more" than these; or, to express the matter better, our understanding of these as "transcendental" realities is now raised to a deeper and more inclusive level, one that embraces (in a way that is yet to be clarified) even what appears (from a merely inner-worldly perspective) to be irrational, disordered, lacking in attractiveness and goodness. "In this self-declaration [*viz.*, in Christ] ... God's beauty embraces death as well as life, fear as well as joy, what we might call the ugly as well as what we might call the beautiful."[73]

The perception of this dimension of divine beauty, the ability to feel its attractiveness, its goodness *for us* demands certain subjective conditions: namely, self-transcendence toward God to the degree of being able to see things, not merely *sub specie aeternitatis,* but from the perspective of God's creative agapé. But this involves a conversion that is perceived by the unspiritual ego as "death." For this reason, God may appear to us as "unattractive" in two ways.

First, as Barth saw, God's "glory" can also "unleash fear and terror" in the sinful soul. "It works by contraries on the man who cannot have it."[74] In Hindu and Mahayana Buddhist iconography, the gods are frequently portrayed in a fierce, destructive, and terrifying aspect, symbolizing the fact that the divine is terrible to our sinful or false or unenlightened selves and that vice, ignorance, and illusion must be destroyed.[75] (See especially the remarkable representations of "The Goddess," Kali, who is regularly portrayed standing, tongue hanging out, on the corpse of Siva, of whom she is the "energy"; she is adorned with human skulls and carries a bloody sword and a decapitated head.)

Because of the divine transcendence, God may be imagined as terrifying, as a strange, alien power. A sense of this dark vision is communicated in some of Ingmar Bergman's films. In *Through a Glass Darkly*, the mentally ill Karin reports her experience of a theophany:

> "I was suddenly afraid. The door opened. But the god that came out was a spider. He came towards me and I saw his face. It was a horrible, stony face. He crawled up me and tried to press into me, but I defended myself. The whole time I saw his eyes. They were calm and cold. And he couldn't force his way into me. He climbed onto my breast, onto my face, and on up the wall. I have seen God."[76]

Some Christian art renders the crucifixion of Christ as a scene of grotesque horror (see, for example, Grünewald's crucifixion panel for the Isenheim altar [Figure 5], or his small crucifixion of 1510). Such portrayals generally express some version of the Anselmian "satisfaction" theory of redemption. This is easily extended to the notion that the cross is the manifestation of God's wrath against sin, which Christ takes upon himself in our stead.[77]

On the other hand, the God revealed in the cross of Christ may be unattractive for the opposite reason: not because of the divine transcendence or its wrathful manifestation against sin, but because of the divine *identification* with the subhuman, the suffering, the poor, the ugly (as in the passages from Endo quoted above). If the crucified Christ is the most profound and positive image of God, a God who suffers along with humanity,[78] then divinity seems to be found, not in what is beautiful and world-affirming, but in association with powerlessness and death.

Here we must tread carefully and distinguish more clearly in what way what is represented by the cross—abasement, suffering, death—is the revelation of God, so that by extension the poor and mistreated remain a word, image, and presence of God for us.

Perhaps we may best begin on the level of imagination and proceed by contrast. In Dostoievsky's novel *The Idiot*, Prince Myshkin is impressed by a painting that he sees in the house of Rogozhin, a painting of the Savior who has just been taken from the cross, a copy of a Holbein.[79] The image of the spider recurs in the description the dying consumptive Ippolit later gives of the effect the picture has on him:

> "I suddenly recalled a picture I had seen at Rogozhin's, over the door of one of the dreariest of his rooms. He showed it me himself in passing. I believe

I stood before it for five minutes. There was nothing good about it from an artistic point of view, but it produced a strange uneasiness in me.

The picture represented Christ who has only just been taken from the cross. I believe artists usually paint Christ both on the cross and after He has been taken from the cross, still with extraordinary beauty of face. They strive to preserve that beauty even in His most terrible agonies. In Rogozhin's picture there's no trace of beauty. It is in every detail the corpse of a man who has endured infinite agony before the crucifixion; what has been wounded, tortured, beaten by the guards and the people when He carried the cross on His back and fell beneath its weight, and after that has undergone the agony of crucifixion, lasting for six hours at least (according to my reckoning). It's true it's the face of man *only just* taken from the cross—that is to say, still bearing traces of warmth and life. Nothing is rigid in it yet, so that there's still a look of suffering in the face of the dead man, as though he were still feeling it (that has been very well caught by the artist). Yet the face has not been spared in the least. It is simply nature, and the corpse of a man, whoever he might be, must really look like that after such suffering. I know that the Christian Church laid it down, even in the early ages, that Christ's suffering was not symbolical but actual, and that His body was therefore fully and completely subject to the laws of nature on the cross. In the picture the face is fearfully crushed by blows, swollen, covered with fearful, swollen and blood-stained bruises, the eyes are open and squinting, the great wide-open whites of the eyes glitter with a sort of deathly, glassy light. But, strange to say, as one looks at this corpse of a tortured man, a peculiar and curious question arises; if just such a corpse (and it must have been just like that) was seen by all His disciples, by those who were to become His chief apostles, by the women that followed Him and stood by the cross, by all who believed in Him and worshipped Him, how could they believe that that martyr would rise again? The question instinctively arises: if death is so awful and the laws of nature so mighty, how can they be overcome? How can they be overcome when even He did not conquer them, He who vanquished nature in His lifetime, who exclaimed, 'Maiden, arise!' and the maiden arose—'Lazarus, come forth!' and the dead man came forth? Looking at such a picture, one conceives of nature in the shape of an immense, merciless, dumb beast, or more correctly, much more correctly, speaking, though it sounds strange, in the form of a huge machine of the most modern construction which, dull and insensible, has aimlessly clutched, crushed and swallowed up a great priceless Being, a Being worth all nature and its laws, worth the whole earth, which was created perhaps solely for the sake of the advent of that Being. This picture expresses and unconsciously suggests to one the conception of such a dark, insolent, unreasoning and eternal Power to which everything is in subjection. The people surrounding the dead man, not one of whom is shown in the picture, must have experienced the most terrible anguish and consternation on that evening, which had crushed all their hopes, and almost their convictions. They must have parted in the most awful terror, though each one bore within him a mighty thought which could never be wrested from him. And if the Teacher could have seen Himself on the eve of the crucifixion, would He have gone up to the cross and died as He did? That question too rises involuntarily, as one looks at the picture.

All this floated before my mind by snatches, perhaps in actual delirium, for fully an hour and a half before Kolya went away, sometimes taking definite shape. Can anything that has no shape appear in a shape? But I seemed to fancy at times that I saw in some strange, incredible form that infinite Power, that dull, dark, dumb force. I remember that some one seemed to lead me by the hand, holding a candle, to show me a huge and loathsome spider, and to assure me, laughing at my indignation, that this was that same dark, dumb and almighty Power."[80]

In response to this image we must clarify what it means theologically to say that God is found in the cross of Christ and in the history of human suffering in general. If God is conceived transcendentally as the absolute, as the horizon and condition of possibility of human reason and freedom, then the message of the cross cannot mean simply the defeat of God by a dark and deadly power of irrational "nature," as the fevered imagination of Ippolit suggests. Much less can it mean that death, suffering, and sorrow form part of God's very being. Some contemporary thinkers have gone in this direction in response to the problem of evil, as a reaction against the image of an "apathetic" God. (This, of course, means taking the Aristotelian/Patristic doctrine of God's ἀπάθεια on the *imaginative* level, rather than as a theoretical statement of negative theology, whose positive correlate is the statement that God is pure Act. In the Christian Scholastic context, the Aristotelian doctrine is taken to imply that God's relationship [*habitudo*—see *ST*, I, q. 13, a. 7, *ad* 1um] to creatures is totally creative and "agapic" rather than dependent and "erotic.")

If the Christian is to *imagine* God, it must be as God is portrayed in the Scriptures—that is, as compassionate, not as "unfeeling." But this correct *image* does not preclude a (negative) *theoretical* understanding of the transcendence of God's being (knowledge) in terms of nonreceptivity. As Rahner notes, Christian theodicy must take account of the ultimate incomprehensibility or "mystery" of God's relationship to the world.[81] I will suggest below that God is not merely in "solidarity" with human suffering, but is also genuinely identified with it, and that the proper context for understanding this statement is an appreciation of God's transcendental "immanence." At the same time, God's eternity implies that for God the "eschatological" triumph of good is present to every moment, so that "God has in his nature the knowledge of evil, of pain, and of degradation, but it is there as overcome with what is good."[82]

Therefore, if the image and presence of God are found in the poverty, ugliness, and suffering of the world, it is precisely as the hope and the promise of transcending these conditions. A transcendentally conceived theology cannot fall into the delusion of a mysticism of evil, placing it somehow at the center of Being itself. There can be no question here of what Rahner calls "a theology of absolute paradox . . . a Schelling-like projection into God of division, conflict, godlessness, and death."[83]

It is not possible here to enter more deeply into the question of how and in what sense it may be said that God "suffers" along with creation and still remains the ever-blessed God who alone can save creation from evil. (As Rahner says: "To put it crudely, it does not help me to escape from my mess and mix-up and despair if God is in the same predicament."[84]) I believe that Rahner has indicated the direction in which such a discussion might go in his formula that God suffers *in* God's "other" (meaning not only Christ but also all of creation). To appreciate the meaning of this, one would have to come to an understanding that what is meant by God's "immanence" is not merely a "closeness" to creation (balanced by the "distance" of transcendence) but rather consists in the fact that the "otherness" of creation from God is a distinction *within* God's being: "The difference between God and the world is of such a nature that God establishes and *is* the difference of the world from himself, and for this reason he establishes the closest unity precisely in the differentiation. . . . [T]he difference itself comes from God, and, if we can put it this way, is itself identical with God."[85]

It is, in any case, clear that God's presence in the poor and suffering cannot be taken to mean that these conditions are "godly," but that they contain within themselves an inextinguishable possibility of transcending the present evil in the direction of goodness. This means that God's presence is experienced by the suffering as hope, and by those who encounter the suffering as the imperative to be engaged in the reversal of their suffering condition.

Likewise, the cross of Christ must be seen always in the light of the resurrection. Barth has said, "If the beauty of Christ is sought in a glorious Christ who is not the crucified, the search will always be in vain."[86] But by the same token, the beauty of the crucified cannot be separated from his victory over death as the sign of God's victorious life in human history. The cross is not beautiful or good in itself: it is beautiful only insofar as it represents Christ's ultimate faithfulness and self-gift to God, even to the point of death, and insofar as this act is given eternal validity by God's overcoming of death itself. That is, the cross only has beauty as the expression of an act of love; and love is "beautiful," theologically speaking, precisely because it is finally not defeated, but victorious. Love is godly and therefore in itself the participation in and anticipation of the divine form of life. The fulfillment of that anticipation by God is revealed historically and in definitive form in Christ's resurrection as the sign that confirms the validity and shows the final victorious nature of all human self-giving in love.

The cross, then, is not a beautiful thing; it is the symbol of a beautiful *act*—on Jesus' part, as self-giving, and (inseparably) on the part of the Father, in raising Jesus from death. When the Christian speaks of the beauty of the cross, it is seen, not as a self-contained object or event (such as might be represented in a naturalistic picture), but as moment in God's *poiesis*,[87] an element in the theo-*drama* of salvation, whose significance is therefore incomplete except in the *dénouement* of the narrative.

(This is the reason that through the ages most Christian pictorial art, with certain exceptions, has not attempted to represent the crucifixion with "photographic" realism, but has treated the cross symbolically, making it already the manifestation of glory.[88] As we saw earlier, in pictorial art, in contrast to narrative, movement is fixed and representation is "complete" and unchanging over time. Hence it can only show the true meaning of the cross by visually combining two "moments," representing the cross in the aura of the resurrection.[89] The representation of the crucifixion by itself is "abstract," from a theological point of view, unless it is seen in this light. In this sense, the representation of the cross in most Christian art is already a kind of "theodicy": it shows evil overcome, transformed into good. The danger of this, as of any theodicy, explicit or implicit, is that it may be used as a "short-cut" through the problem of evil, in which the negative moment is simply overlooked or is not felt with its full power. Of course, Christians believe that Christ has delivered us not only from the power of death and evil but also from anxiety about them; the danger of a misused theodicy is not that it produces peace of mind, but that it may allow us to escape from a compassionate love that shares the sufferings of others.)

The cross does not mean the ultimate subjection of even God to the power of death (as seems to be implied in some theories of redemption as "ransom"). Rather, it means that God in Christ has conquered the "powers" that threaten our existence (Col. 2:15; Rom. 8:38f.; John 12:31, 14:30, 16:11; 1 Pet. 3:22) and remains in us as the ability to conquer them (Eph. 6:12). Similarly, the gospel blessing on the poor, on those who weep, and on those who are engaged in Jesus' work (Matt. 5:3–12; Luke. 6:20–23) is not an exaltation of suffering, but a statement about its reversal by God's "kingdom." The triumph of God's love is manifest above all in those who have only God as their hope. In this consists the beauty of God seen by faith in the cross and in all suffering. It is the beauty of God's active presence as the power of the future that creates hope; it is the light that shines in the darkness, which cannot conquer it (John. 1:5).

The pains and sorrows of the world are a word of God: a word about overcoming and an invitation to engagement. Hence Christian devotion to the cross must eschew the kind of *Kreuzseligkeit* that is a religiously disguised form of masochism. The beauty of the cross is not the contradiction of what we experience through "worldly" beauty, but is the elevation of the latter to its fullest and most complete level, that of interpersonal communion among humans and with God.[90]

The Aesthetic and Asceticism

This having been said, it is all the more clear that the Christian message demands a kind of engagement with the world in which a purely "aesthetic" attitude, in the sense described and criticized by Kierkegaard and Blondel, is impossible.[91] Christian spirituality by its nature demands a certain asceticism. The love of God in and through the love of others (especially those in sorrow and need) involves the relativization, if not the renunciation, of all lesser goals, however good they may be "in themselves"; and in the actual situation of human existence, one may have to choose between the higher good and a lower. The cross is hence the symbol of the "purity of heart," the singlemindedness that is demanded by God's "kingdom," the accomplishment of God's way of love for humanity, including the "poor."

Hence Christian asceticism is not to be understood only as a matter of pluck-ing out the offending eye (Matt. 5:29); nor should it be conceived simply as re-nunciation of "the world" for the sake of an other-worldly salvation (although it cannot be denied that the notion that "the form of this world is passing away" [1 Cor. 7:31] has historically been an influential element in Christian asceticism). Rather, the "asceticism" of the Christian should be seen also (and primarily) as "witness" to the reality and primacy of God's Kingdom, as voluntary solidarity with "the cross" as manifest in those who are involuntarily deprived of the goods of this world, and as a means of attaining freedom for the service to others (see, for example, Matt. 19:10–12; Col. 1:24; 1 Cor. 7:32–35; 9:3–15).

The ascetical element in Christianity includes a certain practical caution con-cerning the arts and beauty. These are not evil, but de facto they usually seem to be connected with wealth. G. B. Shaw makes the realistic point that art is expen-sive, as is the cultivation of the "soul":

> ELLIE: Old fashioned people think you can have a soul without
> money. They think the less money you have, the more
> soul you have. Young people nowadays know better. A
> soul is a very expensive thing to keep: much more so
> than a motor car.
>
> CAPTAIN SHOTOVER: Is it? How much does your soul eat?
>
> ELLIE: Oh, a lot. It eats music and pictures and books and moun-
> tains and lakes and beautiful things to wear and nice
> people to be with. In this country you can't have them
> without lots of money: that is why our souls are so hor-
> ribly starved.[92]

But the dangers of wealth are frequently and forcefully stated in the gospel and other New Testament writings (see especially Luke. 6:24–26: the "woes" pro-claimed on the rich, those who laugh now, those who are filled; also Matt. 6:19–21 [= Luke 12:33–34]; Mark. 10:17–27 [= Matt. 19:16–30, Luke. 18:18–30]; Luke 16:13 [= Matt. 6:24]; Luke. 16:20–25; 1 Tim. 6:10; Heb. 13:5; James 1:9–11; etc.).

In short, the pursuit of beauty (like any form of human self-fulfillment) may serve as a vehicle of escapism, fostering an egotistical occupation with pleasure and providing a distraction from the love of neighbor. (Already in the Book of Amos the "complacent" who are condemned are satirized as being preoccupied with luxury and art—"improvising to the music of the harp, like David, they devise their own accompaniment" [Amos 6:5]—rather than being concerned with the ills of the nation. And did not Leo Tolstoy, who struggled with the problem all his life, declare that the closer one approaches to beauty, the further one moves from goodness?) As Van der Leeuw puts it: "Religion gives to culture again and again the command Jesus gave the rich young man: 'Sell all that thou hast.' "[93]

Even where hedonism is avoided, the danger remains that a preoccupation with the aesthetic may engender a kind of contemplative attitude that finds itself in competition with the moral imperative for action. In Pasternak's great novel, the heroine Lara reflects, standing at the grave of Zhivago: "The riddle of life, the riddle of death, the enchantment of genius, the enchantment of discovery— that, yes, please, that we understood. But the small practical squabbles—about things like reshaping the earth—that, no thank you, that was not for us."[94] (It is also significant that Zhivago, Pasternak's Christ figure,[95] begins as a doctor but abandons healing for art.) Again, there is a fear that the good as the present satisfaction provided by beauty may undermine the power of the future good to inspire engagement to change the world.

Moreover, even if we accept that beauty can be a way to God, a theology that takes seriously the idea that the lives of the saints are a genuine theological source[96] must conclude that while "whoever has beauty, has God . . . there is also a possession of God which does not lead to beauty."[97] Similarly, Rahner writes:

> We might defend the thesis that real saints are those who have developed all their human potentialities. When people are fully attuned to life, have wholly developed their power of seeing and hearing, their experience is at once identical with their religious attitude. . . . That is one side.
>
> However, if we proceed empirically, we may easily reach an opposite opinion. Are there not people who are really genuine saints, who love God and their neighbor in a radically unselfish way, and who, nevertheless, have hardly developed any artistic capabilities, who in matters of art are real lowbrows, capable only of rudimentary reactions? On the other hand, there are those who have developed an extraordinary artistic sensibility without being saints. We probably have once more to distinguish here between innate and freely accepted religious possibilities.[98]

More than this: must we not say that there could be those who are prevented from being saints precisely because of their aesthetic "humanism," as Kierkegaard claimed? And, on the other hand, that there are those for whom the offending eye that must be plucked out in attaining holiness is precisely the eye for beauty?[99]

The practical tension that we are speaking of here (as distinguished from the more theoretical issues involved, for example, in the iconoclast controversy) is one that has manifested itself repeatedly in the history of Christian spirituality. We have already earlier referred to Augustine's ambivalence with regard to the pleasures of music, even in the liturgy, and we have cited the Abbot Suger's defense of the arts and earthly splendor as a means of ascent to God for the weak human mind. A few further examples must suffice to illustrate how the resolution of the tension differed according to circumstances and personalities.

In a sermon on the love of the poor, St. Gregory Nazianzen takes a positive stance toward earthly beauty and uses it as a motivation for generosity.[100] As examples of blessings that have been received from God he names "the arts" and the "life of humanity and culture," along with physical life, the reasoning mind, the beauties of nature, human friendship, family, and finally divine filiation. The grateful response for such gifts should be generosity toward others, for God intends that the goods of creation should be shared by all:

Brethren and friends, let us never allow ourselves to misuse what has been given us by God's gift. If we do, we shall hear Saint Peter say: *Be ashamed of yourselves for holding on to what belongs to someone else. Resolve to imitate God's justice, and no one will be poor.* Let us not labor to heap up and hoard riches while others remain in need.[101]

Already in classical Greek, the word "beautiful" (καλός) combined the meanings "useful," "virtuous," and "attractive." Gregory expands the notion to include the specifically Christian dimensions of life. Faith, hope, and love are "a beautiful (or "good") thing" (καλόν). So likewise are hospitality, fraternal love, benevolence, patience, mildness, zeal, the castigation of the body, prayer, chastity and virginity, continence, solitude, a modest way of living, humility, poverty, and contempt for money.[102]

John Chrysostom in a similar vein addresses Christians who wish to honor the eucharist with splendid vessels and to adorn God's house with beauty. With the tradition in general, he finds this laudable,[103] but he exhorts them to attend first to the body of Christ in the poor.

Do you want to honor Christ's body? Then do not scorn him in his nakedness, nor honor him here in the church with silken garments while neglecting him outside where he is cold and naked. Give him the honor prescribed in his law by giving your riches to the poor. For God does not want golden vessels but golden hearts.

Now, in saying this I am not forbidding you to make such gifts; I am only demanding that along with such gifts and before them you give alms. He accepts the former, but he is much more pleased with the latter. In the former, only the giver profits; in the latter, the recipient does too. A gift to the church may be taken as a form of ostentation, but an alms is pure kindness.

Of what use is it to weigh down Christ's table with golden cups, when he himself is dying of hunger? First, fill him when he is hungry; then use the means you have left to adorn his table. Will you have a golden cup made but not give a cup of water? What is the use of providing the table with cloths woven of gold thread, and not providing Christ himself with the clothes he needs? What profit is there in that? Tell me: if you were to see him lacking the necessary food but were to leave him in that state and merely surround his table with gold, would he be grateful to you or rather would he not be angry? What if you were to see him clad in worn-out rags and stiff from the cold, and were to forget about clothing him and instead were to set up golden columns for him, saying that you were doing it in his honor? Would he not think he was being mocked and insulted?

Apply this also to Christ when he comes along the roads as a pilgrim, looking for shelter. You do not take him in as your guest, but you decorate floor and walls and the capitals of the pillars. You provide silver chains for the lamps, but you cannot bear even to look at him as he lies chained in prison. Once again, I am not forbidding you to supply these adornments; I am urging you to provide these other things as well, and indeed to provide them first. Do not, therefore, adorn the church and ignore your afflicted brother, for he is the most precious temple of all.[104]

Just at the time that Abbot Suger was celebrating the richness of decoration of his church, the Cistercians and Carthusians were engaged in a vociferous protest against the "excesses" of ecclesial art. Bernard of Clairvaux, Alexander Neckham, and Hugh of Fouilloi were among those who condemned the luxury and the distracting qualities of church decoration.[105] In his well-known "Apologia" to William, the abbot of St.-Thierry, St. Bernard not only takes a dim view of the characteristics of the nascent Gothic style but also stresses the inappropriateness of artistic riches for those who have dedicated themselves to the ascetical life:

I say naught of the vast height of your churches, their immoderate length, their superfluous breadth, the costly polishings, the curious carvings and paintings which attract the worshiper's gaze and hinder his attention, and seem to me in some sort a revival of the ancient Jewish rites. Let this pass, however: say that this is done for God's honour. But I say, as a monk, ask of my brother monks as the pagan asked of his fellow-pagans: "Tell me, O Pontiffs" (quoth he) "what doeth this gold in the sanctuary?" So say I, "Tell me, ye poor men" (for I break the verse to keep the sense) "tell me, ye poor (if, indeed, ye be poor), what doeth this gold in *your* sanctuary?" And indeed the bishops have an excuse which monks have not; for we know that they, being debtors both to the wise and the unwise, and unable to excite the devotion of carnal folk by spiritual things, do so by bodily adornments. But we who have now come forth from the people; we who have left all the precious and beautiful things of the world for Christ's sake; who have counted but dung, that we may win Christ, all things fair to see or soothing to hear, sweet to smell, delightful to taste, or pleasant to touch—in a word, all bodily delights—whose devotion, pray, do we monks intend to excite by these things? What profit, I say, do we expect therefrom? The admiration of fools, or the oblations of the simple? Or, since we are scattered among the nations, have we perchance learnt their works and do we yet serve their graven images? To speak plainly, doth the root of all this lie in covetousness, which is idolatry, and do we seek not profit, but a gift? . . . [F]or at the very sight of these costly yet marvelous vanities men are more kindled to offer gifts than to pray. Thus wealth is drawn up by ropes of wealth, thus money bringeth money; for I know not how it is that, wheresoever more abundant wealth is seen, there do men offer more freely. Their eyes are feasted with relics cased in gold, and their purse-strings are loosed. . . . Hence the church is adorned with gemmed crowns of light—nay, with lustres like cart-wheels, girt all round with lamps, but no less brilliant with the precious stones that stud them. Moreover, we see candelabra standing like trees of massive bronze, fashioned with marvelous subtlety of art, and glistening no less brightly with gems than with the lights they carry. What, think you, is the purpose of all this? The compunction of penitents, or the admiration of the beholders? O vanity of vanities, yet no more vain than insane! The church is resplendent in her walls, beggarly in her poor; she clothes her stones in gold, and leaves her sons naked; the rich man's eye is fed at the expense of the indigent. The curious find their delight here, yet the needy find no relief. ... And, lastly, what are such things as these to you poor men, you monks, you spiritual folk? Unless perchance here also ye may answer the poet's question in the words of the Psalmist:

"Lord, I have loved the habitation of Thy House, and the place where Thine honour dwelleth." I grant it, then, let us suffer even this to be done in the church; for, though it be harmful to vain and covetous folk, yet not so to the simple and devout. But in the cloister, under the eyes of the Brethren who read there, what profit is there in those ridiculous monsters, in that marvelous and deformed comeliness, that comely deformity? To what purpose are those unclean apes, those fierce lions, those mounting centaurs, those half-men, those striped tigers, those fighting knights, those hunters winding their horns. ... In short, so many and so marvelous are the varieties of divers shapes on every hand, that we are more tempted to read in the marble than in our books, and to spend the whole day in wondering at these things rather than in meditating the law of God. For God's sake, if men are not ashamed of these follies, why at least do they not shrink from the expense?[106]

Interestingly, Bernard (somewhat begrudgingly?) agrees with Suger's contention that art is needed for the *un*spiritual mind to reach God, and hence may be necessary in the ministry of the secular clergy. He also takes for granted that the "honoring" of God is a legitimate motivation for beautification of the church. But he echoes, in much more strident terms, Chrysostom's contrast between the ornamentation of the church and the neglect of Christ's living members: "The church is resplendent in her walls, beggarly in her poor; she clothes her stones in gold, and leaves her sons naked; the rich man's eye is fed at the expense of the indigent."

This last is perhaps the most powerful of the arguments for a certain caution on the part of the Christian with regard to the realms of the aesthetic. Bernard has in effect introduced a kind of "hermeneutic of suspicion" regarding the rationalization of aesthetic pursuits. In the light of contemporary philosophy and theology, we may go further in applying the same to aesthetic experience itself, as well as to its conceptual justification. The questions raised by such a hermeneutic are in line with Bernard's concerns. We may ask, for example, what is the concrete perception of beauty in any particular case based on? What social structures are co-affirmed or presupposed in it? Καλόν ἡσυία, proclaimed the Greeks: leisure is a beautiful, noble thing. But the leisure that permitted the glories of Greek civilization was based on slave labor. The medieval "mirror" of the celestial hierarchy—"Jacob's ladder," as Santayana calls it—served as a justification for the feudal system. There is a danger that beauty may both propagate and depend on ideology. Such considerations add a further dimension to the tension between the aesthetic and the ascetical.

Feeling, Art, and Beauty in the Spirit of Christ

Up to this point we have been considering the problems and tensions that may arise when the aesthetic realm is confronted with the values of ethical and religious (specifically Christian) conversion. It is not the purpose of this concluding section to achieve a complete theoretical resolution of the issues that have been raised. On the contrary: a certain tension between the beautiful and the good, between art and religion, is a permanent part of our existential condition—as is also that between imagination and concept, feeling and thought, as we have seen earlier. We should expect that the practical courses taken by people of faith and goodness on the place of the aesthetic in religious life—and in theology—will be determined by prudent judgments within particular situations, and will therefore exhibit pluralism, as they have historically.

Nevertheless, the legitimate cautions and hesitations raised by Christian faith should not be the last word on this topic. Christian spirituality, frequently centering itself on the "imitation of Christ," has perhaps traditionally been too exclusively preoccupied with renunciation, and has taken too little account of the fact that Jesus, in contrast to the ascetical John the Baptist, came in a spirit of celebrating the arrival of God's kingdom (Matt. 11:18–19, Luke 7:33–34); that the resurrection proclaims that despite (and indeed through) Jesus' passion and death, the power of God's kingdom, the outpouring of God's transforming spirit has in fact taken place (John. 20:19–23; Acts 2:1–41; Rom. 8:12–17; Col. 3:1–4; etc.); and that therefore the Christian exists in joy and hope, even while struggling against evil and embracing the self-giving attitude of the cross (Rom. 8:35–39; Phil. 2:1–11, 4:4–6; 1 Thes. 5:16–19; etc.). A spirituality based on a simple dualistic rejection of the body or of matter or of the world, which has not infrequently colored Christian thinking, should be excluded (1 Tim. 4:1–5). "True Christianity knows that body and soul were both equally created by God, equally attacked by corruption, and equally saved by Christ."[107]

This book has been based on the idea that there is in Christianity a positive and necessary place for the aesthetic in all its dimensions. However, feeling and imagination, art, and the quest for beauty are transformed and deepened by the encounter with the transcendent values of God's kingdom. In the following pages, building on what has already been said, I will attempt to suggest the outlines of a theological understanding of how these realities may be transfigured by the Christian appropriation of revelation, and how they may serve the ideal of self-giving love while retaining their proper human integrity.

Christian "Conversion" and the Aesthetic

Balthasar writes that

> when we approach God's revelation with the category of the beautiful, we quite spontaneously bring this category with us in its this-worldly form. It is only when such a this-worldly aesthetics does not fit revelation's transcendent form that we suddenly come to an astonished halt and conscientiously decline to continue on that path.[108]

We have already noted that although we may say that God is "objectively" beautiful, in an eminent way, whether God—in particular God as revealed in Christ—appears to any particular person as "beautiful" (and hence desirable and lovable) depends on subjective conditions: above all, on one's degree of self-transcendence. The ability to judge and feel value "from God's point of view" is the result of what Lonergan calls "religious conversion": that is, what is variously described as acceptance of the gift of "sanctifying grace," as "being in love with God" in an unrestricted way, as God's Spirit "flooding our hearts" (Rom. 5:5), as the human acceptance of the divine self-communication and consequent sharing of the divine life.[109]

In the terminology of Scholastic theology, the "natural" human desire for God opens onto a supernatural desire to share God's very life; and the actuation of the later brings about an ontological reorientation of human being and consciousness, a "supernatural intentionality."[110] Hence religious conversion has an "aesthetic" dimension. "Being in love" with God unrestrictedly[111] means first of all the transformation of the eros of the human spirit[112]—the "higher" affects and spiritual operations that define us as persons. But the aesthetic dimension of conversion also includes the erotic in the psycho-sexual sense.[113] Not only does it reach our "higher" (spiritual) operations and affects, transforming their finality, but insofar as our spirit "informs" our material, biological being, this dimension of conversion affects our bodiliness as well.

To put it another way, "grace" and conversion reach also into our "lower" affects, feelings, and imagination, the sensible parts of our conscious being that are the psycho-physiological "underpinning" of all our spiritual activity. If the process of conversion did not affect our spontaneous desires, our human reality would be schizophrenic:

> The various operations that constitute the creative vector in human consciousness are permeated by feelings. To the extent that these feelings are not congruent with the self-transcendent objectives of their corresponding operations, to the extent that one does not *desire* meaning, truth, the real, the good, and attunement with a world-transcendent God whose Word and Love are incarnate in Christ Jesus, to that extent the *operations* of conscious intentionality are inhibited from reaching their objectives. The automatisms and complexes of our psychic sensitivity interfere with the spontaneous unfolding of the normative order of the search for direction in the movement of life.[114]

Along with the "intellectual" and "moral" conversions referred to by Lonergan,[115] we may therefore also speak of an "aesthetic conversion"[116] that takes place when "beauty," or the object of our affective intentionality (as discussed above in chapter 3), is anticipated and defined not merely as what produces feelings of pleasure, or as "accord" with the proportions of our senses, but as "form," understood as perceivable order, intelligibility, and value. In other terms, the "beauty" intended by the aesthetically converted subject may be heuristically defined as that which is in accord with the deepest desire of the "heart," the personal dimension of our being.

More concretely, in what way must our notion and our concept[117] of the beautiful be transformed in order to correspond to Christian religious conversion?

The fact that we are called to religious conversion means that we must "learn" from God what is ultimately beautiful and desirable, what is our real fulfillment as persons. The medieval mystic Dame Julian of Norwich expresses this idea in a justly celebrated passage in which she imagines God speaking these words:

> It is I, the strength and goodness of Fatherhood.
> It is I, the wisdom of Motherhood.
> It is I, the light and grace of holy love.
> It is I, the Trinity, it is I, the unity.
> I am the sovereign goodness in all things.
> It is I who teach you to love.
> It is I who teach you to desire.
> It is I who am the reward of all true desiring.[118]

Religious and aesthetic conversion do not replace the "natural" dynamism toward beauty that is proportionate to our being as spatio-temporal and sensitive, but they "sublate" this dynamism into a new horizon,[119] which is the eternal divine life. Human eros, as Augustine saw, is at its root directed toward the infinite good, which is God; only God can satisfy this drive or desire. But the divine life, on the transcendental view that I have espoused, is intrinsically agapic. To the extent that humans attain the goal of union with God, to the extent that they participate in the divine life, the dynamism of human eros is sublated into agapé.[120]

Hence "grace" or "being in love with God" is the principle not only of the possibility of faith and hope[121] but also of the possibility of loving God "unselfishly"—that is, for God's self—rather than simply as the fulfillment of *our* being (happiness or beatitude).[122] Or, to put it another way, our final way of attaining fulfillment is discovered to be "ecstatic"—centered in the Other.[123] Here also arises the possibility of loving others in the same way—that is, self-sacrificially, "as Christ loved us" (John. 13:34; 15:12–13; Rom. 5:6ff.; 1 John 3:16).[124] It is by the Spirit of God in us that we become able to see beauty in and positively to desire a way of being that appears to spontaneous subjectivity as "death," and to experience joy in despite of self-loss and suffering (see Matt. 5:11–12; Luke 6:23; 2 Cor. 6:8–10; Rom. 5:3; Phil. 2:17; Col. 1:11; 1 Pet. 1:6, 8; 4:13; etc.).

The interaction of religious and aesthetic conversion in transforming the idea of "beauty" is also relevant to Ricoeur's comments on "pleasure" and "happiness," since "the beautiful" is classically defined as that which, being perceived, brings pleasure.[125] As we have seen above, Plato and many of his followers warn of the spiritual danger of pleasure: namely, that it threatens to close off the "affective horizon" within itself. Nevertheless, it need not do so: only by willing it are we at the mercy of pleasure. Plato himself recognized that we must take "the good" as a criterion for distinguishing between "true" and "false" pleasures.[126] To overlook this is the mistake of philosophies that make pleasure itself an evil,[127] or even attempt to suppress affect altogether, like Stoicism.[128]

Pleasure can also lead, in a dialectical way, to true happiness, which is not its negation but its "recovery and reaffirmation,"[129] or, in the term I have been using, its "sublation." This dialectic, Ricoeur points out, "is internal to pleasure itself," since there is already a natural hierarchy of pleasures: the enjoyment of sensible beauty; play; the joy of learning and activity; and openness to another in friendship.[130] Hence even on the "worldly" level, we may postpone particular satisfactions for the sake of a higher enjoyment. "The suspension of pleasure aims at restoring the dynamism and the hierarchy of human action and ultimately at finding the *supremely pleasant*"—which for a spiritual being is ultimately identical with "the good"[131] or "value."

It is "reason"—in the Kantian sense of a demand for totality—that distinguishes the intention of happiness from that of mere pleasure.[132] The demand for totality is "opposed to the individuality of an existential perspective"[133]—that is, it transcends the "bias" of egotism.[134] But in order to be an effective motivation for action, the demand of reason must be "enriched" by affectivity, so that its goal of happiness (which includes relation to the totality) can be seen as the "most excellent form of pleasure"[135]—that is, as supremely beautiful. "Being in love with God" gives us the proleptic anticipation of the beatitude of the eschatological "resurrection," the form of our final life in God, which includes the total good of all creation: the final *shalom* of God's "Kingdom."[136] The present anticipation of this goal through the life of faith and hope allows us to be moved by its supreme beauty,[137] and gives us, in Ricoeur's words, an "affective figuration" of beatitude. This in turn allows us to forgo present "lower" satisfactions for the sake of happiness[138]—which is not simply future, but is already anticipated in the joy of the Spirit (Rom. 5:2, 11; 14:17; Gal. 5:22; Phil. 3:1; 4:4–8; 1 Thess. 1:6, 5:15–19; etc.).[139]

Likewise, "religious conversion" or life in God's Spirit allows us to love our fellow creatures in excess of their beauty[140]—that is, of their appeal to "natural" eros; we find ourselves called to love them "absolutely," in a way that could not be justified by a creature per se.[141] By means of the divine life in us and (at least as a potentiality) in every other, we are motivated to love others in their limitations, their need, and even their sinfulness. God's love, being totally agapic, is totally creative: it gives both existence and lovability to the object of its love. This is true also of the order of "grace": as St. Paul tells us, the greatness of God's love is shown in that God loved us while we were still sinners (Rom. 5:8; cf. 1 John. 4: 10). The gift of "grace" allows us to love in an analogous way. We are still motivated by the perception of a good,[142] but a good that transcends the horizon of finite desires. The "beauty" that motivates the engraced act of love is protological and eschatological.[143] To the extent that we participate in the divine mode of life, we see others neither simply as a function of our selves nor solely in their present condition. By virtue of our graced anticipation of the totality of all things in God (an anticipation analogous to the *Vorgriff* of being),[144] we ourselves and all others appear in the light of God: first, as the creator, the free giver of existence, of the dynamism to self-transcendence, and of the relational ordering of things to one another and to the whole; and second, as the "pleroma," the "locus" of the eschatological communion of all with all.

Hence, although the other may not be beautiful, generous self-giving love for the needy other is nevertheless perceived by the eyes of faith as a (morally, spiritually) beautiful act in the "theo-drama" being created by God's artistry: an act that anticipates the eschatological beauty of God's "Kingdom." The same may be said for the disciplining of the self. It is in this sense that we may speak of the "beauty" of the cross.

This understanding implies that the exercise of agapic love does not simply find beauty, but creates it: totally and absolutely in God's case, subordinately and relatively in ours. Our ability to love the needy and the sinful other is based on the intrinsic value of the other's being, insofar as this is seen not as closed off within itself, but as essentially "open" to union with the totality. In the light of God's agapic love, even the "need" of the other is not simply a lack but also an openness, a possibility for fulfillment; even sin is not merely negation but also an invitation to its own reversal.[145] The act of love itself, as a gratuitous affirmation that meets evils with good, creates a new possibility for overcoming the self-isolating quality of sin and constitutes a concrete invitation to a self-transcending response.[146] Thus St. John of the Cross counsels: *"adonde no hay amor, ponga amor, y sacaras amor"*—"where there is no love, put love; then you will get love." Similarly for beauty.

Thus far, in speaking of "conversion" (i.e., the human categorical appropriation and achievement of what is given as God's self-gift),[147] I have presented it in its ideal full and integral achievement. But in fact conversion (of every kind) is a life-long process, with stages, with advances and declines, with many combinations of integration and nonintegration of the different forms of conversion with each other and with the internal and external plurality that characterizes the human condition. Lonergan reminds us that

> love is the utmost in self-transcendence, and [human] self-transcendence is ever precarious. Of itself, self-transcendence involves tension between the self as transcending and the self as transcended. So human authenticity is never some pure and serene and secure possession. It is ever a withdrawal from unauthenticity, and every successful withdrawal only brings to light the need for still further withdrawals.[148]

According to Lonergan's analysis, conversion generally begins with God's self-gift (which is also self-revelation). The perception of its "beauty" follows: "first there is God's gift of his love. Next, the eye of this love reveals values in their splendor."[149] This is the beginning of "aesthetic," as well as religious conversion. Moral and intellectual conversion follow from this affective perception and the desire it inspires. As St. Paul testifies, however, this integration is difficult to achieve. The resistance of the "flesh" to the "spirit" may even be felt as a battle within the self (Rom. 7:14–25).

Finally, as we have noted above, the gift of God's love not only redirects our freedom but also heals the affective "aesthetic undertow" of spiritual being.[150] This process constitutes the prolongation of aesthetic conversion: the integration of the dramatic subject's affects, "tastes," habitual inclinations, and desires with the spirit's direction toward God and others. "Charity" or "being in love with God" provides a principle of integration for the whole of life. Nevertheless, on the psycho-physical level a certain plurality ("concupiscence") will always be present: First, because of the intrinsic incompleteness, ambiguity, and complementarity of finite values; hence there will be different and complementary concrete "ways" to the good. Second, because conversion itself is not complete, or not totally appropriated or not adequately formulated. Because God's gift must be humanly appropriated, we must *learn* to take pleasure in the "things of the spirit," rather than reducing the spirit to our measure of momentary enjoyment. In this process, there is an important place for both asceticism and—I shall argue—art.[151]

Beauty and Goodness: Art as the Mediator of Virtue

A few words remain to be said regarding the place of art in religion, and specifically in relation to moral goodness.

In the course of this study, we have encountered two basic kinds of theological objection against the arts. First, there is the problem of idolatry. The imaginative presentation of God may become an obstacle to encounter with the living God; a projection of human qualities, corresponding to human feeling and desire, may replace the challenge of God's Word; human imagination may substitute for God's self-revelation.

Second, there is the problem of "distraction." Art is a form of "riches," and like all riches, is dangerous to the spirit: it may lead to a more subtle form of "idolatry." The pursuit of pleasure, even at the "high" level of art, may lead away from the love of neighbor, especially the poor and suffering. Because it does represent a genuine human "good," art may prevent us from seeking a higher interpersonal good; it may provide a plausible rationalization for escaping from the reality of the cross by providing a "short-cut" to glory. Even when art is used in the service of the "word," there is a tension. Art tends to become its own master and to have an agenda of its own that can compete with the religious message.

In response to these objections, we have seen that the danger of "idolatry" applies to word and concept (including those used in the Scriptures) as much as it does to other forms of representation; that human feeling and desire may be the expression of revelation rather than an escape from it; and that revelation must always take place through the mediation of human agency. On the other hand, purely conceptual or verbal expressions of revelation may also lead away from the encounter with the living God; and self-conscious symbol rather than concept may be a more adequate expression of the infinite mystery, and is indeed necessary for complete human appropriation of God's self-gift.[152] It is true that art may pursue a different end than the propagation of a religious message. But if that end is beauty, then it is also a revelation of God, albeit of another sort.

Art, like other human goods, may provide an escape from "the cross." But it may also provide a means of communicating the latter's meaning. "The cross" itself is a highly charged symbolic image. In fact, unless they take refuge in a totally negative theology, presenting the Ultimate in terms of an impersonal, imageless Void, neither philosophy nor theology can do without metaphor—and metaphor cannot be controlled or communicated without art of some kind.[153] The resolution of the problem of idolatry, in both its intellectual and its ascetical dimensions, is to be found in intellectual, moral, aesthetic, and religious conversion, rather than in the renunciation of any intrinsic dimension of human being.

Moreover, we have seen that there is a permanent priority of the poetic and symbolic over the conceptual. This is particularly true of the sphere of religion. If we are to encounter and communicate God's self-revelation within human history, it will be primarily on the "aesthetic" (imaginative and artistic) level. We speak religiously of God and of God's relation to us above all in the analogies of art, not those of metaphysics.[154] Lonergan summarizes nicely:

though the solution [to the problem of salvation] as a higher integration will be implemented principally in man's intellect and will through conjugate forms of faith and hope and charity, it must also penetrate to the sensitive level and envelop it. For, in the main, human consciousness flows in some blend of the dramatic and practical patterns of experience and, as the solution harmoniously continues the actual order of the universe, it can be successful only if it captures man's sensitivity and intersubjectivity. Moreover, as has been seen, all exercise of human intelligence presupposes a suitable flow of sensitive and imaginative presentations and, again, inasmuch as intelligence and reasonableness and will issue into human words matched with deeds, they need at their disposal images so charged with affects that they succeed both in guiding and propelling action.... It follows, then, that the emergent trend and the full realization of the solution must include the sensible data that are demanded by man's sensitive nature and that will command his attention, nourish his imagination, stimulate his intelligence and will, release his affectivity, control his aggressivity and, as central features of the world of sense, intimate its finality, its yearning for God.[155]

Therefore, the aesthetic dimension can and must play an important role in the concrete working out of the divine "solution" to the human dilemma, and in the recognition that this "solution" consists in the transformation of this world, not its rejection or destruction.[156]

Within the larger field of "the aesthetic" art has a particular role to play in the economy of salvation. In its very performance of creating order out of disorder, art can be both a symbol of the redemptive process[157] and an element in its accomplishment: an aspect of our present sharing in God's glory and an anticipation of its final victory. As Nicholas Wolterstorff puts it, "Art can serve as instrument in our struggle to overcome the fallenness of our existence, while also, in the delight which it affords, anticipating the shalom which awaits us."[158] In this sense, Patrick Sherry points out, the destruction of beauty or the creation of ugliness is a sin against the Spirit.[159]

As we have seen earlier, findings of contemporary neuroscience support the view that affect is important to thinking, even in the most abstract realms. Feeling subtly and subconsciously pervades and accompanies all thought. Hence the perception of beauty, in its various kinds, is also crucial to the working of the good. To feel the "beauty" of thought, even when abstract, is important: such feelings make us more capable of thinking. The accompaniment of positive feelings produces efficiency in the cognitive process: images are generated more quickly, associations are more fruitful, inference is easier.[160] Naturally, the beauty that produces positive feeling has different levels. The attainment of beauty in thinking may require discipline and learning; in mathematics or science, for example, one must know the "language" before one can appreciate the "beauty" of equations or hypotheses.

In other spheres of life, beauty may be introduced purposely through art in order to facilitate learning. Despite the dangers that we have spoken of, in the light of what has been said concerning the need for conversion we may recognize that art, especially insofar as it seeks and mediates beauty, has a place in the pursuit of the good. Indeed, when aesthetic conversion is achieved in art, it becomes particularly relevant to moral conversion. Like morality, art can transcend the realm of pure immediacy. In his scattered and unsystematic remarks about art, Wittgenstein points out that

> The work of art is the object seen *sub specie aeternitatis*, and the good life is the world seen *sub specie aeternitatis*. This is the connection between art and ethics. The usual way of looking at things sees objects as it were from the midst of them, the view *sub specie aeternitatis* from outside. In such a way that they have the whole world as background.[161]

That is, art can lead us to view things or events in the perspective of a "total" horizon that invites us to break out of the narrowly restricted concerns of the ego.

Iris Murdoch makes a similar point in response to Plato's objections: the experience of the beautiful

> may provide our first and possibly our most persisting image (experience) of transcendence. . . .
> Good art, thought of as symbolic force rather than statement, provides a stirring image of a pure transcendent value, a steady visible enduring higher good, and perhaps provides for many people, in an unreligious age without prayer or sacraments, their clearest *experience* of something grasped as separate and precious and beneficial and held quietly and unpossessively in the attention.[162]

Murdoch argues strongly for art's morally educative possibilities. Plato saw the dangers of art, but did not do justice to its "unique truth-conveying capacities."[163] "Art," she declares, "is far and away the most educational thing we have, far more so than its rivals, philosophy and theology and science."[164] Despite Plato's fears of distraction, art is in fact "therapy" for the soul; it is "about the pilgrimage from appearance to reality," just as philosophical dialectic is.[165]

> Art is a special discerning exercise of intelligence in relation to the real . . . form in art, as form in philosophy, is designed to communicate and reveal. In the shock of joy in response to good art, an essential ingredient is a sense of the revelation of reality, of the really real, the ὄντως ὄν: the world as we were never able so clearly to see it before.[166]

Murdoch admits that art can be misled and misleading. "Magic in its unregenerate form as the fantastic doctoring of the real for consumption by the private ego is the bane of art as it is of philosophy." The solution to this problem lies in what I have called "conversion." The "prescription for art is the same as for dialectic: overcome personal fantasy and egoistic anxiety and self-indulgent daydream. . . . Learning to detect the false in art and enjoy the true is part of a lifelong education in moral discernment."[167] The notion of "aesthetic conversion" implies that one may make value judgments about art not only with regard to such criteria as skill, imagination, formal excellence, and so on, but also on the basis of its relation to the revelation of the true and the good. Paul Tillich's categories of "authentic" and "inauthentic" art are relevant here. Corresponding to truth and untruth in the cognitive realm is authenticity or inauthenticity of expressive form. Art can be inauthentic in two ways: "either because it copies the surface instead of expressing the depth or because it expresses the subjectivity of the creating artist instead of his artistic encounter with reality." On the other hand, the "work of art is authentic if it expresses the encounter of mind and world in which an otherwise hidden quality of a piece of the universe (and implicitly of the universe itself) is united with an otherwise hidden receptive power of the mind (and implicitly of the person as a whole)."[168]

Despite its dangers, then, art can play a significant part in the moral educative process. Murdoch recognizes that the "fundamental school of virtue" is the "practice of personal relations": "The spiritual revelations involved in dealing with people are in an evident sense more important than those available through art, though they tend to be less clear."[169] But, prescinding from direct personal engagement, art has a certain advantage over other forms of learning about "the good." It is more efficacious, in Murdoch's view, than the example of good people. When we see persons of virtue, as Kierkegaard says, "we admire and relax." "Good art, on the other hand, provides work for the spirit."[170] Art gives us pictures of other worlds;[171] it allows us to enter with sympathy into contexts that would otherwise be alien to us; it gives us a universal "language."[172]

Art is an effective moral educator in that it portrays vice and virtue rather than legislating about them or explaining them in theoretical terms. Narrative art is particularly apt at teaching about human fallibility. The fundamental moral evil of "seeing the worse for the better," for example, "is more informatively (though of course less systematically) carried out by poets, playwrights, and novelists" than by moral philosophers and theologians.[173] Likewise, virtue is more convincing and imitable when it is embodied concretely in art than when it is commanded or expounded theoretically. "Perhaps in general art *proves* more than philosophy can."[174] Art need not be didactic in order to serve the good—although there is clearly also a place for beauty and art in preaching and teaching, as in every form of communication. Art as communication can have a transformative effect on the person because it can literally give us a new way of seeing, hearing, feeling, and so on.[175] Moreover, the kind of art that serves beauty, as Balthasar says, "brings with it a self-evidence that enlightens without mediation."[176]

This self-evidence of beauty is the ultimate connection between art and goodness, and is a fitting point on which to end these considerations. The good, in order to be morally effective, must also appear good; that is, its connection with our final end, with our deepest desire, must be perceivable. The good must be seen as beautiful, as joy-filled and fulfilling. God's self-revealing love in our hearts is necessary for this perception to occur at its deepest level: for us to recognize beauty in the drama of the Christ event and to be attracted to its imitation. But God's self-gift is always also a human achievement. Human collaboration is no less called for in the revelation of beauty than in the transmission of truth and the teaching of virtue. Michelangelo tells us (in a poem!) that art can be an idol; but it can also be the means by which the heart's terror is overcome, and it opens to the nearness of the transcendent: to "that divine love / which opened its arms on the cross to take us."

There always remains for the Christian the need to make prudent decisions about the use of the world and its goods. The poor are always with us (Mark 14: 7; Matt. 26:11; John. 12:8); and it is not always clear in the concrete whether the more "beautiful work" of love (Mark. 14:6, Matt. 26:10) is in meeting their material needs or in nourishing the spirit's hunger. We do not live by bread alone; and the inspiration of hope through artistic beauty can also be a "word from the mouth of God" (cf. Matt. 4:4). Finally, as Barth says, it "belongs to the essence of the glory of God not to be *gloria* alone but to become *glorificatio*."[177] The glorifying of God demands from us above all the spiritual beauty of agapic love; but it includes as well the integration of human creativity and sensitivity in the praise of God through art.

The need for art in conjunction with religion is perhaps especially crucial today, when the world has been transformed by human intervention and so many of the earth's inhabitants live in an environment far removed from any natural beauty. St. Thomas quotes with approval the passages in Aristotle's *Ethics* in which he says that "no one can remain long without delectation," and that "those who cannot rejoice in spiritual pleasures will turn to corporeal ones."[178] "Sadness" about the spiritual realm—a lack of experience of the beauty of what is truly good, a lack of "taste" for the holy—turns people away from the value of communion with others and toward the pursuit of material pleasure. Humankind is more and more responsible for our environment and our relations with each other. Crucial decisions that affect the future of our species—and of large parts of the nonhuman world as well—increasingly depend upon human insight and virtue. But our ability to be intelligent and responsible will depend largely on our having a vision of the good that touches and convinces us. A form of art is needed to produce such a vision.

In his lecture written on the occasion of receiving the Nobel Prize for Literature, Alexander Solzhenitsyn quotes a phrase spoken by Dostoievsky's Prince Myshkin, the Christ-like hero of *The Idiot:* "Beauty will save the world." In the novel Myshkin is mocked for his naiveté, but in the light of the above we may perhaps agree with Solzhenitsyn that the words convey a deep truth, or at least a deep hope:

> "Beauty will save the world." What does this mean? For a long time it seemed to me that it was merely a phrase. How could such a thing be possible? When in our bloodthirsty history did beauty ever save anyone, and from what? It has ennobled, elevated, yes; but whom has it saved?
>
> Only there is something so peculiar at the core of beauty, a peculiarity in the position of art: the conviction carried by a genuine work of art is absolute and conquers even a resisting heart....
>
> A work of art contains its verification in itself: artificial, strained concepts do not withstand the test of being turned into images; both concepts and images fall to pieces, they show themselves to be sickly and pale, they

convince no one. But works which draw on truth and present it to us concentrated and alive seize us, powerfully join us to themselves—and no one ever, even centuries from now, will come forth to refute them.

Then perhaps the old tri-unity of Truth, Goodness, and Beauty is not simply a showy, worn-out formula as we thought in the time of our self-confident, materialistic youth? If the tops of these three trees meet, as scholars have declared, but the too obvious, too straight sprouts of Truth and Goodness have been knocked down, cut off, and do not grow—then perhaps the capricious, unpredictable, unexpected sprouts of Beauty will force their way through and rise *to that very same place*, and thus carry out the work for all three?

And then it is not a mistake, but a prophecy that we find written in Dostoievsky: "Beauty will save the world."[179]

Original Texts of Poetry
Quoted in Translation

Rainer Maria Rilke

Der Schauende

Ich sehe den Bäumen die Stürme an,
die aus laugewordenen Tagen
an meine ängstlichen Fenster schlagen,
und höre die Fernen Dinge sagen,
die ich nicht ohne Freund ertragen,
nicht ohne Schwester lieben kann.

Da geht der Sturm, ein Umgestalter,
geht durch den Wald und durch die Zeit,
und alles ist wie ohne Alter;
die Landschaft, wie ein Vers im Psalter,
ist Ernst und Wucht und Ewigkeit.

Wie ist das klein, womit wir ringen,
was mit uns ringt, wie ist das groß;
ließen wir, ähnlicher den Dingen,
uns *so* vom großen Sturm bezwingen—
wir würden weit und namenlos.

Was wir besiegen, ist das Kleine,
und der Erfolg selbst macht uns klein.
Das Ewige und Ungemeine
will nicht von uns gebogen sein.
Das ist der Engel, der den Ringern
des Alten Testaments erschien:
wenn seiner Widersacher Sehnen
im Kampfe sich metallen dehnen,
fühlt er sie unter seinen Fingern
wie Saiten tiefer Melodien.

Wen dieser Engel überwand,
welcher so oft auf Kampf verzichtet,
der geht gerecht und aufgerichtet
und groß aus jener harten Hand,
die sich, wie formend, an ihn schmiegte.
Die Siege laden ihn nicht ein.
Sein Wachstum ist: der Tiefbesiegte
von immer Größerem zu sein.

Friedrich Nietzsche

Mitternachtslied

O Mensch! Gib Acht!
Was spricht die tiefe Mitternacht?
'Ich schlief, ich schlief—
aus tiefem Traum bin ich erwacht:—
Die Welt ist tief,
und tiefer als der Tag gedacht.
Tief ist ihr Weh—,
Lust—tiefer noch als Herzeleid.
Weh spricht: Vergeh!
doc all Lust will Ewigkeit—,
—will tiefe, tiefe Ewigkeit!'

Rainer Maria Rilke

Die Neunte Elegie

Warum, wenn es angeht, also die Frist des Daseins
hinzubringen, als Lorbeer, ein wenig dunkler als alles
andere Grün, mit kleinen Wellen an jedem
Blattrand (wie eines Windes Lächeln)—: warum dann
Menschliches müssen—und, Schicksal vermeidend,
sich sehnen nach Schicksal? . . .

Oh, *nicht*, weil Glück *ist*,
dieser voreilige Vorteil eines nahen Verlusts.
Nicht aus Neugier, oder zur Übung des Herzens,
das auch im Lorbeer *wäre*.. . . .

Aber weil Hiersein viel ist, und weil uns scheinbar
alles das Hiesige braucht, dieses Schwindende, das
seltsam uns angeht. Uns, die Schwindendsten. *Ein* Mal
jedes, nur *ein* Mal. *Ein* mal und nichtmehr. Und wir auch
ein Mal. Nie wieder. Aber dieses

ein Mal gewesen zu sein, wenn auch nur *ein* Mal:
irdisch gewesen zu sein, scheint nicht widerrufbar.

Und so drängen wir uns und wollen es leisten,
wollens enthalten in unsern einfachen Händen,
im überfülltcren Blick und im sprachlosen Herzen.
Wollen es werden.—Wem es geben? Am liebsten
alles behalten für immer ... Ach, in den andern Bezug,
wehe, was nimmt man hinüber? Nicht das Anschaun, das hier
langsam erlernte, und kein hier Ereignetes. Keins.
Also die Schmerzen. Also vor allem das Schwersein,
also der Liebe lange Erfahrung,—also
lauter Unsägliches. Aber später,
unter den Sternen, was solls: *die* sind *besser* unsäglich.
Bringt doch der Wanderer auch vom Hange des Bergrands
nicht eine Hand voll Erde ins Tal, die Allen unsägliche, sondern
ein erworbenes Wort, reines, den gelben und blaun
Enzian. Sind wir veilleicht *hier*, um zu sagen: Haus,
Brücke, Brunnen, Tor, Krug, Obstbaum, Fenster,—
höchstens: Säule, Turm ... aber zu *sagen*, verstehs,
oh zu sagen *so*, wie selber die Dinge niemals
innig meinten zu sein. Ist nicht die heimliche Lust
dieser verschwiegenen Erde, wenn sie die Liebenden drängt,
daß sich in ihrem Gefühl jedes und jedes entzückt?
Schwelle: was ists für zwei
Liebende, daß sie die eigne ältere Schwelle der Tür
ein wenig verbrauchen, auch sie, nach den vielen vorher
und vor den Künftigen. . . . , leicht.

Hier ist des *Säglichen* Zeit, *hier* seine Heimat.
Sprich und bekenn. Mehr als je
fallen die Dinge dahin, die erlebbaren, denn,
was sie verdrängend ersetzt, ist ein Tun ohne Bild.
Tun unter Krusten, die willig zerspringen, sobald
innen das Handeln entwächst und sich anders begranzt.
Zwischen den Hämmern besteht
unser Herz, wie die Zunge
zwischen den Zähnen, die doch,
dennoch, die preisende bleibt.

Preise dem Engel die Welt, nicht die unsägliche, *ihm*
kannst du nicht großtun mit herrlich Erfühltem; im Weltall,
wo er fühlender fühlt, bist du ein Neuling. Drum zeig
ihm das Einfache, das, von Geschlect zu Geschlectern gestaltet,
als ein Unsriges lebt, neben der Hand und im Blick.
Sag ihm die Dinge. Er wird staunender stehn; wie du standest
die dem Seiler in Rom, oder beim Töpfer am Nil.
Zeig ihm, wie glücklich ein Ding sein kann, wie schuldlos und unser,

wie selbst das klagende Leid rein zur Gestalt sich entschließt,
dient als ein Ding, oder stirbt in ein Ding—, und jenseits
selig der Geige entgeht.—Und diese, von Hingang
lebenden Dinge verstehn, daß du rühmst; vergänglich,
traun sie ein Rettendes uns, den Vergänglichsten, zu.
Wollen, wir sollen sie ganz im unsichtbarn Herzen verwandeln
in—o unendlich—in uns! Wer wir am Ende auch seien.

Erde, ist est nicht dies, was du willst: *unsichtbar*
in uns erstehn?—Ist es dein Traum nicht,
einmal unsichtbar zu sein?—Erde! unsichtbar!
Was, wenn Verwandlung nicht, ist dein drängender Auftrag?
Erde, du liebe, ich will. Oh glaub, es bedürfte
nicht deiner Frühlinge mehr, mich dir zu gewinnen, einer,
ach, ein einziger ist schon dem Blute zu viel.
Namenlos bin ich zu dir entschlossen, von weit her.
Immar warst du im Recht, und dein heiliger Einfall
ist der vertrauliche Tod.

Siehe, ich lebe. Woraus? Weder Kindheit noch Zukunft
werden weniger. . . . Überzähliges Dasein
entspringt mir im Herzen.

Die Spanische Trilogie (I)

Aus dieser Wolke, siehe: die den Stern
so wild verdeckt, der eben war—(und mir),
aus diesem Bergland drüben, das jetzt Nacht,
Nachtwinde hat für eine Zeit—(und mir),
aus diesem Fluß im Talgrund, der den Schein
zerrissner Himmels-Lichtung fängt—(und mir);
aus mir und alledem ein einzig Ding
zu machen, Herr: aus mir und dem Gefühl,
mit dem die Herde, eingekehrt im Pferch,
das große dunkle Nichtmehrsein der Welt
ausatmend hinnimmt—, mir und jedem Licht
im Finstersein der vielen Häuser, Herr:
ein Ding zu machen; aus den Fremden, denn
nicht Einen kenn ich, Herr, und mir und mir
ein Ding zu machen; aus den Schlafenden,
den fremden alten Männern im Hospiz,
die wichtig in den Betten husten, aus
schlaftrunknen Kindern an so fremder Brust,
aus vielen Ungenaun und immer mir,
aus nichts als mir und dem, was ich nicht kenn,
das Ding zu machen, Herr Herr Herr, das Ding,
das welthaft-irdisch wie ein Meteor

in seiner Schwere nur die Summe Flugs
zusammennimmt: nichts wiegend als die Ankunft.

Giaccomo Leopardi

L'Infinito

Sempre caro mi fu quest'ermo colle
e questa siepe che da tanta parte
del ultimo orizonte il guardo esclude.
Ma sedendo e mirando, interminati spazi di là da quella
e sovr'umani silenzi, e profondissima quiete
io nel pensier mi fingo;
ove per poco il cuor non si spaura.
E come il vento odo stormir tra queste piante,
io quel infinito silenzio a questa voce vo comparando
e mi sovien l'eterno, e le morte staggioni
e la presente e viva, e il suon di lei.
E così tra quest'immensità s'annega il pensier mio;
e il naufragar m'è dolce in questo mare.

Michelangelo Buonarroti

Sonnetto

Giunto è già 'l corso della vita mia,
con tempestoso mar, per fragil barca,
al commun porto, ov'a render si varca
conto e ragion d'ogni opra trista e pia.

Onde l'affettüosa fantasia
che l'arte mi fece idol e monarca
conosco or ben com'era d'error carca
e qual c'a mal suo grado ogn'uom desia.
Gli amorosi pensier, già gani e lieti,
che fien or, s'a due morti m'avvicino?
D'una so 'l certo, e l'altra mi minaccia.
Nè pinger nè scolpir fie più che quieti
l'anima, volta a quell'amor divino
c'aperse, a prender noi, 'n croce le braccia.

Notes

Introduction

1. Mary Gerhart, "Dialogical Fields in Religious Studies," *Journal of the American Academy of Religion*, vol. LXII no. 4 (winter, 1994), 999.

2. Bruce B. Lawrence, "Toward a history of global religion(s) in the twentieth century, parachristian sightings from an interdisciplinary Asianist." Sixteenth Annual University Lecture in Religion, Arizona State University, March 23, 1995. Lawrence further suggests that the recent interest in these areas of religious studies has been accompanied by a decline in the study of theology.

3. Already classic are Hans Urs von Balthasar, *The Glory of the Lord. A Theological Aesthetics*, vol. 1, trans. by E. Leiva-Merikakis, edited by Joseph Fessio and John Riches (San Francisco: Ignatius Press, 1982), and Gerardus van der Leeuw, *Sacred and Profane Beauty. The Holy in Art*, trans. by David E. Green (New York: Holt, Rinehard and Winston, 1963). More recent works that explicitly attempt an integration of theology and aesthetics are: Frank Burch Brown, *Religious Aesthetics. A Theological Study of Making and Meaning* (Princeton, N.J.: Princeton University Press, 1989); Aiden Nichols, *The Art of God Incarnate* (New York: Paulist Press, 1980); Jeremy S. Begbie, *Voicing Creation's Praise. Towards a Theology of the Arts* (Edinburgh: T&T Clark, 1991); Günter Pöltner and Helmuth Vetter, eds., *Theologie und Ästhetik* (Wien, Freiburg, Basel: Herder, 1985); Patrick Sherry, *Spirit and Beauty. An Introduction to Theological Aesthetics* (Oxford: Clarendon Press, 1992); J. Daniel Brown, *Masks of Mystery. Explorations in Christian Faith and the Arts* (Lanham, New York, London: University Press of America, 1997); Nicholas Wolterstorff, *Art in Action. Toward a Christian Aesthetic* (Grand Rapids, MI: William B. Eerdmans, 1980); Garrett Green, *Imagining God. Theology and the Religious Imagination* (San Francisco: Harper & Row, 1989); Richard Harries, *Art and the Beauty of God* (London: Mobray, 1993); John Navone, *Toward a Theology of Beauty* (Collegeville: Liturgical Press, 1996).

4. Frank Burch Brown, *Religious Aesthetics. A Theological Study of Making and Meaning* (Princeton, N.J.: Princeton University Press, 1989), p. 37.

5. Hans Urs von Balthasar, *The Glory of the Lord. A Theological Aesthetics. Volume 1: Seeing the Form*. Translated by Erasmo Leiva-Merikakis. Edited by Joseph Fessio, S.J., and John Riches (San Francisco: Ignatius Press, 1982), p. 17.

6. Hans Georg Gadamer, *Truth and Method* (New York: Crossroad, 1982), p. 346.

1. The context is Barth's consideration of "God and nothingness."

2. Barth had written earlier about the eighteenth century: "It is surely no accident that precisely this century brought forth the best music of all time up to the present: J. S. Bach and G. F. Handel, Gluck and Haydn, and W. A. Mozart, the Incomparable. *Kirchliche Dogmatik* III, i (Zurich: Zollikon, 1932ff.), p. 465.

3. Barth's text substitutes the indicative *lucet* for the subjunctive *luceat* in the second phrase of the Introit of the requiem mass: *Requiem aeternam dona eis Domine, et lux perpetua luceat eis* ("Eternal rest grant unto them, O Lord, and may perpetual light shine upon them")—so that the last phrase is no longer a prayer, but a statement of fact: "eternal light shines upon them."

4. Karl Barth, *Kirchliche Dogmatik* III, 3, 337–340 (my translation).

5. Gerardus van der Leeuw, *Sacred and Profane Beauty. The Holy in Art*, trans. by David E. Green (New York: Holt, Rinehart and Winston, 1963), p. 242.

6. Ibid.

7. Ibid.

8. Hans-Georg Gadamer, *Truth and Method* (New York: Crossroad, 1982), p. 11. References to Gadamer will normally be to the English edition; where clarification of the translation is needed I will include in brackets [] a reference to the original: *Wahrheit und Methode. Grundzüge einer philosophischen Hermeneutik* 4 Auflage. (Tübingen: J. C. B. Mohr, 1975) (henceforth *WM*).

9. James Alfred Martin, *Beauty and Holiness. The Dialogue between Aesthetics and Religion* (Princeton: Princeton University Press, 1990), pp. 36–37.

10. *Aesthetica*, no. 1, 14; *Metaphysica*, 607, 662. Quoted in Iesu Iturrioz, S.J., "Metaphysica generalis," in Professores Societatis Iesu Facultatum Philosophicarum in Hispania, *Philosophiae Scholasticae Summa*, vol. I (Madrid: Biblioteca de Autores Cristianos, 1957), p. 614.

11. "*Aesthetices finis est perfectio cognitionis sensitivae, qua talis. Haec autem est pulchritudo.*" *Aesthetica*, no. 14, quoted loc. cit.

12. Friedrich Schiller, *On the Aesthetic Education of Man in a Series of Letters (Über die Ästhetische Erziehung des Menschen)*, German and English texts, edited and trans. with an Introduction and Commentary and Glossary of Terms by Elizabeth M. Wilkinson and L. A. Willoughby (Oxford: Clarendon Press, 1967), s.v. *"ästhetisch,"* p. 304.

13. Ibid.; cf. Iturrioz, *Metaphysica*, p. 615.

14. Hans Urs Von Balthasar, *The Glory of the Lord. A Theological Aesthetics*, Volume 1: Seeing the Form. Translated by Erasmo Leiva-Merikakis. Edited by Joseph Fessio, S.J., and John Riches. (San Francisco: Ignatius Press, 1982), p. 50.

15. Augustinus Karl Wucherer-Huldenfeld, "Sein und Wesen des Schönen," in Günter Pöltner and Helmuth Vetter (eds.), *Theologie und Ästhetik* (Wien, Freiburg, Basel: Herder, 1985), pp. 20–34, at pp. 23, 24–26.

16. Iturrioz, *Metaphysica*, p. 615.

17. Georg Wilhelm Friedrich Hegel, *On Art* (translation of *Vorlesungen über die Ästhetik*) in Hegel, *On Art, Religion, Philosophy. Introductory Lectures to the Realm of Absolute Spirit*, edited by J. Glenn Gray (New York: Harper & Row, 1970), p. 22.

18. Schiller, *Über die Ästhetische Erziehung des Menschen*, XX. 4, n. (p. 140).

19. "*Sie wollen mir also vergönnen, Ihnen die Resultate meiner Untersuchungen über das Schöne und die Kunst in einer Reihe von Briefen vorzulegen*" (emphasis original). Ibid., I.1 (p. 2).

20. Ibid., XX. 4, n., pp. 140–143. Translation modified.

21. Ibid.

22. James Alfred Martin, *Beauty and Holiness. The Dialogue between Aesthetics and Religion* (Princeton: Princeton University Press, 1990), p. 29.

23. On this topic see also Brown, *Religious Aesthetics*, pp. 21ff. On the replacement of "beauty" with the notion of the *"ästhetische Zustand"* in contemporary aesthetics, see Helmuth Vetter, "Ästhetik und Schönheit," in Günter Pöltner and Helmuth Vetter (eds.), *Theologie und Ästhetik* (Wien, Freiburg, Basel: Herder, 1985), pp. 35–47, at p. 43.

24. Gadamer, *Truth and Method*, p. 54. Naturally, the validity of this insight does not settle the question of whether there is an ultimate criterion of "beauty" or of "artistic taste."

25. Oscar Wilde, "The Decay of Lying," in *Intentions and the Soul of Man* (1891), quoted in Melvin Rader, ed., *A Modern Book of Esthetics. An Anthology* (New York: Holt, Rinehart and Winston, 1960), p. 21.

26. Gadamer, *Truth and Method*, p. 434. Cf. Maritain: "beauty, which is of no use." Jacques Maritain, *Creative Intuition in Art and Poetry* (New York: Meridian Books, 1955), p. 41.

27. Ibid., p. 444 [*WM* 463].

28. Karl Rahner, "Art against the Horizon of Theology and Piety," in *Theological Investigations* XXIII, trans. by Joseph Donceel, S.J., and Hugh M. Riley (New York: Crossroad, 1992), p. 162.

29. Mikel Dufrenne, ed., *Main Trends in Aesthetics and the Sciences of Art*, in *Main Trends of Research in the Social and Human Sciences*, Part 2, Vol. 1 (The Hague: Mouton Publishers/UNESCO, 1978), 491. quoted in Martin, *Beauty and Holiness*, p. 164.

30. Maritain, *Creative Intuition*, pp. 31–32; cf. Martin, *Beauty and Holiness*, p. 12.

31. *Posterior Analytics*, bk. 1, lect. 1, no. 1.

32. Maritain, *Creative Intuition*, pp. 31–50.

33. Rader, *A Modern Book of Esthetics*, presents a useful collection of writings representing different theories.

34. *Kritik der Urteilskraft*, 1799, no. 45; quoted in Gadamer, *Truth and Method*, p. 48.

35. Martin, *Beauty and Holiness*, p. 12.

36. Thus Paul Tillich states that aesthetic enjoyment "is based on the expressive power of an aesthetic creation even if the subject matter expressed is ugly or terrifying." *Systematic Theology*, vol. III (Chicago: University of Chicago Press, 1951), p. 257.

For an examination of modern aesthetics that replaces beauty with what Paul Valéry called *"valeurs de choc"*—in particular novelty, intensity, and foreignness (*la nouveauté, l'intensité, l'étrangeté*)—for the sake of transforming the subject's way of experiencing, see Helmuth Vetter, "Ästhetik und Schönheit," in Günter Pöltner and Helmuth Vetter (eds.), *Theologie und Ästhetik* (Wien, Freiburg, Basel: Herder, 1985), pp. 35–47. Vetter explores in particular Rimbaud's influence on this new approach to aesthetics.

37. Gadamer, *Truth and Method*, p. 64.

38. Martin, *Beauty and Holiness*, p. 114.

39. On the other hand, a good deal of popular (and even some "classic") religious art may be deemed kitsch, but to what extent does this impede its effectiveness as communicative art? On kitsch in religious art, see below, ch. 5.

40. Maritain, *Creative Intuition*, p. 15.

41. Martin, *Beauty and Holiness*, p. 140.

42. Ibid., p. 141.

43. Gadamer, *Truth and Method*, p. 64.

44. David Tracy, *The Analogical Imagination. Christian Theology and the Culture of Pluralism* (New York: Crossroad, 1981), p. 112. Tracy categorizes various theories of art according to the elements of the experience that they emphasize: the creative artist (expressive

theories); the work itself (objective, frequently formalist theories); the world the work creates or reveals (mimetic theories); the audience the world affects (pragmatic theories). Ibid.

45. Hans Küng and David Tracy, eds., *Paradigm Change in Theology*, trans. by Margaret Köhl (New York: Crossroad, 1989).

46. Thomas Aquinas, *Summa Theologica*, I, q. 1, a. 7, c.

47. *Omnia autem pertractantur in sacra doctrina sub ratione Dei vel quia sunt ipse Deus; vel quia habent ordinem ad Deum, ut ad principium et finem.*

For Aquinas "salvation history," including the Christ event, is theology's object in the same sense: *Quidam vero, attendentes ad ea quae in ista scientia tractantur, et non ad rationem secundum quam considerantur, assignaverunt aliter subiectum huius scientiae: vel res et signa, vel opus reparationis, vel totum Christum, idest caput et membra. De omnibus enim istis tractatur in ista scientia, sed secundum ordinem ad Deum.* Ibid.

In Roman Catholic theology, under the influence of neo-Scholasticism, this conception perdures well into the modern age. Thus the "earlier" Lonergan argues for the Thomistic position against the notion of theology as *Glaubensverständnis* or *Glaubenswissenschaft*. See Lonergan, "Theology and Understanding," in *Collection. Papers by Bernard Lonergan, S.J.*, edited by F. E. Crowe, S.J. (New York: Herder and Herder, 1967), p. 125 and n. 7.

48. See, for example, Lonergan, "Theology in its New Context," in *A Second Collection. Papers by Bernard J. F. Lonergan, S.J.*, edited by William F. J. Ryan, S. J., and Bernard J. Tyrrell, S.J. (London: Darton, Longman & Todd, 1974), p. 67; "Revolution in Catholic Theology," in ibid., p. 237; *Method in Theology* (New York: Herder and Herder, 1972), pp. 125–145; 267, 331, and *passim*.

49. Thus the "later" Lonergan in *Method in Theology*, p. 350.

50. Karl Rahner, "The Future of Theology" in *TI*, vol. XI, trans. by David Bourke (New York: Seabury, 1974), p. 144. Cf. "Reflections on Methodology in Theology" in ibid., p. 76.

Lonergan makes a distinction between theology proper and theological methodology; see, for example, *Method in Theology*, pp. xii, 355. Nevertheless, if a theological methodology appeals to such categories as "religious conversion" (in Lonergan's sense of the term), it is in fact taking the point of view of "faith seeking understanding" and may be seen as an extension of critical reflection on religious experience. In my view, theological methodology may be seen as an element of fundamental theology.

51. Karl Barth, *Church Dogmatics*, edited by G. W. Bromiley and T. F. Torrence (Edinburgh: T&T Clark, 1970), vol. II, part 1, p. 656.

52. Hans Urs Von Balthasar, *The Glory of the Lord*, p. 18.

53. Alois Gügler, *Die heilige Kunst* (Landshut, 1814), quoted in ibid., p. 102.

54. Rowan Williams, "Balthasar and Rahner," in John Riches, ed., *The Analogy of Beauty. The Theology of Hans Urs von Balthasar* (Edinburgh: T&T Clark, 1986), p. 24.

55. It is relevant in connection with this point that Balthasar never held a regular academic post.

56. Balthasar, *The Glory of the Lord*, p. 19.

57. Bruce B. Lawrence, "Toward a history of global religion(s) in the twentieth century, parachristian sightings from an interdisciplinary Asianist." Sixteenth Annual University Lecture in Religion, Arizona State University, March 23, 1995, p. 5.

58. For a study of one of the pioneers in restoring the imaginative dimension to Roman Catholic theology, see Gerald J. Bednar, *Faith as Imagination. The Contribution of William F. Lynch, S.J.* (Kansas City: Sheed & Ward, 1996).

59. "The fact that the primary language of religion is markedly poetic, mythic, and otherwise aesthetic means that it is with such language that theology repeatedly begins and that it is to such language that theology must often return." Frank Burch Brown, *Religious*

Aesthetics. A Theological Study of Making and Meaning (Princeton, N.J.: Princeton University Press, 1989), p. 193.

60. Rahner, "Reflections on Methodology in Theology," in *TI*, vol. XI, trans. by David Bourke (New York: Seabury Press, 1974), pp. 105–110.

61. Rahner, "A Theology That We Can Live With," in *TI*, vol. XXI, trans. by Hugh M. Riley (New York: Crossroad, 1988), pp. 111–112.

62. Rahner, "Art against the Horizon of Theology and Piety," p. 164.

63. Martin, *Beauty and Holiness*, p. 191.

64. I use this term without any of the pejorative sense that it has in Balthasar's work. In the term "aesthetic theology" (as opposed to "theological aesthetics") he takes "aesthetic" to mean "worldly" and "limited." In this sense of the word (as in Kierkegaard) the "merely" aesthetic is contrasted with genuine Christian values. See *The Glory of the Lord*, pp. 38, 79.

65. Amos Niven Wilder, *Theopoetic. Theology and the Religious Imagination* (Philadelphia: Fortress Press, 1976), p. 3.

66. Frank Burch Brown, *Religious Aesthetics. A Theological Study of Making and Meaning* (Princeton, N.J.: Princeton University Press, 1989), p. 42. Brown's book provides an excellent survey of modern aesthetics and "anti-aesthetics," as well as the foundations of a "neo-aesthetic" theory that can include religious objects.

67. Tracy, *The Analogical Imagination*, p. 408.

68. Rahner, "Art against the Horizon of Theology and Piety," p. 165.

69. Martin Heidegger, *Identität und Differenz* (Pfullingen, 1957), p. 70; quoted in Johannes Baptist Lotz, S.J., *Die Identität von Geist und Sein. Eine Historische-Systematische Untersuchung* (Roma: Università Gregoriana Editrice, 1972), p. 199f.

Lotz notes that Heidegger's remark shows that he is thinking in terms of rationalist philosophy [Spinoza?], for *causa sui* is not an accurate designation for God in the Aristotelian-Thomistic tradition: "*Statt 'causa sui' müßte man, streng genommen, 'ratio sui' sagen: denn Gott verursacht nicht sich selbst, was eine contradictio in adiecto wäre, wohl aber ist er der Grund seiner selbst.*" Ibid., n. 207.

70. See, for example, Messiaen's notes on his *Méditations sur le mystère de la sainte Trinité*.

71. Blaise Pascal, *Pensées* (Paris: Éditions Garnier Frères, 1964), p. 4.

72. "An Interview with Fr. Bernard Lonergan, S.J." in *A Second Collection*, p. 227; cf. *Method in Theology*, p. 266.

73. Lonergan, *Method in Theology*, p. 364.

74. Ibid., p. 362.

75. Brown, *Religious Aesthetics*, pp. 87–88.

76. David Tracy cites Friedrich von Hügel's enumeration of three fundamental elements of every great religion: the institutional, the intellectual, and the "mystical." The last Tracy thinks is more exactly called the "religious" element, and includes the realm that is here called "aesthetic." See Tracy, "The Uneasy Alliance Reconceived: Catholic Theological Method, Modernity, and Postmodernity," in *Theological Studies*, vol. 50, no. 3 (September 1989), pp. 548–570, at p. 548.

77. Van der Leeuw, *Sacred and Profane Beauty*, p. 11.

78. Tracy, "The Uneasy Alliance," p. 564.

79. As Frank Burch Brown points out, it is not merely the individual works but the various "styles" of art that serve as embodiments of the Christian classic. *Religious Aesthetics*, p. 168.

80. Karl Rahner, "The relation between theology and popular religion," in *TI*, vol. XXII, translated by Joseph Donceel, S.J. (New York: Crossroad, 1991), p. 140.

81. Ibid., p. 142.

82. Ibid., p. 145.

83. Tracy, "The Uneasy Alliance," p. 548. Arguing a similar point, Rahner asks rhetorically: "What faith (of the Church) does theology, in its own self-understanding, presuppose as its object of study? Only the one laid down in the canonical Scriptures? . . . Would it then be possible for theology to understand popular religion as nothing more than human (religious and sociological) objectifications falling under the judgment (of rejection or forgiveness) of Scripture? But if we accepted this understanding and were then to discover in normative Scripture itself ('sola Scriptura') more popular religion, and would thus again have to look for a canon within the canon, what then?" "The relation between theology and popular religion," p. 141.

84. Tracy, "The Uneasy Alliance," p. 548.

85. Ibid., p. 549. Tracy sees much of the study of this "religious" element of the church as the work of social scientists, anthropologists, and historians; but it is in theology and philosophy that their findings "come home for reflection." Ibid., p. 549f.

86. Margaret R. Miles, *Image as Insight. Visual Understanding in Western Christianity and Secular Culture* (Boston: Beacon Press, 1985), p. 9.

87. Ibid., p. xi.

88. Ibid., p. 9.

89. Patrick O'Brian, *Post Captain* (New York: W. W. Norton & Co., 1990), p. 470. In another volume of the series, O'Brian's Captain Aubrey struggles with a violin partita by Bach and "thinks" the music as a form of discourse. See *The Ionian Mission* (New York: W. W. Norton & Co., 1994), p. 155f.

The historical setting of the fictional doctor's insight (the Napoleonic era) is plausible. As Balthasar shows in his historical overview, the "rehabilitation" of feeling and imagination as modes of knowing, in opposition to Enlightenment rationalism, began within the Enlightenment period itself, with such figures as Rousseau, Herder, and Chateaubriand. See Balthasar, *The Glory of the Lord*, p. 91.

90. Gadamer, *Truth and Method*, p. 87.

91. Rahner, "Art against the Horizon of Theology and Piety," p. 162.

92. Karl Rahner, "The Theology of the Religious Meaning of Images" in *TI*, vol. XXIII, trans. by Joseph Donceel, S.J., and Hugh M. Riley (New York: Crossroad, 1992), p. 156. Rahner notes that the intrinsic intelligibility of the nonverbal element has frequently been neglected in sacramental theology: "one has the impression that the 'matter' of the sacraments (washing, anointing, imposition of hands) is only a more or less arbitrarily prescribed ceremony, which could just as well have been replaced by another." Ibid.

93. Rahner remarks: "The water which is seen by *the human being*, which is praised by the poet, and which is used by the Christian in baptism—this water is not a poetic glorification of the chemist's water, as if the latter were the true realist. On the contrary, the 'water' of the chemist is much rather a narrowed down, technified derivation of a secondary kind from the water of humanity." Karl Rahner, "Priest and Poet," in *Theological Investigations*, vol. III, translated by Karl-H. and Boniface Kruger (New York: Seabury Press, 1974), p. 296 [pronouns in translation altered].

94. See Lonergan, *Method*, p. 73.

95. David Freedberg's study of people's responses to images, *The Power of Images. Studies in the History and Theory of Response* (Chicago and London: Chicago University Press, 1989), which gives many examples drawn from sacred art, discusses and illustrates the difficulties inherent in such a project.

96. With regard specifically to painting, Michael Baxendale refers to the need for the viewer to develop a "period eye": i.e., to retrieve the "equipment" that its contemporary public brought to a painting. *Painting and Experience in Fifteenth-Century Italy* (London:

Oxford University Press, 1972), p. 102. Compare Lonergan's statement that the task of "interpretation" of a text must include an understanding of the "common sense" of the author. *Method in Theology* (New York: Herder and Herder, 1972), p. 161. On the other hand, David Freedberg warns us against a "strict and unthinking contextualism." *The Power of Images*, p. 439; cf., p. 431.

97. Tracy, *The Analogical Imagination*, p. 124.

98. "The artist speaks through matter of which he/she is not completely the master, in a language of which he/she is not the inventor except to a small extent." P.-M. Léonard, S.J., *s.v.* "Art" in *Dictionnaire de Spiritualité*, edited by Marcel Viller, S.J. (Paris: Beauchesne, 1937), tome. 1, col. 907.

99. Rahner, "Art against the Horizon of Theology and Piety," p. 165.

100. Ibid., p. 163.

101. See Rahner, "Theology and popular religion," pp. 143–144.

102. Ibid.

103. Paul Tillich, *Systematic Theology*, vol. 1 (Chicago: University of Chicago Press, 1951), p. 3. David Tracy reformulates Tillich's method in terms of a critical correlation of "common human experience and language" with "Christian texts" or of "the tradition" with "the contemporary situation." Tracy, *Blessed Rage for Order. The New Pluralism in Theology* (New York: Seabury Press, 1975), p. 53; "The Uneasy Alliance," p. 550. See the last named for Tracy's defense of correlational method in the light of "postmodern" criticisms.

104. Ibid., p. 4.

105. Ibid., pp. 3–4.

106. So, for example, Garrett Green, *Imagining God. Theology and the Religious Imagination* (San Francisco: Harper & Row, 1989). Green writes: "The hermeneutical function of Christian theology implies that its proper form is not 'systematic' in the philosophical or foundational sense. . . . Rather, theology as an interpretive discipline ought to be 'local' or topical, the elaboration of specific *loci*, whose relationships to one another are ad hoc rather than a priori. . . . Doing theology this way is more like doing literary criticism than elaborating a philosophical system." P. 148.

107. For an analysis and critique of two examples, see Paul Lauritzen, "Is 'Narrative' Really a Panacea? The Use of 'Narrative' in the Work of Metz and Hauerwas," in *The Journal of Religion*, 67 (1987), pp. 322–339.

108. In the terminology I have adopted "theological aesthetics" in the wide sense designates (1) the theological use of or (2) the theological account of the aesthetic. In "aesthetic theology," as described here, one has equally an "aesthetic" account of theology—e.g., a conception of its method (at least in part) in terms of narrative or of literary hermeneutics.

109. Balthasar, *The Glory of the Lord*, p. 79.

110. *Dogmatik* I, § 17, n. 240ff. Quoted by Balthasar in ibid., p. 107. Scheeben is echoed by contemporary Hamburg theologian and pastor Harmut Sierig: "*Als Buch der Bilder könnten wir die Bibel in ihrer Gesamtheit bezeichnen. Wer sie unbefangen ließt, wird zuerst — vor allen wissenschaftlichen, philosophischen und theologischen Fragen — von ihrer Ausdrucksmächtigkeit, ihrer malerischen Intellektualität ergriffen.*" Harmut Sierig, *Über den garstigen Graben. Der dritte Standpunkt im Grundriß* (Hamburg: Agentur des Rauhen Hauses, 1967), p. 33.

111. Balthasar, *The Glory of the Lord*, p. 84. Balthasar notes that for some Romantic thinkers, notably Herder, the level of image and sensibility (*Empfindung*) is valued more highly than that of abstract thought, which belongs to the "fallen" level of alienation. Ibid., p. 86.

112. Lawrence, "Toward a history of global religion(s)," p. 6.

113. Williams, "Balthasar and Rahner," p. 27.

114. Martin, *Beauty and Holiness*, p. 95. Cf. Nicholas Lash, "Ideology, Metaphor, and Analogy," in Stanley Hauerwas and L. Gregory Jones, eds., *Why Narrative? Readings in Narrative Theology* (Grand Rapids: William B. Eerdmans Publishing, 1989). Lash seems to favor a narrower definition of "theology": "I suggest that the distinction between narrative, metaphorical discourse, and those non-narrative modes of discourse to which reflection on the metaphorical gives rise appears, within Christianity, as a distinction between religious practice and critical reflection on that practice: between 'religion' and 'theology' " (p. 119; cf. p. 137).

This usage of the word "theology" seems to me overly restrictive. In its wide sense, at least, "theology" can include a "logos" or understanding about God that is narrative, metaphorical, and precritical.

Lonergan schematically divides the "realms" of meaning into "common sense" (the sphere of practical life: the particular, relative, imaginable; its language is descriptive rather than explanatory), theory, interiority, and transcendence. (See *Method in Theology*, pp. 81ff.). Religion, in its mode of teaching and preaching, occurs in the realm of "common sense" (ibid., p. 114). So does a great deal of its theology. Lonergan remarks that "Augustine is just in the world of common sense, a beautiful rhetorician; Newman too" ("Interview," p. 227; cf. *Method in Theology*, p. 261, where he adds Descartes and Pascal). The "systematic" and "critical" exigencies, leading to the differentiation of the realms of abstract theory and of interiority, are significant developments for "scientific" theology, but do not define theology's limits.

On the other hand, I will argue that philosophical and specifically metaphysical thought have a crucial (although not exclusive) role to play in theology.

I emphasize once again that the use of the term "aesthetic" for movements like narrative theology is in no way pejorative, but stems from their method. As Lash says, "there does seem to be a sense in which narrative construction is more patently a 'work of art' than is the elaboration of scientific theory. And if this is so, then that sense may be closely connected with the apparently more pervasive presence of the metaphorical in narrative than in theoretical discourse."

115. The whole of Lonergan's *Insight* (New York: Philosophical Library, 1957) is relevant; see especially pp. 175–179, ch. VI–VII *passim*, pp. 390–391, 417–421; *Method in Theology*, pp. 81–84, 302–318; cf. Lash, "Ideology, Metaphor, and Analogy," p. 119.

116. Lash, "Ideology, Metaphor, and Analogy," p. 136. The internal quote is from Brian Wicker, *The Story Shaped World* (London, 1975), p. 27.

117. Lash, "Ideology, Metaphor, and Analogy," p. 118.

118. Ibid., p. 117.

119. Balthasar, *The Glory of the Lord*, p. 81.

120. Lash, "Ideology, Metaphor, and Analogy," p. 120.

121. Ibid., p. 116. Note that Lash speaks of an "aspiration" to universality and timelessness, not its actual achievement by theoretical or "scientific" language.

Contemporary critical metaphysics admits that all concepts and all modes of reasoning, including the abstract and theoretical, are both "linguistically rendered" and "historically embedded" (Tracy, "The Uneasy Alliance," p. 559). Although, as Tracy remarks, many forms of classical and modern theology have failed to pay sufficient attention to this fact, it is presumed by transcendental philosophers like Johannes Baptist Lotz (e.g., *Die Identität von Geist und Sein* [Roma: Università Gregoriana Editrice, 1972], p. 157, where he speaks briefly of what he calls "acquired" a prioris of knowledge) and is made an explicit theme by others, like José Gómez Caffarena (e.g., *Metafísica Fundamental* [Madrid: Ediciones de la Revista de Occidente, 1969]). It is also present in nonmetaphysical theologians like Schillebeeckx (see, for example, *Christ. The Experience of Jesus as Lord* [New York: Seabury Press, 1980], pp. 31–61). Although Karl Rahner is generally more concerned with the "transcendental" element in knowledge, he is perfectly aware of its linguistic and historical relativity. (See, for example, his 1973 article "Faith between rationality and emotion," in *Theological Investigations*, vol. XVI, trans. by David Morland, O.S.B. [New York: Crossroad, 1983], p. 62, where he speaks of the dependence of rationality on social conditions, historically conditioned language, and a general horizon of understanding, conscious and unconscious).

If reason is not conceived rationalistically but historically, as a self-corrective process, as it is most explicitly in Lonergan's cognitional theory, then it is able to achieve a "partly history-transcending character" (Tracy, ibid., p. 567) and a relative universality. However, as this book is intended to argue, the relative adequacy that can be hoped for in theology must occur in relation to other embodiments of the spirit: ethics, science, history, other religions, and art (Tracy, *The Analogical Imagination*, p. 422).

122. Ibid., p. 120.

123. Ibid., p. 120.

124. Tracy, *The Analogical Imagination*, p. 346.

125. Ibid., p. 133.

126. It is notable that although earlier conflicts between science and religion have largely been reconciled on the *theological* level, they remain actual in the minds of many ordinary believers and many empirical scientists. Paul Davies, professor of Natural Philosophy at the University of Adelaide, Australia, and winner of the 1995 Templeton Prize for Progress in Religion, commented that "The gap is not between science and the theologians. That gap is really rather small. The gap is between the theologians and the ordinary believers." (Gustav Niebuhr, "Scientist Wins Religion Prize of $1 Million," in the *New York Times*, Thursday, March 9, 1995, p. A13). Many teachers of theology have no doubt shared the experience of meeting this gap in their students.

127. Wolfe's once admired poetry is now practically unavailable except in Holst's song settings. "Betelgeuse" is found in the cycle "The Dream City." There is an excellent recording by soprano Patrizia Kwella with the City of London Sinfonia, conducted by Richard Hickox. Hyperion CDA 66099.

128. Cf. Lonergan, *Method in Theology*, p. 66.

129. Lauritzen, "Is 'Narrative' Really a Panacea?," p. 339.

130. Ibid., p. 339. Lauritzen illustrates this point with reference to the theologies of Metz and Hauerwas, who both appeal to narrative, but draw strongly opposed practical conclusions from their readings of the Christian story.

Tracy remarks: "For Christian systematic theology, the first clue for an appropriate response to the radical pluralism of the contemporary situation is the need to reflect upon the pluralism *within* the Christian tradition in order to reflect upon the pluralism *among* the religious traditions or the pluralism *among* the analyses of the situation." *The Analogical Imagination*, pp. 447–448.

131. Lash, "Ideology, Metaphor, and Analogy," p. 119.

132. Ibid., p. 123. Cf. Lonergan, *Method in Theology*, p. 66.

133. Ibid., p. 124.

134. Ibid., pp. 125–126.

135. Ibid.

136. Ibid., pp. 121–123.

137. Lauritzen, "Is 'Narrative' Really a Panacaea?," p. 339.

138. Paul Ricoeur, *The Symbolism of Evil* (Boston: Beacon Press, 1967), pp. 347–357. Quoted in Tracy, *The Analogical Imagination*, p. 13.

139. See David Tracy, *Blessed Rage for Order* (New York: Seabury Press, 1975), p. 78f.; *The Analogical Imagination*, pp. 112ff.

140. The other great twentieth-century theologian who has dealt extensively with aesthetics in theology (but without formulating an explicit and systematic "theological aesthetics") is Paul Tillich. I shall make some references to Tillich's work in later chapters, but because his ideas on art are scattered through many essays, and because they are comprehensible only in the context of the whole of Tillich's ontology and theology, I have not attempted to treat them in an extensive or systematic way. A systematic exposition, contextualization, and critique of Tillich's "latent" philosophy of art is given in Jeremy S. Begbie, *Voicing Creation's Praise. Towards a Theology of the Arts* (Edinburgh: T&T Clark, 1991).

141. Gerardus Van der Leeuw, *Religion in Essence and Manifestation*, trans. by J. E. Turner (New York: Harper & Row, 1963).

142. Van der Leeuw, *Sacred and Profane Beauty. The Holy in Art*, trans. by David E. Green (New York: Holt, Rinehart and Winston, 1963).

143. See ibid., p. 227.

144. Ibid., p. 328.

145. Ibid., p. 336.

146. Ibid., p. 5.

147. Ibid., p. 6.

148. Ibid., p. 8.

149. Ibid., p. 266.

150. Ibid., p. 265.

151. Ibid., p. 265.

152. Ibid., p. 327; cf. pp. 8, 318, 328.

153. Noel O'Donaghue, "A Theology of Beauty" in Riches, ed., *The Analogy of Beauty*, p. 3.

154. Abraham Kuyper and his followers to some extent anticipated Barth in their theology of the divine glory (*Herrlijkheid*) and its relation to beauty. For a treatment of these Dutch Neo-Calvinists, see Begbie, *Voicing Creation's Praise*, pp. 82–146. Barth was acquainted with the work of the Kuyperians, and attacked them for what he considered their incipient "natural theology." Ibid., p. 146.

155. Barth, *Church Dogmatics*, vol. II, part 1, p. 641.

156. Ibid., p. 641.

157. Ibid., p. 643.

158. Ibid., p. 644.

159. Ibid., p. 645.

160. Ibid., p. 646.

161. Ibid., p. 648.

162. Ibid.

163. Ibid., p. 653.

164. Ibid.

165. Ibid.

166. Ibid., p. 654.

167. Ibid., pp. 650–651.

168. Ibid., p. 659.

169. Ibid., p. 664.

170. Ibid., p. 662. Ibid., pp. 657–661.

171. Beauty that is beyond human understanding.

172. Ibid., p. 656.

173. Ibid., p. 657.

174. Ibid.

175. Ibid., p. 655.

176. Ibid., p. 652.

177. Ibid., p. 655.

178. Ibid., p. 666.

179. Ibid.

180. Ibid., p. 653.

181. Ibid., p. 652. The "other concepts" to which Barth refers are act, love, and freedom. The perfections of loving are conceptualized as grace and holiness; mercy and righteousness; patience and wisdom. The perfections of freedom are unity and omnipresence; constancy and omnipotence; eternity and glory. Ibid., pp. 257–678.

182. Barth, *Church Dogmatics*, vol. I, part 2, p. 840. The essence of the "Church attitude" that theology must take is to "listen to that which is the voice of its prayer as the final meaning of all its speaking."

183. Ibid., p. 648.

184. Ibid., pp. 841–842.

185. Ibid., p. 651.

186. Barth, *Church Dogmatics*, vol. II, part I, p. 652.

187. Ibid., p. 651.

188. Ibid., p. 652.

189. Ibid., p. 655.

190. Balthasar, *The Glory of the Lord*, pp. 45ff., 48; cf. Donaghue, "A Theology of Beauty," p. 3.

191. Balthasar, *The Glory of the Lord*, p. 67.

192. Ibid., p. 70.

193. Ibid., p. 13.

194. Ibid., p. 80.

195. Ibid., p. 38.

196. Ibid., p. 13.

197. Balthasar, "Another Ten Years," trans. by John Saward, in John Riches, ed., *The Analogy of Beauty. The Theology of Hans Urs von Balthasar* (Edinburgh: T&T Clark, 1986), p. 224.

198. Ibid.

199. Ibid., pp. 224–225.

200. Balthasar, "In Retrospect" (adapted from *Rechenschaft 1965* by Kenneth Batinovich, N.S.M.) in Riches, *The Analogy of Beauty*, p. 217.

201. Balthasar, "Another ten years," p. 225.

202. Ibid., p. 226.

203. Balthasar, "In retrospect," p. 218.

204. Balthasar, *The Glory of the Lord*, pp. 13–14.

205. Balthasar, "In Retrospect," p. 214.

206. Ibid., p. 216.

207. Ibid., p. 217.

208. Balthasar, *The Glory of the Lord*, p. 125.

209. Ibid., p. 117.

210. Balthasar, "In Retrospect," p. 217.

211. Balthasar, *The Glory of the Lord*, vol. I p. 69.

212. Ibid., p. 124. This does not mean that the divine beauty can only be examined in the context of God's actions in history; but the latter must be the starting point even for the examination of the divine attributes *in se*. Ibid., p. 125.

213. Ibid., p. 69.

214. Ibid., p. 29.

215. Ibid., p. 70.

216. Balthasar, "Another Ten Years," p. 224.

217. Ibid., p. 213.

218. Balthasar, "In Retrospect," pp. 213–214.

219. *The Glory of the Lord*, vol. 1, p. 38.

220. Ibid., p. 41 and *passim*.

221. Cf. Barth's comments on Mozart, above: the "light, shines so brightly, because it shines forth from the shadows."

222. Balthasar, *The Glory of the Lord*, vol. 1, p. 124.

223. John Riches, "Afterword" in Riches, ed., *The Analogy of Beauty*, p. 181.

224. Ibid.

225. Balthasar, *The Glory of the Lord*, vol. 1, p. 121.

226. Corresponding to St. Thomas's *"species"* or *"forma"* and *"lumen"* or *"splendor."* Ibid., p. 118.

227. Ibid., p. 119.

228. Ibid., p. 118. Balthasar notes that classical art emphasizes form containing the depths; Romantic art emphasizes the pointing beyond to the boundless.

229. Ibid.

230. Ibid., p. 32. As John Riches notes, for Balthasar there is not merely a formal similarity between aesthetics and theology: they also have a common content, insofar as in art, literature, and music we perceive something of the truth of being. Riches, "Afterword," p. 182.

231. *The Glory of the Lord*, vol. 1, p. 120.

232. Ibid., p. 33.

233. Ibid., p. 121.

234. John Riches, "Balthasar and the analysis of faith" in Riches, ed., *The Analogy of Beauty*, p. 36.

235. Balthasar, *The Glory of the Lord*, vol. 1, p. 126.

236. Balthasar's emphasis on the cross distinguishes his theological aesthetics from earlier attempts to formulate an "aesthetic" apologetic for Christianity. Chateaubriand, for example, starting from the premise that beauty is a criterion for truth, had proposed an apologetic based on Christianity's effect on art, philosophy, etc., as well as on the *charme* of the Christian mysteries. Balthasar remarks that such an apologetic fails because its criterion of beauty is this-worldly and cultural. It may show that Christianity had positive effects, but it does not touch the essence of Christian faith. In contrast, Balthasar holds that revelation brings its own criterion for beauty, by which culture must be measured. *The Glory of the Lord*, vol. 1, pp. 92–94.

237. Ibid., p. 14.

238. Balthasar, *The Glory of the Lord*, vol. 1, p. 34.

239. Riches, "Balthasar and the analysis of faith," pp. 51, 54.

240. Ibid., pp. 46–47; cf. "Afterword," p. 181.

241. Balthasar, "Another Ten Years," p. 227.

242. Riches, "Balthasar and the analysis of faith," p. 47.

243. Balthasar, *The Glory of the Lord*, vol. 1, p. 33.

244. See, for example, the First Vatican Council's dogmatic constitution "*Dei Filius*," ch. 3, "*De fide*," where faith in God's revelation is said to be "*propter auctoritatem ipsius Dei revelantis.*" (*DS* 3008).

245. See ibid., ch. 4, "*De fide et ratione*": "*Neque solum fides et ratio inter se dissidere numquam possunt, sed opem quoque sibi mutuam fuerint, cum recta ratio fidei fundamenta demonstret . . .*" (*DS* 3019). Cf. Canon 3 to chapter 3, which condemns the reduction of the motive of faith to purely internal experience: "*Si quis dixerit, revelationem divinam externis signis credibilem fieri non posse, ideoque sola interna cuiusque experientia aut inspiratione privata homines ad fidem moveri debere: anathema sit*" (*DS* 3033).

246. Balthasar acknowledges the *ad intra* quality of his work; see, for example, "Another Ten Years," p. 229.

247. Lash, "Ideology, Metaphor, and Analogy," p. 134.

In this connection, Balthasar is sometimes accused of using the Scriptures in an uncritical manner. Certainly his use of them takes their inspiration for granted; but his notion of what this implies seems to presuppose a great deal. To take a single example, he writes of the eyewitnesses to Christ: "just as the Holy Spirit was in their eyes so that the image should spring into view, so, too, was he in their mouth and in their pen so that the likeness (*Nachbild*) which they drew up of the original image (*Ur-Bild*) should correspond to the vision which God's Holy Spirit himself possesses of God's self-representation in the flesh." *The Glory of the Lord*, p. 31. For a brief overview of Balthasar's view of the Scriptures, see Medard Kehl, "Hans Urs von Balthasar: A Portrait," in Medard Kehl, S.J., and Werner Löser, S.J. (eds.) *The Von Balthasar Reader* (Edinburgh: T&T Clark, 1985), p. 36.

Balthasar takes from Origen a sacramental-symbolic idea of the Scriptures; they are an extension of the Incarnation, the primal sacrament. He frequently proclaims the inadequacy of a historical-critical approach to Scripture, and declares the need for a "spiritual" exegesis based on dogmatic theology. The basic exegetical principle is the indissolubility of "form." In the last analysis, "God is his own exegete" (the title of an article by Balthasar in *Communio* [Winter, 1986]); that is, Jesus is the self-interpretation of the Father; and Jesus is known through the Church's Spirit-filled reading of the Scriptures.

Here as elsewhere in Balthasar we come against the "self-authenticating" nature of revelation that resists critical examination.

248. O'Donaghue, "A Theology of Beauty," p. 9.

249. Barth, *Church Dogmatics*, vol. 2, part 1, p. 654.

250. O'Donaghue, "A Theology of Beauty," p. 9.

251. Ibid., p. 7.

252. Tracy, "Theologies of Praxis," in Matthew Lamb (ed.), *Creativity and Method: Essays in Honor of Bernard Lonergan, S.J.* (Milwaukee: Marquette University Press, 1981), p. 51. (This essay has been incorporated as part of ch. 2 of *The Analogical Imagination*.)

253. Tracy, *The Analogical Imagination*, p. 57.

254. Ibid., p. 97, n. 114; cf. "Theologies of Praxis," p. 51.

255. Tracy, *The Analogical Imagination*, p. 57.

256. Ibid., p. 97, n. 114.

257. Ibid., p. 57.

258. Ibid., p. 97, n. 114. Cf. George Lindbeck, *The Nature of Doctrine* (Philadelphia: Westminster Press, 1984), p. 112. For Lindbeck, systematic or dogmatic theology is concerned with faithfulness, practical theology with applicability, foundational theology with intelligibility. (Note that Lindbeck speaks of "intelligibility" rather than "truth.") Tracy also emphasizes "reasonability"—but "truth" is the guiding value. Compare both with Wolfhart Pannenberg, for whom the goal of "intelligibility" belongs to systematics, which

includes much of what the Catholic tradition usually calls "fundamental" theology. See *Systematic Theology*, vol. 1, trans. by Geoffrey W. Bromiley (Grand Rapids: William B. Eerdmans Publishing Co., 1991), pp. 1–26, 48–61.

259. A transcendental notion of revelation—like that of Rahner alluded to above—promises to give a more positive evaluation of the presence of divine beauty and truth in non-Christian religions than one finds in some of the statements of Balthasar. In his concern to preserve the uniqueness of Christ, he sometimes devaluates not only the secular, but also every other encounter with the sacred. He writes, for example, that "the religious and aesthetic enthusiasms of extra-Biblical religions with all their empty systems of divine epiphanies and avatars" are to be understood as "impotent and distorted sketches of such a desperately needed and yet unimaginable fulfillment" as God provides in Christ. Without Christ, these systems would remain "at the stage of ineffective rhetoric which is the most man's religious *eros* can attain to once one excludes God's redemptive grace." *The Glory of the Lord*, vol. 1, p. 123.

260. Cf. Tracy, *The Analogical Imagination*, p. 86, n. 34: "Dialectical arguments, as necessary abstractions from the concrete and as formulated in fundamental theology in ultimately transcendental or metaphysical terms, remain true and therefore relevant to claims operative in (and abstractable from) the fuller symbolic expressions of systematic theology and the fuller praxis realities of practical theology."

261. Nicholas Lash defines "rationalism" as "an approach according to which the practice of faith is judged at best irresponsible and at worst superstitious, except insofar as its grounds have been established and secured by techniques of verification that are independent of specifically religious considerations." "Ideology, Metaphor, and Analogy," p. 134. Foundational theology, while incorporating philosophical methods and categories, attends to the specific nature of transcendental and religious experience.

262. See Tracy, "The Uneasy Alliance," 559ff.

263. Tracy writes: "Each journey through the concreteness of a particular vision or tradition today must be undertaken on behalf of the proleptic concreteness of that future global humanity which the present suggests and the future demands." *The Analogical Imagination*, p. 449.

264. See Balthasar, *Love Alone*, trans. and edited by Alexander Dru (New York: Herder and Herder, 1969), p. 8.

Chapter 2

1. Discography: Arnold Schoenberg, *Moses und Aron*. Sir Georg Solti, conductor; Chicago Symphony Orchestra and Chorus; members of the Glen Ellyn Children's Chorus; Moses: Franz Maura; Aron: Philip Langridge. Performed in Orchestra Hall, Chicago 1984. Notes by Paul Griffiths. London CD #414 264–2. There is also a more recent recording by Pierre Boulez, conductor; The Royal Concertgebouw Orchestra and Netherlands Opera Chorus; Moses: David Pittman-Jennings; Aron: Christ Merritt. Deutsche Grammophon CD 449 174–2. (For a comparison of the merits of these two interpretations, see David Schiff, "Exodus, 'Moses' and a Lot of Gaps," *New York Times*, "Recordings View," 25 May 1997, sec. 2, pp. 25, 29.)

Das Chorwerk. Includes "Friede auf Erden," op. 13; "Kol Nidre," op. 39; "Drei Volkslieder," op. 49; "Zwei Kanons nach Goethe"; "Drei deutsche Volkslieder"; "Vier Stücke," op. 27; "Drei Satiren," op. 28; "Sechs Stücke," op. 35; "Dreimal tausend Jahre," op. 50A; "Psalm 130," op. 50B; "Moderner Psalm no. 1," op. 50C; "A Survivor from Warsaw," op. 46. Pierre Boulez, conductor; BBC Singers, BBC Chorus, BBC Symphony Orchestra; members of the London Sinfonietta. Includes texts in German and English and an introductory essay,

"Zu Schönbergs Chormusik," by Clytus Gottwald (complete only in German; a summary is given in English). Sony CD S 2K 44571.

2. Schoenberg had converted to Lutheranism in 1898, at the age of 24. He formally returned to the Jewish faith in 1933, after his emigration from Berlin. The immediate context of his conversion was an act of solidarity with Hitler's victims; but he had been contemplating the move for some time previous. According to Schoenberg's letters, the idea for *Moses und Aron* can be dated back at least as far as 1923. In 1928 he drafted a text for an oratorio on the subject. The opera was begun in 1930, and the first two acts were completed in 1932. Schoenberg worked on the music for the third act in 1937, during his exile in the United States; but the work was unfinished at his death in 1951.

3. David Schiff calls the opera an example of *midrash*. While this may be to some degree an apt comparison, the similarity to the ancient Jewish genre should not be pressed too far. Schoenberg's viewpoint is distinctly modern and his use of the text has more in common with contemporary dramatic forms than with the ancient genre.

4. Schoenberg enunciates these three ideas as his principal themes in a 1933 letter to Eidlitz: *"Ich habe aus dem mächtigen Stoff vor allem diese Elemente in den Vordergrund gerückt: Der Geganke des unvorstellbaren Gottes, des auserwählten Volkes und des Volksführers."* Quoted in Clytus Gottwald, "Zu Schönbergs Chormusik" in Arnold Schonberg, *Chorus Music*, conducted by Pierre Boulez (Sony CD #S 2K 44571), p. 11.

5. Griffiths, p. 13.

6. The title purposely evokes the language of Luther's German translation, which Schoenberg valued for its eloquence.

7. Quoted in Pamela C. White, *Schoenberg and the God-idea: The Opera "Moses und Aron"* (Ann Arbor, Mich.: UMI Research Press, 1985), p. 85.

8. Schoenberg here has adapted the biblical account to his own purposes. In the book of Exodus, Moses destroys the tablets of the law when he sees the people's idolatry on his descent from the mountain (Ex. 32:19).

9. Schoenberg has once again taken liberty with the biblical text. In Deut. 9:20, Moses says, "With Aaron, too, the Lord was deeply angry, and would have killed him had I not prayed for him also at that time."

10. In his notes to the London recording, Paul Griffiths speculates concerning the "autobiographical" element in the title figures of *Moses und Aron*. "Given . . . Schoenberg's absolute conviction of his mission, it is very tempting to see Moses as a self-portrait. . . . But Schoenberg is Aron too (Aron = Arnold). . . . After all, Moses would never have composed an opera. The work that exists, incomplete though it may be, is the creation of Aron-Arnold, doing his best to be just in his treatment of Moses, but pointing out too the weaknesses and absurdities in the prophetic stance. . . . Far from being a glorification of his own role as a prophet . . . *Moses und Aron* may therefore be a work of unyielding self-criticism in which Schoenberg made himself face the question of whether musical difficulty might not be an end in itself and not an inevitable concomitant of the need to express difficult ideas. He would go on expressing those ideas: he was Moses as well as Aron. But he would go on making them, as he had in the opera, as amenable as possible to human understanding, and even as exciting: he was Aron as well as Moses" pp. 13–14).

11. Eugen Biser, "Der unvorstellbare Gott: das Geheimnis ins Bild gebracht," in Kraus et al., *Moses und Aron: zur Oper Arnold Schönbergs* (Bensburg: Thomas-Morus-Akademie Bensburg, 1979), p. 41.

12. *"Statt prinzipieller Abwertung gewinnen die Bilder für Schönberg hingegen einen positiven und unerläßlichen Stellenwert, sobald vom Gottesgedanken ausgegangen wird und im steten Festhalten dieses Ursprungs die Bilder, Vorstellungen, Manifestationen Gottes zum zeitweilen und wechselnden Ausdruck des dominierenden Gottesgedankens werden, der sie immer übersteigt."* Odil

236 Notes to Pages 49–52

Hannes Steck, *Moses und Aron: die Oper Arnold Schönbergs und ihr biblischer Stoff* (München: Chr. Kaiser, 1981), p. 47.

13. White, p. 73.

14. The inability of words to express the divine is for Schoenberg the most extreme case of the general inadequacy of language to embody thought. Schoenberg refers to this in his text to the satirical song, "Hemmung" ("Inhibition"), the first of his *Six Pieces for Male Chorus*, op. 35:

> Does speech fail them?
> Or do they not feel it?
> Do they have nothing to say?
>
> But they speak all the more fluently,
> the less they are hemmed in by a thought!
> How difficult it is to speak a thought!

15. Biser points out that for Schoenberg, the meaning of words is reduced to their concrete content (p. 39). This notion will contrast with the Scholastic notion of meaning as defined by intentionality.

16. Steck, p. 63.

17. Ibid., p. 46; Biser, p. 43.

18. Compare Schoenberg's words in the second stanza of "Thou shalt not; thou must," quoted above.

19. Rainer Maria Rilke, "Der Schauende" in Rilke, *Gedichte. Eine Auswahl* (Stuttgart: Reclam, 1968), pp. 13–14.

20. White, p. 85.

21. Cf. Hans-Joachim Kraus, "Moses und der unvorstellbare Gott," in Kraus et al., p. 5.

22. White, p. 67.

23. Cf. Biser, p. 41. For Schoenberg, "any display of magic is a misrepresentation of divine authority, which ought to be recognised by the free act of the intellect" (Griffiths, p. 10). Schoenberg sees the true "miracle" in God's creation of order in the world. In his text for "The Law" (the second of his *Six Pieces for Male Chorus*, op. 35), he writes:

> If things turn out as we're used to them,
> it's all right: that we can understand.
> But if it turns out otherwise, its a miracle (*Wunder*).
> But just think:
> the fact that things always come out the same,
> that's really the miracle
> that should seem incomprehensible to you:
> the fact that there's a law
> that things obey,
> as you obey your Lord;
> a law that commands things,
> as your Lord commands you:
> This is what you should recognize as a miracle!
> The fact that someone refuses is banal—it's to be expected.

24. The feast commemorates the revindication of icons under the Empress Theodora in 843. See Mahmoud Zibawi, *The Icon. Its Meaning and History* (Collegeville: Liturgical Press, 1993), p. 11; also Hans Belting, *Likeness and Presence. A History of the Image before the*

Era of Art, trans. by Edmund Jephcott (Chicago and London: University of Chicago Press, 1994), p. 148.

25. Ibid., p. 11.

26. Gerhard Von Rad, *Theology of the Old Testament*, vol. II, pp. 381–383.

27. Ibid.

28. Aidan Nichols, O.P., *The Art of God Incarnate. Theology and Image in Christian Tradition* (New York: Paulist Press, 1980), pp. 21–33, 35, 50.

29. See *TDNT s.v.* "εἰκών." (A similar usage is to be found in early Christian and in Byzantine art; see, for example, the mosaic of the sacrifice of Abraham in the Church of San Vitale in Ravenna.)

30. Van der Leeuw, *Sacred and Profane Beauty*, p. 182.

31. Ibid., p. 177.

32. For a detailed study of the earliest Christian attitudes and their philosophical background, and especially of the apologists, see Paul Corby Finney, *The Invisible God. The Earliest Christians on Art* (New York and Oxford: Oxford University Press, 1994). Finney points out that although the apologists, like Philo before them, presumed a continuity between the Jewish aniconic taboo and Greek apophaticism, it was the latter that was foremost in their arguments, the former serving as "a kind of secondary corroboration" (p. xi). He argues persuasively that the absence of identifiably Christian forms of art before the year 200 cannot be construed as due to a theological opposition to all imagery, and that there is evidence, on the contrary, that the earliest Christians were striving to make their religion visible. At the same time, he strongly supports the point I am making here: that the religion they wished to make visible involved the worship of the *invisible* transcendent God (p. 291 and *passim*). See also David Freedberg, *The Power of Images. Studies in the History and Theory of Response* (Chicago and London: Chicago University Press, 1989), p. 62.

33. For example, in the Christian "church" at Dura Europus; however, it is perhaps significant that the cult aula has no figurative decorations.

Finney argues that the appearance of Christian art dates from no earlier than 200; but he further insists that this late development was "an unintended consequence of political, social, and economic factors." *The Invisible God*, p. 291.

34. Ibid., p. 281.

35. On the other hand, some contemporary scholars believe that nineteenth-century scholarship seriously exaggerated early Christian hostility to art and introduced a misleading contrast between aniconic church leaders and iconophilic laity. See Nichols, *The Art of God Incarnate*, pp. 49–54; Finney, *The Invisible God*, pp. 7–10, 290–291.

36. Cf. Freedberg, *The Power of Images*, p. 60. Freedberg speaks of the "myth" of aniconism, citing evidence of the presence of images in all cultures, even where there is a prohibition and/or an equation between "higher" thought and absence of images. Ibid., pp. 54–65.

37. For a number of texts, see Nichols, *The Art of God Incarnate*, pp. 54ff.

38. Zibawi, *The Icon*, p. 24.

39. *PG* C 757; quoted in Zibawi, *The Icon*, p. 24.

40. "There must be no pictures in the church, lest they depict on the walls what is bowed down to and adored." Mansi, II, col. 11.

41. Van der Leeuw comments that in this controversy "two different religions are battling each other: the rational, exalted, deistic religion of the emperors under Mohammedan influence, and the primitive, but strongly Christian, religion of the women and the monks." *Sacred and Profane Beauty*, p. 185.

For a brief but illuminating discussion of the issues raised by the iconoclast controversy, see Jaroslav Pelikan, *Jesus Through the Centuries. His Place in the History of Culture* (New

Haven: Yale University Press, 1985), pp. 83–94. Useful summaries are also found in Nichols, *The Art of God Incarnate*, pp. 76–88; and Belting, *Likeness and Presence*, pp. 144–163. See also Freedberg, *The Power of Images*, pp. 378–428.

42. Nichol notes that there is evidence of *proskynesis* before the cross as early as the end of the fourth century; but the earliest literary witness to similar veneration of images dates from more than a century later. See Nichol, *The Art of God Incarnate*, pp. 53ff.

43. Karl Rahner, "The Theology of the Symbol," in *TI*, vol. 4, trans. by Kevin Smith (Baltimore: Helicon Press, 1966), p. 243.

44. Balthasar, *The Glory of the Lord*, p. 40.

45. See *DS* 600ff.

46. An unfortunate Latin translation of the council's decrees seems to have been in part responsible for this rejection. See *DS* 600.

For a detailed overview of iconoclasm in the West, with an emphasis on the Reformation period, see Helmut Feld, *Der Ikonoclasmus des Westens. Studies in the History of Christian Thought*, edited by Heiko A. Oberman, vol. XLI (Leiden, New York, København, Köln: E. J. Brill, 1990).

47. "*Imagines . . . in templis praesertim habendas et retinendas, eisque debitum honorem et venerationem impertiendam, non quod credatur inesse aliqua in iis divinitas vel virtus.*" *DS* 1823.

Aiden Nichols, arguing the importance of art in the church, states that "An ecumenical Council [Second Nicaea] recognized that art has a virtually sacramental power to bring the intangible within our touching" (*The Art of God Incarnate*, p. 5). While I agree with the substance of Nichols's position, I think this particular statement should be qualified by the recognition of Western theology's resistance to the idea of an image's functioning in a "virtually sacramental" way.

48. Van der Leeuw, *Sacred and Profane Beauty*, p. 185.

49. John Calvin, *Institutes of the Christian Religion*, trans. by Ford Lewis Battles, bk. I, ch. 11–12, n. 109, in John T. McNeill, ed., *The Library of Christian Classics* (Philadelphia: Westminster Press, 1960), vol. XXI.

50. Gregory argues that through pictures the illiterate are able to "read": "*Nam quod legentibus scriptura, hoc idiotis praestat pictura cernentibus, quia in ipsa ignorantes vident quod sequi debeant, in ipsa legunt qui litteras nesciunt.*" *Ep. "Litterarum tuarum primordia," DS* 477.

51. Green, *Imagining God*, p. 95. Gregory's point, however, is not that pictures communicate better than stories, but that it is only through pictures that the biblical stories were generally accessible to an illiterate populace. Of course, the invention of the printing press and the spread of literacy had changed the situation by Calvin's time.

52. Van der Leeuw, *Sacred and Profane Beauty*, p. 186.

Paul Tillich remarks that "there can be no doubt that the arts of the eye are more open to idolatrous demonization than the arts of the ear." *Systematic Theology*, vol. III (Chicago: University of Chicago Press, 1963), p. 200. But Frank Burch Brown notes that the question of why this should be so—i.e., the "question of how visual images could potentially be more conducive to idolatry than the mental images produced by verbal eloquence"—has rarely been raised in Western theology. Frank Burch Brown, *Religious Aesthetics. A Theological Study of Making and Meaning* (Princeton, N.J.: Princeton University Press, 1989), p. 2.

53. Cf. Sierig, *Über den garstigen Graben*, pp. 34–35.

54. Raimon Pannikar, *The Trinity and the Religious Experience of Man* (New York: Orbis Books, 1973), p. 13.

55. "Even today," he writes—that is, at the time of the liturgical renewal and *aggiornamento* that was to be institutionalized by the Second Vatican Council—"it is again

making itself felt in church architecture and in every realm of church art." Balthasar, *The Glory of the Lord*, vol. 1, p. 41.

56. Green, *Imagining God*, p. 91.

57. Eberhard Jungel, *God as the Mystery of the World*, trans. by Darrell L. Guder (Grand Rapids: William B. Eerdmans, 1983), p. 232. Jüngel's discussion of the history of the notion of God's ineffability is valuable.

58. Ibid., p. 233.

59. John L. McKenzie, "Aspects of Old Testament Thought," in *JBC*, pp. 739–740.

60. *Critique of Judgment*, II, 274.

61. Song 29. *PG*, XXXVII, 507f.

62. "What is invisible in itself, became visible among us; the ungraspable wished to be grasped."

63. "We firmly believe and plainly confess that there is but one true God, eternal, immeasurable and unchangeable, ungraspable [incomprehensible], omnipotent and ineffable."

64. "There is one supreme reality, ungraspable [incomprehensible] and ineffable, which truly is the Father, and the Son, and the Holy Spirit."

65. "If you understand it, it is not God."

66. See *The Divine Names*, ch. 7, no. 3; *The Mystical Theology*, ch. 5, in Pseudo-Dionysius, *The Complete Works*, trans. by Colm Luibheid (New York: Paulist Press, 1987), pp. 108–109, 141.

67. Karl Rahner, "An investigation of the incomprehensibility of God in St. Thomas Aquinas," in *TI*, vol. XVI, trans. by David Morland, O.S.B. (New York: Crossroad, 1983), p. 229. (Henceforth, "Incomprehensibility").

68. Ibid.

69. *Ex quo intellectus noster divinam substantiam non adaequat, hoc ipsum quod est Dei substantia remanet nostrum intellectum excedens et ita a nobis ignoratur et propter hoc illud est ultimum cognitionis humanae de Deo, quod sciat se Deum nescire, inquantum cognoscit illum quod Deus est omne ipsum quod de eo intelligimus excedere. De Potentia*, q. 7, a. 5.

70. Karl Rahner, "The human question of meaning in face of the absolute mystery of God," in *TI*, vol. XVIII, trans. by Edward Quinn (New York: Crossroad, 1983), p. 94.

71. Rahner, "Incomprehensibility," p. 252.

72. Ibid., 236f.

73. Karl Rahner, "The Concept of Mystery in Catholic Theology," in *TI*, vol. 4, trans. by Kevin Smith (Baltimore: Helicon Press, 1966), p. 41; cf. "The human question of meaning," p. 91f.; "An investigation of the incomprehensibility of God in St. Thomas Aquinas," p. 246.

74. Rahner, "The Human Question of Meaning," p. 104.

75. Van der Leeuw, *Sacred and Profane Beauty*, p. 186.

76. Sierig, *Über den garstigen Graben*, p. 20. Of course, Sierig adds, neither Michelangelo nor his contemporaries saw it this way; it is only in retrospect that we can see Renaissance humanism as the start of "modernity."

77. Jungel, *God as the Mystery of the World*, p. 141. Descartes holds that the existence of the "innate" idea of God in the subject can only be explained if we posit its production by God—hence his "ontological" argument for God's existence. (See *Méditations Métaphysiques*, III and V). I take Jungel's point to be that for Descartes the connection between the idea and the reality is extrinsic (God creates this idea in us) rather than intrinsic (the light of the human mind through which we know God is a participation in the divine being). Of course, creation itself can be thought of in terms of participation; but Descartes' objectifying notion of substance militates against this insight.

78. Balthasar, *The Glory of the Lord*, vol. 1, p. 75.

79. Sierig, *Über den garstigen Graben*, p. 16.

80. Immanuel Kant, *Critique of Pure Reason*, trans. by F. Max Müller (Garden City: Doubleday & Co., 1966), Preface to the Second Edition, p. xxxix.

81. Ibid., p. 456.

82. Ibid., p. 453; *cf.* p. xxxvii.

83. Ibid., pp. 442, 444.

84. *"Denn auf welcherlei Art auch ein Wesen als **Gott** von einem anderen bekannt gemacht und beschrieben worden, ja ihm ein solches auch (wenn das möglich ist) selbst erscheinen möchte, so muß er diese Vorstellung doch allerst mit seinem Ideal zusammen halten, un zu urteilen, ob er befugt sei, es für eine Gottheit zu halten und zu verehren. Aus bloßer Offenbarung, ohne jenem Begriff **vorher** in seiner Reinigkeit, als Probierstein, zun Grunde zu legen, kann es also keine Religion geben und alle Gottesverehrung würde **Idolatrie** sein."* Kant, *Die Religion innerhalb der Grenzen der bloßen Vernunft*, ed. Rudolf Malter (Stuttgart: Philipp Reclam, 1974), p. 222n.

Wolfhart Pannenberg follows Kant in assigning a "regulative" function to the metaphysical conception of God in the conflict of religious claims—even though he also agrees with Kant that "metaphysics can make no final judgment about the existence of God." *Systematic Theology*, vol. 1, p. 176. Metaphysics allows us to judge whether what religion is speaking of can genuinely be called "God." See pp. 68, 95.

85. Ibid.

86. Ibid., p. 224.

87. Green, *Imagining God*, pp. 14–15.

88. Johann Gottlieb Fichte, *Der Herausgeber des philosophischen Journals gerichtliche Verantwortungsschriften gene die Anklage des Atheismus*, in *Sämmtliche Werke*, ed. I. H. Fichte (Berlin, Veit & Co., 1845, 1971), V, pp. 266–267; quoted in Jungel, *God as the Mystery of the World*, pp. 127, 141.

89. Georg Wilhelm Friedrich Hegel, *Glauben und Wissen, oder die Religionsphilosphie der Subjectivität, in der Vollständigkeit ihrer Formen als Kantische, Jacobische, und Fichtesche Philosophie*, in *Sämmtliche Werke*, 24 vols., ed. Hermann Glockner (Stuttgart-Bad Cannstatt: Friedrich Frommann Verlag, 1965), vol. 1, p. 286.

90. Ibid., p. 282.

91. Ibid., p. 279.

92. Ibid. Cf. Hegel, *Vorlesungen über die Philosophie der Religion*, in *Sämmtliche Werke*, vol. XVI. E.t. *Lectures on the Philosophy of Religion*, trans. by E. B. Speirs and J. Burdon Sanderson, ed. E. B. Speirs (New York: The Humanities Press, 1962). This classic English translation has drawbacks because of its lack of a consistent vocabulary for translating technical terms. For a more contemporary version: Hegel, *Lectures on the Philosophy of Religion. One Volume Edition. The Lectures of 1827*, trans. by R. F. Brown, P. C. Hodgson, and J. M. Stewart, ed. by Peter C. Hodgson (Berkeley: University of California Press, 1988).

93. Hegel, *On Art (Vorlesungen über die Aesthetik)*, trans. Bernard Bosanquet, in Hegel, *On Art, Religion, Philosophy*, ed. J. Glenn Gray (New York: Harper & Row, 1970), p. 29.

94. Ibid., pp. 29–30.

95. Hegel, *Vorlesungen über die Philosophie der Religion*, p. 37f.; cf. Hegel, *The Phenomenology of Mind*, trans. by J. B. Baillie (New York: Harper & Row, 1967), p. 801.

96. Hegel, *Vorlesungen über die Philosophie der Religion*, pp. 47ff.

97. Ibid., pp. 47, 58.

98. Hegel, *The Phenomenology of Mind*, p. 789.

99. Hegel, *Vorlesungen über die Philosophie der Religion*, p. 44.

100. Green, *Imagining God*, p. 17; see also Hegel, *Vorlesungen über die Philosophie der Religion*, p. 42; Hegel, *The Phenomenology of Mind*, pp. 709–808.

101. This previously unedited letter was published by H. Grassl in *Hegel Studien*, II. The text is given in Cornelio Fabro, *God in Exile*, trans. and ed. by Arthur Gibson (New York: Newman Press, 1968), pp. 621–622.

102. Until fairly recently Roman Catholic theology tended to see Hegel's *Aufhebung* of religion into philosophy as an implicit affirmation of the absolute autonomy of reason, the negation of the supernatural, and the denial of God's transcendence. For a typical view, see Edgar Hocedez, S.J., *Histoire de la Théologie au XIX Siècle* (Paris: Desclée de Brouwer, 1948), vol. II, p. 27. Cornelio Fabro states that contemporary atheism "goes back principally to one thinker, and that is Hegel" (*Introduzione all'Atheismo Moderno* [Roma: Editrice Studium, 1964], p. 534.) On the other hand, Franz Grégoire (in *Études Hégéliennes: Les Points Capitaux du Système* [Louvain: Publications Universitaires, 1964] and subsequent studies), gives a sympathetic view of Hegel's system and sees the accusation of rationalism as based on a misunderstanding of Hegel's intent. Hegel's absolute philosophy, according to Grégoire, should be understood "existentially" as the extension of revelation into the realm of abstract thought—in other words, as "faith seeking understanding."

103. Green, *Imagining God*, p. 22.

104. Ibid., p. 23.

105. Karl Rahner, "The Concept of Mystery in Catholic Theology," in *TI*, vol. 4, trans. by Kevin Smith (Baltimore: Helicon Press, 1966), p. 36f.

106. Green, *Imagining God*, p. 12.

107. Ibid., p. 10.

108. See Rahner, "Art against the Horizon of Theology and Piety," p. 165.

109. Martin, *Beauty and Holiness*, p. 114.

110. Ibid., p. 108f. The quote is from Santayana, *Interpretations of Poetry and Religion* (New York: Charles Scribner's Sons, 1900), p. 290.

In his only novel, Santayana summarizes his ideas about religion succinctly in the words of his main character: "Originally . . . Christianity was partly poetry and partly delusion. The Roman Church clings to both parts equally; Protestantism has kept the delusion and destroyed the poetry; and only the Anglican tradition is capable of preserving the poetry, while sweeping the delusion away. Now, the poetry of Christianity doesn't mean much to me as yet, because I wasn't brought up in it; but I admire and envy . . . all pious people for being able to feel it, provided it doesn't lead you to turn the truth upside down, as people do who think they are inspired, and mistake their poetry for literal fact." *The Last Puritan* (New York: Charles Scribner's Sons, 1936), p. 474.

111. Balthasar, *The Glory of the Lord*, p. 91.

112. Balthasar, *The Glory of the Lord*, p. 22.

113. Tracy, *The Analogical Imagination*, p. 109.

114. Rahner, "The Theology of the Religious Meaning of Images," p. 157.

115. *Church Dogmatics*, vol. II, part 1, p. 666.

116. Ibid., pp. 40–41.

117. Wolfhart Pannenberg, *Anthropology in Theological Perspective*, trans. by Matthew J. O'Connell (Philadelphia: Westminster Press, 1985), pp. 385–386. Cf. *Anthropologie in theologischer Perspektive* (Göttingen: Vandenhoeck & Ruprecht, 1983), pp. 373, 374f. On the mythological underpinnings of the notion of revelation as "word," see also *Systematic Theology*, vol. 1, trans. by Geoffrey W. Bromiley (Grand Rapids: William B. Eerdmans, 1991), ch. 4, #4, esp. pp. 254ff.

118. Rahner, "The Theology of the Religious Meaning of Images," p. 157.

119. *Il Milione*, ch. 31, 32.

120. "I should not care if it was proved by someone that the man called Jesus never lived, and that what was narrated in the Gospels was a figment of the writer's imagination.

For the Sermon on the Mount would still be true to me." "To those who live the Sermon, the birth, death, and continued presence of Christ are not historical but ever-recurring eternal events in the moral life of every individual or corporate self engaged in sacrificial love." Quoted in M. M. Thomas, *The Acknowledged Christ of the Indian Renaissance* (London, SCM, 1969), pp. 202f., 207.

 121. Edward Schillebeeckx, *Christ. The Experience of Jesus as Lord*, trans. by John Bowden (New York: Seabury Press, 1980), p. 465.

 122. This is to some extent true already in the New Testament; the "picture" of Jesus in John's gospel is quite different from that in Mark.

 123. See Robert Briner, *The Management Methods of Jesus* (Nashville: Thomas Nelson, 1996).

 124. Jungel, *God as the Mystery of the World*, pp. 187–188.

 125. Alfred North Whitehead, *Religion in the Making* (New York: Macmillan, 1927), p. 101.

Chapter 3

 1. I have used Philo's word for the Platonic "ideas."

 2. Origen, *Commentaire sur Saint Jean. Texte Grec*, edited by Cécile Blanc. *Sources Chrétiennes*, vol. 120 (Paris: Les Éditions du Cerf, 1966), no. 104, 105, 107, 108, 243–245, pp. 114–116, 180–182.

A similar Platonic exemplarist scheme is found in Origen's *De Principiis*. After identifying Christ with Wisdom, Origen explains how all was created through him:

> We must therefore believe that Wisdom was engendered without any beginning that can be named or thought. In this subsistent being of Wisdom the entirety of the future creation was virtually present and formed; whether it be primary beings or accidental and accessory realities, everything was pre-formed and disposed according to divine foreknowledge. Because of these creatures that were designed and prefigured in her, Wisdom says by the mouth of Solomon that she was established as the "beginning of God's ways," since she contains in herself the beginnings, the reasons, and the forms of all creation.... (I, 2, 2)
>
> ...In this Wisdom, then, which was always with the Father, creation was always present in a delineated and formed condition, and there was never a time when Wisdom did not contain the prefiguration of everything that would come to be in the future.
>
> ...If absolutely everything was made in Wisdom, then because Wisdom has always existed, everything was prefigured and pre-formed in Wisdom before being made substantial later on....If then every thing under the sun already existed in the centuries that preceded us (since nothing is new under the sun), then without doubt all the genuses and species always existed, and perhaps even individual beings.... (I, 4, 4–5)

Origen, *Traité des Principes*, tome I. Introduction, critical text of the version of Rufinus, and trans. by Henri Crouzel and Manlio Simonetti. *Sources Chrétiennes*, vol. 252 (Paris: Les Éditions du Cerf, 1978), pp. 112–114, 170–173.

For a more systematic and more critical treatment of Plato's "ideas" in a Christian exemplarist context, see Augustine: *De Diversis Quaestionibus*, q. 46 ("*De ideis*"), *PL* 40:29–31. Cf.*De Civitate Dei* 1, 12 c. 26, *PL* 41: 375; *Expos. in Ev. Io.* tract 1, *PL* 35:1387; *De Genesi ad literam*, 60, 61, *PL* 34, 243–244.

 3. Green, *Imagining God*, p. 42.

4. Ibid., p. 84.

5. Ibid., p. 40.

6. Ibid., p. 39.

7. Pannenberg, *Anthropology in Theological Perspective*, p. 387 (the words in brackets are added from the original, *Anthropologie in theologischer Perspective* (Göttingen: Vandenhoeck & Ruprecht, 1983), pp. 375–376).

8. Rahner, "The Body in the Order of Salvation," in *TI*, vol. XVII, trans. by Margaret Kohl (New York: Crossroad, 1981), pp. 83, 84, 85.

9. Rahner, "The Theology of the Religious Meaning of Images," pp. 149–150. The unity of the intellectual-spiritual with sense knowledge is the crucial point of difference between transcendental Thomism and Kant. According to Lonergan, Kant's critique was not actually directed at "pure reason," but at the human mind as conceived by Scotus: "for Scotus, understanding was preceded by conceptualization which is a matter of metaphysical mechanics. It is the latter position that gave Kant the analytic judgments which he criticized; and it is the real insufficiency of that position which led Kant to assert his synthetic apriori judgments; on the other hand, the Aristotelian and Thomist positions both consider the Kantian assumption of purely discursive intellect to be false, and, indeed, to be false, not as a point of theory, but as a matter of fact." That is, against Kant's assumption that the intellect is purely discursive and all intuitions sensible, the Thomist phenomenology of knowledge sets the fact of insight arising from sense images. Lonergan, *Verbum. Word and Idea in Aquinas*, ed. by David B. Burrell, C.S.C (Notre Dame: University of Notre Dame Press, 1967), p. 25f. and n. 122.

10. Rahner, loc. cit.

11. Rahner, *Spirit in the World*, trans. by William Dych, S.J. (Montreal: Palm Publishers, 1968), pp. 2, 10 [I have given my own translation of the Latin text].

12. See, for example, Lonergan, *Insight*, pp. 8–10, 34–35; *Verbum*, pp. 28–31. For the Thomistic notion of "phantasm," see Lotz, *Metaphysica Operationis Humanae Methodo transcendentali explicata* (Rome: Gregorian University Press, 1972), pp. 75ff.; Rahner, *Spirit in the World*, pp. 237ff.

13. In Scholastic cognitional theory, the construction of the "phantasm" or image presupposes the prior integration of the different kinds of sense data through the *"sensus communis."* For the distinction between the two, see Lotz, *Metaphysica*, p. 75f.; *Die Identität von Geist und Sein*, pp. 165ff.

14. Lonergan, *Insight*, pp. 88–89.

15. See Lotz, *Metaphysica Operationis Humanae*, pp. 17–18.

16. See Lonergan, *Insight*, pp. 113ff., 399–400.

17. See ibid., pp. 554–555. Aristotle had already noted that the perception of an individual thing among the data of sensation involves abstraction; for the adult, acts of perception are themselves normally functions of meanings that have been learned (although it is also possible to question or reevaluate these). See Gadamer, *Truth and Method*, pp. 81–82.

18. José Gómez Caffarena, *Metafísica Fundamental* (Madrid: Ediciones de la Revista de Occidente, 1969), p. 268.

19. Pannenberg, *Anthropology*, p. 383; *Anthropologie*, p. 371. Lonergan's treatment (aside from using terms somewhat differently) would emphasize that the essential function of the concept is performed neither in the comparison nor the formation of representations, but in the occurrence of insight into the intelligibility inherent in them.

20. Ibid., p. 340.

21. Ibid.

22. Rahner, "Priest and Poet," in *TI*, vol. III, p. 295.

244 Notes to Pages 80–84

23. On "meaning" as mediating and constituting the human "world," see Lonergan, *Method in Theology*, pp. 77–79.

24. Gadamer, "To what extent does language preform thought?" Supplement II to the English edition of *Truth and Method*, p. 493. Gadamer traces the origins of contemporary linguistic relativism to Humboldt, who held that language is the necessary condition for thought, and that every language imparts a particular worldview.

25. Pannenberg, *Anthropology*, p. 343, 344.

26. Pannenberg, *Anthropology*, p. 339.

27. Ibid., p. 343.

28. Pannenberg, *Anthropology*, p. 345.

29. Ibid., pp. 346–361.

30. Tracy, *The Analogical Imagination*, p. 146 n. 80.

31. Gadamer, "To what extent...", pp. 495, 496.

32. Antonio Damasio, *Descartes' Error. Emotion, Reason, and the Human Brain* (New York: Avon Books, 1994), p. 166. Damasio uses the word "language" in the narrow sense of verbal formulations.

33. Pannenberg, *Anthropology*, pp. 381, 382f.; *Anthropologie*, pp. 369, 370f.

34. Ibid., p. 383 (German ed., p. 371).

35. Ibid., n. 183 (German ed., n. 181).

36. Rahner, "The human question of meaning," pp. 96–97.

37. Rahner, "Thomas Aquinas on Truth," in *TI*, vol XIII, trans. David Bourke (New York: Crossroad, 1983), p. 24; cf. Rahner, *Hörer des Wortes* (Munich: Kössel-Verlag, 1963), p. 76.

38. Rahner, "Thomas Aquinas on Truth," p. 25.
On the distinction between the human intellect's "proper" object (the intelligible in the sensible) and its "formal" object (being), see also Lonergan, "*Insight*. Preface to a Discussion," in *Collection*, pp. 152–168; "Christ as Subject: a Reply," in ibid., p. 189; cf. Pierre Rousselot, S.J., *The Intellectualism of St. Thomas*, trans. by James E. O'Mahony (New York: Sheed and Ward, 1935), p. 71.

39. Rahner, "The concept of mystery," p. 52.

40. Rahner, "Faith between rationality and emotion," p. 68.

41. See Rahner, *Hörer des Wortes*, p. 180, n. 3.

42. Green, *Imagining God*, p. 26. David Tracy also notes that contemporary science has found the resources to overcome positivism, to become "a nature-participatory, a non-spectatorial, a value-concerned, 'postmodern' science." Nevertheless, Tracy notes, this ideal is not necessarily lived by scientists, among whom positivism is still alive. *The Analogical Imagination*, p. 343.

43. Green, *Imagining God*, pp. 75, 77. As I have noted above, Green uses the term "imagination" in a wide sense that overlaps with what Lonergan means by "insight."

44. Lonergan, *Insight*, p. 251.

45. Ibid., p. 206; cf. pp. 252–253.

46. Aside from Lonergan's work, especially valuable is Michael Polanyi, *Personal Knowledge. Towards a Post-Critical Philosophy* (Chicago: University of Chicago Press, 1962).

47. Lonergan, *Insight*, p. 250.

48. This parallel is the basis for Lonergan's use of scientific method as the basis for a "generalized empirical method" that applies also to metaphysics and to theology. *Insight*, pp. 72, 243; see also pp. xxi–xxii. Cf. Garrett Green: "Natural scientific and theological methodologies are comparable because of an important, though negative, parallel between their objects: both nature and God transcend the mesocosmic world, the knowledge of

which is the specialty of both common sense and modern [as opposed to contemporary] science." *Imagining God*, p. 75.

49. Lonergan, *Insight*, p. 250. Hence the difference between scientific knowledge and what we mean by "knowledge" in the sphere of everyday life simply provides a dramatic example of the complexity and polymorphism of human cognition in general. Lonergan refers several times to Sir Arthur Eddington's contrast of his "two tables": "the bulky, solid, colored desk at which he worked, and the manifold of colorless 'wavicles' so minute that the desk was mostly empty space." Lonergan, *Method in Theology*, p. 84 (see also pp. 258, 274). José Ortega y Gasset had earlier developed the same example for a similar purpose. See *Unas Lecciones de Metafísica* (Madrid: Alianza Editorial, 1966), p. 157. The polymorphism of cognition leads Lonergan to distinguish diverse "realms" of meaning (common sense, theory, interiority, transcendence) that are based on different exigencies of the mind (Lonergan, *Method in Theology*, pp. 81–85) and are related to various "patterns" of experience (biological, aesthetic or artistic, intellectual, dramatic) (*Insight*, pp. 181–189).

50. Damasio, *Descartes' Error*, p. 106.

51. This sense of "imagination" therefore can include (but is not limited to) the production of works of art. See Tracy, *The Analogical Imagination*, p. 128.

52. Damasio, *Descartes' Error*, p. 107.

53. Ibid., p. 189.

54. Greene, *Imagining God*, p. 66.

55. Ibid., p. 44.

56. Ibid., p. 77.

57. As Gómez Caffarena notes, "admiration" is not the only object of artistic expression; but it is *"su más decisiva razón antropológica." Metafísica Fundamental*, p. 268; cf. p. 485.

58. Unfortunately, the meanings assigned to the different terms applied to this area—feeling (*Gefühl*), mood (*Stimmung*), sensation (*Empfindung*), emotion (*Emotion*), affect (*Affect*), heart (*Gemüt*)—and their relation with one another, are rather inconsistent and confused. See Pannenberg, *Anthropology*, p. 244 (*Anthropologie*, p. 237).

Pannenberg gives a useful history of the concept of "feeling" and its theological use. See ibid., pp. 244–256 (German, pp. 237–250); for his own treatment, see especially pp. 256–265 (250–258). Complementary historical insights are found in Gadamer, *Truth and Method*, especially pp. 27–38. In the contemporary context, a seminal work in the area is Strasser's *Das Gemüt. Grundgedanken zu einer phänomenologischen Philosophie und Theorie des menschlichen Gefühlslebens* (1956). Also important is the work of Paul Ricoeur. In particular, see *Fallible Man*, trans. by Charles A. Kelbley (New York: Fordham University Press, 1986). Andrew Tallon has produced several significant studies relating these and other works to the Thomistic notions of "intentionality" and "connaturality" and to the insights of contemporary Thomists like Rahner and Lonergan. See especially "The Concept of Heart in Strasser's *Phenomenology of Feeling*," in the *American Catholic Philosophical Quarterly*, vol. LXVI, no. 3 (Summer 1992), pp. 341–360; "Affection, Cognition, Volition: the Triadic Meaning of Heart in Ethics," in the *American Catholic Philosophical Quarterly*, vol. LXVIII, no. 2 (Spring 1994), pp. 211–232; "Rahner's Philosophy of Mysticism," in *Theological Studies*, vol. 53, no. 4 (Dec. 1992), pp. 700–728. Tallon's *Head and Heart. Affection, Cognition, Volition as Triune Consciousness* (New York: Fordham University Press, 1997) provides a phenomenology showing that some affections are spiritual acts, as intentional as are cognition and volition, as well as a metaphysical theory of the place of affect in consciousness. See also Rahner, "Faith between rationality and emotion," pp. 62ff.

For a complementary view from the perspective of contemporary neuroscience, see Damasio's already cited work *Descartes' Error*. From his studies of the neural underpinnings of reason, Damasio concludes that "certain aspects of the process of emotion and feeling are indispensable for rationality" (p. xiii).

59. Cf. Damasio: "the essence of a feeling may not be an elusive quality attached to an object, but rather the direct perception of a specific landscape: that of the body." Damasio thinks of feeling as a momentary view of the structure and state of the body accompanied by a corresponding mode of thinking. Feeling is juxtaposed in time with the perception or memory of something that is not part of the body; hence feelings become "qualifiers" (philosophically, one might say "symbols") of that thing. *Descartes' Error*, p. xiv, xv, 145f., 159.

60. Tallon, "The Concept of Heart," p. 346.

61. Tallon, "Affection, Cognition, Volition," p. 230. Cf. Lonergan, *Method in Theology*, pp. 30–41. For the physiological side, see Damasio, *Descartes' Error*, pp. 172–179.

62. Might we say that affect is itself a kind of "representation," in which one's bodily and psychic state is the real symbol of the union of the object with the subject?

63. On the use of images in this way in meditation, see David Freedberg, *The Power of Images. Studies in the History and Theory of Response* (Chicago and London: Chicago University Press, 1989), pp. 161–191, especially pp. 188–191 on the necessity of images for thought.

64. Tallon quotes Alexius Meinong's contention that under certain conditions, a feeling or desire can be substituted for an idea as a means of presentation in the mind. The imagination as representational allows us to apprehend in memory our past emotional experiences, without having to depend on ideas. Tallon, "Affection, Cognition, Volition," p. 219 n. 13.

See also Frank Burch Brown, *Religious Aesthetics* (Princeton: Princeton University Press, 1989), pp. 96–100.

65. Popular language frequently calls this mode of reasoning "intuitive." I have avoided this word because of its technical meaning. Strictly speaking, we have no intuitions but those of sensation. We might, with Tallon, speak of "affective connaturality" as a "quasi-intuitive" way of knowing and loving. See Tallon, "Affection, Cognition, Volition," p. 215, n. 10.

Damasio gives a physiological explanation of the mechanism "by which we arrive at the solution of a problem *without* reasoning toward it." According to his thesis, when an act of what is popularly called "intuition" occurs, explicit imagery generated in the brain, instead of producing perceptible changes in the body's state, covertly advances or inhibits the regulatory neural circuits in the brain core that mediate appetitive behavior. *Descartes' Error*, pp. 187–188.

66. Tallon, "Rahner's Philosophy of Mysticism," p. 711.

67. Tracy, *The Analogical Imagination*, pp. 125–126. Cf. Gadamer: "aesthetic experience is not just one kind of experience among others, but represents the essence of experience itself." ("Experience" here is *Erlebnis*: what establishes itself in memory and is distinct from the rest of life in which "nothing" is "experienced.") *Truth and Method*, pp. 61, 63.

68. Aidan Nichols similarly points out that art communicates in two ways (Nichols is explicitly referring to visual art, but his analysis may I think be extended to the arts in general): first, as part of an iconology, a network of visual images which form a sign-system analogous to a language; second, by the "expressiveness" of the individual work: its communication of a singular affective quality which is parallel to intellectual insight. See Aidan Nichols, O.P., *The Art of God Incarnate. Theology and Image in Christian Tradition* (New York: Paulist Press, 1980), pp. 94–98.

It should be noted that what is said here about "affective/intellectual" communication does not imply that this is the exclusive mode of artistic operation. Many forms of art are mixed: music can set texts, paintings can have titles or captions, narratives can contain abstract conceptual formulations. In such cases, the affective/intellectual can be combined with the conceptual/intellectual mode of thinking.

69. Paul Tillich, *Systematic Theology*, vol. I (Chicago: University of Chicago Press, 1951), pp. 76–77. The aesthetic realm is not restricted to the passive or contemplative activity of the mind, however: indeed, the principal function of art for Tillich is "expression:" "The intention of finding truth is only one element in the aesthetic function. The main intention is to express qualities of being which can be grasped only by artistic creativity." *Systematic Theology*, vol. III (Chicago: University of Chicago Press, 1963), p. 64.

70. Paul Tillich, *Systematic Theology*, vol. III (Chicago: University of Chicago Press, 1963), p. 62.

71. Ibid.

72. Tillich, *Systematic Theology*, vol. I, p. 77.

73. Ibid.

74. Gadamer, *Truth and Method*, p. 87 (German ed., p. 92).

75. Ibid.

76. Tracy, *The Analogical Imagination*, p. 114.

77. Ibid., p. 115. Tracy notes that it is of course possible to refuse to enter into engagement with the work's revealing and challenging possibilities.

78. Ibid., p. 110.

79. Gadamer, *Truth and Method*, p. xii; cf. Gómez Caffarena, *Metafísica Fundamental*, p. 485. These areas constitute "the most pressing challenge to scientific consciousness to acknowledge its own limits." (ibid., p. xiii). As I have noted above, contemporary philosophy of science (although not all scientists) has largely recognized these limits. Lonergan's *Insight* attempts to show that the dynamism of mind that motivates scientific inquiry is identical with that which underlies common sense, metaphysics, and religion. In the same light, Tracy replies to Heidegger's critique of science and technology that "scientific inquiry does not necessitate dominance, mastery, control; it bears within itself its own immanent norms of critical, emancipatory self-transcendence opening it to values, ethics, art, religion, to the fundamental questions." *The Analogical Imagination*, p. 353.

80. This methodological abstraction typifies the legitimate functional specialization of the sciences, and need not imply conflict with those areas of thought that deal with the subjective and/or the transcendent.

81. Gadamer notes that all creations of human culture, including nonlinguistic ones, seek to be understood linguistically. *Truth and Method*, p. 365. Hence there is a particular importance to imagination as mediating between linguistic and nonlinguistic fields of knowledge.

82. I am using the words "analogy" and "metaphor" here to indicate two connected but distinct ways of employing language. "Analogy" refers specifically to the use of language in an ontological context; "metaphor" to the less systematic drawing of comparisons between different things or events. The doctrine of analogy is the ontological explanation of the legitimacy of metaphorical language.

83. Green, *Imagining God*, pp. 127–128. Umberto Eco remarks that "Scholasticism, unlike modern theories, could not envisage the possibility that poetry might reveal the nature of things with an intensity and a breadth lacking in rational thought. This was because of its commitment to a didactic conception of art." Eco, *Art and Beauty in the Middle Ages*, trans. by Hugh Bredin (New Haven and London: Yale University Press, 1986), p. 106.

84. Of course, it is true that the most general ontological categories—"being," "the real," etc.—refer to the whole of reality in its totality, subjective and objective; but they do so in a merely heuristic and abstract way, and to this extent they are lacking in content.

As the Scholastic adage has it, they express the whole, but not wholly (*totum, sed non totaliter*).

85. *"Denn es gibt auch 'geschichtliche Ereignisse, die wie Sinnbilder über den Zeiten stehen.' Es gibt — wie Reinhold Schneider hervorgehoben hat — in der Tat historische Situationen, die in sich selbst so verdichtet sind, daß sie 'typisch' gennant werden können."* Sierig, *über den garstigen Graben*, p. 32.

86. On inverse insight, see Lonergan, *Insight*, pp. 19–25.

87. Lonergan is particularly wary of the dangers of confusing different types of knowing. "The perennial source of nonsense is that, after the scientist has verified his hypothesis, he is likely to go a little further and tell the layman what, approximately, scientific reality looks like!" *Insight*, p. 253. "The unity . . . of differentiated consciousness is, not the homogeneity of undifferentiated consciousness, but the self-knowledge that understands the different realms and knows how to shift from any one to any other." *Method in Theology*, p. 84.

88. See Lonergan, *Insight*, pp. 560–561, on the place of imagination in self-appropriation and the process of learning.

89. See Lonergan, *Insight*, pp. 25–32.

90. Green, *Imagining God*, p. 70. Green goes on to say that the "spectrum from image to concept also clarifies the relationship between religion and theology." Religion, that is, occurs on the level of imagination, while theology is conceptual, having the task of articulating and interpreting religious images, not in order to "progress" beyond them, but in order to return to lived religion in an enriching way (ibid., p. 71). As I have noted above, I prefer to use the term "theology" more widely, so that it can include an "aesthetic" and imaginative as well as a "scientific" conceptual form; and I think that lived "religion," although it occurs primarily on the "common sense" and imaginative level, can include abstract theological formulations of doctrine without being identical with systematic theology. That is, I see the boundary between "religion" and "theology" as more fluid and complex than seems the case when one describes theology as the interpretation of religious images. Concepts and images are both interpretive; and while the latter are usually prior in religion, the former may in certain circumstances have a first-level religious function.

91. Lonergan characterizes these as the "biological" and "intellectual" patterns of experience, and distinguishes also "aesthetic" (i.e., artistic) and "dramatic" or existential-ethical patterns. See *Insight*, pp. 182–189. Lonergan recognizes that insight and judgment occur in the common sense and aesthetic realms; from this point of view, I find his use of the term "intellectual" to refer exclusively to the abstract "scientific" mode of knowing to be unfortunate.

92. Lonergan, *Method in Theology*, pp. 85, 95.

93. The most obvious example is in gestural sign languages (like those used by the deaf) and in written languages that are pictorial rather than alphabetic in form, like ancient Egyptian or Chinese. (In the latter case, ideograms have become so conventionalized and complex that their original pictorial function is generally unrecognizable except to an expert. And, of course, many ideograms—like those for "is" or "not"—represent no material thing, but are simply signs for spoken words). But one might also think of examples of paintings, statues, dances, and music that can in certain contexts serve as languages that symbolize abstract ideas.

94. Paul Ricoeur, *Fallible Man*, p. 27.

95. Rahner, "Faith between rationality and emotion," p. 61.

96. Cf. Van der Leeuw: "The doctrine of the image of God includes the entire theological aesthetics or aesthetical theology." *Sacred and Profane Beauty*, p. 327.

I am here subsuming the notion of "word" into the larger category of "image." One could, of course, also examine the image of humanity as the "word" of God.

97. The latter seems to be the original point of reference for the use of the phrase בְּצַלְמֵנוּ in Gen. 1:26, while the following בִּרְמוּתֵנוּ appears to qualify the boldness of the statement. See S. Otto, *s.v.* *"Bild"* in Heinrich Fries, ed., *Handbuch Theologischer Grundbefriffe* (Munich: Kösel-Verlag, 1962).

For a more extended treatment of the biblical background of the notion of "image" in Genesis, see Aidan Nichols, O.P., *The Art of God Incarnate. Theology and Image in Christian Tradition* (New York: Paulist Press, 1980), pp. 13–20.

98. Pannenberg, *Systematic Theology*, vol. 2, p. 204.

99. For a systematic treatment of the theme of God's image in humanity, based on but going beyond the scriptural use of the term, see Pannenberg, *Systematic Theology*, vol. 2, pp. 202–231. Pannenberg also refers to some of the major theological interpretations of the idea. Also useful is Maurizio Flick, S.J. and Zoltan Alszeghy, S.J., *Fondamenti di una antropologia teologica* (Florence: Libreria Editrice Fiorentina, 1969), pp. 59–146, especially pp. 62–73.

100. *ST*, q. 93, a 1 and 6. Thomas calls the prior dimensions of likeness God's "vestiges" in creation.

Humanity may also be said to be God's image in other respects—for example, because the soul is omnipresent in the body, as God is omnipresent in the world; but the primary reason is in the mind's capacity for knowledge and love (q. 93, a 3).

It is to be noted that for St. Thomas, "mind" is identified with the "soul," which is the real image of God; the body is the soul's "representation" and is a "vestige" of God (q. 93, a 6). But this "spiritualizing" of the image of God seems to be in tension with some of Thomas's own basic positions: for he insists that the human mind knows only through sensibles, and exists as spirit through material embodiment.

101. See *Insight*, pp. 644ff., for a discussion of this notion. Lonergan here extends his cognitional theory to support the classical theistic position that "the unrestricted act of understanding, inasmuch as it understands itself, also grasps everything about everything else." *Insight*, p. 660; cf. pp. 646, 648, where Lonergan speaks of the primary and secondary "components" of the Idea of Being.

102. *Foundations of Christian Faith*, trans. by William Dych (New York: Seabury Press, 1978), p. 63; cf. "The Concept of Mystery," p. 51.

103. *"Non propterea est Dei imago in mente, quia sui meminit, et intelligit et diligit se: sed quia potest etiam meminisse, intelligere et amare Deum, a quo facta est."* Augustine, *De Trinitate*, XIV, c. 12 (ML 42, 1048).

From the point of view of transcendental theology, it would be better to say that the mind's openness to God is what constitutes its ability to know itself.

104. *"Imago Dei attenditur in anima secundum quod fertur, vel nata est ferri, in Deum."* *ST*, I q. 93, a. 8.

St. Thomas discerns three ways in which humanity is God's image: (1) insofar as humanity has the capacity for the knowledge and love of God: this aptitude is constituted by the very nature of mind; (2) insofar as we activate that capacity, knowing and loving God actually and habitually through grace; (3) insofar as we know and love God perfectly in the state of glory. *ST*. q. 93, a 4.

105. See Pannenberg, *Systematic Theology*, vol. 1, pp. 107ff.; vol. 2, p. 229.

106. Cf. Emerich Coreth, *Metaphysics*, edited by Joseph Donceel (New York: Herder and Herder, 1968), p. 182; Rahner, *Hörer des Wortes*, pp. 76–79.

107. Rahner, "The Concept of Mystery," p. 52.

108. Ibid., p. 50.

109. Rahner, "The Concept of Mystery," p. 50.

110. This statement presupposes a cognitional theory that recognizes human "knowledge" as a matter of reasonable judgments of being, not merely encounter with sensations.

111. The explication of this statement is the core of the transcendental approach to the judgment of God's existence. See Coreth, *Metaphysics*, p. 174; Rahner, *Hörer des Wortes*, p. 83; *Geist in Welt*, pp. 193–194 (= *Spirit in the World*, p. 184); Lotz, *Metaphysica*, pp. 50, 109; *Die Identität von Geist und Sein*, p. 233–235; Lonergan, *Insight*, ch. XIX.

112. Rahner, "The Concept of Mystery," p. 39.

113. Ibid. p. 54.

114. Rahner, "The human question of meaning," p. 102; cf. "The Concept of Mystery," p. 55.

115. Rahner, "Faith between rationality and emotion," p. 68.

116. Rahner, "The human question of meaning," p. 100.

117. This theme is enunciated many times throughout Rahner's writings. As he puts it succinctly in *Spirit in the World*, "the free spirit becomes, and must become, sensibility in order to be spirit" (p. 406).

118. *ST*, I, q. 75, a. 5; q. 76, a. 2, obj. 2; q. 79, a. 6.

119. Although we may say with Jungel that the mode of the human receiver is "changed" by the very fact that God communicates God's self, still this communication presupposes a subject capable of that change; i.e., a "spiritual" being. But human spirit, even in grace, is always realized through corporeal being in the world. Cf. Jungel, *God as Mystery of the World*, p. 295.

120. Rahner sees the final "beatific vision" as in some way overcoming our present condition of mediated knowledge, in which the mystery of God is accessible to us only (1) in our experience of subjective transcendence (i.e., as the goal of that unlimited transcendence); and (2) as the condition of possibility of our categorical knowledge. In the beatific vision, for Rahner, God becomes immediate to the human spirit, while remaining always absolute mystery. See "The Concept of Mystery," pp. 55–56; "The incomprehensibility of God in St. Thomas Aquinas," p. 246. Nevertheless, even in the final state a kind of "mediation" by the world and history is not excluded (see "The Theology of the Religious Meaning of Images," p. 151). Likewise, insofar as our present life participates already in an eschatological mode of existence, we can speak of a certain "immediacy" of God already; but this remains a "mediated immediacy."

121. The quotation marks around the word "also" are meant to indicate that it is not a matter of two independent revelations that are accidentally joined, but of two dimensions of a single reality. Its two "aspects" may be distinguished by reflection in the same manner that classical philosophy distinguishes between a finite being's "matter" and "form," while acknowledging that neither exists without the other.

122. Rahner, "The Word and the Eucharist" in *TI*, vol. 4, trans. by Kevin Smith (Baltimore: Helicon Press, 1966), pp. 258–259.

123. God's transcendence and immanence, when thought of in imaginative terms, seem to be "opposites" (transcendence = "distance"; immanence = "closeness"), but in fact they are two aspects of the same reality: God's infinity, from which follows the uniqueness of the "distinction" of God from all that is not God. See above. Cf. Jungel, *God as Mystery of the World*, p. 295.

124. For a discussion of the idea of God's "action" in history as variously conceived in fundamentalist, existential, process, and nondualist interpretations, and a comparison with the transcendental understanding presented here, see Viladesau, *Answering for Faith*.

Christ and the Human Search for Salvation (New York: Paulist Press, 1987), pp. 49–70. The limit case of "miracles" is also briefly treated.

125. For Rahner, this causality is not merely "efficient" but also "quasi-formal"; that is, it goes beyond the creation of something finite that is "other" than God, and effects an intimate participation in the divine being. See Rahner, "The Theology of Symbol," in *TI*, vol. IV, trans. by Kevin Smith (Baltimore: Helicon Press, 1966), pp. 245–247.

126. Naturally, in order to avoid any notion of synergy, one must keep in mind Rahner's principle of the direct relation of human categorical causality and divine transcendental causality ("efficient" and "quasi-formal"), so that the free acceptance of God's grace is itself a gift.

127. Rahner, "Faith between rationality and emotion," p. 69.

128. Cf. *Answering for Faith*, p. 61.

129. For a succinct summary of Rahner's idea of revelation as transcendental and categorical, see *Foundations of Christian Faith*, pp. 87ff.

It should be noted that for Rahner God's grace is universally offered; hence the entirety of human history is also "salvation history" or "general categorical revelation"; the history of religion is the most explicit part of this, and the history of the Christ event (including its preparation in the Jewish people) is its "special" and final accomplishment.

130. Pannenberg, *Anthropology*, p. 395. We must beware of restricting the notion of "word" in this context to its literal, verbal sense. On the other hand, as we have pointed out above and as Pannenberg emphasizes, verbal language is peculiarly apt for expressing what is "hidden" and for evoking not only the present object of experience, but also its context. For this reason it is also the usual means of the expression of the context of "totality" that is involved in God-language.

131. Cf. Jungel, *God as Mystery of the World*, p. 300.

132. Ibid., p. 289.

133. Alfred North Whitehead, *Religion in the Making* (New York: Macmillan, 1926), p. 33.

134. The "excess" referred to here includes both the primary movement of spirit, in its activity, toward the infinity and incomprehensibility of God and the free human acts by which we accept God's self-communication (which once again, at a new level, orders our being to God's mystery). In this latter sense, it is the activity of faith, hope, and love. Rahner, "The incomprehensibility of God in St. Thomas Aquinas," p. 254.

135. See Rahner, *Foundations*, p. 87.

136. A similar answer may be formulated to Schoenberg's problem concerning prayer, both as petition and as "hearing" God: we petition God rightly and we "hear" insofar as God's Spirit prays in us. In St. Thomas's felicitous formulation, the prayer of petition is *spei interpretativa*: its essence is in the virtue of hope, which is a supernatural anticipation of beatitude; but it is necessarily also a categorical (and therefore fallible) *interpretation* and concretization of the good that is experienced as the goal of a transcendental dynamism. See *ST* II IIae, q. 4, a 2, 2 and ad 2.

In accord with his view of divine causality, Rahner explains prayer similarly. It is both the expression of our own mental state and activity and God's "word" to us. The criterion of its genuineness is our "unconditionally openness toward God"—so that its categorical contents are always conditional. See Rahner, "Dialogue with God?" in *Theological Investigations*, vol. XVIII, trans. by Edward Quinn (New York: Crossroad, 1983), esp. pp. 123, 128, 130–131.

137. "Because they do not wish to make themselves better, they make God worse." Augustine, *En. in Ps. LXXIV*, n. 25.

138. Rahner, *s.v.* "Revelation," in *CSM.*

139. *"Durch die Einfälle der Phantasie kann Gott zum Menschen sprechen, wenn dieser reinen Herzens auf das Ganze seiner Lebenswelt und auf Gott als auf ihren Grund und ihr Ziel hin geöffnet ist. Wenn aber die Aufmerksamkeit des Menschen das Ganze seines Lebens mit anderen Themenbereichen so verknüpft, daβ sie nicht mehr Gott als Grund und Vollendung aller Dinge bezeugen, sondern davon losgelöst das ganze Interesse des Menschen in Anspruch nehmen, dann wird auch das Leben der Phantasie durch solche Verkehrtheit des Menschen korrumpiert."* Pannenberg, *Anthropologie,* p. 370 (English ed., pp. 381–382). Pannenberg is speaking here specifically of imaginative life, but he applies the same principle to the word (p. 383; English ed., p. 394f.).

140. Insofar as Christ is the perfect expression of God's being outside Godself, and God creates the world for the sake of just such a perfect sharing in the divine being, the Fathers speak of Christ as the "exemplar" of creation: a theme widely influential in Christian art. See the artistic "prologue" to this chapter.

141. Pannenberg, *Anthropology,* p. 396.

142. Cf. Pannenberg's statement that only the Easter event makes it clear that God spoke in Jesus. *Anthropology,* p. 396.

143. I have prescinded here from the question of the relation of Jesus to other revelations of God in history, particularly in the world religions. The exact meaning of Jesus' "absoluteness," and whether it necessarily implies exclusivity, are important and much debated questions, and ones that are sharpened by the perspective of theological aesthetics. The understanding of revelation as "sign" raises the problem already anticipated by Kierkegaard: can any finite "form" be a *definitive and final* representation of the divine? On this, see Viladesau, "How is Christ Absolute? Rahner's Christology and the Encounter of World Religions" in *Philosophy and Theology,* vol. II (spring, 1988), pp. 220–240; also *Answering for Faith,* pp. 232–251, and the literature there cited.

144. See, for example, Van der Leeuw, *Sacred and Profane Beauty,* pp. 318, 328. Aiden Nichols, following the general lines of Balthasar's thought, goes beyond the latter by providing a theology of revelation directly modeled on our experience of art. See *The Art of God Incarnate,* especially pp. 91–156.

145. Rahner, *Foundations,* p. 304.

146. For explication of this notion, see Rahner, "The Theology of the Symbol."

147. As we have noted above, the latter is the basis for Augustine's psychological analogy of the Trinity in the human mind. It is significant that in Augustine, humanity is God's image not by being "pure" spirit but by being spirit that comes to self-consciousness through word (or image) and love: concretely, by being spirit-in-world.

148. Theology can legitimately take its starting point from either of these elements. (See above on the distinction between "systematic" and "fundamental" theologies.) If we take it as a "given" of faith that God is revealed definitively in Christ, then the explanation of the legitimacy of verbal and imaginative presentations of God and of the holy is relatively unproblematic. As Van der Leeuw says, anthropomorphism is legitimate because God has, in fact, assumed human form (*Sacred and Profane Beauty,* p. 326). But a fundamental theology asks also about the truth of what is given in faith—that is, it asks how we can responsibly affirm that God is revealed in human form, and how we can know that it is in fact *God* that is represented, rather than a mere projection of our own being. These questions demand an examination of the anthropological conditions of possibility of revelation.

149. That is, what is distinct from God in the sense that its being is derivative and experienced only within the infinitely greater totality. This is not the same as saying that we can determine what God is "not": to do so would be to determine God as a being over

against other beings, and so to lose God's infinity. Strictly speaking, God is opposed only to complete nonbeing.

150. Tracy, *The Analogical Imagination*, p. 408.

151. This is true even of those "transcendental" terms whose "proper" referent is God—for example, "being," "goodness" or "truth." Cf. St. Thomas: "*Quantum igitur ad id quod significant huiusmodi nomina [scl. "bonitas," "vita," etc.], proprie competunt Deo, et magis proprie quam ipsis creaturis, et per prius dicuntur de eo. Quantum vero ad modum significandi, non proprie dicuntur de Deo: habent enim modum significandi qui creaturis competit . . .*"; "*quantum ad rem significatum per nomen, per prius dicuntur de Deo quam de creaturis. . . . Sed quantum ad impositionem nominis, per prius a nobis imponuntur creaturis, quas prius cognoscimus.*" *ST*, q. 13, a. 3 and 6.

152. Cf. Rahner: "There exist in religious language very concrete concepts, representations, and images, and beside them a language that, as we say, sounds abstract, imageless, purely conceptual. But, in the final analysis, even in the religious domain, concepts and words can only be understood if and insofar as they contain a sensory moment." "The Theology of the Religious Meaning of Images," p. 150.

153. St. Thomas holds that this relation is "real" only on the side of the creature. Without engaging in a full discussion of his position, which is complicated by Thomas's technical terminology, I suggest that its basis is the insight into the uniqueness of God's "distinction" from all that is other than God. See above, p. 197.

154. It is instructive to compare Kant's treatment of analogy with that of Aquinas. As Jüngel remarks, Kant came up with an idea of analogy very like the classical, although he was probably unaware of it (Jüngel, *God as the Mystery of the World*, p. 263). According to Kant, we may indeed conceive God "according to the analogy of realities in the world." But God's essence remains unknowable, for "all the categories by which I can try to frame to myself a concept of such an object [*scl.* the transcendental ground of the world and its order, or God] admit of none but an empirical use, and have no meaning at all, unless they are applied to objects of possible experience, that is, to the world of sense. Outside that field they are mere titles of concepts, which we may admit, but by which we can understand nothing." *Critique of Pure Reason*, trans. by F. Max Müller (Garden City: Doubleday & Co., 1966), pp. 443, 453. What is lacking in Kant is the basis for a metaphysics that allows us to affirm the reality of God and the "similarity" of what is known through concepts derived from sensible perception to their transcendental condition of possibility. For transcendental Thomism, as we have seen, the "transcendence which is the enabling condition of judgments upon, and *a priori* knowledge of, objects of the world of perception, must necessarily be a transcendence extending beyond the world, and hence is accepted to be such in every kind of knowledge belonging to this world. Once this transcendental deduction is carried through, then that condition is fulfilled under which even Kant is prepared to recognize a metaphysic as valid." Rahner, "Thomas Aquinas on Truth" in *TI* XIII, trans. by David Bourke (New York: Crossroad, 1983), p. 25. In that case, a genuine analogy of being—not merely of concepts—becomes possible.

155. For a more extensive discussion of these points, see Viladesau, *The Reason for Our Hope. An Introduction to Christian Anthropology* (New York: Paulist Press, 1984), pp. 157–162, and the literature there cited. See also Jüngel, *God as the Mystery of the World*, pp. 236–284. Jüngel intends to refute the "traditional" position that we can have only negative knowledge of God (p. 231). He thinks that the standard Protestant objection to the *analogia entis* frequently misses the point completely: the danger of the analogy of being is not that it makes God too "close" to humanity, but that it makes God a totally inaccessible mystery (p. 283). But, he points out, if we speak about God analogously, God cannot be simply unknown: God must be expressible (*as* the unknown) in terms of a known and nameable

relationship to the world. God relates to the world in a way we know of. The "unknown-ness" of God is the unknownness of our origin, or of the condition for the existence of the world, ourselves, and our language (p. 277). Jungel's position thus far seems essentially in accord with St. Thomas's. However, Jungel ultimately concludes that the "unknowability" of God in metaphysics is incompatible with the gospel (p. 284), and that the theologian is forced to renounce the traditional concept of God and begin anew from God's self-revelation in Jesus (pp. 187–188). Jungel seems to overlook the essentially positive quality of our ability to *know* God as (conceptually) "unknowable." As Rahner points out, this is the correlate to God's being genuinely, personally known precisely as divine, in God's infinite being: God would not be divine if God ceased to be mystery ("The Concept of Mystery," p. 54). As Nicholas Lash remarks with regard to Aquinas's "agnosticism," "The lover does not . . . infer from his inability to 'capture the beloved in language' that the beloved is not, after all, known." "Ideology, Metaphor, and Analogy," p. 132.

156. *ST*, I, q. 13, a. 6.

157. Lash, "Ideology, Metaphor, and Analogy," p. 129.

158. We might say that the transcendental concepts express the unity of being, and God's mysterious presence as the act of being in every being; while metaphor takes its start in what is constituted as "other" than God, yet reflects God's being and is referred to it.

159. Rahner, "Art against the Horizon of Theology and Piety," p. 164. Cf. "The Theology of the Symbol," p. 239: "Every God-given reality, where it has not been degraded to a purely human tool and to merely utilitarian purposes, states much more than itself: each in its own way is an echo and indication of all reality." Creation as such can have no absolute mysteries; but all created things partake of the mysterious character of God because they are intrinsically "referred" to God. "The Concept of Mystery," p. 62. For this reason they can "image" God's mystery in concrete finite form, or be God's "symbol."

160. Martin, *Beauty and Holiness*, p. 71.

161. *"Als Buch der Bilder könnten wir die Bibel in ihrer Gesamtheit bezeichnen. Wer sie unbefangen ließt, wird zuerst — vor allen wissenschaftlichen, philosophischen und theologischen Fragen — von ihrer Ausdrucksmächtigkeit, ihrer malerischen Intellektualität ergriffen."* Sierig, *Über den garstigen Graben*, p. 33.

162. Green, *Imagining God*, p. 6. Green evokes Calvin's celebrated metaphor of the Scriptures as a "lens" that we do not look at, but rather look through, in order to make an intelligible pattern of what we see. While there is truth in this idea, it should not be forgotten that there is also plurality within the tradition itself, and that the normativity of its "viewpoint(s)" must be subjected to critical examination.

163. Ibid., p. 99.

164. Ibid., p. 101. In contrast to Green, however, I would hold that one can legiti-mately speak of an ontological dimension to this image.

165. Tracy, *The Analogical Imagination*, p. 451.

166. Cf. ibid., p. 411; Green, *Imagining God*, p. 80.

167. Tracy, *Plurality and Ambiguity. Hermeneutics, Religion, Hope* (San Francisco: Har-per & Row, 1987), p. 77.

168. Ibid., p. 66.

169. Cf. ibid., p. 90.

170. For a treatment of the hermeneutical task that arises for theology out of this multiple dialectic, see ibid., esp. pp. 38–61; also, "Hermeneutical Reflections in the New Paradigm," and "Some Concluding Reflections" in Hans Küng and David Tracy, eds., *Paradigm Change in Theology* (New York: Crossroad, 1989).

171. Tracy, *The Analogical Imagination*, p. 408.

172. Ibid., p. 411.

173. Aquinas prefaces his discussion of the "attributes" of God—simplicity, goodness, infinity, omnipresence, immutability, eternity, unity—in part I, q. 3–11 of the *Summa*, with the remark that *"quia de Deo scire non possumus quid sit, sed quid non sit, non possumus considerare de Deo quomodo sit, set potius quomodo non sit"* (q. 3).

174. Cf. Pannenberg: "Philosophical reflection on the anthropological necessity of elevation to the thought of the infinite and absolute . . . retains the critical function of the natural theology of antiquity relative to every form of religious tradition, i.e., that of imposing minimal conditions for talk about God that wants to be taken seriously as such." *Systematic Theology*, vol. 1, p. 107; see also pp. 69–72.

175. Tracy, *The Analogical Imagination*, p. 410. This danger, as Lonergan sees, is characteristic of the polymorphism of human consciousness when it has not been reflexively differentiated. In that case,

> Man affirms the divine, and obscurely he knows what he means. As best he can, he expresses his meaning, but his resources for expression are unequal to the task. He can give God a name, but there are many tongues, and so there are many names. He can indicate divine attributes by analogy, but he cannot dissociate the analogies he employs from their imperfections. To make God a cause is also to relegate him to the past; to make him an end is to postpone him to the future; to insist upon his immediacy and relevance to the world and to human living is to involve him in the hearth and the family, in the emphases of patriarchal and matriarchal arrangements, in the concerns of hunters and fishers, of agriculturalists, craftsmen, and nomads, in the interests of property and the state, in the occupations of peace and war. The fourfold bias of the dramatic and practical subject of common sense re-appears in the conception of the divine. *Insight*, p. 681

176. Jungel remarks that the Scriptures present the problem of anthropomorphism in a drastic way; however, it must be recalled that *all* human speech is "anthropomorphic," because language itself implicitly or explicitly expresses the human way of being. *God as the Mystery of the World*, p. 258. This insight is in accord with what we have said above. St. Thomas would also agree: human language, which must be formulated as subject and predicate, necessarily fails to convey the absolute simplicity of God's being. See Lash, "Ideology, Metaphor, and Analogy," p. 128.

177. I am thinking here primarily of the picture or statue; but these remarks may be extended, *mutatis mutandis*, to physical objects or gestures that are used to signify the divine action or presence, in particular the "matter" of the sacraments.

178. Lonergan, *Insight*, pp. 439–440, 533.

179. See Rahner, "The Word and the Eucharist," pp. 266f., on the way in which sacraments partake of the quality of word.

180. Rahner, "The Theology of the Religious Meaning of Images," p. 158.

181. See Green, *Imagining God*, pp. 93, 94, for his distinction between "imagining" the divine paradigmatically and "picturing" the divine.

182. Maximus the Confessor, *Myst.*, 2, quoted in Zibawi, *The Icon*, p. 11.

Chapter 4

1. I have translated *Lust* as "joy"; it can also have the sense of "pleasure" or even of "desire."

2. For the original text, see Appendix I. A moving performance of Mahler's setting is given by Helga Dernesch in the 1982 recording by Sir Georg Solti, conducting the Chicago Symphony Orchestra. Decca no. 414 268–2.

3. Hans Urs von Balthasar. *The Glory of the Lord. A Theological Aesthetics*. Trans. by Erasmo Leiva-Merikakis. Vol. I. (New York: Crossroad, 1982).

4. On the meaning of this disputed term and its relation to systematic theology, see Wolfhart Pannenberg, *Systematic Theology*, vol. 1, pp. 73–82.

5. The main lines of my approach to this question have been anticipated in my article, "Natural Theology and Aesthetics: An Approach to the Existence of God from the Beautiful?" in *Philosophy and Theology*, vol. 3, 2 (Winter 1988), pp. 145–160. I have subsequently found a similar line of thought on the ontological nature of the beautiful—although without the application to knowledge of God's existence—in Günter Pöltner, "Die Erfahrung des Schönen," in Günter Pöltner and Helmuth Vetter (eds.), *Theologie und Ästhetik* (Wien, Freiburg, Basel: Herder, 1985), pp. 9–19.

My perspective here will be limited to the Western and Christian traditions. In Hindu thought there is also an important tradition that sees beauty (*rasa*) as a way to the ultimate. For an introductory survey, see James Alfred Martin, *Beauty and Holiness. The Dialogue between Aesthetics and Religion* (Princeton: Princeton University Press, 1990), pp. 146ff.

6. Gerhard von Rad, *Old Testament Theology*, vol. 1, trans. by D. M. G. Stalker (New York: Harper & Row, 1962), pp. 364–365.

7. See Kittel, *TDNT, s.vv.* καλός and δόξα. For a brief but enlightening discussion of the biblical notion of "glory" and its relation to "beauty," see Raphael Schulte, "Die Biblische Erfahrung der Herrlichkeit," in Günter Pöltner and Helmuth Vetter (eds.), *Theologie und Ästhetik* (Wien, Freiburg, Basel: Herder, 1985), pp. 48–64.

Patrick Sherry enumerates several terms used of God in the Hebrew Bible (other than *kabod*, "glory") that may be translated as "beauty": *nō am* (favor, sweetness; Ps. 27:4, cf. Ps. 90:17); *hāh-dāhr* (splendor, majesty, pride, glory; Ps. 145:5); *tiphāhrāh* (splendor, pride, glory, honor; Ps. 71:8); *yōphee* (beauty; Zech. 9:17, Mazoretic text). Patrick Sherry, *Spirit and Beauty. An Introduction to Theological Aesthetics* (Oxford: Clarendon Press, 1992), p. 63.

8. Balthasar, *The Glory of the Lord*, vol. 1, p. 43. For a comparison of Wis. 13 with Psalm 8, see Schulte, "Die Biblische Erfahrung der Herrlichkeit," p. 56f.

9. See Pannenberg, *Theological Anthropology*, p. 260.

10. For a number of texts from the Eastern Fathers, see Patrick Sherry, *Spirit and Beauty*, pp. 61–63. Particularly evocative of the Platonic tradition is the following from Gregory of Nyssa:

> Hope always draws the soul from the beauty which it seeks to what is beyond, always kindles the desire for the hidden through what is constantly perceived. Therefore the ardent lover of beauty, although receiving what is always visible as an image of what he desires, yet longs to be filled with the very stamp of the archetype.
>
> And the bold request which goes up the mountains of desire asks this: to enjoy the Beauty not in mirrors and reflections, but face to face.

Gregory of Nyssa: The Life of Moses ii, 231–2 (PG 401d-404a), trans. by A. Malherbe and E. Ferguson (New York: Paulist Press, 1978), p. 114f., quoted in ibid., pp. 62–63.

11. The translation attempts to preserve a play on words that occurs in the Greek text: ὡς πάντα πρὸς ἑαυτὸ καλοῦν (ὅθεν καὶ κάλλος λέγεται): "as calling (καλοῦν) all things toward itself—for this reason it is also named the beautiful (κάλλος)."

12. Dionysius the Areopagite, *The Divine Names*, trans. by C. E. Holt (London, 1920),

pp. 95–96. Quoted in Umberto Eco, *Art and Beauty in the Middle Ages*, trans. by Hugh Bredin (New Haven: Yale University Press, 1986), p. 18.

13. See James Alfred Martin, *Beauty and Holiness. The Dialogue between Aesthetics and Religion* (Princeton: Princeton University Press, 1990), p. 19.

14. Augustine, *Ennar.in Ps. 94*, 2. Quoted in Pannenberg, *Theological Anthropology*, p. 259.

15. *De Vera Religione*, 32. Cited in Eco, *Art and Beauty in the Middle Ages*, p. 71.

16. *Confessions*, bk. X, ch. XXVII (my translation).

17. Eco, *Art and Beauty in the Middle Ages*, p. 66. Cf. Aquinas, for whom both hearing and seeing are "*maxime cognoscitivi.*"

18. Jesu Iturrioz, S.J., "Metaphysica generalis," in Professores Societatis Iesu Facultatum Philosophicarum in Hispania, *Philosophiae Scholasticae Summa*, vol. 1 (Madrid: Biblioteca de Autores Cristianos, 1957), p. 614.

19. This distinction had already been made by Cicero; however, Augustine does not say that this was his source. See Eco, *Art and Beauty in the Middle Ages*, p. 15.

20. *Confessions*, bk. IV, ch. XIII (Cambridge: Harvard University Press, 1977), p. 182f.

21. Augustine. *Enn. in Ps. CXLIV*, n. 13; PL 37, 1878–9.

22. *Confessions*, bk. X, ch. XXXIV.

23. Following the magistral studies of Edgar de Bruyne, *Études d'esthétique médiévale*, 3 vols. (Bruges, 1946); *L'esthétique au Moyen Age* (Louvain, 1947). Eco also cites Henri Pouillon, "La Beauté, propriété transcendentale chez les scholastiques," in *Archives d'histoire doctrinale et littéraire du moyen age*, XXI (1946), pp. 263–329. Eco has outlined the course of medieval aesthetic theory leading up to the thought of Aquinas: of this development we will touch briefly only on those points most directly relevant to our question.

24. Eco, *Art and Beauty*, p. 58.

25. Ibid., p. 66.

26. Cf. John Scotus Eriugena, *On the Division of Nature*, III, 6; cited in ibid., p. 18.

27. *In Hierarchiam Coelestem*, II; PL 175, col. 949. Quoted in ibid., p. 58.

28. *Sermones in Cantica*, LXXV, 11; PL 183, col. 1193. Quoted in ibid., p. 10.

29. *Tractatus de Bono et Malo*. Quoted in ibid., p. 22. Eco comments on the difference between the medieval and modern worldviews: "Whenever contemporary man finds that art and morality are in conflict, this occurs because he is trying to reconcile a modern conception of the aesthetic with a classical conception of the moral.... For the Medievals, a thing was ugly if it did not relate to a hierarchy of ends centered on man and his supernatural destiny; and this in turn was because of a structural imperfection which rendered it inadequate for its function." Ibid., p. 80.

30. *De Anima*, V, 18. Quoted in ibid., pp. 18–19.

31. The word I have translated "rises" is "*resurgit*": the word used for the rising of Christ from the dead, the resurrection.

The original of the whole inscription reads as follows.
(On the left door):

> *Portarum quisquis attollere queris honorem*
> *aurum nec sumptus operis mirare laborem*
> *nobile claret opus sed opus quod nobile claret*
> *clarificet mentes ut eant per lumina vera*

(On the right door):

> *ad verum lumen ubi Christus ianua vera*
> *quale sit intus in his determinat aurea porta*

mens hebes ad verum per materialia surgit
et demersa prius hac visa luce resurgit.

See also the passages from *The Book of Suger, Abbot of St-Denis, on what was done under his administration*, quoted in Elizabeth Gilmore Holt, ed., *A Documentary History of Art*, vol. 1 (Garden City: Doubleday, 1957), p. 25.

32. Ibid., p. 33.

33. Ibid.

34. Ibid., pp. 31–32.

35. Ibid. Far from thinking that there is anything reprehensible in the enriching of the church's ornamentation, Suger expects that his efforts will bring him eternal reward. He had inscribed the following prayer in verse to the basilica's patron:

> For the splendor of the church that has fostered and exalted him,
> Suger has labored for the splendor of the church.
> Giving thee a share of what is thine, O Martyr Denis,
> He prays to thee to pray that he may obtain a share of
> Paradise ..." (Ibid., p. 24)

36. Ibid., p. 30.

37. Eco, *Art and Beauty*, p. 22. There was some effort to preserve Augustine's distinction between the beautiful (*pulchrum*) and the useful (*aptum*). Isidore of Seville, for example, echoes Augustine in saying that *pulchrum* refers to what is beautiful in itself, while *aptum* refers to what is beautiful with regard to something else. *Sententiarum Libri*, I, 8, 18; pl 83, cols. 551–2. Cited in Eco, p. 15. But Western medieval views of art—especially religious art—stressed its didactic as well as its beautifying function. As we have seen, from Carolingian times medieval defenses of art against iconoclasm stressed its importance for teaching, and the saying attributed to Gregory the Great—that pictures are the books of the unlearned—was frequently repeated. Therefore, as we have seen in the writings of the abbot Suger, the ideas of beauty and usefulness were frequently combined. See also ibid., pp. 15–16.

38. *Summa Aurea*. Quoted in ibid., p. 19.

39. On the emergence of theoretical understanding in the thirteenth century, see Bernard Lonergan, *Verbum. Word and Idea in Aquinas* (Notre Dame: University of Notre Dame Press, 1967).

40. Eco, *Art and Beauty*, pp. 19–20.

41. On the critical place of Philip in the development of abstract scholastic reasoning, see Bernard Lonergan, *Grace and Freedom. Operative Grace in the Thought of St. Thomas Aquinas*, edited by J. Patout Burns, S.J. (New York: Herder and Herder, 1971), pp. 15–19. Lonergan notes that Philip was the first to recognize that the distinction between "nature" and "grace," although "real," is to be understood as purely explanatory, and not as a designation of different existent states. Similarly, Philip's treatment of the transcendentals requires the recognition of the category of "purely rational" distinctions.

42. Eco, *Art and Beauty*, p. 20.

43. Quoted in ibid., p. 23.

44. Now considered to have been written by John of la Rochelle and a certain "Brother Considerans" as well as Alexander. See ibid., p. 23.

45. Ibid., p. 23.

46. Quoted in ibid., p. 25.

47. Ibid., p. 70.

48. Ibid., p. 26.

49. Ibid., p. 25.

50. Bonaventure, *Itinerarium Mentis in Deum*, in *Opera Omnia*, edited by A. C. Peltier (Paris: Ludovicus Vives, 1868), vol. XII, ch. 1, p. 4.

51. Ibid.

52. The *Itinerarium* is organized according to the schema: God in the world—God in the mind—God above the world and the mind. In this sense, it follows an "ascending" pattern. But it treats the effects of grace on the subject at the second level, prior to dealing with the innate "light" of God's presence in the concepts of being and the good (since the latter are the reflected presence of God in God's self, not merely God in the creature).

53. *Circa speculum sensibilium, non solum contingit contemplari Deum per ipsa tanquam per vestigia, verum etiam in ipsis in quantum est in eis per essentiam, potentiam, et praesentiam.* Ibid., cap. II, p. 6.

54. "*[I]n omne re quae sentitur, sive quae cognoscitur, interius lateat ipse Deus.*" Bonaventure, *Opusculum de Reductione Artium ad Theologiam*, in *Opera Omnia*, edited by A. C. Peltier (Paris: Ludovicus Vivès, 1866), vol. VII, p. 505.

55. *Itinerarium*, cap. II, pp. 7–8.

56. "*[C]um ergo omnia sint pulchra, et quodam modo delectabilia.*" Ibid., cap. II, p. 9.

57. Ibid. In Bonaventure's presentation here the link between created beauty and the divine Beauty is proportion: the beauty and delightfulness of things depend on their proportion, which in turn depends on number; so number (i.e., the principle of order) is the primary exemplar in the soul of the Creator.

58. Ibid., cap. II, p. 10.

59. Ibid., cap. III.

60. *In Librum Primum Sententiarum*, q. II, in *Opera*, vol. I, pp. 148–150.

61. *Itinerarium*, cap. III, p. 11.

62. Ibid., cap. IV, p. 16. Cf. Augustine, *De Diversis Quaestionibus*, LXXXIII, q. DII, n. 2, 4.

63. *Itinerarium Mentis in Deum*, cap. II, *Opera*, vol. XII, p. 8.

64. "*[M]agis est in experientia affectuali, quam in consideratione rationali.*" *Itinerarium*, cap. IV, p. 14.

Pannenberg remarks that Luther, like St. Bernard, would follow Bonaventure in placing "affect" at a higher level than reason: "*fides non intellectum illuminat, immo excaecat, sed affectum: hunc enim ducit quo salvetur, et hoc per auditum verbi.*" (WA 4, 356; quoted by Pannenberg, *Theological Anthropology*, p. 259, n. 60). While this may be true, the context is clearly different: Bernard's monasticism was suspicious of nascent Scholastic reasoning, and Luther's nominalist background led him to mistrust it. Bonaventure values the "affective" without devaluating reason and intellect.

65. *Itinerarium.*, cap. iv, p. 14.

66. Ibid., cap. VII, p. 20.

67. Ibid., cap. V, p. 16.

68. Ibid., cap. VI, p. 18.

69. "*Postquam mens nostra contuita est Deum extra se per vestigia, et in vestigiis; intra se per imaginem, et in imagine; supra se per divinae lucis similitudinem super nos relucentem, et in ipsa luce, secundum quod possibile est secundum statum viae, et exercitium mentis nostrae: cum tandem in sexto gradu ad hoc pervenerit, ut speculetur in principio primo et summo, et mediatore Dei et hominum Jesu Christo, ea quorum similia in creaturis nullatenus reperiri possunt . . . restat ut haec speculando transcendat, et transeat non solum mundum istum sensibilem, verum etiam semetipsam.*" Ibid., cap. VII, p. 21.

70. Quoted in Eco, *Art and Beauty*, p. 24. Eco remarks that Bonaventure's position is

similar to that of Maritain, who sees beauty as the "splendor of all the transcendentals together." *Art and Scholasticism*, p. 132 n. 63b.; quoted loc. cit.

71. Thomas Aquinas, *Commentarium in librum De Divinis Nominibus* (Opusculum VII), in *Sancti Thomae Aquinatis Opera Omnia*, vol. XV (Parma: Petrus Fiaccadorus, 1864).

72. *"Pulchritudo autem [est] participatio primae causae, quae omnia pulchra facit. Pulchritudo enim creaturae nihil est aliud quam similitudo divinae pulchritudinis in rebus participata."* Ibid., lectio V, p. 506.

73. In the *Summa*, Aquinas adds "integrity" to these (I, q. 39, a. 8, c.). The terminology is somewhat confused by the fact that integrity may be called "proportion," and "proportion" is sometimes substituted for Dionysius's "consonance."

74. Ibid.

75. Ibid.

76. Ibid.

77. *"Ostendit [Dionysius] qua ratione Deus superpulcher, inquantum in seipso habet excellenter, et ante omnia alia fontem totius pulchritudinis. In ipsa enim natura simplici et supernaturali omnium pulchrorum ab ea derivatorum, praeexistunt omnis pulchritudo et omne pulchrum, non quidem divisim, sed uniformiter, per modum quo multiplices effectus in causa praeexistunt."* Ibid., pp. 506–507.

78. Ibid., lect. VI, p. 509.

79. *"[E]x pulchro isto provenit esse omnibus existentibus. Claritas enim est de consideratione pulchritudinis . . . Omnis autem forma, per quam res habet esse, est participatio quaedam divinae claritatis."* Ibid., p. 507; *"forma autem est quaedam irradiatio proveniens ex prima claritate."* Ibid., lectio VI, p. 508.

80. Ibid., lect. VI, p. 508.

81. *"Qui enim propriam pulchritudinem habet, vult eam multiplicare sicut possibile est, scilicet per communicationem suae similitudinis."* Ibid., p. 507; cf. Bonaventure, *Itinerarium*, cap. VI: *"bonum dicitur diffusivum sui."* (In this text Bonaventure uses the saying with regard to the Trinity; but it is also applied to creation.)

82. *"[H]ujus signum est, quod nullus curat effigiare vel repraesentare nisi ad pulchrum."* In *lib. de Div Nom.*, lect. v, p. 507.

83. *"Quamvis autem pulchrum et bonum sint idem subjecto, quia tam claritas quam consonantia sub ratione boni continentur, tamen ratione differunt: nam pulchrum addit super bonum ordinem ad vim cognoscitivam illud esse hujusmodi."* Ibid.

84. *ST*, I, q. 5, a. 4 ad 1. Quoted in Eco, *Art and Beauty*, p. 70. Eco thinks that there is implied here (he cites also *Comm. de Anima* III, 2) a kind of "ascent" from physical beauty to the beauty of the mind, as in Augustine and Bonaventure: for Aquinas, he explains, "when we reflect upon the objective and rule-governed character of perceived phenomena, we discover our own connaturality with their proportions, that there are proportions also in ourselves." Ibid., p. 77.

85. *"Pulchrum autem dicatur id cuius ipsa apprehensio placet."* *ST*, Ia IIae, q. 27, a. 1 ad 3; cf. I, q. 5, a. 4, ad 1.

86. Eco, *Art and Beauty*, p. 71; cf. Louis De Raeymaker, *Metaphysica Generalis*, tomus I (Louvain: Imprimerie "Nova et Vetera", 1931), p. 70. See *ST*, I, q. 67, 1; Ia IIae q. 77, a.5 ad 3.

87. Eco, *Art and Beauty*, pp. 72–73.

88. Beauty always satisfies a "cognitional" appetite; but this can be on the level of appearance or of knowledge: *"ad rationem pulchri est quod in eius aspectu seu cognitione quietatur appetitus."* *ST*, I, q. 5, a. 4 ad 1. It remains true, however, that Aquinas seems to presume a certain "objectivity" to beauty ("right" proportion, or proportion that corresponds to the human mind) even on the level of appearance.

89. *ST*, I, q. 2 a. 3 c. Patrick Sherry notes that the "ascent" of the mind from the beauty of the world to God as Beauty also has affinities with the "argument from design." Sherry, *Spirit and Beauty*, p. 72.

90. See Avicenna, *Metaphysices Compendium (Nadjât)*, trans. by Carame (Rome: Pontificium Institutum Orientalium Studiorum, 1926), lib. II, tract. VIII, cap. III (initium).

91. See Jacques Maritain, *Approaches to God*, trans. by Peter O'Reilly (New York: Collier Books, 1962), pp. 52ff.

92. Paul Ricoeur, "Préface à Raphael Célis: *L'oeuvre et l'imaginaire. Les origines du pouvoir-être créateur.*" (Bruxelles: Publ. des Fac. Universitaires Saint-Louis, 1977).

93. Jean-Dominique Robert, O.P., *Essai d'Approches Contemporaines de Dieu en Fonction des Implications Philosophiques du Beau* (Paris: Beauchesne, 1982).

94. Ibid., 327.

95. Ibid.

96. Jacques Maritain also delineates an "approach" to God through poetic experience and artistic creativity. He considers this a "way" of the "practical intellect" rather than a speculative demonstration. In artistic creation, says Maritain, there is implied a "poetic" knowledge not directly of God, but of the "mirrors" of God—"either in the being of things or, by privation, in the hollow of their nothingness." The artist encounters a twofold absolute: the demands of the beauty that must pass into work, and the demands of the poetry that incites him or her to create. This encounter can be the beginning of the "natural" knowledge of God. Beauty in creative experience gives an "affective and nostalgic" knowledge of infinite Beauty through connaturality. But this incipient knowledge is vulnerable, because it is disengaged from the light of intelligence; there is the danger of stopping at God's beautiful reflections, and not proceeding toward their Author. See *Approaches to God*, trans. by Peter O'Reilly (New York: Collier Books, 1962), pp. 79–82. As will be seen, Robert's approach manifests several similarities to this line of thinking, in particular with regard to the absolute (Robert: "a priori") demands ofeauty on the artist.

97. Robert, *Essai*, p. 328.

98. Ibid., p. 329.

99. Ibid., p. 330.

100. Ibid., p. 332.

101. Ibid., p. 349. A succinct account of the reductionist argument is given by a character in John Updike's novel *Roger's Version*, the biologist Professor Kriegman. After explaining to a dumbfounded divinity student at a cocktail party how life arose from matter by pure chance, Kriegman concludes that the fact of "mind" requires no reference to God, either: " 'Mind is just a manner of speaking. It's what the brain does. The brain is what's evolved to operate our hands, mostly.' " John Updike, *Roger's Version* (New York: Fawcett Crest, 1986), p. 331.

102. Ibid., p. 339.

103. Ibid., pp. 322–325.

104. Compare Hans Küng's mode of argument in his *Does God Exist?* (New York: Vintage Books, 1981). Küng also stresses that the affirmation of the existence of God as the explanation of "radically uncertain" human experience can only be the result of an option; but he stresses that such an option is radically rational and in a sense inevitable, while its refusal involves one ultimately in a radical irrationality. See pp. 568–575 and the treatment of Küng's position below.

105. I am here describing "transcendental method" in a way that is closest to Lonergan's formulation of it; but I believe the description can be applied as well to thinkers like Coreth and Rahner, despite their less differentiated approach to the question of cognitional theory.

106. See Rahner, *Geist in Welt* (Munich: Kösel-Verlag, 1964), pp. 193–194 (English translation: *Spirit in the World*, trans. by William Dych, S.J. [Montreal: Palm Publishers, 1968], p. 184).

107. See Lotz, *Die Identität von Geist und Sein*, pp. 235–236; also Emerich Coreth, *Metaphysik. Eine Methodische-Systematische Grundlegung* (Innsbruck: Tyrolia Verlag, 1964), pp. 285–289.

108. See Rahner, *Hörer des Wortes* (Munich: Kösel-Verlag, 1963), p. 84; cf. *Geist in Welt*, pp. 396–397 (*Spirit in the World*, pp. 396–398); *Foundations of Christian Faith* (New York: Seabury Press, 1978), pp. 51–71.

109. See Lonergan, *Insight*, pp. 280, 284, 354ff.

110. J. L. Mackie, *The Miracle of Theism. Arguments for and against the existence of God* (Oxford: Clarendon Press, 1982), pp. 85–86. (For Mackie, the same applies to values, which are human inventions; they neither have nor need any further ground [p. 247]. For a discussion of this aspect, see below on Küng).

111. Leszek Kolakowski, *Religion. If There is no God... on God, the devil, sin, and other worries of the so-called philosophy of religion* (New York: Oxford University Press, 1982), pp. 88–90.

112. Ibid., p. 85.

113. This is a restatement of St. Thomas's contention that *"Omnia cognoscentia cognoscunt implicite Deum in quolibet cognito."* *De Veritate*, q. 22, a. 2, ad. 1.

114. Lonergan, *Insight*, p. 683.

115. See Hans Küng, *Does God Exist? An Answer for Today*, trans. by Edward Quinn (New York: Random House, 1981), p. 547f.; cf. p. 572. Küng here speaks of asking about "the condition of the possibility of this wholly and entirely uncertain reality." For the central argument, see pp. 552–576.

116. Ibid., p. 570.

117. For example, ibid., p. 550, 574.

118. Küng, *Does God Exist?*, p. 447.

119. Ibid., p. 571.

120. Ibid., p. 574.

121. Emerich Coreth, *Metaphysics* (ed. by Joseph Donceel) (New York: Herder and Herder, 1968), p. 181. Lonergan similarly states that there are as many "proofs" for God as there are aspects of incomplete intelligibility in the universe of proportionate being (i.e., being as known through sense perception): for God is the answer to the intellect's drive for complete intelligibility, which cannot be had from finite beings. *Insight*, p. 678. See also Karl Rahner, *Grundkurs des Glaubens* (Freiburg, Basel, Wien: Herder, 1976), p. 77.

122. See Coreth, *Metaphysik*, pp. 323–396 (this is the original version of the work cited above; unfortunately, the English translation omits significant portions of the text, in particular the detailed historical perspectives). Also: Fernand Van Steenberghen, *Ontologie* (Louvain: Publications Universitaires de Louvain, 1952), pp. 58–59; Johannes Baptist Lotz, S.J., *s.v.* "Transcendentals" in Karl Rahner, ed., *The Concise Sacramentum Mundi* (New York: Seabury, 1975), pp. 1746–48; *Metaphysica operationis humanae*, pp. 122–125.

123. See Coreth, *Metaphysik*, p. 397.

124. For a brief history of the scholastic treatment of the transcendentals and the proponents of different views, see De Raeymaeker, *Metaphysica Generalis*, vol. 2, pp. 250–254; cf. Lotz, "Transcendentals," pp. 1746f.; Van Steenberghen, *Ontologie*, p. 75.

125. Iesu Iturrioz, S.J., "Metaphysica generalis," in Professores Societatis Iesu Facultatum Philosophicarum in Hispania, *Philosophiae Scholasticae Summa*, vol. I (Madrid: Biblioteca de Autores Cristianos, 1957).

126. It is noted that Maritain in *Art et Scholastique* proposed an argument for beauty as a transcendental; "sed et refutata, *peculiariter a P. de Munnynck...*" Ibid., p. 620, n. 8.

127. Iturrioz, *"Metaphysica Generalis,"* p. 620. Cf. Patrick Sherry, *Spirit and Beauty. An Introduction to Theological Aesthetics* (Oxford: Clarendon Press, 1992), p. 44. Sherry considers being a "transcendental" in the sense that it may be ascribed to different categories of being; but he is "less happy" about saying that being per se is beautiful, "since there is a risk that such a generalized claim makes the notion vacuous."

128. Iturrioz, *"Metaphysica Generalis,"* p. 616.

129. Ibid., p. 620.

130. *"Dicendum est, si proprie loquamur et non fingamus distinctiones minime necessarias, tres tantum esse proprias passiones entis, scilicet* transcendentale *unum, verum, et bonum."* Suarez, *Disput. Metaph.*, disp. 4–11; quoted by De Raeymaker, *Metaphysica*, vol. II, p. 254.

131. *"Quodammodo omnia, scl. omnia cognoscere et appetere valet."* ibid., p. 39.

132. Ibid.

133. Ibid.

134. *ST*, Ia, q. 5, a. 4, ad 1; 1a 2ae, q. 27, a. 1, ad 3.

135. De Raeymaeker, *Metaphysica*, pp. 69–70.

136. Ibid., pp. 70f. Cf. Iturrioz, *"Metaphysica generalis,"* p. 616f. for a similar neo-Scholastic view on the psychology of aesthetics. Aesthetic apprehension is based on intellectual cognition, not merely sensitive perception; hence animals do not have a sense of beauty. At the same time, although it is a spiritual act, it is the fruit of the whole person and is usually founded in the "higher" senses (i.e., especially hearing and sight).

137. De Raeymaeker notes that the "pleasure" involved in the perception of beauty is *"complacentia,"* not the love of concupiscence. Insofar as we tend to possession, we lose the sense of aesthetic enjoyment. *Metaphysica*, p. 71.

De Raeymaeker further follows Kant in distinguishing the beautiful from the "sublime." The latter designates the beautiful insofar as it transcends our faculties of apprehension and is beyond comparison. The apprehension of the sublime is therefore not purely delightful, as is the apprehension of beauty; it is rather a mixed state (like Otto's sense of the numinous as both *fascinans* and *tremendum*). In fact, only God is properly sublime; all other intimations of sublimity are foreshadowings of the vision of God. Ibid., p. 80.

138. In explaining this idea De Raeymaeker quotes from Sertillanges: *"[Le beau] exprime l'être en tant qu'il rapporte aux puissances connaissantes, mais non pas en tant qu'elles connaissent simplement, ce qui appartient au vrai, mais selon qu'il s'éveille en elles, sous le contact de l'idéal de la contemplation, une complaisance qui tient à ce que d'une certaine manière elles s'y retrouvent."* A.-D. Sertillanges, O.P., *Saint Thomas d'Aquin* (Paris: 1925), tome 1, p. 30; quoted in ibid., p. 71.

139. *"Addit super bonum ordinem ad vim cognoscitivam illius esse hujusmodi."* In 1 *De Divinis Nominibus*, c. 4, lect. 5. *in fine*.

140. De Raeymaeker, *Metaphysica*, pp. 72, 77.

141. Ibid., p. 77. Cf. *ST*, I, 5, 4. For St. Thomas, the beautiful is defined in terms of knowledge, the good in terms of desire.

142. Ibid.

143. François de Sales, *Traité de l'amour de Dieu*, 1, I, ch. 1, in *Oeuvres*, tome 4 (Annency: 1894), pp. 23–24. Quoted in ibid., p. 72, n. 3.

144. Ibid., p. 73.

145. Van Steenberghen, *Ontologie*, pp. 59–60.

146. Ibid., pp. 74–75. Lotz points out, however, that "similarity" may be reduced to "determinate agreement" and is an aspect of the transcendental "unity." Lotz, "Transcendentals," p. 1747.

147. Van Steenberghen, *Ontologie*, p. 75.

148. Ibid., p. 75.

149. Ibid., p. 76.

150. Coreth, *Metaphysik*, pp. 323–324, 394, 395.

151. Lotz, "Transcendentals," p. 1748. Although Lotz devotes a great part of his *Metaphysica Operationis Humanae* to the exposition and explanation of the transcendentals, in this text he renounces the effort to demonstrate why beauty should be enumerated among them (p. 122f.), and concentrates only on the traditional triad of the one, the true, and the good.

152. *ST*, I, 5, 4, ad 1; II IIae, 27, 1, ad 3.

153. Coreth, *Metaphysik*, p. 396.

154. Ibid., p. 398.

155. Ibid., p. 397.

156. Ibid., p. 399. Similarly Günther Pöltner: "*Bonum und verum sind im pulchrum in ihrer ursprünglichen Einheit gegenwärtig.*" The experience of beauty tells us that it is good to be, and that this is true. Hence it proclaims the "given" character of being (*der Gabecharakter [das Sich-Gegeben-Sein] des Seins*). *Schönheit. Eine untersuchung zum Ursprung des Denkens bei Thomas von Aquin* (Wien: 1978), pp. 171, 173, quoted in Augustinus Karl Wucherer-Huldenfeld, "Sein und Wesen des Schönen" in Günter Pöltner and Helmuth Vetter (eds.), *Theologie und Ästhetik* (Wien, Freiburg, Basel: Herder, 1985), pp. 20–34, at p. 32. Wucherer himself, following Balthasar, sees the particularity of "beauty" as a transcendental in its manifestation of the "ungroundedness" (*Grundlosigkeit*) of the ground of being itself; it is the pure "shining forth" of goodness and truth in and for themselves. This accounts for the disinterestedness (*Interesselosigkeit*) of the experience of beauty. Ibid., p. 33.

157. For the differences between Lonergan's and Coreth's views of transcendental method and its implications for metaphysics, see Lonergan, "Metaphysics as Horizon," in *Gregorianum*, 44 (1963) (reproduced in *Collection. Papers by Bernard Lonergan* [New York: Herder and Herder, 1967]); Coreth, "Immediacy and the Mediation of Being: An Attempt to Answer Bernard Lonergan," in *Language Truth and Meaning. Papers from the International Lonergan Congress 1970*, edited by Philip McShane, S.J. (Notre Dame: University of Notre Dame Press, 1972). Lotz's method in approaching the transcendentals shows significant convergences with Lonergan's. See his discussion in *Metaphysica Operationis Humanae*, pp. 138ff.

158. On the distinction between "notion" and "concept," see Lonergan, *Insight*, pp. 359–361.

159. Lonergan, *Method in Theology*, p. 12.

160. Ibid., p. 35; cf. p. 282.

161. Ibid., pp. 74, 105.

162. Ibid., p. 20; cf. pp. 53, 302.

163. Ibid., pp. 11–12.

164. See, for example, *Insight*, pp. 673, 676.

165. See *Insight*, pp. 509–520, esp. p. 520.

166. Lonergan, *Method in Theology*, p. 9. Later brief descriptions of this level also presume an essentially ethical focus: "the drive to value rewards success in self-transcendence with a happy conscience and saddens failures with an unhappy conscience" (p. 35); "Being responsible includes basing one's decisions and choices on an unbiased evaluation of short-term and long-term costs and benefits to oneself, to one's group, to other groups" (p. 53).

167. See ibid., p. 37.

168. As Lonergan himself says, we not only can deliberate about courses of action but can also deliberate whether our deliberation itself is worth while. Ibid., p. 101.

169. Lonergan, *Insight*, p. 182. For the extended treatment, see pp. 181–189.

170. Lonergan, *Method in Theology*, p. 286.

171. Frank Burch Brown's "neo-aesthetics," although it does not refer to Lonergan, deals extensively with what the latter calls the "aesthetic pattern of experience" as well as its intersections and combinations with other "patterns" in the existential subject. See Frank Burch Brown, *Religious Aesthetics. A Theological Study of Making and Meaning* (Princeton, N.J.: Princeton University Press, 1989), especially chapters 2 and 3, pp. 16–76.

172. Lonergan, *Insight*, p. 184.

173. Ibid., p. 185.

174. Ibid.

175. Cf. Sertillanges, above, n. 137.

176. Iturrioz, "*Metaphysica Generalis*," p. 616.

177. Pöltner, "Die Erfahrung des Schönen," p. 16.

178. I believe this suggested understanding of "beauty" accounts for the two positive characteristics mentioned by Iturrioz ("*1. pulchrum est quod habet formam finalitatis sine representatione finalitatis. 2. pulchrum est quod est objectum beneplaciti universalis.*" "*Metaphysica Generalis*," p. 615)—perhaps even better than his own nontranscendental explanation.

179. Gadamer, *Truth and Method*, p. 438.

180. Lonergan, *Method in Theology*, p. 120.

181. Pöltner, "Die Erfahrung des Schönen," pp. 12–14.

182. Ibid., p. 15.

183. Augustinus Karl Wucherer-Huldenfeld, "Sein und Wesen des Schönen" in Günter Pöltner and Helmuth Vetter (eds.), *Theologie und Ästhetik* (Wien, Freiburg, Basel: Herder, 1985), pp. 20–34, at 21. Wucherer-Huldenfeld further comments that the reduction of beauty to the object of "aesthetics"—conceived as the field of sense perception—led to the modern loss of the ontological notion of beauty, and finally to the loss of beauty altogether.

184. Gadamer, *Truth and Method*, p. 439. The manifestation, however, may not be clear to all; beauty is the evident lovability of something as it appears to at least some subject.

185. Cf. Tallon, "The Concept of Heart."

186. Gadamer, *Truth and Method*, p. 439.

187. Lotz, "Transcendentals," p. 1748.

188. See, for example, Joseph de Finance, *An Ethical Inquiry* (Roma: Pontificia Universitas Gregegoriana, 1991), pp. 261 ff. De Finance himself presumes and attempts to overcome a separation of the idea of "the good" as [moral] "end" and as "value." See ibid., p. 271 and *passim*.

189. Boris Pasternak, Доктор Живаго (Paris: Société d'Édition et d'Impression Mondiale, 1959), p. 527f. [E.t. *Doctor Zhivago*, trans. by Max Hayward and Manya Harari (New York: New American Library, 1958).] (It will be noted that the words "delight" and "joy" in my translation both correspond to "счастье," which might also be rendered as "happiness.")

190. *ST* Ia, q. 5, 4, 1m; *Commentarium de Divinis Nominibus*, lect. VI.

191. Cf. Pöltner, "Die Erfahrung des Schönen," p. 17: there is a sense in which we are truly "all eyes" or "all ears"; that is, sensation is an act of the whole person, not merely of the senses.

192. "*Schönheit—das ist das offen zutage liegende und zu erfahrbarer Realität gewordene Wunder, daß es solch Beglückendes, Hinreißendes oder still Umgebendes überhaupt gibt. Diesem vor Augen liegenden Wunder entspricht auf unserer Seite das Staunen, das sich in den Dank vollendet.*" Ibid., p. 16.

193. Hans Urs von Balthasar, *The Glory of the Lord*, vol. 1, p. 118. See above, p. 59.

194. It seems to me significant that Pasternak writes that art is a "recounting" about

the joy of existence (рассказ о счастье существования—literally, a "tale" or narrative about the joy of existence), not simply (as the published English translation more freely says) that art "expresses the joy of existence." Art may be "about" the joy of existence, even when the emotion it "expresses" is not joy.

195. See Miguel de Unamuno, *Del Sentimiento Tragico de la Vida* (Madrid: Espasa-Calpe, 1966), pp. 36–49.

196. Charles Baudelaire, "Théophile Gautier" in *L'Art Romantique*, quoted in Maritain, *Approaches to God*, p. 80.

197. Quoted in Richard Harries, *Art and the Beauty of God. A Christian Understanding* (London: Mowbray, 1993), p. 92.

198. Schlegel, "On the Limits of the Beautiful" (1794), in E. J. Millington (ed.), *The Aesthetic and Miscellaneous Works of Friedrich von Schlegel* (London, 1860), p. 419, quoted in Sherry, *Spirit and Beauty*, p. 56.

199. *Wer, wenn ich schriee, hörte mich denn aus der Engel*
Ordnungen? und gesetzt selbst, es nähme
einer mich plötzlich ans Herz: ich verginge von seinem
stärkeren Dasein. Denn das Schöne ist nichts
als des Schrecklichen Anfang, den wir noch gerade ertragen,
und wir bewundern es so, weil es gelassen verschmäht,
uns zu zerstören. Ein jeder Engel ist schrecklich.

Rainer Maria Rilke, *Duino Elegies*. The German text, with an English translation, introduction, and commentary by J. B. Leishman and Stephen Spender (New York: Norton, 1963).

200. Pasternak, *Doktor Zhivago*, p. 107 (my translation).

201. Paul Ricoeur, *Fallible Man*, trans. by Charles A. Kelbley (New York: Fordham University Press, 1986), p. 106.

202. This is to some extent what Van der Leeuw does in his *Sacred and Profane Beauty*.

203. In a similar vein, Pöltner explains: "*Für gewöhnlich sind wir des Ganzen nur unausdrücklich inne. In der Schönheitserfahrung jedoch wird uns das Ganze des Seins auf ausdrückliche Weise* **mit-gegen**wärtig *(Ausdrücklich meint nicht, daβ das Ganze au einem Gegenstand über oder hinter anderen würde)*." Pöltner, "Die Erfahrung des Schönen," p. 18.

204. Küng, *Does God Exist?*, p. 571ff. We may also note a certain similarity to the argument from hope as formulated by the Catholic Tübingen school in the last century.

205. Lonergan, *Insight*, pp. 673ff.

206. If one takes "beauty" in its transcendental sense, then my argument can be stated in a way exactly parallel to Lonergan's: if "the real" in its totality is beautiful (i.e., worthy of joyous affirmation), then God exists. But I have purposely attempted to formulate the reasoning so that it does not depend on the acceptance of beauty as a transcendental, but applies as well to "the beautiful" as a perfection found only in certain beings.

This line of thought is at the opposite pole from radical deconstructionism (the death of the author implies the death of the Author), for it holds that the possibility of art implies what Bonaventure calls the "Eternal Art:" God, seen as the source of hope and of the dynamism to goodness, joy, and beauty.

207. The contention that joy or bliss is an essential attribute or "name" of God follows directly from metaphysical theology. But even Karl Barth, who eschews its method, acknowledges that "Joy in and before God . . . has an objective basis. It is something in God, the God of all perfections, which justifies us in having joy, desire, and pleasure toward Him, which indeed obliges, summons and attracts us to do this." It is because God's "glory" is also "joy" that it "radiates" and awakens joy in creatures, rather than simply

"awe, gratitude, wonder, submission and obedience." *Church Dogmatics*, vol. II, part 1, p. 655.

208. *Church Dogmatics*, vol. II, part 1, p. 654. (In support of this assertion Barth cites a number of Scriptural passages that speak of rejoicing in or because of God).

209. Robert, *Essai*, p. 267.

210. I have prescinded here from a discussion of the relation between the "natural" knowledge of God and grace. It must suffice here to note several points that I think would be important for the clarification of that issue: that the concept of "nature" is, as Rahner says, an abstract *Restbegriff*, not a description of the existential situation; that the "natural knowledge" of God is to be conceived as "natural" *revelation*, i.e., as God's self-revelation in and through creation and the mind; that the existential "goal" of the preapprehension (*Vorgriff*) of the human mind is "supernatural;" that the latter cannot be distinguished from the "natural" or intrinsic infinite openness of finite spirit by introspection, but only by subsequent theological reflection.

To Karl Barth's rhetorical question—"Is it possible to hear the answer given by God and the Gospel themselves, that pleasure and desire are evoked and enjoyment created by the eternal beauty, and still to seek another mode of enlightenment apart from the Gospel of God?" (*Church Dogmatics*, vol. II, part 1, p. 666)—I would reply (1) that the "natural theology" of beauty that stems from human rationality, formulated in transcendental metaphysics, is not "apart" from God's self-revelation, but is an intrinsic element in it; (2) that it formulates the transcendental a priori that constitutes the precondition for every categorical revelation, and hence provides a necessary hermeneutical key to the latter; (3) that Barth himself surreptitiously introduces such a principle of interpretation when he draws from the Scriptures the theology of "eternal beauty," of desire and of joy that he expounds.

Chapter 5

1. Gadamer, *Truth and Method*, p. 102 (*WM*, 108).

2. Ibid., pp. 76–77. Gadamer reminds us that it was only in the high Renaissance that pictures began to stand entirely "by themselves," outside a connection to some nonaesthetic life-function. Ibid., p. 120.

3. Frank Burch Brown, *Religious Aesthetics. A Theological Study of Making and Meaning* (Princeton, N.J.: Princeton University Press, 1989).

4. Ibid., p. 22.

5. Ibid., p. 55.

6. Ibid., p. 76.

7. Ibid.

8. Ibid., pp. 50–51.

9. Ibid., p. 55; cf. p. 76.

10. Ibid., p. 77.

11. Ibid., p. 78; cf. pp. 12–13, 72.

12. Ibid., pp. 67–68, 70–73.

13. Ibid., p. 72.

14. Ibid., p. 86.

15. Ibid.

16. Ibid., p. 88. Brown notes that these definitions presume that the identification of "art" is not absolute: things may be more or less artistic. Brown also gives several qualifications to his definition: the "artificial" aspect of art may derive from arrangement and display, rather than complete fabrication; what makes something a work (or performance) of art need not necessarily be directly perceived by the senses, although "it must have some

imaginative appeal"; and the work "need not be made with the conscious and express intention of producing an *aesthetic object*." Ibid., p. 90.

17. See also, for example, the presentation of "formalistic" ("*also von der 'Logizität' bestimmten*") aesthetics given in Helmuth Vetter, "Ästhetik und Schönheit," in Günter Pöltner and Helmuth Vetter (eds.), *Theologie und Ästhetik* (Wien, Freiburg, Basel: Herder, 1985), pp. 35–47.

18. James Martin echoes artists like Bernini and philosophers like Hegel in holding that art embodies a "higher" beauty than nature because it involves (human) freedom and spirit. (Of course, one may argue for seeing subhuman creation as expressing divine Spirit— as indeed Hegel does. The point is that art as a human creation mediates that same universal creative spirit on a higher level.) See Martin, *Beauty and Holiness* (Princeton, N.J.: Princeton University Press, 1990), p. 61. We shall prescind from this question, as from the related question of whether nature's fascination and attraction should be included under the category of "beauty" or distinguished from it by some such concept as "sublime," as Kant suggests.

19. In classical Scholastic language, the *cognitio Dei insita* is constituted by the same intrinsic structures of human spirit that constitute the *potentia obedientialis*.

20. See Lonergan, *Method in Theology*, pp. 105ff.

21. Rahner, "Art Against the Horizon of Theology and Piety," p. 166.

22. Ibid. This statement does not imply that the artist necessarily intended such a reaction, or experienced it him/herself. The theological-aesthetic appreciation of a work of art involves a complex interaction among the artist, the work, and the viewer or hearer, in which both the work's original context and the existential situation of the viewer or hearer (permitting a new interpretation) may be involved to different degrees.

23. Van der Leeuw, *Sacred and Profane Beauty*, p. 277.

24. Gregory Petrov, Kontakion 2 from "Acathist of Thanksgiving," translated by Mother Thekla, abbes of the Monastery of the Assumption; quoted from the text booklet to the recording: John Tavener, "Acathist of Thanksgiving," Sony CD #SK64446.

25. Van der Leeuw, *Sacred and Profane Beauty*, p. 266.

26. As both Tracy and Gadamer note, this mediation involves restoring to art connections that it has largely lost in the contemporary world. Gadamer sees modern art as isolated by the "aesthetic differentiation"; Tracy, defining art more broadly, sees it as having been privatized: "art" is the attractive or repulsive expression of a private self and its sentiments. This is why it has become increasingly marginalized in our society: "art seems to live principally in the realm of private taste and omnivorous consumption. The claim that the work of art, often through its powerful conscious or unconscious negations of present actuality, discloses a truth about our common human condition often strikes both artists and the general public as counterintuitive." Tracy, *The Analogical Imagination*, p. 12; cf. p. 112.

27. Hans Urs von Balthasar, *The Glory of the Lord*, vol. 1 (San Francisco: Ignatius Press, 1983), p. 36.

28. Van der Leeuw, *Sacred and Profane Beauty*, p. 270. Cf. Gadamer's statement that the difference between secular and sacred art is only relative: "A work of art always has something sacred about it." *Truth and Method*, p. 133.

29. Cf. *ST*, Ia, q. 5, 4, ad 1am; *Commentarium in de Divinis Nominibus*, lect. VI.

30. Thomas Aquinas, *Commentarium in De Divinis Nominibus*, lect. V.

31. Oscar Söhngen, "Music and Theology: A Systematic Approach," in *Sacred Sound. Music in Religious Thought and Practice*, edited by Joyce Irwin. *Journal of the American Academy of Religion Thematic Studies*, vol. L, no. 1 (Scholars Press: Chico, Calif., 1983), pp. 1–20, at p. 3.

32. Bk. III, ch. iii. Quoted in ibid.

33. Söhngen, loc. cit.

34. *Paradiso* XXXIII, 143, 145.

35. See *Paradiso*, XXVII to XXIX; cf. Boethius, *The Consolation of Philosophy*, bk. II, ch. VIII, and bk. III, ch. IX.

36. " 'Glory to the Father, to the Son, to the Holy Spirit,' began singing all Paradise, in such a way that the sweet song inebriated me. What I saw seemed to me a smile of the universe; for my inebriation entered both by hearing and by sight." *Paradiso*, XXVII.

37. See Olivier Messiaen's note on his score of *Méditations sur le mystère de la Sainte Trinité*, quoted below.

38. Susanne K. Langer, *Feeling and Form* (New York: Charles Scribner's Sons, 1953), p. 27. The musical theory of the Baroque age in particular subscribed to the idea of a natural and direct musical symbolism of feelings.

39. For a brief survey of theories on how music can communicate meaning, see Lois Ibsen al Faruqi, "What Makes 'Religious Music' Religious?" in Irwin, *Sacred Sound*, pp. 21–34, at pp. 25ff.

40. Carroll C. Pratt, *The Meaning of Music: A Study in Psychological Aesthetics* (New York and London: McGraw-Hill., 1931), pp. 228ff. Cited in ibid., p. 26.

41. This "naturalistic" theory of music's association with meaning is expounded for example, by George Santayana, *The Sense of Beauty* (New York: Charles Scribner's Sons, 1896). The related notion that beauty is a matter of correspondence between experience and the proportions inherent in the organs of sense is already found in Aquinas. See *ST* I, a. 5, q. 4, ad 1.

42. Leonard B. Meyer, *Emotion and Meaning in Music* (Chicago: University of Chicago Press, 1961), p. 260. Quoted in al Faruqi, "What Makes 'Religious Music' Religious," p. 26.

43. Rudolf Otto, *The Idea of the Holy* (London: Oxford University Press, 1969).

44. Lois Ibsen al Faruqi argues both these points. See "What Makes 'Religious Music' Religious," pp. 27–31.

45. Van der Leeuw, *Sacred and Profane Beauty*, p. 279.

46. Gadamer, *Truth and Method*, p. 111.

47. Tracy, *The Analogical Imagination*, p. 112.

48. Van der Leeuw, *Sacred and Profane Beauty*, p. 279.

49. Gadamer, *Truth and Method*, p. 63.

50. Ibid., p. 113: in the work of art, says Gadamer, "It is the truth of his own world, the religious and moral world in which he lives, which presents itself to [the subject of aesthetic experience] and in which he recognizes himself."

51. For Gadamer, "representation" (*Darstellung*) is the essential "mode of being" of works of art (ibid., p. 104; *WM*, p. 110)—although not all representation is art (ibid., p. 134). What is represented in art is the "being there" (*Dasein*) and the "essence" of what is represented: in artistic representation the subject's unity and identity emerge (ibid., pp. 109, 118; *WM*, pp. 110, 127). This means the revelation that what is represented is not merely "there," but also has come into presence "there" (*ins Da gekommen ist*) (ibid., p. 103; *WM*, p. 109). Hence the "world which appears in the play of representation does not stand like a copy next to the real world, but is the latter in the heightened truth of its being" (ibid., p. 121).

Karl Albert explicitly relates art, especially twentieth-century art, to the "ontological experience" that is the root not only of art but also of philosophy and religion. It is particularly in its "ontological" character, according to Albert, that art touches on the "sacred." Karl Albert, "Zur Ontologie des Sakralen in der Kunst," in Günter Pöltner and Helmuth Vetter (eds.), *Theologie und Ästhetik* (Wien, Freiburg, Basel: Herder, 1985), pp. 65–76, at pp. 66, 76.

52. Gadamer, *Truth and Method*, p. 63.

53. In this context Pannenberg underlines the connection of art with "play": in real social life, our interaction with the world usually includes elements of conflict and compulsion. It is only in the context of an interaction that is free of these cares that the mind is able to attend to the beauty and wonder of being. See Pannenberg, *Anthropology in Theological Perspective*, p. 336 (German edition, p. 326).

54. Jacques Maritain, *Approaches to God* (New York: Collier Books, 1954), p. 18.

55. Boris Pasternak, *Doctor Zhivago* (New York: New American Library, 1958), p. 417.

56. Rainer Maria Rilke, *Die Spanische Trilogie*, I.

57. Rainer Maria Rilke, "Ich finde dich in allen diesen Dingen."

58. "For in man / God wishes to be advised."

Rainer Maria Rilke, from the uncollected poems ("Da dich das geflügelte Entzücken") in *The Selected Poetry of Rainer Maria Rilke* (bilingual edition), edited and trans. by Stephen Mitchell (New York: Random House, 1984), p. 260.

59. The translation attempts to be as literal as possible, and hence loses the 17 syllable (5–7–5) form that defines haiku. The original reads:

Furu-ike / ya // kawazu / tobi-komu // mizu-no-oto
Old-pond / : // frog / jump-in // water-sound.

The text is taken from Harold G. Henderson, ed. and trans. *An Introduction to Haiku. An Anthology of Poems and Poets from Bashō to Shiki* (Garden City: Doubleday, 1968), p. 19.

60. Greg Whincup, ed. and trans., *The Heart of Chinese Poetry* (New York: Doubleday, 1987), p. 169. Two other translations and a discussion of their merits are given in Sven P. Birkerts, ed., *Literature. The Evolving Canon* (Boston: Allyn and Bacon, 1993), pp. 634ff.

61. Rahner, "The Theology of the Religious Meaning of Images," in *TI*, vol. XXIII, trans. by Joseph Donceel, S.J., and Hugh M. Riley (New York: Crossroad, 1992), p. 159.

62. Rahner, "Art against the Horizon of Theology and Piety," p. 163.

63. Ibid.

64. Ibid., p. 166.

65. Rahner, "The Theology of the Religious Meaning of Images," p. 158. Eugen Biser's remarks about the Scholastic theory of images remind us of the antecedents of Rahner's thinking on the subject. According to Biser, in scholastic thinking images "illumine:" "*Sie lassen die von ihnen versinnbildeten Dinge nicht in ihrer Faktizität stehen, sondern heben sie über die Ebene des Faktischen hinaus. . . . In diesen Sinn sind Bilder Fenster, die sich in das je größere Weltgeheimnis hinein öffnen und den Blick auf das freigeben, was den Dingen als ein noch uneingelöstes Versprechen zugrunde liegt.*" "Der unvorstellbare Gott," p. 40.

66. Cf. J.-B. Lotz's treatment of "*das dem Einzelnen entsprechende apriori*" in *Die Identität von Geist und Sein* (Roma: Università Gregoriana Editrice, 1972), pp. 162–174.

67. Blaise Pascal, *Pensées*, edited by Ch.-M. Des Granges (Paris: Éditions Garnier Frères, 1964). One might also think of Rilke's line from the first Duino Elegy, quoted above: "*jeder Engel ist schrecklich.*"

68. See Augustine, *The Trinity*, Bk. XIV, ch. 3 (end) and 4 (beginning). Augustine's idea of *memoria* "demythologizes" Plato's ἀναμνήσις, replacing the memory of a past heavenly existence with the experience of consciousness as God's image, in which God's eternity and infinity are (in Rahner's phrase) "pre-apprehended."

69. Although I have deferred discussion of Christian art to the next section, it might be remarked here that the golden or azure backgrounds of medieval paintings—even when they include a stylized "landscape"—produce much the same effect: the subject is seen against the backdrop of the "heavens," the cosmos, rather than merely earth and sky.

70. This notion of "suchness" is related to the Scotist idea of *haecceitas* as used by

Gerard Manley Hopkins to explain his poetic theory of "inscape" and "instress." At a further remove, there is perhaps at least an analogy with the Mahayāna Buddhist concept of *tathātā* (suchness), as the positive aspect of the Void (*śūnya*).

71. Rilke made somewhat similar comments on Cézanne's paintings when he first encountered them in Paris: Cézanne's painting says of its object, "here it is" (*hier ist es*) (Letter of 13/10/1907 to his wife Clara). Fruit in a Cézanne still life appears, not as something edible, but as simply unconsumable in its obstinate existence (*so einfach unvertilgbar in ihrer eigensinnigen Vorhandenheit*). Letters of 13/10/1907 and 8/10/1907 to his wife Clara, quoted in Albert, "Zur Ontologie des Sakralen in der Kunst," pp. 67–68.

72. Augustinus Karl Wucherer-Huldenfeld, "Sein und Wesen des Schönen," in Günter Pöltner and Helmuth Vetter (eds.), *Theologie und Ästhetik* (Wien, Freiburg, Basel: Herder, 1985), pp. 20–34, at 21.

73. A performance supervised by the composer is recorded on the Varèse Sarabande label: VCD 47213. In his notes on the piece, Takemitsu explicitly refers to the "metaphysical" quality of the music.

74. See Rahner, "Art against the Horizon of Theology and Piety," p. 167.

75. Ibid.

76. Van der Leeuw, *Sacred and Profane Beauty*, p. 230.

77. Rahner, "Art against the Horizon of Theology and Piety," p. 167.

78. John Ruskin goes further: "I cannot answer for the experience of others, but I never yet met with a Christian whose heart was thoroughly set upon the world to come, and, so far as human judgment could pronounce, perfect and right before God, who cared about art at all . . . the general fact is indeed so, that I have never known a man who seemed altogether right and calm in faith, who seriously cared about art; and when casually moved by it, it is quite impossible to say beforehand by what class of art this impression will on such men be made. Very often it is by a theatrical commonplace, more frequently still by false sentiment." *The Stones of Venice*, Vol. II, ch. iv, no. 58, in *Ruskin Today*, chosen and annotated by Kenneth Clark (Hammondsworth: Penguin Books, 1964), p. 201.

79. Rahner, "The Theology of the Religious Meaning of Images," p. 160.

80. Van der Leeuw, *Sacred and Profane Beauty*, pp. 302, 333.

81. Ibid., pp. 328–329.

82. Ibid., p. 303. Rahner applies a similar insight in his discussion of the use of images in prayer. Christianity, "in its efforts to arrive at the absolute God, intends to take along the earth as a whole, the glorified earth." It is only this that can explain the Ignatian method of prayer. Despite the ideal of "contemplation without an object," Ignatius considers the "application of the senses" to be "not the lowest, but a most sublime level of meditation." Rahner, "The Theology of the Religious Meaning of Images," p. 156.

83. Ibid., pp. 302, 328. Oscar Söhngen suggests the possibility of a Trinitarian schema for a theology of music, according to its three functions with regard to the sacred: (1) music "in the realm of creation" (i.e., music as expressive of mathematical order); (2) music in its specifically cultic (as distinguished from "religious") use; and (3) religious music, both in combination with Word and in separation from it, as the work of the Spirit and anticipation of the eschaton. See Söhngen, "Music and Theology: A Systematic Approach," p. 15.

84. As we have seen, Gadamer in particular decries the tendency to look at religious (or indeed any) art works of the past from a purely "aesthetic" point of view, in abstraction from their "life-function": "it cannot be doubted that the great ages in the history of art were those in which people without any aesthetic consciousness and without our concept of 'art' surrounded themselves with creations whose religious or secular life-function could be understood by everyone and which to no-one gave solely aesthetic pleasure. Can the

272 Notes to Pages 166–171

idea of the aesthetic experience be applied to these without reducing their true being?" *Truth and Method*, p. 73.

85. I use the term "symbol" in differentiation to the arbitrary "signs" that constitute writing: "A symbol is the coincidence of sensible appearance and supra-sensible meaning . . . not a subsequent coordination, as in the use of signs." Gadamer, *Truth and Method*, p. 69. However, the relation of pictorial symbols and written or spoken signs can be complex, as the examples will show.

86. Although this kind of pictorial symbol is not an ideogram in the strict sense, since its symbolic functioning depends on the evocation of an alphabetically written word, we may nevertheless include it as "ideographic" in a broad sense.

87. Rahner, "The Theology of the Religious Meaning of Images," p. 157. Emphasis added.

88. Garrett Green, *Imagining God*, pp. 95, 149.

89. Ibid., p. 95.

90. Wolfhart Pannenberg, *Anthropology in Theological Perspective*, p. 329 n. 41.

91. Ibid., pp. 328–329.

92. Rahner, "The Theology of the Religious Meaning of Images," p. 160. Cf. William M. Thompson, *The Struggle for Theology's Soul* (New York: Crossroad, 1996), p. 27: "The use of the senses in the service of the Christian arts . . . seems dependent upon the verbal revelations as orally and then scripturally communicated for coherence of meaning and truth through the forms."

93. Rahner, op. cit., p. 153.

94. Gadamer, *Truth and Method*, p. 104. Gadamer indeed would expand this insight about specifically religious works to art in general: "no one can doubt that the aesthetic differentiation, e.g. of a 'beautiful' ceremony or of a 'good' sermon is, in view of the appeal that is made to us, misplaced. Now I maintain that the same thing is basically true for the experience of art" Ibid., p. 113. That is, as we have discussed above, all art, even if it is not religious, must be related to a revelation of truth, not merely appreciated "aesthetically."

95. Rahner, "The Theology of the Religious Meaning of Images," p. 155.

96. Ibid., p. 156.

97. Gadamer, *Truth and Method*, pp. 345, 350f., 496.

98. Ibid., p. 146

99. As Gadamer says, "The picture points by causing us to linger over it." *Truth and Method*, p. 135.

100. Cf. Rahner's affirmation that the function of mediating the absolute should not belong exclusively to word. "The Theology of the Religious Meaning of Images," p. 157.

101. For a summary of Trinitarian theology compatible with this theological view, see Piet Schoonenberg, *Der Geist, das Wort und der Sohn* (Regensburg: Verlag Friedrich Pustet, 1992), pp. 145–218.

102. Gadamer, *Truth and Method*, p. 127 (137).

103. Ibid., p. 126. "*Wort und Bild . . . lassen das, was sie darstellen, damit erst ganz sein, was es ist*" (136).

104. Ibid., p. 131 (141).

105. Ibid., p. 132 (142).

106. Ibid., p. 126.

107. Ibid., p. 135. The picture's "being is . . . not absolutely different from what it represents, but shares in the being of that . . . what is represented comes to itself in the picture. It experiences an increase in being." Ibid. This "increase" is precisely the heightened presence or manifestation of what is represented.

108. Gadamer, *Truth and Method*, pp. 135–137 (146–147).

109. *"[I]maginibus non exhibetur religionis cultus secundum quod in seipsis considerantur, quasi res quaedam: sed secundum quod sunt imagines ducentes in Deum incarnatum. Motus autem qui est in imaginem prout est imago, non sistit in ipsa, sed tendit in id cuius est imago(ST,* II-IIae, q. 81, a 3, ad 3am).

110. *"[D]uplex est motus animae in imaginem: unus quidem in imaginem ipsam secundum quod est res quaedam; alio modo, in imaginem inquantum est imago alterius . . . secundus autem motus, qui est in imaginem inquantum est imago, est unus et idem cum illo qui est in rem. Sic igitur dicendum est quod imagini Christi inquantum est res quaedam, puta lignum sculptum vel pictum, nulla reverentia exhibetur: quia reverentia debetur non nisi rationali naturae. Relinquitur ergo quod exhibeatur ei reverentia solum inquantum est imago. Et sic sequitur quod eadem reverentia exhibeatur imagini Christi et ipsi Christo. Cum igitur Christus adoretur adoratione latriae, consequens est quod eius imago sit adoratione latriae adoranda.* Ibid., III, q. 25, a. 3, c.

111. (Objection:) *"Christo debetur adoratio latriae ratione divinitatis, non ratione humanitatis. Sed imagini divinitatis eius, quae animae rationali est impressa, non debetur adoratio latriae. Ergo multo minus imagini corporali, quae repraesentat humanitatem ipsius Christi."* (Response:) *"Ad tertium dicendum quod creaturae rationali debetur reverentia propter seipsam. Et ideo, si creaturae rationali, in qua est imago, exhiberetur adoratio latriae, posset esse erroris occasio; ut scilicet motus adorantis in homine sisteret inquantum est res quaedam, et non ferretur in Deum, cuius est imago. Quod non potest contingere de imagine sculpta vel picta in materia insensibili."* Ibid., III, q. 25, a. 3, 3 *et ad* 3.

112. Rahner, "The Theology of the Religious Meaning of Images," p. 161.

113. Hence Gadamer refers to the icon as a "picture sign" (*Bildzeichen*). *Truth and Method*, p. 120; *WM*, p. 129.

114. *"Eiusmodi vero amantissima cognitio, qua divinus Redemptor a primo Incarnationis suae momento nos prosecutus est, studiosam quamlibet humanae mentis vim exsuperat; quandoquidem per beatam illam visionem, qua vixdum in Deiparae sinu exceptus, fruebatur, omnia mystici Corporis membra continenter perpetuoque sibi praesentia habet, suoque complectitur salutifero amore."* DS 3812.

115. Green, *Imagining God*, p. 87.

116. Quoted in Green, *Imagining God*, p. 95.

117. Paul Ricoeur, *Fallible Man*, pp. 53–54.

118. Van der Leeuw, *Sacred and Profane Beauty*, p. 190.

119. Ibid.

120. Ibid., p. 191.

121. Ibid.

122. For a recent discussion of Tillich's contribution to theological aesthetics, see Jeremy Begby, *Voicing Creation's Praise. Towards a Theology of the Arts* (Edinburgh: T&T Clark, 1991), part I. Begby presents a chronological survey of Tillich's theology, tracing the development of his "latent" philosophy of art. Michael Palmer, in *Paul Tillich's Philosophy of Art* (Berlin and New York: de Gruyter, 1984), provides a thematic approach to the topic.

123. Paul Tillich, "Art and Ultimate Reality" in Tillich, *On Art and Architecture*, ed. by John Dillenberger, trans. by Robert P. Scharlemann (New York: Crossroad, 1987), p. 143.

124. Ibid., p. 143.

125. Ibid., pp. 145–146.

126. Ibid., p. 147. Tillich remarks, "I came to the conclusion that an apple of Cézanne has more presence of ultimate reality than a picture of Jesus by Hofmann." Ibid., p. 144. Tillich uses a still life by Cézanne as an example of "numinous realism." I would classify the same painting under "descriptive realism." Its "sacramental" character, it seems to me, is a function of the viewer's attitude in approaching it. Cf. Rahner's remark, quoted above, on Dürer's picture of a hare.

It should be noted that "descriptive realism" can take on another dimension of connection with the sacred when what is depicted is human life lived in virtue, even if religious values are not explicitly invoked. As Rahner says, "Faithfulness, responsibility, resignation to the mystery of life, *et cetera* are, even when they are mentioned in a context that is not explicitly religious, references to that of which theology expressly speaks." "Art against the Horizon of Theology and Piety," p. 165.

127. Ibid.

128. Ibid., p. 148.

129. Ibid., pp. 148–149. Cf. Martin, *Beauty and Holiness*, p. 94.

130. Ibid., p. 150.

131. Martin, *Beauty and Holiness*, p. 96. On the other hand, John Dillenberger complains that some writers on art and theology dismiss Tillich's views without providing contrary evidence or engaging in debate. See Dillenberger's review of the papers collected in *Sacred Imagination: The Arts and Theological Education* in *ARTS. The Arts in Religious and Theological Studies*, vol. 7, no. 1 (1994), pp. 15–18, at p. 15.

132. We shall have occasion to mention below the negative side of the use of music in prayer—for example, the fact that chant removes a text from ordinary discourse and obviates the possibility of dramatizing its different meanings and emphases by the differences in pitch we would use in speaking or reading. Chant submits the text instead to an artificial pattern that in some cases (psalmody, for example) is the same for each line, or in others (composed settings for particular antiphons, for example) imposes a preestablished stylized decoration as its means of adding emphasis.

133. Of course, the actual religious use of such music may have another focus, depending on concrete situations. Gregorian chant, for example, serves quite a different function for people who are meditating on the words and for those who do not know Latin and hence are ignorant of the meaning of the text being sung. In the latter case, it is the cadence and solemnity of the tones, the long historical association with the sacred, and perhaps the beauty of the singing that set a religious or at least reflective mood.

134. Söhngen, "Music and Theology," p. 14.

135. From Messiaen's note on his score of *Méditations sur le mystère de la Sainte Trinité*, trans. by Felix Aprahamian, reproduced in the text booklet to the recording by Jennifer Bate. Unicorn-Kanchana Records, DKP(CD)9024/25, 1982.

136. Bach apparently adopted this device from Reinhard Keiser, who seems to have introduced it (as well as the use of the orchestra not merely for accompaniment, but also for "word painting") in his *Passion According to St. Mark*.

137. Ibid., p. 231.

138. Ibid., p. 235. Van der Leeuw's brief description does not fully convey the tension that Beethoven builds by the multiple repetition first of the full phrase and then of its concluding words. I am grateful to Frank Burch Brown for pointing this out.

139. Ibid.

140. Ibid., pp. 237f.

141. Ibid., p. 236. The works of Arvo Pärt, mentioned above, are perhaps an even better example of what Van der Leeuw calls the *chiaroscuro* technique.

142. Ibid., pp. 220f.

143. Ibid., p. 294.

144. Schopenhauer, *Die Welt als Wille und Vorstellung* (Wiesbaden, 1949), quoted in ibid., p. 245.

145. Martin, *Beauty and Holiness*, p. 21.

146. Gadamer, *Truth and Method*, p. 82.

147. For this distinction, see Lois Ibsen al Faruqi, "What makes 'Religious Music'

Religious?," in *Sacred Sound. Music in Religious Thought and Practice*, Journal of the American Academy of Religion Thematic Studies, vol. 50, no. 1, edited by Joyce Irwin (Chico, Calif.: Scholars Press, 1983], pp. 21–34, at p. 32, n. 5.

148. Rahner, "Art against the Horizon of Theology and Piety," p. 163. (Note Rahner's assumption that revelation is also about humanity, not simply the unveiling of God).

149. Van der Leeuw, *Sacred and Profane Beauty*, pp. 270–271.

150. *"Ac ratio quidem, fide illustrata, cum sedulo, pie et sobrie quaerit, aliquam Deo dante mysteriorum intelligentiam eamque fructuosissima assequitur tum ex eorum, quae naturaliter cognoscit, analogia, tum e mysteriorum ipsorum nexu inter se et cum fine hominis ultimo."* Constitutio de fide catholica, cap. 4; DS 3016.

151. Gadamer, *Truth and Method*, p. 85.

152. Ibid., p. 83.

153. Ibid., p. 87.

154. Van der Leeuw, *Sacred and Profane Beauty*, p. 335.

155. Ibid., p. 333.

156. Ibid.

Chapter 6

1. David Freedberg points out that pagan Roman writers as well as Jews and Christians not only rejected anthropomorphic images of the deity but in general also associated the pursuit of the arts with loose morals and/or softness. *The Power of Images. Studies in the History and Theory of Response* (Chicago and London: Chicago University Press, 1989), pp. 63–65.

2. Van der Leeuw, *Sacred and Profane Beauty*, pp. 97ff.

3. Ibid., p. 53.

4. Ibid., pp. 53–55. Early Christian "puritanism" stemmed both from Jewish scandal at the ways of the "impure Greeks" and Hellenistic soul-body dualism; so that, as Van der Leeuw remarks, bodily pleasure could never be completely innocent.

5. For a detailed study of early Christian "musical puritanism," see Johannes Quasten: *Music and Worship in Pagan and Christian Antiquity.* (Washington, D.C.: National Association of Pastoral Musicians, 1983). For a collection of relevant texts from the patristic period, see James McKinnon (ed.), *Music in Early Christian Literature* (Cambridge: Cambridge University Press, 1987).

6. The most obvious and extreme example is Islam, which not only bans images of God but also frequently places restrictions on all figurative art, rejects most forms of theater, and in some sects severely limits the use of music except for the chanting of the Qur'an. The Zen reaction against the perceived excesses of Mahayana Buddhism included the destruction of images of Buddha and the creation of a simplified painting style that Iris Murdoch calls "art as anti-art," oriented to metaphysical insight rather than to figurative representation. See Iris Murdoch, *The Fire and the Sun. Why Plato Banished the Artists* (Oxford: Clarendon Press, 1977), pp. 71–73.

7. Quoted in Sierig, *Über den garstigen Graben*, p. 15.

8. Friedrich Gundolf, *Goethe* (Berlin, 1925), quoted in Van der Leeuw, *Sacred and Profane Beauty*, p. 190.

Whitehead's philosophy goes so far as to consider beauty the one self-justifying aim. In aesthetic experience "the art object insists that it be experienced as an end in itself. It temporarily short-circuits the long-range, overarching subjective aims that shape life-patterns or dominate ordinary living." Donald W. Sherburne, *A Whiteheadian Aesthetic* (New Haven: Yale University Press, 1961), p. 143; quoted in Martin, *Beauty and Holiness*, p. 120f.

9. Van der Leeuw, *Sacred and Profane Beauty*, p. 5.

10. John Dewey, "Having an Experience," in *Art as Experience* (New York: Capricorn Books, 1959), p. 55, quoted in Martin, *Beauty and Holiness*, p. 113.

11. Van der Leeuw, *Sacred and Profane Beauty*, p. 178. Mircea Eliade, in his "Preface" to Van der Leeuw's book, makes the same point: the ancient Greeks did not put Phideas's masterpieces in their temples, but rather awkward archaic statues or the xoanon. Ibid. p. viii.

12. Van der Leeuw, *Sacred and Profane Beauty*, pp. 255, 291.

13. Hans Gerth and C. Wright Mills, eds., *From Max Weber: Essays in Sociology* (New York: Oxford University Press, 1946), p. 342. Quoted in Nicholas Wolterstorff, *Art in Action. Toward a Christian Aesthetic* (Grand Rapids: William B. Eerdmans, 1980), pp. 49f. and p. 227, n. 25.

14. Paul Tillich, *Systematic Theology*, vol. III (Chicago: University of Chicago Press, 1963), p. 65.

15. *Wisdom* 13:1–7. Finally, however, those who are distracted by the beauty of the world are not to be excused:

> But again, not even these are pardonable,
> For if they so far succeeded in knowledge
> that they could speculate about the world,
> how did they not more quickly find its Lord? (v. 9)

16. Cf. Rahner, *Foundations of Christian Faith*, pp. 84ff.

17. Van der Leeuw, *Sacred and Profane Beauty*, p. 334. Tillich argues that the substitution of the aesthetic for the religious is untrue to the human situation and to aesthetics itself. "A work of art is a union of self and world with limitations both on the side of the self and on the side of the world." On the side of world, the union is limited because through the artwork a single otherwise hidden quality is reached, but not ultimate reality, which transcends all qualities. On the side of self, the encounter is limited because "in the aesthetic function the self grasps reality in images and not with the totality of its being. The effect of this double limitation is to give union in the aesthetic function an element of unreality. It is 'seeming'; it anticipates something that does not yet exist." *Systematic Theology*, vol. III, p. 65.

It might be added that the positive side of the real but limited union of self and reality through art and beauty is that they are therefore capable of being "signs" and anticipations of the total, eschatological union with the transcendent.

18. Murdoch, *The Fire and the Sun*, p. 72. Murdoch intentionally focuses one-sidedly on the extremes of Plato's opposition to the arts. She is well aware of the fact that he thought that the arts could also play a legitimate role (namely, in discerning the harmony of nature and giving it emphatic expression in simple ways—ibid., p. 57). Murdoch's emphasis, however, suits our present purposes of presenting the negative ("dualistic") side of the Platonic attitude toward art and earthly beauty.

19. Ibid., pp. 32; see also pp. 2 and 17 and *passim*. There is, of course, a profound irony in Plato's denigrating of art. As Nietzsche noted, it was he who invented the artistic form of dialogue to expound his philosophy, and he could not do without imaginative forms to represent the divine. Van der Leeuw, *Sacred and Profane Beauty*, p. 134.

20. See, for example, *Republic*, bk. III, 398f.

21. Murdoch, *The Fire and the Sun*, p. 65.

22. Ibid., p. 6.

23. Ibid., p. 5.

24. Ibid., p. 32.

25. Yet, as Murdoch points out, Plato himself cannot avoid using images or myths as a part of his conversations. Ibid., p. 67.

26. Ibid., p. 2. Cf. Lonergan on "intellectual conversion" from the "already-out-there-now" to the real as the object of true affirmation, and moral conversion from the ego to the object of judgments of value.

27. Ibid., p. 34.

28. Ibid., pp. 35–36.

29. Ibid., p. 39.

30. Pannenberg, *Anthropology in Theological Perspective*, p. 257.

31. Murdoch, *The Fire and the Sun*, p. 40.

32. Ibid., p. 55.

33. Ibid., p. 43.

34. Ibid., p. 66.

35. Ibid.

36. Ibid.

37. Ibid., p. 69.

38. Augustine's imperative always to go beyond the present finite good (*"ambulent, ambulent"*) is expressed dramatically in Goethe's version of the Faust legend. Faust's bargain with the devil allows him to experience everything; but he will lose his soul only if the beauty of the moment causes him to find repose in it, rather than moving onward:

> *Werde ich zum Augenblicke sagen,*
> *"Verweile dich, du bist so schön,"*
> *Dann kannst du mich in Fesseln schlagen;*
> *Dann will ich gern zu Grunde gehen.*

Naturally, in Goethe's context the idea has more in common with pagan humanism than with Augustine's Christian morality, despite the use of Christian symbolism in the play.

39. Recall Kant's distinction between the "beautiful" and the "sublime": the sublime is disturbing, and awakens our spiritual nature, but we rest in the beautiful. Murdoch, *The Fire and the Sun*, p. 20.

40. Frank Burch Brown, *Religious Aesthetics. A Theological Study of Making and Meaning* (Princeton, N.J.: Princeton University Press, 1989), p. 105.

41. Ibid., pp. 65, 70.

42. Ibid., p. 70.

43. Ibid., pp. 69, 70.

44. Aristotle here quotes *The Iliad*, bk III (γ), 156–160.

45. Sigmund Freud, *The Relation of the Creative Writer to Day-Dreaming*, in *Collected Works*, vol. IV; quoted in Murdoch, *The Fire and the Sun*, p. 38.

46. Paul Ricoeur, *Fallible Man*, trans. by Charles A. Kelbley (New York: Fordham University Press, 1986), p. 127.

47. The Stoics first made a distinction between "pleasure" and "joy" or "happiness." This distinction influenced Christian terminology, in which "joy" is consistently good, and "pleasure" negative. Pannenberg, *Theology in Anthropological Perspective*, p. 256. See TDNT *s.v.* χαίρω, ‛ηδονη.

48. Ibid., p. 94. Cf. Balthasar's explanation of Nebel's idea of "daimonic" beauty: "Daimonic beauty is concerned with the present moment, with making it eternal." That is, it commits the sin for which Goethe's Faust bargains that he should be damned: it says to the present moment, *"Verweile doch, du bist so schön!"*

49. Ibid.

50. Ibid., p. 93.

51. Ibid., p. 131.

52. Murdoch, *The Fire and the Sun*, p. 70.

53. Nicholas Wolterstorff, *Art in Action. Toward a Christian Aesthetic* (Grand Rapids: William B. Eerdmans, 1980), p. 83.

54. Ricoeur, *Fallible Man*, p. 131.

55. For a succinct resumé of the relevant texts, see *s.v.* σταυρός in TDNT.

56. We prescind here from the question of the pre-Pauline origin of the hymn. Its import for our concern lies in its use by Paul to give his readers a model to follow.

57. Taking the word ἀντί in the phrase ἀντὶ τῆς προκειμένης αὐτνῷ χαπᾶς in its normal sense of "instead of." In this case, the "joy" referred to is earthly. The phrase may also mean "for the sake of" the joy before him—that is, after death, with God. Each meaning places the stress differently, but nevertheless each implies the other: Jesus renounces earthly joys and endures the cross for the sake of his exaltation by God.

58. The Johannine text reads:

I solemnly assure you,
unless the grain of wheat falls to the earth and dies,
it remains just a grain of wheat.
But if it dies,
it produces much fruit.
The one who loves his life loses it,
while the one who hates his life in this world
preserves it to life eternal.
If anyone would serve me,
let him follow me . . .

59. Among the many Pauline texts bearing on this theme, see, e.g., Rom. 5:24f., 6:1–10; Col. 3:1–17. Perhaps the most explicit succinct statements of this theme are found in 1 John.: "That we have passed from death to life we know because we love the brothers" (3:14); "we too must lay down our lives for our brothers" (3:16).

60. As we saw above, Tillich considered that most religious art of the "idealist" style fails to attain to spiritual depth. The reason is that such art ignores the existential "estrangement" of humanity; in other terms, it overlooks the reality of sin and he fact that its overcoming always involves "the cross."

61. Cf. Tallon, "The Concept of Heart in Strasser's *Phenomenology of Feeling*," p. 355.

62. Shusaku Endo, *Silence*, trans. by William Johnston (New York: Taplinger Publishing, 1980), p. 38.

63. Ibid., p. 116.

64. Balthasar, *The Glory of the Lord*, p. 124. See above, ch. 1, p. 58.

65. "*[D]as Schöne ist nichts als des Schrecklichen Anfang.*" Cf. Balthasar, *The Glory of the Lord*, p. 65.

66. It is clear that this passage, which is still used liturgically as the first reading of the Good Friday service, already colored the passion narratives in the gospels, and was considered in the early church to be a prophetic foretelling. It is possible that the figure of the Isaian "servant" also formed part of Jesus' own self-consciousness as he approached the end of his life. For discussion of these points, see Raymond Brown, S.S., *The Death of the Messiah* (New York: Doubleday, 1994), especially pp. 234, 1457–1459, 1471–1473, 1480f., 1485–1487.

67. Barth, *Church Dogmatics*, vol. II, part 1, p. 665.

68. Balthasar, *The Glory of the Lord*, p. 117.

69. "Things are not beautiful because they give pleasure, but they give pleasure because they are beautiful."

70. "Those things are beautiful that, being perceived [literally, "seen"], give pleasure."

71. "God is not God because of being beautiful, but rather God is beautiful because of being God."

72. Ibid., p. 656. Through most of his life Barth rejected the ontological notion of the analogy of being; to the extent that he might include this within the meaning of "preconceived ideas," the position I have argued differs from his. The analogy of being (beauty) holds that "our creaturely conceptions of the beautiful," *if* they are arrived at by true judgments of value, will in fact "rediscover" themselves—in "eminent" form—in the divine beauty. Nevertheless, Barth's statement is correct even from the point of view of analogy, which, as we have seen, is based on a "pre-grasp" (*Vorgriff*) of God's being, not a conception or "idea" that describes or contains it.

Hence we may say that "supernatural" revelation introduces a "new" element in our notion of beauty—recognizing, however, that supernatural revelation is not restrictively Christian, but is in some sense co-extensive with human history; so that the "novelty" is in comparison to the abstract notion of human "nature," not necessarily to historical human achievement, which is already within the perspective of "grace." Therefore I would hold (as will be seen from what follows) that the insight into God's "beauty" that Christians attain from the cross of Christ may also be found in other religions, insofar as they are existentially media of "grace." Naturally, the insight of "the cross" will be found outside Christianity only in analogous form and without the concreteness and "absoluteness" (however this may be defined) of God's self-revelation in Jesus.

73. Barth, *Church Dogmatics*, p. 665.

74. Ibid., p. 653.

75. In some forms of Tantric Hinduism, however, the symbols are taken in a more radical sense: the divinity is totally beyond our ideas of good and evil, and is indifferent to all created things.

76. Nietzsche also, but with disdain, calls the Christian concept of God, "God as spider": *The Anti-Christ*, no. 18, in Friedrich Nietzsche, *Twilight of the Idols and The Anti-Christ*, trans. by R. J. Hollingdale (Middlesex: Penguin Books, 1975), p. 128.

77. The notion of a vicarious "penal substitution" of Christ for sinners was influential in late-medieval spirituality. Several of the Reformers developed it in an extreme form, in which Christ actually experiences the pains of hell in our stead. (Jürgen Moltmann continues this line of thinking in contemporary theology in his discussion of the real abandonment of Jesus by the Father.) The most radical understandings of this theory were rejected by Tridentine Catholic theology; but elements of the idea of penal substitution nevertheless remained important in a number of strands of Catholic theology and spirituality, although theoretically divorced from both a "real" abandonment or punishment of Christ by the Father and from what Trent considered a merely "juridical" view of salvation through Christ's "substitution" for us. For a rather positive interpretation of the idea of penal substitution from a Catholic point of view, see Thompson, *The Struggle for Theology's Soul*, pp. 186–199.

78. One of the most moving contemporary expressions of this idea is found in the oft-cited incident related by Elie Wiesel in *Night*: when a child is hanged in the concentration camp, a voice in the crowd asks, "Where is God now?" "And I heard a voice within me answer him: 'Where is He? Here He is—He is hanging here on this gallows.'" Elie Wiesel, *Night*, trans. by Stella Rodway (New York: Hill and Wang, 1960), pp. 74–76.

79. The picture actually has some of the characteristics of the crucifixions by Grünewald mentioned above.

80. Fyodor Dostoievsky, *The Idiot*, trans. by Constance Garnett (New York: Bantam Books, 1983), pp. 395–396.

81. Rahner, "The human question of meaning in face of the absolute mystery of God," *TI*, vol. XVIII, p. 95.

82. Alfred North Whitehead, *Religion in the Making* (New York: New American Library, 1960), p. 149.

83. Rahner, *Karl Rahner in Dialogue. Conversations and Interviews, 1965–1982.* Edited by Paul Imhof and Hubert Biallowons; trans. edited by Harvey D. Egan (New York: Crossroad, 1986), p. 127. Rahner sees the possibility of such a projection in the theology of Moltmann.

84. Ibid.

85. Rahner, *Foundations of Christian Faith*, trans. by William Dych (New York: Crossroad, 1990), p. 62f. Emphasis added.

86. Barth, *Church Dogmatics*, p. 665.

87. Cf. Balthasar, "In Retrospect," p. 217.

88. In paintings like those by Grünewald mentioned above the crucifixion is also treated symbolically, not realistically, but there it is a symbol of the pains of hell, which Christ suffers in place of sinners.

89. This perspective is already present in the gospel narrative itself, although the following resurrection accounts are its explanation.

90. By contrast, the moral fault of "aestheticism," as Tillich says, is to enjoy, but withdraw from participation. *Systematic Theology*, vol. III, p. 257.

91. Balthasar points out that Kierkegaard's thought on "the aesthetic" undergoes an evolution from the second volume of *Either/Or* to the more negative stance in *Stages on Life's Way*. See Balthasar, *The Glory of the Lord*, p. 50.

92. George Bernard Shaw, "Heartbreak House," in *Six Plays by Bernard Shaw* (New York: Dodd, Mead & Co., 1945), p. 664.

93. Van der Leeuw, *Sacred and Profane Beauty*, p. 5.

94. Pasternak, **Доктор Живаго**, p. 581.

95. This is not the place for an analysis of the theme, but it should be noted that the very name Zhivago (in Old Church Slavonic, the genitive/accusative form of the noun meaning "the living one") is the title given to Christ by the angels at the tomb after the resurrection: "Why do you seek the Living One (живаго) among the dead?" Luke. 24:5.

96. This idea is important in William M. Thompson, *The Struggle for Theology's Soul. Contesting Scripture in Christology* (New York: Crossroad, 1996), p. 23. See also the more extensive treatment in the same author's *Fire and Light: the Saints and Theology* (New York: Paulist Press, 1987).

97. Van der Leeuw, *Sacred and Profane Beauty*, p. 284.

98. Rahner, "Art against the Horizon of Theology and Piety," pp. 167–168. Cf. the remarks of John Ruskin quoted above, ch. 5, n. 78.

99. See George Santayana, *The Last Puritan* (New York: Charles Scribner's Sons, 1936), p. 7. Santayana uses this phrase to describe what he calls "puritanism." He says to his fictional interlocutor: "You and I are not puritans; and by contrast with our natural looseness, we can't help admiring people purer than ourselves, more willing to pluck out the eye that offends them, even if it be the eye for beauty, and to enter halt and lame into the kingdom of singlemindedness." He adds: "I don't prefer austerity for myself as against abundance, against intelligence, against the irony of ultimate truth. But I see that in itself, as a statuesque object, austerity is more beautiful, and I like it in others."

100. Gregory of Nazianzen, *Oratio 14, De Pauperum Amore*, pp. 23–25; *PG* 35, 887–890.

101. Ibid.

102. Ibid., pp. 859–863.

103. The liturgy of St. John Chrysostom includes in its concluding prayers (the "prayer behind the ambo") the petition, "sanctify those who love the beauty of your house." The "beauty" of God's house is first of all "ontological;" the temple is beautiful because the One who dwells there is beautiful. (Cf. Psalm 27:4: "One thing have I asked of the Lord, that will I seek after: that I may dwell in the house of the Lord all the days of my life, to behold the beauty of the Lord, and to inquire in his temple;" Ps. 96:6: "Honor and majesty are before him; strength and beauty are in his sanctuary;" see also Ps. 50:2). But the artistic beautification of the church seems to follow logically, and is also in accord with the example of the Old Testament, where the beautification of the priestly garments and of the sanctuary is commanded (Exod. 28:2ff., 40; 35–39).

104. John Chrysostom, *Homilies on the Gospel of St. Matthew*, no. 50, pp. 3–4; *PG* 58, 508–509.

105. Umberto Eco, *Art and Beauty in the Middle Ages*, trans. by Hugh Bredin (New Haven: Yale University Press, 1986), p. 6.

106. Bernard of Clairvaux, "'Apologia' to William, abbot of St.-Thierry, in *A Documentary History of Art, Vol. I: The Middle Ages and the Renaissance*, edited by Elizabeth Gilmore Holt (Garden City: Doubleday, 1957), pp. 19–22; *PL* 182, 914–916.

107. Van der Leeuw, *Sacred and Profane Beauty*, p. 55.

108. Balthasar, *The Glory of the Lord*, p. 37. Calvin Seerveld carries this line of thinking even further, to the point of renouncing the common neo-Calvinist idea that beauty is grounded in the divine glory. The latter, for Seerveld, "speaks of God's grace in action, supremely in the 'unlovely form' of Jesus Christ." The key to art and beauty is in creaturely reality, not a divine attribute. Jeremy Begbie, *Voicing Creation's Praise*, p. 134.

109. Lonergan, *Method in Theology*, pp. 105–107, 112; Rahner, *Foundations of Christian Faith*, pp. 116–126, 198–203, and *passim*; see also *s.v.* "grace" in *CSM*. On the notion of conversion in general, see *Method in Theology*, pp. 130–131. On conversion as being at once "gift" and human "achievement" of transcendence, and for a comparison with Rahner's categories of understanding, see my *Answering for Faith. Christ and the Human Search for Salvation* (New York: Paulist Press, 1987), pp. 81–82.

Roberto Goizueta provides a fruitful comparison and synthesis of Lonergan's idea of conversion (as expanded to include the psychic realm) with Enrique Dussel's "analectical" understanding of conversion to the personal Other (an idea largely inspired by the philosophy of Levinas). Goizueta's remarks on the connection of Lonergan's theory with "praxis," as understood in political and liberation theology, are also enlightening. See Roberto S. Goizueta, *Liberation, Method and Dialogue. Enrique Dussel and North American Theological Discourse* (Atlanta: Scholars Press, 1988), ch. 5, especially pp. 111–125.

110. See Juan Alfaro, *Fides, Spes, Caritas* (Roma: Pontificia Universitas Gregoriana, 1968), pp. 234–280, 322–333.

111. Lonergan, *Method in Theology*, p. 105 and *passim*.

112. Ibid., p. 13.

113. Cf. Goizueta, *Liberation, Method and Dialogue*, pp. 123–124.

114. Doran, "Theological Grounds," pp. 109–110.

115. See especially *Method in Theology*, pp. 238–241. Moral conversion "changes the criterion of one's decisions and choices from satisfactions to values." Intellectual conversion means that "the real" is seen as the object of true judgments, rather than as the object of sense perception.

116. What I have called "aesthetic conversion" coincides substantially with what Robert Doran calls "psychic conversion." See Robert M. Doran, "Theological Grounds for a

World-Cultural Humanity," in *Creativity and Method: Essays in Honor of Bernard Lonergan, S.J.*, edited by Matthew L. Lamb (Milwaukee: Marquette University Press, 1981), pp. 104–122, especially 111–112; also his *Subject and Psyche: Ricoeur, Jung, and the Search for Foundations* (Washington, D.C.: University Press of America, 1977); *Psychic Conversion and Theological Foundations: Towards a Reorientation of the Human Sciences* (Chico, Calif.: Scholar's Press, 1982).

Although in substantial agreement with Doran's treatment, my own differs in several respects: (1) although he recognizes that it is analogously realized, Doran speaks of "psychic conversion" primarily in terms of the *self-appropriation* of one's "aesthetic intentionality" ("Theological Grounds," pp. 110, 113). Therefore for Doran "The modality of psychic conversion that is to be included as a dimension of these theological foundations [viz., Lonergan's] *follows upon intellectual conversion* and enables the self-appropriation of moral and intellectual conversion" (ibid., p. 113; emphasis added). I refer primarily to the level of unthematic accomplishment, rather than its formulation through self-appropriation; hence "aesthetic" conversion (in my sense) need not necessarily follow upon the intellectual, but might in some cases precede and enable it. However, I agree with Doran that conversion must attain intellectual formulation "in order to be self-critical and to progress, in order to be communicated with others, and in order to establish a measure of objective control over one's actions" (*Answering for Faith*, p. 88). (2) On the other hand, Doran defines "aesthetic intentionality" and the "transcendental notion of the beautiful" in terms of *sensitive* consciousness (ibid., p. 112), while I refer primarily to the spiritual level of intentionality (while acknowledging that this level presupposes and "sublates" a psycho-physical substratum). (3) For this reason, Doran deals extensively with the psychic dimensions of "affect" and "feeling" that are only marginally referred to in my treatment. For Doran, "theological aesthetics" would be "a methodical psychology grounded in self-appropriation," i.e., "an explicit integration through self-appropriation of our intention of the beautiful with our notions of the intelligible, the true, the real, and the good." Doran also explicitly treats the socio-political possibilities ("world-cultural humanity") that would flow from "psychic conversion." Doran's work is therefore a valuable complement to the more limited form of fundamental "theological aesthetics" I have attempted here.

117. I continue to use the word "notion" in Lonergan's sense of an unthematic heuristic preapprehension, and "concept" in the sense of a thematic understanding.

118. This text has been effectively set to music by the contemporary composer William Mathias in the anthem known by its opening words, "As truly as God is our Father." The piece has been recorded by the Christ Church Cathedral Choir under Stephen Darlington on the compact disk *William Mathias. Church and Choral Music.* Nimbus Records, 1990; NI 5243.

119. As the Scholastic maxim says, *"gratia naturam praesupponit et perficit."*

The category of "sublation" is used in a sense derived from the Hegelian philosophical use of the term *Aufhebung*—i.e. a preservation and at the same time raising to a new level. The term applies not only to the relation of "grace" to "nature," but also to the various "ascending" levels that we observe in the process of "active self-transcendence" in the evolution of life and spirit, since the "lower" levels of intelligibility remain intact when they are subsumed into a "higher" level. See Viladesau, *The Reason for Our Hope* (New York: Paulist Press, 1984), pp. 28–33; Lonergan, *Insight*, pp. 70–89, 103–115, 451–452; Rahner, *Foundations of Christian Faith*, p. 183ff. On the notion of the "sublation" of the different levels of conversion (intellectual by moral, and both by religious conversion) see Lonergan, *Method in Theology*, pp. 241–243. Note that in these cases the idea of "sublation" does not imply the temporal priority of the "lower" level.

120. From another point of view, it might be said that in the light of Christian revelation the distinction between the two is not so absolute as it appears, for example, in

Nygren's famous study. See Anders Nygren, *Eros and Agape*, trans. by Philip S. Watson (New York: Harper & Row, 1969). Might one redefine (engraced) "eros" not in terms of self-seeking, but as the "unitive" element in love, while agapé is seen as the "estimative" dimension?

121. Recall St. Thomas's definition of faith: *"fides est habitus mentis, qua incohatur vita aeterna in nobis, faciens intellectum assentire non apparentibus"* (*ST* II, II, q. IV, a. 1.); similarly on the "supernatural intentionality" of hope (*ST* II, II, q. 17, a. 2).

122. Cf. St. Thomas: *"caritas igitur facit hominem Deo inhaerere propter seipsum, mentem hominis uniens Deo per affectum amoris"* (*ST* II, II, q. 17, a. 6; cf. q. 23, a. 1–8).

123. For a discussion of the political implications of this idea, see Goizueta, *Liberation, Method and Dialogue*, p. 123f. and *passim*.

124. This does not contradict the fact that "altruistic" behavior in humans, as in other mammals, has a genetic and biological basis as well; we are speaking here of an act undertaken in freedom and, significantly, one in which the idea of the "neighbor" to whom such love is extended, is open-ended and not tied to familial or tribal interests. Here again, "grace" presupposes and perfects "nature."

125. See *ST* I, q. 5, a4, ad 1; II, II, q. 27, a1 ad 3.

126. Pannenberg, *Theology in Anthropological Perspective*, p. 250.

127. Ricoeur, *Fallible Man*, pp. 94–95.

128. The Stoics radicalized Plato's doctrine by rejecting the affective dimension of human life because it disturbs the harmony of the soul and hinders its integration in the cosmos. The Christian tradition, despite Platonic influences, has on the whole rejected the ideal of ἀπάθεια as being impossible for our kind of being. See Pannenberg, *Anthropology in Theological Perspective*, pp. 251–253.

129. Ibid.

130. Ibid., pp. 95–96. It is the last—loving encounter with another person—that "breaks the finite, cyclic pattern of the sensible appetite" (ibid., p. 111).

131. Ibid., p. 97. Ricoeur remarks that the "Greek theory of 'virtue' has no other intention than that of restoring the primordial amplitude of the pleasant, through 'suspension' of pleasure ... temperance is the 'practical' ἐποχή of pleasure, thanks to which the dynamism of preference is put back into movement" when it has been disturbed by the temptation of present satisfactions (ibid).

132. Ibid., p. 102.

133. Ibid., p. 99.

134. See Lonergan, *Insight*, pp. 191–203, 218–242, especially 218–222.

135. Ricoeur, *Fallible Man*, p. 99.

136. Nicholas Wolterstorff, going beyond the Calvinist tradition's justification of art (as well as science and technology) by a "cultural mandate" given at creation, emphasizes the present experience of God's eschatological *shalom* as the theological justification of aesthetic enjoyment: the end of humanity is God's

"shalom, eirene, peace—of man [*sic*] dwelling at peace in all his [*sic*] relationships: with God, with himself, with his fellows, with nature. . . . To dwell in shalom is to enjoy living before God, to enjoy living in nature, to enjoy living with one's fellows, to enjoy life with oneself. . . .

Aesthetic delight is a component within and a species of that joy which belongs to the shalom God has ordained as the goal of human existence, and which here already, in this broken and fallen world of ours, is to be sought and experienced.

Wolterstorff, *Art in Action*, pp. 79, 169, 177.

137. Cf. Balthasar's comment on Nebel: the beauty acceptable to faith can only be protological or eschatological. *The Glory of the Lord*, p. 64.

138. Cf. Wolterstorff, *Art in Action*, p. 174. Wolterstorff agrees that the Christian will be willing to sacrifice aesthetic enjoyment in favor of morality when there is conflict between the two; but he gives as the reason a calculation based on the idea that aesthetic joy is momentary, while moral behavior is habitual in character. While this may generally be true, it seems to me to miss the more profound motivation pointed to by Ricoeur. Wolterstorff's view of the aesthetic as radically independent of the moral and religious (ibid., pp. 172f.) and his affirmation that beauty is neither truth nor goodness (ibid., p. 173) seems to stem both from what Frank Burch Brown calls a "purist" notion of aesthetics (see Brown, *Religious Aesthetics*, pp. 5–6 and *passim*) and from the lack of an ontological perspective on beauty (see especially the remarks of von Balthasar, above, ch. 1). For this reason it seems to me that Wolterstorff, while affirming the validity of aesthetics within the religious perspective, misses the deeper links between aesthetic, moral, and religious levels of conversion. For this reason also, even though he strongly affirms the usefulness of art in the religious life, Wolterstorff insists on a strict demarcation between the aesthetic realm and supernatural revelation: "Art does not provide us with the meaning of human existence. The gospel of Jesus Christ does that. Art is not a way of rising toward God. It is meant instead to be in service of God" (ibid., p. 196). At the same time, he admits that God's working is not confined to the church (ibid., p. 197). Is this a possible opening to a wider view of "categorical" revelation, such as the one I have presented—one which includes the aesthetic as an intrinsic element?

139. The letter of James, however, warns that joy can be delusive (James 4:10). This is because of the intrinsic connection between "joy" and "pleasure" referred to above. See Pannenberg, *Theology in Anthropological Perspective*, p. 256.

As Barth writes, joy in God "has nothing whatever to do with an optimistic glossing over of the need and the condition of mankind. On the other hand, the latter cannot alter but is confuted and overcome by the fact that God must be the object of joy. 'Thou hast turned for me my mourning into dancing: thou hast put off my sackcloth, and girded me with gladness' (Ps. 30:11)." *Church Dogmatics*, p. 654. See above, ch. 4, n. 207.

140. See Tallon, "The Concept of Heart," p. 355.

141. Conversely, the call to engage in this kind of love is the sign or "evidence" of God's presence in us. See Viladesau, *The Reason for Our Hope*, pp. 201f.; Rahner, *Do You Believe in God?*, trans. by Richard Strachan (New York: Newman Press, 1969), pp. 112–113; *s.v.* "Jesus Christ" in *CSM*, pp. 753–754.

142. On the presence of *eros* in finite *agapé*, see Viladesau, *The Reason for Our Hope*, p. 153; cf. *ST* II, I, q. 5, a. 8; Blaise Pascal, *Pensées*, no. 169, 425 (Paris: Éditions Garnier Frères, 1964), pp. 119, 176.

143. Cf. Balthasar, *The Glory of the Lord*, p. 64.

144. Existentially, the *Vorgriff* of being is not adequately distinguishable from the "supernatural intentionality" that characterizes the engraced spirit.

145. See Viladesau, *The Reason for Our Hope*, p. 194; cf. Lonergan, *De Verbo Incarnato* (*ad usum auditorum*, Roma: Pontificia Universitas Gregoriana, 1961), p. 506.

146. On "supernatural" love as a "solution" to the problem of evil, see Lonergan, *Insight*, pp. 694–696, 698–700, 724.

147. This description applies not only to "religious" conversion, which directly regards "grace," but also to the intellectual, moral, and aesthetic levels of conversion. In theory, these are independent from each other and from grace; but existentially, each kind of conversion calls out for the others, and normally our entire process of achieving self-transcendence is a function of God's "grace," even if it is not explicitly adverted to. Lo-

nergan admits that it is possible, in exceptional cases, that aspects of intellectual conversion (for example) might precede religious conversion (see *Method in Theology*, p. 339). But even on the level of "creation," abstracting from grace, we may correctly speak of God's self-gift to God's "other," since existence itself is already a finite participation in God's being, albeit at a different "level" from that of grace.

148. Lonergan, *Method in Theology*, p. 110. Cf. pp. 252, 284.

149. Lonergan, *Method in Theology*, p. 243. Lonergan does not explicitly advert to the "aesthetic" dimension of conversion, but it is implied, as he agreed in response to commentators on his work.

150. Doran, "Theological Grounds," p. 110.

151. It should be recalled, however, that "aesthetic conversion" does not per se *guarantee* a high level of aesthetic development in the artistic sense.

152. To say this is by no means to devaluate the importance of word and abstract concept. As Iris Murdoch says, the fact that there are ultra-verbal insights, that the ultimate is ineffable, is clearly not an argument against careful verbalization on a "lower" level. "The careful responsible skillful use of words is our highest instrument of thought and one of our highest modes of being." Murdoch, *The Fire and the Sun*, pp. 87–88.

153. Ibid., pp. 87–88. Murdoch complains that "as religion and metaphysics in the West withdraw from the embraces of art, we are it might seem being forced to become mystics through the lack of any imagery which could satisfy the mind."

154. See Viladesau, *The Reason for Our Hope*, p. 196. Cf. Brown, *Religious Aesthetics*, p. 193.

155. Lonergan, *Insight*, pp. 723–724.

156. This theme is prominent in the Dutch Neo-Calvinist theologians. Herman Bavinck writes that earthly beauty is "a prophecy and pledge that this world is not meant for destruction, but for glory, the nostalgic longing for which dwells in every heart." Herman Bavinck, "Van Schoonheid en Schoonheidsleer," in *Verzamelde Opstellen* (Kampen: Kok, 1921), p. 280; quoted in Begbie, *Voicing Creation's Praise*, p. 99. His predecessor Kuyper likewise taught that art recollects our pre-fallen state and anticipates the new creation. Ibid., p. 98.

157. Jeremy S. Begbie, *Voicing Creation's Praise. Towards a Theology of the Arts* (Edinburgh: T&T Clark, 1991), pp. 212, 215.

158. Wolterstorff, *Art in Action*, p. 84; cf. Brown, *Religious Aesthetics*, p. 104.

159. Patrick Sherry, *Spirit and Beauty. An Introduction to Theological Aesthetics* (Oxford: Clarendon Press, 1992), p. 181. I would qualify Sherry's statement by pointing out that the *artistic* creation of ugliness may in some cases be a means of communicating a moral message.

The theme of Sherry's book, the relationship of beauty to the Spirit, is a logical systematic extension of the fundamental theological perspectives that have been treated here. Paul Tillich also sees aesthetics in the light of the Spirit: the principal treatment of aesthetics in his *Systematic Theology* occurs in Part IV, "Life and the Spirit," within a discussion of the functions of the church. Tillich's "economic" approach to Trinitarian theology is more in line with the Rahnerian theology of revelation that has been adopted here than is Sherry's presentation, which relies largely on an older, more "dogmatic" approach to the Trinity (even though it attempts to begin "from below" in its consideration of "inspiration").

160. Damasio, *Descartes' Error*, pp. 163–164.

161. Ray Monk, *Ludwig Wittgenstein* (Vintage, 1991), p. 143; quoted in Harries, *Art and the Beauty of God*, pp. 110–111.

162. Murdoch, *The Fire and the Sun*, pp. 36, 76f.

163. Ibid., p. 85.

164. Ibid., p. 86.

165. Ibid., p. 80.

166. Ibid., p. 78.

167. Ibid., pp. 79, 83.

168. Tillich, *Systematic Theology*, vol. III, p. 64.

169. Ibid., p. 77. "'Falling in love,' a violent process which Plato more than once vividly describes (love is abnegation, abjection, slavery) is for many people the most extraordinary and most revealing experience of their lives, whereby the center of significance is suddenly ripped out of the self, and the dreamy ego is shocked into awareness of an entirely separate reality." Ibid., p. 36.

170. Ibid. However, as Gadamer points out, when art is approached with a purely "aesthetic" frame of mind it may also serve as a way of escaping from the moral dimension. Good art may provide work for the spirit; but the work may be toward art "for its own sake" rather than toward the moral good. It must also be noted that Murdoch does not resolve the perennial problem of what constitutes "good" art. Moreover, she explicitly avoids the question of whether "bad" art is morally damaging (ibid., p. 77), and seems to overlook the possibility that something artistically good may be morally counterproductive if it presents an evil as beautiful. Nevertheless, to the extent that aesthetic conversion is in process, Murdoch's point retains validity.

171. Ibid., p. 86.

172. Ibid.

173. Ibid., p. 81.

174. Ibid., p. 83.

175. Helmuth Vetter, "Ästhetik und Schönheit," in Günter Pöltner and Helmuth Vetter (eds.), *Theologie und Ästhetik* (Wien, Freiburg, Basel: Herder, 1985), pp. 35–47, at p. 43.

176. Balthasar, *The Glory of the Lord*, p. 36. However, this same bearing of "self-evident" value (i.e., of beauty) makes art dangerous when it is not combined with intellectual, moral, and religious conversion.

177. Barth, *Church Dogmatics*, p. 667.

178. *ST* II, II, q. 35, a. 4, ad 2, quoting from *Ethics* VIII and X.

179. Alexander Solzhenitsyn, *Nobel Lecture* (Нобелевская Лекция) (New York: Farrar, Strauss and Giroux, 1972), pp. 40–42. This bilingual edition also contains an English translation by F. D. Reeve; see pp. 6–8.

Index

Adam, 59, 73
aesthetics
  meanings of, 5, 6–11, 23, 32, 103
  as a source for theology, 3, 15–19, 86
  theological
    concept of, 4–11, 30, 32, 37, 38, 51,
      103, 227n. 108
    divisions of, 11–19
    objects of, 11
    place in theology, 35–38
    as practice, 11–15
    as study of art, 141–182
    as study of beauty, 103–140, 191–214
    task of, 68–71, 97, 104
    as theory, 23–24, 90–96
  theories of, 51, 96, 144–145
agapé, 191–193, 196, 198, 207–208, 209,
    213, 283n. 120
Albertus Magnus, 111, 115
Alighieri, Dante. *See* Dante
Alexander of Hales, 111
Ambrose, 106
analogy, 20, 22, 30, 59, 71, 77, 90, 97, 98,
    99, 100, 101, 120, 135, 193, 207,
    247n. 82, 253n. 154, 279n. 72
anamnesis, 160, 187
Anknüpfungspunkt. See revelation, capacity
    for
Anselm of Canterbury, 28, 194
anthropomorphism, 42, 55, 56, 63, 89, 100,
    252n. 148, 255n. 176
apologetics, 35, 104, 232n. 236
a priori, linguistic, 88
Aquinas, Thomas, 14, 22, 33, 34, 58, 77,
    78, 80, 82, 90, 91, 97, 98, 100, 114–

117, 119, 126, 127, 128, 132, 135,
    171, 213
architecture, 148
Aristotle, 9, 77, 110, 115, 135, 143, 150,
    188, 196, 213
art
  Christian, 53, 66
  authentic vs. inauthentic, 212
  as communication, 153
  creation as, 108, 113, 115
  and the cross, 189–198
  dangers of, 55, 182–214
    in Christian perspective, 189–198
    in Platonic perspective, 186–189
  definition of, 8–11, 143–146
  eternal, 113, 115
  as a form of knowledge, 17, 61, 85, 86,
    87
  Indian, 10, 174
  in Islam, 275n. 6
  Jewish, 53
  as language, 148
  meaning of, 8, 9, 130–131, 184–185
  as object of aesthetics, 8, 9, 11
  and ontological insight, 152–162
  phenomenology of, 24–25
  and religion, 16, 141–182, 184–214
  as revelation, 145, 146–182
  sacred, 10, 32, 52, 53, 101, 144–145, 163–
    163, 168–182
  and theology, 5, 24, 32, 164–165
  useful vs. fine, 9–10
  visual, 53, 64, 101, 148, 164–165, 168–
    177, 275n. 6
  as a way to God, 118–119

CPSIA information can be obtained
at www.ICGtesting.com
Printed in the USA
BVOW11s2338210917
495468BV00002B/23/P